# Nature, Culture, Imperialism

*Essays on the Environmental History of South Asia*

# Nature, Culture, Imperialism

## *Essays on the Environmental History of South Asia*

*edited by*

DAVID ARNOLD

and

RAMACHANDRA GUHA

OXFORD
UNIVERSITY PRESS

OXFORD
UNIVERSITY PRESS

Oxford University Press is a department of the University of Oxford. It furthers the University's objective of excellence in research, scholarship, and education by publishing worldwide. Oxford is a registered trademark of Oxford University Press in the UK and in certain other countries

Published in India by
Oxford University Press
YMCA Library Building, 1 Jai Singh Road, New Delhi 110001, India



First Edition published in 1995
Oxford India Paperbacks 1996



ISBN-13: 978-0-19-564075-5
ISBN-10: 0-19-564075-6

Typeset by Rastrixi, New Delhi 110 070

Printed in India by Repro Knowledgecast Limited, Thane

# Acknowledgements

The essays that appear in this volume were first presented at a conference entitled 'South Asia's Changing Environment', held at the Bellagio Conference Center, Lake Como, Italy, between 16 and 20 March 1992. The editors, who were the organizers of that conference, are grateful to the Ford Foundation in New Delhi for providing the financial support which made that conference possible, and to the Rockefeller Foundation for making available their splendid facilities at Bellagio. We could not have wanted a more hospitable environment for our deliberations. We would also like to thank the other participants in the conference, Rita Brara, Richard Grove, Christopher V. Hill, Mahesh Rangarajan, Ravi Rajan, R. Sudarshan and Francis Zimmermann, for their very valuable contributions to the proceedings; equally, we thank our two discussants, Michael Adas and Madhav Gadgil, for stimulating comments and criticisms.

DAVID ARNOLD
RAMACHANDRA GUHA

# Contents

# Notes on Contributors

MICHAEL R. ANDERSON is Lecturer in Law at the School of Oriental and African Studies, London. He has published articles on Indian legal history, the Bhopal litigation and international environmental law. He is currently working on the history of labour legislation in India.

DAVID ARNOLD is Professor of South Asian History at the School of Oriental and African Studies, London. His published work includes *Police Power and Colonial Rule: Madras, 1859–1947* (1986), *Famine: Social Crisis and Historical Change* (1988), and *Colonizing the Body: State Medicine and Epidemic Disease in Nineteenth-Century India* (1993).

NEELADRI BHATTACHARYA is at the Centre for Historical Studies, Jawaharlal Nehru University, New Delhi. His work has been mainly on the agrarian history of Punjab. He is an editor of *Studies in History* and *Tracts for the Times.*

MADHAV GADGIL currently holds the Astra Professorship in Biological Sciences at the Indian Institute of Science, Bangalore. His interests range widely over population biology, conservation biology, human ecology and ecological history. With Ramachandra Guha he is the author of *This Fissured Land: An Ecological History of India* (1992).

DAVID GILMARTIN is Associate Professor of History at North Carolina State University, Raleigh. He is the author of *Empire and Islam: Punjab and the Making of Pakistan* (1988), and is currently working on a history of Indus Basin irrigation from the eighteenth to the twentieth centuries.

RAMACHANDRA GUHA is a Professorial Fellow at the Nehru Memorial Museum and Library, New Delhi. His books include *The Unquiet Woods* (1989), *Wickets in the East* (1992), and, with Madhav Gadgil, *Ecology and Equity* (to be published in 1995).

DAVID HARDIMAN, the author of *Peasant Nationalists of Gujarat: Kheda District, 1917–34* (1981) and *The Coming of the Devi: Adivasi Assertion in Western India* (1987), is currently working on moneylenders in Western India. He was a Simon Fellow at the University of Manchester in 1992–93.

ATLURI MURALI is Reader in History at the Central University Hyderabad. He has published on the nationalist movement in Andhra Pradesh and is currently conducting research on environmental change in South India.

MARK POFFENBERGER has conducted research on both South and South East Asia. He edited *Keepers of the Forest: Land Management Alternatives in Southeast Asia* (1990). He is currently at the School of Natural Resources, University of California, Berkeley.

JACQUES POUCHEPADASS is Directeur de recherche (History) at the National Centre for Scientific Research (CNRS), Paris, and was Director of the French Institute, Pondicherry. His publications include *Planteurs et paysans dans l'Inde coloniale* (1986) and *Paysans de la plaine du Gange: Croissance agricole et societe dans le district de Champaran (Bihar), 1860–1950* (1989).

R. PRABAKHAR trained in engineering at the Indian Institute of Technology, Madras, before completing a Ph.D at the Centre for Ecological Sciences, Bangalore, on resource use patterns and ecological change in the Nilgiri area of southern India. In 1993–4 he was a Macarthur Fellow in population and development at Harvard University.

PETER REEVES, Professor of South Asian History and Director of the South Asia Research Unit, School of Social Science, Curtin University, Australia, is currently studying the history of artisanal fisheries in colonial India, *c.* 1793–1947. In 1991 he published *Landlords and Governments in Uttar Pradesh.*

CHETAN SINGH is Assistant Professor in the Department of History, Himachal Pradesh University, and is also a Fellow at the Indian Institute of Advanced Studies, Shimla. Since publishing *Region and Empire: Panjab in the Seventeenth Century* (1991), he has been working on environment, society and economy in the Himachal Himalaya, 1800–1950.

ELIZABETH WHITCOMBE is currently a Senior Lecturer in the Department of Physiology, University College, London. Her major publications include *Agrarian Conditions in Northern India: The United Provinces under British Rule, 1860–1900* (1972); 'Whatever Happened to the Zamindars?' in *Peasants in History: Essays in Honour of Daniel Thorner* (1980), and 'Irrigation' in the *Cambridge History of India*, vol. II (1983).

# Introduction: Themes and Issues in the Environmental History of South Asia

DAVID ARNOLD AND RAMACHANDRA GUHA

If, globally speaking, environmental history may be said to have come of age in recent years, in South Asia it remains by and large in its adolescence. It has produced its prophets and pioneers; it has had moments of precociousness, though these have been born more out of urgent contemporary concerns than from any depth of historical understanding. Environmental history in this region has yet to develop a firm intellectual base, a solid scholarly foundation. One response to this predicament might be to say that South Asia has a lot of catching up to do before it can begin to compare with the meticulous research and scholarly sophistication which has characterized the writing of environmental history elsewhere—for instance in France and the United States. But a different response, closer to the spirit of the present volume, would be to argue that South Asia is beginning to develop its own distinctive contribution to environmental history without being intent merely upon emulation. Before trying to identify the distinctive features of such a history, it may be as well to ask what we mean by environmental history in the first place.

Although the terms 'ecological history' and 'environmental history' are often used synonymously, some distinction might usefully be made between them. The term *oecologie*, as coined by the German zoologist Ernst Haeckel in 1866, embraced 'the science of the relations of living organisms to the external world, their habitat, customs, energies, parasites, etc.' With its distant echoes of the domestic household, ecology implied a family of living organisms, each in close proximity to the other, sharing the same physical space, with conflicting appetites or complementary needs.[1] In practice ecology has tended to focus more narrowly upon the study of 'nature', 'the non-human world, the world we have not in any primary sense created',[2] and to see man as an irrelevant or extraneous factor in shaping the natural environment. From a late-twentieth-century perspective, with images of desertification and deforestation ever-present before us, and with talk of greenhouse gasses and global warming ringing in our ears, such a stark distinction between man and nature might appear dangerously narrow-minded and increasingly artificial. But the value of the stress upon ecology within the environmental/ecological-history continuum has been to direct attention away from an excessively anthropocentric understanding of the world, towards patterns of environmental order and change that have been largely autonomous of man and which draw more heavily upon the natural (rather than the social) sciences for their intelligibility. With the sciences themselves coming increasingly to be scrutinized as cultural and historical constructions, there is besides the possibility of an ecological history which charts the chronological course of the ecological sciences, of the historical observation and shifting scientific interpretation of natural phenomena.[3]

Moving more firmly within the parameters of environmental

[1] Cited in Donald Worster, *Nature's Economy: A History of Ecological Ideas* (1977; republished Cambridge, 1985), p. 192.

[2] Donald Worster, 'Doing Environmental History', in Donald Worster (ed.), *The Ends of the Earth: Perspectives on Modern Environmental History* (Cambridge, 1988), p. 292.

[3] Worster's *Nature's Economy* is an excellent example of this genre, as, for an earlier period, is Clarence J. Glacken, *Traces on the Rhodian Shore: Nature and Culture in Western Thought from Ancient Times to the End of the Eighteenth Century* (Berkeley, 1967).

history *per se*, there is the study of human engagement over time with the physical environment, of the environment as context, agent, and influence in human history. Here, nature figures unabashedly as human habitat, but in a dual capacity. On the one hand are ranged those elements of nature—climate, topography, animal and insect life, vegetation and soils—which directly or indirectly shape human activity and productivity. In affecting land-use and subsistence, they help to promote or prohibit specific forms of social structure, economic organization and belief systems. They also extend the margins of historical analysis and bring centrestage a 'cast of non-human characters' normally ignored, at least until recently, in historical scholarship.[4] But the relationship is a reciprocal one, for man more than any other living organism also alters the landscape, fells trees, erodes soils, dams streams, kills off unwelcome plants and predatory animals, installing favoured species in their stead. The awareness of man's dependence upon nature has a long ancestry; but a sense of man as the maker and unmaker of nature has only more recently dawned upon us, and with it an awesome sense of our own capacity for mischief and mayhem.

In addition, and still within the broad bounds of environmental history, there is a history of the environment as cultural space and ideological artifact, as expressed through the invocation and representation of nature in art and religion, in myth, in ethics and the law. It has recently become fashionable in the West to explore environmental themes in the ideology and iconography and J.M.W. Turner, the novels of James Fenimore Cooper, or the poems of Walt Whitman.[5] But the history of the environment, in

[4] William Cronon, *Changes in the Land: Indians, Colonists, and the Ecology of New England* (New York, 1983), p. vii.

[5] E.g., Denis Cosgrove and Stephen Daniels (eds.), *The Iconography of Landscape: Essays on the Symbolic Representation, Design and Use of Past Environments* (Cambridge, 1988); Hans Huth, *Nature and the American: Three Centuries of Changing Attitudes* (1957; new edn, Lincoln, Nebraska, 1990). Studies of the representation of nature in South Asia have been slow to appear but there are, for example, some suggestive examples in Ray Desmond, *Wonders of Creation:*

both its material and perceptual sense, is also a history of popular perceptions and experience, of folk traditions and religious beliefs which have been more familiar to anthropologists than historians.[6] This kind of environmental history clearly leads us further away from the ecological sciences and closer to anthropology, art, literature and religion. But one of the undoubted attractions of environmental history is its ability to draw upon the insights and techniques of several disciplines, and then to combine them in novel and often provocative ways of its own.

In other parts of the world, especially within France and the United States, environmental history has been for some time a well established sub-field within history. In both countries there has accumulated a substantial body of work that might be classified under 'environmental history', a corpus to which major historians have contributed and which has had a strong impact on the discipline as a whole. In the United States environmental history emerged as a distinct field only in the 1970s, in the wake of the modern environmental movement.[7] While varying widely in their spatial focus, time-frame and mode of analysis, the vast majority of books and articles on American environmental history cluster around two overarching themes: (i) a documentation and analysis of the eco-cultural consequences of the two master processes of American history, namely European colonization and the development of capitalism; and (ii) a celebration of those individuals and organizations that have, however unsuccessfully, challenged the environmental destruction unleashed by colonialism and capitalism.

---

*Natural History Drawings in the British Library* (London, 1986).

6 As in the work of Victor Turner, in books such as *The Forest of Symbols* (Cornell, 1967) and *The Ritual Process* (London, 1967); see also Elisabeth Croll and David Parkin (eds.), *Bush Base, Forest Farm: Culture, Environment, and Development* (London, 1992).

7 For an excellent review, see Richard White, 'American Environmental History: The Development of a New Field', *Pacific Historical Review*, 54:4, 1985, pp. 297–335.

In the first category fall such important works as William Cronon's study of the conflict between colonists and Amerindians in New England, and Donald Worster's exploration of the Dust Bowl and the ethos of capitalist exploitation that underlay it.[8] In the second category are Roderick Nash's wide-ranging history of wilderness thinking in American culture, as well as the numerous biographies of early environmentalists such as John Muir and Aldo Leopold.[9] Proof of the vitality of the field as a whole is the American Society for Environmental History, an organization whose biennial conference features up to two hundred research papers. There are also two scholarly journals—*Forest and Conservation History* and *Environmental History Review.*

By contrast, environmental history in South Asia is at present far from commanding such a high degree of interest among historians. Not only does it have no journal of its own, but there have been no more than a handful of articles in the main South Asia periodicals and no more than a token discussion of environmental issues in the main historical texts.

While the term 'environmental history' does not appear to be in wide circulation in France, work by the leading French historians, particularly those belonging to the Annales school, does answer to that description: this important body of work has also been a major influence on the growth of environmental history elsewhere. In France an ecological approach to history was fostered not by a contemporary environmental movement but by (i) a close and longstanding relationship between history and geography in French intellectual life; and (ii) an appreciation of the fundamental importance of environmental factors to an understanding of agrarian society. What is striking here is the contribution of leading French historians to the making of the field. Among the works of

[8] Cronon, *Changes in the Land*; Worster, *Dust Bowl: The Southern Plains in the 1930s* (New York, 1979).

[9] Nash, *Wilderness and the American Mind* (3rd edn, New Haven, 1982); Michael Cohen, *The Pathless Way: A Study of John Muir* (Madison, 1984); Curt Meine, *Aldo Leopold: A Life* (Madison, 1988).

the first generation Annalists there is, first, Lucien Febvre's lucid and still valuable overview of the match between different natural environments and different forms of resource use; and second, Marc Bloch's great work on French agriculture, a model of ecological analysis in its study of the integration of arable with woodland and pasture.[10]

Among the post-War generation of scholars, both Fernand Braudel and Emmanuel Le Roy Ladurie have in their own writings emphasized—some would say too strongly—the impress of the physical environment on economic life and social organization. The environment appears in such studies largely as a constraining force on agrarian societies, as a series of determining principles and Malthusian checks, rather than as a subject abstracted and considered in isolation. The key organizing concept of much work in the Annales tradition has been the *longue durée*, popularized by Braudel through his work on the Mediterranean. For Braudel the sea, itself unchanging, provides a permanently fixed and supremely powerful environmental context for the evolution of human economies and cultures. The notion of the *longue durée* has also informed studies on French agrarian history, wherein the relative fixity of the natural landscape is invoked in understanding the persistence of the mores of medieval life well into modern times.[11] The absence in France of an agricultural and industrial revolution of the kind that transformed eighteenth- and nineteenth-century Britain has also contributed to the sense of long-term continuity in French historical scholarship.

The approaches adopted by the Annalists and the concept of

[10] Lucien Febvre, *A Geographical Introduction to History* (London, 1950); Marc Bloch, *French Rural History: Its Essential Characteristics* (London, 1952).

[11] See, principally, Fernand Braudel, *The Mediterranean and the Mediterranean World in the Age of Philip II* (1949; republished in English, London, 1972); also 'History and the Social Sciences: The *longue durée*', in Fernand Braudel, *On History* (London, 1980), pp. 25–54; Emmanuel Le Roy Ladurie, *The Peasants of Languedoc* (1966; republished in English, Urbana, 1974); *Times of Feast, Times of Famine: A History of Climate Since the Year 1000* (London, 1972).

the *longue durée* clearly have their attractions for the historian (not least the environmental historian) of South Asia. The antiquity of the region as a lived environment certainly gave rise to a complex process of interaction between people and nature, or, more exactly, between specific sets of human inhabitants and a range of different and changing environmental conditions. Indeed, one of the urgent tasks of environmental history in South Asia is to open up the time-frame for the discussion of environmental change to take long-term developments into account, rather than merely to concentrate upon the developments of the past century or so.[12] South Asia has, for instance, a long and developed history of irrigation and urban settlement, but as yet we know relatively little about how these modified the surrounding environment or gave rise to adverse environmental effects. As major consumers of fuel, fodder, building materials and foodstuffs, cities in South Asia must over time have produced substantial modifications to the environment over a wide area (a development touched on in Chetan Singh's discussion of Mughal India in this volume). Extensive irrigation works and the urban concentration of people must also have considerably modified the environment for disease, particularly through water-borne diseases, the spread of mosquitoes and other insect vectors, and by the sustaining of 'crowd diseases' that might have failed to find an ecological niche among the more scattered or nomadic populations. While these more distant connections remain to be adequately examined, Elizabeth Whitcombe's essay in this volume provides some important evidence for the ecological links between irrigation, disease and other environmental hazards in more recent times.

When dealing with South Asia we need to remind ourselves that we are grappling with a region virtually continental in scale and in its degree of internal diversity. An immense and varied

[12] For an initial attempt at this, see Madhav Gadgil and Ramachandra Guha, *This Fissured Land: An Ecological History of India* (Delhi and Berkeley, 1992); and for Indian prehistory, see D.D. Kosambi's work, especially *Myth and Reality: Studies in the Formation of Indian Culture* (Bombay, 1962), chapter 4.

landscape, South Asia can be mapped out topographically by its mountain ranges and major rivers systems, by its once vast forests, its deserts, its deltas, and its offshore islands. But the region is also defined historically and culturally by its urban centres, and by the crisscrossing routes of pilgrimage and trade. It is divisible into a host of ecological zones and a score or more of linguistic and cultural regions.[13] This diversity and complexity pose particular problems for the historian. What is the appropriate spatial context for historical analysis? At times, in order to be sensitive to the nature of the local ecosystem and to human land-use, it is necessary to concentrate on a very small area, perhaps as small as a village and its immediate environs, or a locality characterized by a particular combination of ecological features and sub-zones (like the Nilgiri hills in Prabhakar and Gadgil's essay). But there is also a danger, as Chetan Singh's account reminds us, of too readily separating off one perceived region from another and not allowing for the exchange of resources and the movement of people and commodities across those boundaries. Are we to take for our analysis the tiny domain of the earthbound villager, the more mobile perspective of the pastoralist, or the worldview of the urban courtier and scribe? All these have their place, but they lead us towards different kinds of ecological understandings of the past. The more we move into the colonial age (and beyond), the more pressing the problem of finding the appropriate level of analysis becomes. The arena for environmental action becomes as large as the Indus river basin (as in David Gilmartin's discussion, in this volume, of irrigation and 'environmental modelling' in Punjab);

[13] How to define the regions of South Asia and how they influence culture, society and politics, has long been a matter for scholarly debate: see, in particular, Bernard S. Cohn, 'Regions Subjective and Objective: Their Relation to the Study of Modern Indian History and Society', in his *An Anthropologist Among the Historians and Other Essays* (Delhi, 1987), pp. 100–35; Francis Zimmermann, *The Jungle and the Aroma of Meats: An Ecological Theme in Hindu Medicine* (1982; republished in English, Berkeley, 1987); David Ludden, 'Ecological Zones and the Cultural Economy of Irrigation in Southern Tamilnadu', *South Asia*, 1:1, 1978, pp. 1–13.

or the state-managed forests of a Presidency (a major part of it features in Atluri Murali's account, herein, of forest policy and its effects in Andhra); or even an empire-wide system of economic extraction and exchange, and environmental ideas and policies.

It is perhaps, then, the sheer ecological and cultural diversity of the Indian subcontinent which most radically and problematically distinguishes its environmental history from the French or American experience. While India, like France, is a predominantly agrarian civilization, the far greater species-diversity of tropical environments here has facilitated and sustained a much greater range of livelihood patterns. For instance, it has long been recognized that the multiplicity of endogamous groups constituting the caste system are sharply differentiated according to occupation and ritual status, but it is only now emerging that they might be further distinguished, in many cases, by highly specific relationships with the natural environment. Field data from western and southern India exemplifies a system where endogamous groups (or *jatis*) within a village often had exclusive access to a particular species, resource or territory, with these individual 'niches' usually having a limited overlap. In some cases this system was elaborated to the extent of two jatis of basket-weavers having exclusive control over different plant species for use as raw material—a situation made possible only by the extraordinarily high biological diversity of their surroundings. While the South Asian landscape is dominated by settled villages, the numerous and widely dispersed communities of hunter-gatherers, swidden cultivators, nomadic pastoralists and fisherfolk have all contributed to a cultural and ecological diversity that is surely unparalleled.[14]

A vital role in sustaining this diversity has been played by the large extent of forest and pasture in the subcontinent. A South Asianist would be struck by the neglect, in a recent round-table of American environmental historians, of these common property resources that provide the larger ecological context for settled agriculture.[15] That neglect was perhaps explicable in terms of the

[14] Gadgil and Guha, *Fissured Land.*

[15] *Journal of American History*, 76:4, 1990, pp. 1087–1147.

symposium's unstated focus on North American industrialized agriculture, where such links might not be so important or apparent. But in the tropics these resources continue to provide crucial inputs into the dominant complex of agriculture and animal husbandry, while also enabling other forms of resource use such as hunting, gathering, swidden cultivation and artisanal production. Given their enormous importance to economic and cultural life, changes in the physical status of forests and pasture, as well as changes in the social institutions governing their use, must form a major area of research for environmental history in South Asia. In particular, the forests of South Asia have (as the articles by Chetan Singh, Atluri Murali and Jacques Pouchepadass in this volume indicate) a wide variety of historical meanings and usages. They served as homes and sources of livelihood for their inhabitants, as well as of fuel, building materials, famine foods and medicines for neighbouring peoples. They provided a home for bandits and rebels, and equally an obstacle to invasion and the expansionist ambitions of the state. They accommodated wild animals and nurtured disease environments that were often fatally inhospitable to outsiders. They defined, in more than one cultural system, the 'primitive' from the civilized. Moreover, in the colonial order of things, they provided a primary source of raw materials and a site for state regulation on a scale massive enough to make the cherished Victorian notion of *laissez-faire* an ecological myth and an economic fantasy.[16]

Especially in the drier parts of the subcontinent, grasslands played a critical role in sustaining rural livelihoods. As much as 6 per cent of India's population has been estimated to be nomadic or semi-nomadic, and a substantial proportion of this is or has been dependent on pastoralism. Pastoral nomads often operated, as Neeladri Bhattacharya shows in his essay, over long distances, being enmeshed in a web of mutual obligations with village society

[16] In addition to the papers in this volume, see also, on forests as lived and changing environments, Gadgil and Guha, *Fissured Land*, especially chapters 5 to 8.

that were not always free from conflict. At the same time, for most settled peasants, too, livestock rearing was a valuable appendage to cultivation. Much pasture land was under community control, but during the colonial period and after, state intervention and the pressures of both population and the market have contributed greatly to the decline and degradation of areas previously held in common.

Several of the essays in this volume address themselves directly to the themes of forest and pasturage, and the ecological, social and political changes that have come to affect these. Others are concerned with water, the other natural resource that looms large over the environmental history of the subcontinent. We noted earlier that Braudel's magisterial work highlighted the importance of the sea as a factor in human history. Following in his footsteps, and influenced too by Braudel's disciple Immanuel Wallerstein, some historians of Asia have emphasized the 'maritime factor' in Indian and Indian Ocean history.[17] But more rewarding still would be work on the great river systems of the Indian land mass that have exercised such a definitive influence on the natural environment, as well as on the economic, social and religious life of the region. Indeed, one might argue that for South Asia, as for many other parts of eastern and western Asia, rivers have been far more important than the adjacent seas and have run like a central silver thread through their history, while maritime trade and contacts have been of only secondary, if not marginal, significance, at least until the opening of the European age.[18]

[17] Most notably K.N. Chaudhuri, in *Trade and Civilisation in the Indian Ocean: An Economic History from the Rise of Islam to 1750* (Cambridge, 1985). But for an earlier and rather different emphasis on the maritime dimension, see K.M. Pannikar, *Asia and Western Dominance* (London, 1969).

[18] See, for instance, Lyman P. Van Slyke, *Yangtze: Nature, History and the River* (Reading, Mass., 1988), which interestingly acknowledges a debt to Braudel's work without seeing any contrast between Europe and China; and, for modern South Asia, A.A. Michel, *The Indus Rivers* (1967). The great rivers of India, though celebrated in ritual and myth, plus countless picture-books and travelogues, have not received similar scholarly treatment.

Under the broad rubric of 'Water in Indian History' a range of exciting research possibilities present themselves. One might thus study the small-scale but often highly sophisticated and effective systems of water use developed by local communities, a theme developed here in David Hardiman's essay on small dams in the Sahyadris; the larger and more centralized systems of irrigation elaborated by both pre-modern and modern states, a subject on which David Ludden has written an important study for south India and on which Elizabeth Whitcombe writes here for northern India;[19] or the changing ecology of subsistence fishing and fishing rights in inland waters, a hitherto neglected topic taken up by Peter Reeves in his contribution to this volume.

Although their importance has been insufficiently recognized in previous work, both forests and water have played a part in the shaping of South Asian history which seems inconceivable in the context of Western cultures and ecosystems. While governmental intervention was not unknown in the pre-colonial period, in the last two centuries these resources have increasingly come under state control. In their different ways, virtually all the essays in this book underline the significance of the state as a leading, often the principal, actor in the environmental history of South Asia. David Gilmartin's discussion of canal irrigation and Peter Reeves' account of inland fisheries bring out this point most strongly, but it is evident in the discussion of forest regulation and legislation as well, and even in the history of urban smoke pollution in colonial Calcutta, which is the subject of Michael Anderson's essay. In many environmental arenas—forests, fisheries, irrigation, urban pollution, epidemic disease—the period 1870–1900 was a remarkably interventionist time, an age of high imperialism and supreme confidence in the capacity of science and technology to rule nature and utilize it to the full.[20] Both colonial and post-

[19] David Ludden, *Peasant History in South India* (Princeton, 1985); the theme was earlier taken up by Nirmal Sengupta for Bihar in 'The Indigenous Irrigation Organization of South Bihar', *Indian Economic and Social History Review*, 17:2, 1980, pp. 157–89.

[20] For forest legislation, see Ramachandra Guha, 'An Early Environmental

colonial states have powerfully influenced environmental change by formulating legislation pertaining to, and assuming control over, resources which were earlier under more informal and decentralized systems of management; by developing and implementing technologies that have dramatically altered the physical environment, as in irrigation works and dam construction; and by creating a transport and communications network (most obviously in India's extensive railway system) that, in aiding the process of commodification, has greatly increased the spatial scale of resource flows. This focus upon the agency of the state, so crucial to discussion of the environmental history of South Asia, also points to an area of enquiry relatively neglected by environmental historians elsewhere.[21]

But these are not the only considerations for an environmental history of South Asia. External contiguity is important as well. Migration and trade, conquest and religion, have for thousands of years exposed South Asia to a host of external environment influences. As K.N. Chaudhuri has shown, the Indian Ocean was an important medium of interaction and exchange long before the arrival of the Portuguese at the end of the fifteenth century, and the process of trans-oceanic exchange as it affected India might as readily apply to plants and pathogens as to more historically familiar items of maritime trade and cultural baggage.[22] Clearly, an environmental history of South Asia cannot meaningfully be an insular history.

---

Debate: The Making of the 1878 Forest Act', *Indian Economic and Social History Review*, 27:1, 1990, pp. 65–84; and for disease control, David Arnold, 'Touching the Body: Perspectives on the Indian Plague', in Ranajit Guha (ed.), *Subaltern Studies V* (Delhi, 1987), pp. 55–90. For the more general point about the West's presumption of mastery over nature, see Michael Adas, *Machines as the Measure of Men: Science, Technology, and Ideologies of Western Dominance* (Ithaca, 1989).

21 But perhaps with important parallels elsewhere in the colonial world, as in Australia, South East Asia and sub-Saharan Africa: on the latter, see David Anderson and Richard Grove (eds.), *Conservation in Africa: People, Parks, Priorities* (Cambridge, 1987).

22 Chaudhuri, *Trade and Civilisation*; A.M. Watson, *Agricultural Innovation*

And yet, despite the appeal of the Braudelian *longue durée* to the recovery of India's environmental history, this must also be a history of fracture and radical disjuncture. Although the ecological rupture may not have been as extreme as that experienced by the Americas in the wake of Columbus's landfall in 1492 (graphically described by Alfred W. Crosby in *The Columbian Exchange*),[23] the effects of European intervention were still very marked starting with the Portuguese arrival. While some recent writers on South Asia have tended to play down the impact of the British on India while stressing deep-seated economic, political and cultural continuities, the contributors to this volume, including Jacques Pouchepadass, Neeladri Bhattacharya, David Hardiman and Peter Reeves, demonstrate how European colonialism in India entailed a rapid and significant modification of the natural environment, which in turn had profound consequences for life in the cities and in the countryside. The pace of ecological change has accelerated still further in recent decades, under the auspices of state-directed economic development in the independent countries of South Asia. This has sucked in even those regions which were once relatively isolated—a process of change discussed here in some detail by Mark Poffenberger.

For the five centuries since Columbus, the concept of the *longue durée* has little meaning for American history either, where, analogous with South Asia, European colonization was a prime agent of environmental and social change. Crosby, one of the leading American scholars in the field, has even suggested that the ecological impact of colonialism has in fact been quite different in the experience of the New World and the Old. In his book, *Ecological Imperialism*, he argues that the main reason for the Europeans' success in conquering and colonizing the New World was not, as has been commonly supposed, their superior weaponry,

---

*in the Early Islamic World: The Diffusion of Crops and Farming Techniques, 700–1100* (Cambridge, 1983); David Arnold, 'The Indian Ocean as a Disease Zone, 1500–1950', *South Asia*, 14:2, 1991, pp. 1–21.

[23] Alfred W. Crosby, *The Columbian Exchange: The Biological and Cultural Consequences of 1492* (Westport, 1972).

but rather their 'portmanteau biota'—the complex of diseases, plants and animals which accompanied them and which devastated indigenous cultures and their supportive ecosystems. This ecological invasion, rather than the feats of famed *conquistadores*, then paved the way for the creation of prosperous colonial settlements founded on European-style agriculture and stock-raising in zones which Crosby describes as 'neo-Europes'.[24] Historians have begun to take Crosby to task for his biological determinism, for it may be wondered whether, even in his 'neo-Europes', the establishment of European power was so closely tied to its biological heritage and epidemiological good fortune. A more serious objection from the viewpoint of South Asia is Crosby's implied argument that European colonialism had correspondingly little ecological impact in the Old World, where the tropical environment was inhospitable to large-scale white settlement and where the populations had greater resistance to diseases, such as smallpox and measles, which had killed Amerindians in their millions. But in fact even in regions like South Asia, and perhaps Africa too, where Europeans did not achieve an automatic, biologically assured domination over the indigenous population, they did succeed—as the essays in this volume clearly show—in fundamentally reshaping the socio-ecological fabric of the colony and the colonized. Having achieved political control through their superior military and technological resources, European colonial regimes were well situated to manipulate a seemingly unfavourable environment to their own advantage and profit.[25] While they escaped genocide, the colonized of South Asia were, nevertheless, exposed to the major ecological consequences of this intervention—namely, growing environmental degradation and restrictions on access to natural resources previously more freely available for their use.

As the essays in this volume also make explicit, the environment in South Asia needs to be understood, too, as a contested

[24] Alfred W. Crosby, *Ecological Imperialism, 900–1900: The Biological Expansion of Europe, 900–1900* (Cambridge, 1986).

[25] For a preliminary critique, see Arnold, 'Indian Ocean'.

space, a site of conflict and confrontation—but also a place of flight and evasion—between competing economic activities and between the social groups dependent upon them. The concern here is not simply with man's place in nature, but with the kinds of men and women who contended for a share in or mastery over natural resources of various kinds. While it is perhaps all too easy to construct the pre-colonial period in South Asia as some kind of golden age, free from environmental strife,[26] the likelihood is that this is an age-old phenomenon, albeit one that was intensified and given fresh impetus by the kinds of changes these essays describe. This kind of history thus needs to draw not only upon the history of the state as a leading environmental actor, but also to explore the course of popular struggles and the ways in which these have been rooted in, and conditioned by, environmental issues.[27]

Moreover, the environment is and has long been a contested site at an ideological as well as material level. It is impossible not to be struck by the multiplicity of ideas, images and meanings the environment conjures up in modern South Asia—the sacred and the scientific, the romantic and the pathogenic, the militaristic, the commercial and the exotic. These may be conflicting understandings when played out at a certain level of abstraction, but they also directly inform the ways in which the environment was historically regulated and contested. We can see suggested in these essays the rich potentialities of investigating science and

26 The 'golden age' syndrome seems particularly entrenched in Vandana Shiva, *Staying Alive: Women, Ecology and Development* (London, 1989).

27 Sumit Sarkar, 'Primitive Rebellion and Modern Nationalism: A Note on Forest Satyagraha in the Non-Co-operation and Civil Disobedience Movements', in K.N. Panikar (ed.), *National and Left Movements in India* (New Delhi, 1980); David Arnold, 'Rebellious Hillmen: The Gudem-Rampa Risings, 1839–1924', in Ranajit Guha (ed.), *Subaltern Studies I* (Delhi, 1982), pp. 88–142; D.E.U. Baker, '"A Serious Time": Forest Satyagraha in Madhya Pradesh, 1930', *Indian Economic and Social History Review*, 21:1, 1984, pp. 71–90; David Hardiman, 'Power in the Forest: The Dangs, 1820–1940', in David Arnold and David Hardiman (eds.), *Subaltern Studies VIII* (Delhi, 1994).

technology, medicine and the law, as colonizing projects in their attempts to bring forests and fisheries, highways and watercourses —and, of course, the people themselves—within expanding systems of comprehension and control.

Thus far we have pointed to the ecological distinctiveness of South Asia and to the specificity of its historical experience. There are two other important, though not always acknowledged, influences at work on the environmental historian—the nature of developments and debates in contemporary South Asia, and a deeper substratum of cultural experience unique to the subcontinent. Indeed, the emergence of environmental history as a special field in South Asia must be linked directly to ongoing processes of ecological degradation and to the growth of a vigorous environmental movement in the region.[28] In the 1970s a series of countrywide protests by peasants and tribals prompted a thoroughgoing critique of forest policy in modern India. The forestry debate in turn led historians to look more closely at the role of forests and forest products in local economies, and to investigate the origins and outcome of state forestry science and legislation. More recently, the politics of water use has replaced the forest question as the most contentious issue on the South Asian environmental agenda, encouraging historians and anthropologists to move into what was previously poorly charted terrain. As we have suggested, forests and water have always been central to the making of South Asian history; yet it has been the visible deterioration of these resources in the present, and the emergence of bitter social conflicts over their control and use, that, more than anything else, have brought them within the orbit of environmental history.

Like other kinds of historians, environmental historians often take their clues from the present. How they then approach the

[28] See, in this connection, Anil Agarwal, *et al.* (eds.), *The State of India's Environment, 1982: A Citizens' Report* (New Delhi, 1982), and *The State of India's Environment, 1984–85: The Second Citizens' Report* (New Delhi, 1985).

problem at hand is also keenly influenced by the cultural milieu in which they work. For example, popular opposition to large dams in the United States has, in markedly nostalgic vein, emphasized the loss of wilderness areas through the construction of dams. In turn, environmental historians of the American West have indicted river valley projects for their destruction of free-flowing rivers and virgin forests.[29] By contrast, resistance to large dams in contemporary South Asia is more strongly human-centred, stressing the displacement of communities from their traditional habitats as well as lopsided resource flows between country and city.[30] Environmentalists have also put forward decentralized, environmentally benign technical alternatives (in the 'small is beautiful' mould) to centralized and destructive patterns of water control. These ideological trends, so different from those prevailing in Western environmentalism, will inevitably influence future histories of dam projects in South Asia.

In India, where there is no greater source of moral authority, Gandhi has emerged as the patron saint of the environmental movement. In providing an environmental gloss on Gandhi's ideas, leading activists have invoked his ethic of self-restraint, his attacks on consumerism, and his celebration of village society as providing building-blocks for the construction of an environmentally and socially harmonious alternative to modern industrial development.[31] By comparison, the cultural icons of the Western

29 See, for example, Tim Palmer, *Endangered Rivers and the Conservation Movement* (Berkeley, 1982); Donald Worster, *Rivers of Empire: Water, Aridity and the Growth of the American West* (New York, 1985).

30 See, for example, Nirmal Sengupta, 'Irrigation: Traditional *versus* Modern', *Economic and Political Weekly*, vol. XX, nos 45–47, November 1985, pp. 1919–38; E. Ganguli-Thukral (ed.), *Big Dams, Displaced People* (New Delhi, 1992).

31 Anil Agarwal and Vandana Shiva, in different ways, show the impact of Gandhi's ideas. See also the history of the Chipko movement in Ramachandra Guha, *The Unquiet Woods: Ecological Change and Peasant Resistance in the Himalaya* (Delhi and Berkeley, 1989); and Ramachandra Guha, 'Ideological Trends in Indian Environmentalism', *Economic and Political Weekly*, vol. XXIII, no. 49, 3 December 1988, pp. 2578–81.

environmental movement are more often individuals, such as John Muir, who have tended to downplay human concerns in their defence of the unspoilt wilderness.[32] Those currents have had a strong impact on the writing of environmental history in the West—and, without all becoming Gandhians, environmental historians of South Asia have had to take some account of the ideas of Gandhi and his modern disciples.

This raises an important final issue, namely that it is important not to assume that environmental ideas current in the West are necessarily of universal applicability. It is possible to see the roots of modern environmentalism in Britain, for instance, in a specific historical and cultural tradition—a tradition of naturalism and rural romanticism, of Gilbert White and John Constable, of Wordsworth and Ruskin, and the impact of the industrial revolution on urban, middle-class sensibilities. Such ideas and concepts were not readily replicated abroad—or had only a limited impact. Gandhi, despite his student days in London and his extensive reading of English works, was hardly indebted for his environmentalist views to Wordsworthian romanticism; and indeed, for all his attachment to the Ruskin of *Unto This Last*, he seems not to have been affected at all by the Ruskin who revelled in nature and rhapsodized over misty mountains and gushing streams: Gandhi's ashram at Sevagram could not have been further, in an intellectual as in a scenic sense, from Ruskin's lakeside home at Brantwood. Rather, Gandhi's environmentalism had its roots in a deep antipathy to urban civilization and a belief in self-sufficiency, in self- abnegation and denial rather than wasteful consumption. Gandhi was not going back to nature but to the village and to the peasantry as the heart and soul of India, to rural asceticism and harmony as against urban bustle and industrial strife.

In all these respects the environmental history of South Asia is a field which, the richness and theoretical sophistication of work on other regions notwithstanding, must develop its own voice,

[32] Stephen Fox, *The American Conservation Movement: John Muir and His Legacy* (Madison, 1985).

vocabulary, and research strategies. Even more so perhaps than social history or women's history, environmental history needs to respond directly—in both theory and practice—to the ecological and cultural distinctiveness of the South Asian experience. It is the distinctive nature of that experience which the following essays set out to examine and address.

Chapter One

# Forests, Pastoralists and Agrarian Society in Mughal India*

CHETAN SINGH

The rural landscape of Mughal India is frequently depicted as a vast expanse of cultivated land peppered with innumerable villages. Its highly differentiated, peasant-centred village community has been graphically described by numerous scholars, along with the hierarchy of ubiquitous revenue officials upon whose diligence the Mughal political edifice ultimately rested. This picture of Mughal rural society, which has emerged through a laborious examination of court chronicles and official revenue records, is coloured by the prejudices of its original creators. What is implicitly articulated in this picture is a self-image of the very society that generated these chronicles and revenue records in the first place. Thus, subtly reasserted in many modern works, has appeared the world-view of the Mughal courtier and the petty revenue official.

For the Mughals, a civilized society was one primarily engaged in agriculture, alongside other more sophisticated commercial activity. It was nurtured by, and conversely lent support to, a state that regarded the protection of the peasant as an essential

* I am grateful to the participants at the conference on 'South Asia's Changing Environment' held at Bellagio in March 1992. Their comments on an earlier version of this paper have helped me immensely. The long discussions I have had with Professor A.R. Khan, my colleague in the History Department at the University of Himachal Pradesh, have been equally useful.

obligation and the extension of agriculture as a cardinal objective. This perception was part of the socio-political thinking amongst dominant elements within the Mughal empire. There was a sound underlying assumption here, namely that the prosperity of the Mughal ruling class hinged upon its success in expanding and strengthening the empire's agrarian foundations.[1]

In reality, however, it was not entirely upon settled villages and revenue-yielding land that the stability of Mughal society depended. What seems to have escaped notice so far is the fact that there was much that lay beyond the agrarian economy of the Mughal heartland. If the Mughal 'system' in its process of expansion gradually created the social and economic context within which it functioned, it was in turn fundamentally affected by the 'others' whom it sought at least to dominate, if not to integrate. Over the long term, Mughal society and polity underwent several changes. In the making of these no small part was likely to have been played by people and areas which were neither fully within the 'system' nor typically 'Mughal'.[2]

The Mughal ruling class did not enjoy an unchallenged monopoly over geographical space and natural resources even within the political confines of the empire. Ecological diversity ensured that these were shared with a host of other social organizations and utilized in different ways by each of them. It can be argued

[1] See Abul Fazl, *Ain-i-Akbari* (New Delhi, 1978), II, pp. 41–2, 46–50, 58–9, for the duties of the *faujdar* and *amalguzar.* Abul Fazl writes that the amalguzar 'should be a friend of the agriculturist . . . He should consider himself the representative of the lord paramount . . . He should strive to bring waste lands into cultivation and take heed that what is in cultivation fall not waste.' See also Irfan Habib, *Agrarian System of Mughal India, 1556–1707* (Bombay, 1963), pp. 249, 251–6.

[2] For arguments regarding the role of tribes within the Mughal empire, see C.A. Bayly, *Rulers, Townsmen and Bazaars: North Indian Society in the Age of British Expansion, 1770–1870* (Cambridge, 1983), pp. 28–30, and his *Imperial Meridian: The British Empire and the World, 1780–1830* (Harlow, 1989), pp. 35–46; Chetan Singh, 'Conformity and Conflict: Tribes and the "Agrarian System" of Mughal India', *Indian Economic and Social History Review* (hereafter *IESHR*), 25:3, 1988, pp. 319–40.

that environmental factors crucially affected the nature of socio-economic developments in the empire, and a proper appreciation of these factors would enable a better understanding of the evolution of state and society in large parts of pre-colonial South Asia.[3] This neglected issue is addressed here: What was the environment of Mughal India, and how did medieval society respond to it?

## I

To begin with, it can be suggested that the extent of forested or uncultivated territory was considerable.[4] Accounts of Mughal forays against hostile local chieftains refer, all too frequently, to the thick jungles and inhospitable uncultivated countryside that the imperialists had to contend with during the course of their expeditions.[5] In the region of Chanderi, for instance, Babur's

[3] François Bernier, *Travels in the Mogul Empire, 1656–1668* (Delhi, 1989), p. 453. About the impact of environment Bernier observed, 'it is often said in the language of Aristotle that Egypt is the workmanship of the Nile, so may it be observed that Bengale is the production of the Ganges.'

[4] Shireen Moosvi, *The Economy of the Mughal Empire, c. 1595: A Statistical Study* (Delhi, 1987), pp. 65–6; Shireen Moosvi, 'Ecology, Population Distribution and Settlement in Mughal India', *Man and Environment,* 14:1, 1989, pp. 109–16. During Akbar's reign the gross cultivated area was unlikely to have been more than 55 per cent of the gross cultivation in 1909–10 of large parts of north India. When compared to the geographical extent of the Mughal *subas* of this region, this would have been even less. Even Bernier's comment can be interpreted in this manner, for he informs us that 'of the vast tracts of country constituting the empire of Hindustan many are little more than sand or barren mountains, badly cultivated, and thinly peopled and even a good portion of the good land remains untilled for want of labourers . . . ' Bernier, *Travels,* p. 205. For a description of dense forests in the *terai* north of Gorakhpur, see Jean Baptiste Tavernier, *Travels in India* (1st edn. 1676; New Delhi, 1972), II, p. 205. See also Habib, *Agrarian System,* pp. 1–24; Irfan Habib, *An Atlas of the Mughal Empire* (Delhi, 1982).

[5] There are also several earlier accounts which show quite clearly that large forested areas were a common feature in north India. During his campaign in the Siwaliks against hill rajas, Timur had to cut his way through thick forests:

artillery was preceded by 'active overseers and a mass of spadesmen to level the road and cut the jungles down . . .'[6] During the time of Akbar, the campaign against Raja Madhukar found the Mughals advancing towards Orchha in a similar fashion. We are told this about the surrounding territories: 'the country was forest, and the marching of the army was difficult, they cut down the trees one day and marched the next.'[7] Even during subsequent reigns the military campaigns in this region were conducted in this manner.[8]

In many parts of Bihar, too, a similar problem was encountered by the Mughal armies. Shahbaz Khan, who was assigned the task of suppressing the rebellion of Gajpati, a zamindar of Jagdishpur in Bihar, had to spend 'nearly two months engaged in cutting down the trees' around the fort before he could capture it.[9] It could be argued that these forts were, for strategic reasons, deliberately built in thickly wooded and isolated areas and that

---

he even ordered that while preparing for battle the soldiers should carry hatchets to 'clear away the jungle': *Mulfuzat-i-Timuri* or *Tuzuk-i-Timuri* (the autobiography of Timur) in H.M. Elliot and J. Dowson, *The History of India as Told by its own Historians* (rpt. Delhi, 1964), III, pp. 463, 469. See Ziauddin Barani, *Tarikh-i-Firoz Shahi* in Elliot and Dowson, *History of India*, III, pp. 103–6, for a description of the thick jungles encountered during campaigns by Balban. Regarding a campaign in Katehar, it is noted that 'Woodcutters were sent out to cut roads through the jungle, and the army passing along these brought the Hindus to submission': Abdul Qadir Badaoni, *Muntakhab-ut-Tawarikh* (rpt. Delhi, 1973), p. 378.

[6] Zahiruddin Muhammad Babur, *Baburnama* (rpt. New Delhi, 1970), p. 572.

[7] Abul Fazl, *Akbarnama* (rpt. Delhi, 1972), III, pp. 324–5.

[8] Abdul Hamid Lahori, *Badshahnama*, in Elliot and Dowson, *History of India*, VII, p. 48, for the campaign against Jajhar Singh Bundela at Chauragarn (near Jabalpur) in 1634.

[9] *Akbarnama*, III, p. 261; *Muntakhab-ut-Tawarik*, II, p. 182. For the area around Gaya, see *Akbarnama*, III, pp. 472–3. See also Nuruddin Muhammad Jahangir, *Tuzuk-i-Jahangiri* (rpt. Delhi, 1968), I, pp. 315–16, for the campaign against Durjan Sal of 'Khokhara' in Bihar.

information pertaining to military campaigns does not necessarily indicate the forested nature of large tracts of territory. While this might be partly true, there were nevertheless many fortresses which were located in, or near, well-populated towns of reasonable importance where the approaches were well forested. A case in point was Kangra. We are told by DeLaet, an early-seventeenth-century traveller, that the only approach to Kangra was 'through a forest 50 *cos* broad', and that while advancing on the fort the Mughals had to cut down the forest as they advanced at a rate of 'about a *cos* a day', and 'finally reached the fortress in the eighth month'.[10] The fortresses of Jasrota and Mau were similarly located in 'impenetrable jungles'.[11] This seems to indicate that many *qasbas*, towns and some adjoining agricultural tracts were still in the nature of clearings in the midst of undisturbed forests. Interestingly, in a letter to the Shah of Iran, Akbar recounted amongst his major achievements his advance into Kashmir, during which thousands of men were employed in 'removing rocks, and in cutting down forests and making roads'.[12]

While their writ ran unchallenged over large agricultural expanses, the Mughals found it difficult to cope in places where forest, desert or topography sheltered strong political entities from their pervasive and expanding influence. Contemporary observers

[10] Joannes DeLaet, *The Empire of the Great Mogol* (Bombay, 1928), p. 195. A much earlier reference to the 'town (*shahr*) of Nagarkot which is a large and important town of Hindustan says that 'the road thither lay through jungles': *Malfuzat-i-Timuri*, in Elliot and Dowson, *History of India*, III, p. 465.

[11] Shaikh Illahadad Faizi Sirhindi, *Akbarnama*, in Elliot and Dowson, *History of India*, VI, pp. 127–8.

[12] *Akbarnama*, III, p. 1010. See also DeLaet, *Empire*, pp. 183–4, regarding a Mughal campaign in Rajasthan during Jahangir's reign: 'the royal army then advanced to Siavend . . . a very strong place, which the Kings of Delhi had never dared to attack on account of the impenetrable wilderness and forests by which it is surrounded. Abdul Chan gave orders that these forests should be gradually cut down ahead of the advancing army . . . ' On reaching the fortress, 'The moat was filled up with logs of trees, and so huge a mound was raised against the walls that at last, the garrison . . . fell.'

repeatedly refer to areas that were not easily amenable to Mughal control.[13] Manucci, who lived and travelled in India for a long time, makes a very interesting observation. He writes:

> There are also in this empire other lords who call themselves zamindars . . . Such men do not maintain cavalry: the greater number live in the midst of jungles, and these usually pay no revenue, unless it be taken by force of arms. At this day, taking the whole Mughal empire, these rajas great and petty and the zamindars, exceed five thousand in number.[14]

While periodic military expeditions ostensibly brought many such areas under imperial paramountcy, the Mughals were still inclined to allow them a large degree of economic and political autonomy.[15] This relative freedom enjoyed by the chieftains was not merely the outcome of a proclaimed policy of magnanimity. The Mughal state, in fact, did not have the military and administrative where-

[13] Apart from the more powerful rulers who ruled over different parts of India. Babur noted that 'there were also, in the hills and jungles, many *rais* and rajas': *Baburnama*, p. 481. Mahomed Kasim Ferishta, *History of the Rise of Mahomedan Power in India till the Year* AD 1612 (rpt. New Delhi, 1981), IV, p. 313, emphasizes Babur's words: 'India abounds with forests and extensive wilderness, full of all sorts of trees; so much so, that these wastes seem to offer inducement, both to rajas and subjects, to revolt from the government.' DeLaet, *Empire*, p. 242, says that 'the empire contains many provinces which are rendered difficult of access on account of their mountainous character and the dense forests with which they are covered. Large armies cannot operate in such districts, which are held by Radias [rajas] . . . If opposed by the Mogols with a greater force than they can cope with, they merely retreat into their mountains and await a better opportunity of success.' Cf. Bernier, *Travels*, p. 205: 'The empire of the Great Mogol comprehends several nations, over which he is not absolute master.'

[14] Niccolao Manucci, *Storia Do Mogor* (rpt. Calcutta, 1965), II, p. 417. Cf. ibid., II, p. 414: 'The roads are not direct, owing to the forests and mountains and the interposition of territories belonging to the different rajas and zamindars who allow no travellers to pass through, out of the fear they have of the Mogul.'

[15] For a detailed description of the political relationship between the chiefs and the Mughal empire under Akbar, see A.R. Khan, *Chieftains in the Mughal Empire during the Reign of Akbar* (Simla, 1977).

withal to directly govern and simultaneously obtain economic benefit from these areas of apparently low productivity.[16] John Fryer observed during the reign of Aurangzeb that the Mughal armies were 'unfit for such barren and uneasy Places . . . .'[17] Moreover, the monetary worth of such territory could not easily be converted into the agricultural revenue statistics to which Mughal revenue officials were more accustomed.

Therefore, the continued existence of autonomous chieftaincies within the Mughal empire was to a great extent the result of the geography and physical environment. If on the one hand the vulnerability of larger cultivated stretches to Mughal military might facilitated close supervision by revenue officials, it was the existence of 'jungles' and 'ravines' within the territory of many of the chieftains, on the other, that probably discouraged direct Mughal interference. While the finances of several of these chiefships drew heavily upon peasant-centred agricultural activity,[18] the proportionally large uncultivated areas within their boundaries must also have necessitated the search for economic alternatives. A wider mix of productive activities utilizing the resources of forests and grassland may thus have become essential. The

[16] Though the Mughal army was successful against Durjan Sal in Bihar, Jahangir says that 'in consequence of the difficult roads and thickness of the jungles they contented themselves with taking two or three diamonds and left him in his former condition': *Tuzuk-i-Jahangiri*, I, p. 315. DeLaet, in *Empire*, p. 243, sees the Mughals' inability to control these areas as a serious political problem: 'The Mogol Emperor has hitherto proved unable to find a cure for these dangerous diseases of the body politic.'

[17] John Fryer, *A New Account of East India and Persia being Nine Years Travels, 1672–1681* (1698; reprinted Liechtenstein, 1967), II, p. 59. This comment was made with reference to the Mughal campaign in the Deccan against Shivaji.

[18] Most of the larger and powerful chiefships maintained a formal state organization in which an important part was played by the land-revenue administration. Two relevant regional studies are G.D. Sharma, *Rajput Polity: A Study of Politics and Administration of the State of Marwar, 1638–1749* (Delhi, 1977), and Dilbagh Singh, *The State, Landlord and Peasants: Rajasthan in the Eighteenth Century* (Delhi, 1990).

relatively greater freedom that peasants probably enjoyed in such an environment may sometimes have been incentive enough for many of them to migrate from the more rigidly administered imperial territories to those controlled by autonomous rajas.[19] Each chieftaincy, influenced as it was by its own peculiar environmental situation, must have developed a suitable balance of a variety of economic activities from which it derived its revenues. Examples of this sort were the principalities located in Rajasthan and Gujarat. According to Ferishta, in the territories of these chiefs 'little other grain but *bajry* and *jowar* are cultivated. The revenue is for the most part derived from horses and camels'.[20]

Any South Asian state attempting to expand to subcontinental dimensions would, therefore, have been confronted with a rich diversity of both physical and socio-economic environments. Furthermore, if it endeavoured to go beyond merely establishing an overarching political suzerainty and sought to squeeze out surplus directly from local-level economies, such a state would have had to evolve a multiplicity of revenue-extracting methods, each suited to a particular socio-economic system. While it had the ability to penetrate down to lower social levels in many agricultural areas, the Mughal revenue machinery relied considerably on intermediaries for its efficient functioning. In regions that were strikingly dissimilar from those where the Mughal revenue officials operated, the autonomy of such intermediaries must have been even greater. This meant that the Mughals were able to obtain a share of the wealth generated in divergent and peripheral economies only in an indirect manner. Very often, a substantial part of the *peshkash* (tribute) that many of the autonomous chiefs sent to the emperor consisted either of forest produce or pastoral products which

[19] Francisco Pelsaert, *Remonstrantie*, published as *Jahangir's India* (Delhi, 1972), p. 47; Bernier, *Travels*, p. 226; Habib, *Agrarian System*, pp. 336–7.

[20] Ferishta, *Mahomedan Power*, IV, p. 318; *Ain-i-Akbari*, II, p. 256.

[21] An earlier reference to how this non-monetary system of tribute extraction worked is obtained from an account of Kabul by Babur for 1519. He fixed the tribute of the Khirichli and Samu-khail Afghans at '4,000 sheep'. A punitive raid on the Waziri Afghans compelled them to proffer a tribute of '300 sheep':

implies the harnessing of grazing land.[21] Despite their inability to exercise direct economic control over these areas of mixed (agrarian, pastoral, forest) economies, the Mughals were thus able to extract from them, over irregular periods, a small portion of their wealth in the form of peshkash. This was perhaps the best available compromise that the Mughal state could strike, through the chieftaincies, with diverse socio-economic systems that were largely different from its own.

Like the Mughal empire, however, most of the autonomous chiefships which interacted with it were reasonably developed state formations. This enabled the Mughals to establish an acceptable political relationship, the principles of which were in fact formulated as early as the reign of Akbar.[22] Amongst these were also to be found tribal chieftaincies that had accepted Mughal suzerainty, or even been incorporated into its military structure. Yet in many parts of Mughal India there existed several tribes which could not be made to conform consistently even to a loosely defined political

---

*Baburnama*, p. 413. Cf. Zain Khan, *Tabaqat-i-Baburi* (rpt. Delhi, 1982), p. 110; *Ain-i-Akbari*, II, p. 183 for honey, wax and wooden-ware from the mountains north of Awadh; DeLaet, *Empire*, p. 59, refers to valuable herbs from the territory of Raja Basu (Nurpur in Kangra). *Tuzuk-i-Jahangiri*, I, p. 218: the peshkash of the Raja of Kumaon included *gunth* ponies, hawks, falcons, 'navels of musk', swords (*khanda*), daggers (*katar*) etc. According to Bernier, *Travels*, pp. 419–20, some areas in Kashmir paid the annual tribute in leather and wool; Tavernier, in *Travels*, II, p. 206, says the Raja of Nepal sent an elephant in tribute annually. See Habib, *Atlas of the Mughal Empire*, p. 41, for elephants taken in tribute from the Morung chiefs. Manucci, *Storia*, II, pp. 415–16, says—with regard to the smaller rajas who had strongholds located north of the Ganges—that they sent the 'rarities produced in their country. Some send gavioens (sparrow-hawks), falcons and other birds of prey, pretty birds, honey and wax. With the last article they produce a waxed cloth for the lining of tents and other uses in the royal household. They also make candles for the harem . . .'

22 Khan, *Chieftains in the Mughal Empire*, pp. 206–24.

23 Bayly, *Rulers, Townsmen and Bazaars*, p. 80: 'in this period the state was only one of the political formations . . . The land-revenue based state and settled agriculture did not occupy the whole of the social and geographical space of the area, and there were large tracts where they were both on the defensive.'

relationship.[23] It was these more fiercely autarchic tribes which probably lay even further from the Mughal 'system'—as it has come to be understood by scholars. Many such tribes were, from time to time, to be found in conflict with Mughal authority and had established a reputation as 'thieves and plunderers' of the 'king's territories'.[24] The topography of the areas they occupied suggests that they relied considerably, though not exclusively, on pastoralism. With this they combined a sense of social or communal cohesion that was characteristically distinct from the differentiated agricultural village communities of the core Mughal areas.

Scattered references in our sources indicate that societies which were predominantly non-agricultural in nature were viewed as primitive and as a threat to the settled agrarian areas where Mughal land revenue regulations were methodically applied. The strangeness of some of these to Mughal society comes through to us from a few stray comments of Abul Fazl. Near the fort of Chunar (in suba Allahabad), we are told, 'is a tribe of men who go naked living in the wilds, and subsist by their bows and arrows and the game they kill.'[25] While hunter-gatherers certainly appeared peculiar to contemporary observers, there were many other tribes which, even though partially agricultural and well known to Mughal society, were also perceived as being socially distinct. The Kolis, Bhils and Gonds (suba Khandesh) are referred to as people who 'can tame lions so that they will obey their commands' and about whom 'strange tales are told'.[26]

[24] Manucci, *Storia*, II, pp. 428, 430. Cf. Singh, 'Conformity and Conflict' pp. 337–8. Forest areas in medieval England were often viewed as being disorderly, as breeding 'atheism and consequently all disobedience of God and King': John Martin, *Feudalism to Capitalism: Peasant and Landlord in English Agrarian Development* (London, 1983), p. 200. See Bayly, *Rulers, Townsmen and Bazaars*, p. 219, for British attitudes to tribes in colonial India, where 'Nomads and wanderers were seen as disorderly elements—carriers of roguery and dissidence.'

[25] *Ain-i-Akbari*, II, p. 170.

[26] Ibid., II, p. 233. See *Muntakhab-ut-Tawarikh*, II, p. 178, for the Kharwaha tribe of sailors, and W.H. Moreland, *India at the Death of Akbar: An Economic Study* (rpt. Delhi, 1974), p. 27.

The Gonds, in particular, are repeatedly mentioned in the *Akbarnama* on account of their considerable population and the large area they controlled.[27] Apart from discovering that the Gonds lived 'in the wilds', we also learn that 'the people of India despise them and regard them as outside the pale of their realm and religion'.[28] Quite clearly, therefore, these peripheral societies were considered by the Mughals as external to their own society. Yet, because they were seen as an occasional hindrance to Mughal hegemony, the imperial authorities intermittently endeavoured to establish a military dominance over these people as a prelude to more fundamental economic inroads into their territories.[29] Also significant is the fact that such societies were not confined to the geographically distant parts of the empire. Some of them were located quite close to important political and military centres,[30] and probably combined the practice of agriculture with a considerable dependence

[27] *Akbarnama*, II, pp. 323–4. According to 'faithful narrators', Garh Katanga 'contained 70,000 inhabited villages'.

[28] Ibid. Their low status did not, however, prevent Salbahan of Ratha, a Chandel raja with declining fortunes, from giving his daughter Durgavati in marriage to Dalpat, the son of Aman Dás, a wealthy Gond chief.

[29] Ibid., pp. 563–4. In 1582 Todar proposed regulations by which Mughal functionaries could take effective action against the 'dwellers in the ravines' who, being of a 'turbulent disposition think the ruggedness of their country a protection and make long the arm of oppression'. The aim was to reduce them to a docile revenue-paying peasantry, and nomads were to be settled as agriculturists. In the context of Kabul, Abdul Fazl notes: 'There are many wild tribes . . . and most of them at the present time have become settled colonists': *Ain-i-Akbari*, II, p. 407. Akbar proudly refers to the suppression of the 'carnivorous Afghans' and the 'wicked Baluchis and other desert-dwellers who are of a bestial nature . . .': *Akbarnama*, III, p. 1010.

[30] Proper control over the fort of Rohtas in Bihar could only be established after the 'bandits of the neighbourhood of the fort' had been coerced by the Mughal army: *Akbarnama*, II, p. 287; cf. ibid., p. 252, where Abul Fazl says that thirty *kos* from Agra, near the town of Sakit, were to be found lawless elements who 'were both ruffians and occupiers of rough places'. The Jats and Mewatis who were to be found at the very centre of the Mughal empire are well-known examples.

[31] Cf. the observation regarding the Roman legions which in the time of

upon pastoralism.[31] What seems to have insulated them from Mughal authority, irrespective of distance, were the densely forested areas which usually surrounded, or were interspersed with, their territories.[32] It was into these forests that they retreated when confronted with stronger Mughal armies. In the arid areas where animal husbandry was a primary occupation, the paucity of water and the inadequacy of local food supplies severely restricted the movement of large invading armies and, therefore, discouraged permanent Mughal occupation. Their own economies being structurally suited to the desert, the pastoralists could seek temporary refuge in terrain where the Mughal forces dare not venture.[33]

At this point, however, it is important to sound a note of caution against overemphasizing the autonomy of the pastoral tribes. They were not totally isolated socio-economic entities, and their distinctiveness from agrarian society did not prevent them from interacting with it. In the north-west many Afghan tribes, particularly the Lohanis, were actively engaged in trading activities that drew them into a fairly close relationship with settled and

---

Caesar encountered Germanic tribes that were 'settled agriculturists, with a predominantly pastoral economy': Perry Anderson, *Passages from Antiquity to Feudalism* (London, 1978), p. 107.

32 *Ain-i-Akbari*, II, pp. 251–2, 254, for the Koli and Jaitwah tribes living in the forests; *Tuzuk-i-Jahangiri*, II, p. 285, for 'villagers' and cultivators', who 'passing their time in the shelter of thick jungles and difficult strong places in stubbornness and fearlessness, would not pay their rents to the *jagirdars*'; DeLaet. *Empire*, pp. 19, 21, 34, 184, for Bhils, 'Grassias' and Kolis, who lived in 'solitary places' and 'trackless retreats'; Manucci, *Storia*, II, p. 428, for Jats; see also Sujan Rai Bhandari, *Khulasat-ut-Tawarikh* (Delhi, 1918), p. 63.

33 DeLaet, *Empire*, pp. 68–70, referring to the area around Thattah, mentions 'savages who recognize no ruler' and were engaged in robbing travellers. Furthermore, 'if the king sends his armed forces against them they burn their huts, which are made of straw, and withdraw to rugged mountains.' See also Khan, *Chieftains*, pp. 63–73.

34 *Baburnama*, p. 235; *Akbarnama*, III, p. 1160; DeLaet, *Empire*, pp. 69–70. See B.R. Grover, 'An Integrated Pattern of Life in the Rural Society of North India During the Seventeenth and Eighteenth Centuries', *Proceedings of the Indian Historical Records Commission*, 1966, p. 5, for Gujars.

commercialized society.[34] Some sections among the Kolis, Bhils, Gonds, Bhattis and probably numerous other tribes were significant elements of the Mughal military force in certain areas.[35] Despite their socially peripheral position, the various tribes of herdsmen scattered all over the Mughal empire would have engaged in various kinds of economic exchange with the adjoining agrarian society. Pastoral products, particularly ghee, were items of commercial value and served as an important linking factor between the two economies.[36] It was probably from such tribes that new social groups were added to the sedentarized agricultural population as and when the need arose.[37]

While he was resident in Kabul and prior to the invasion of Hindustan, Babur seems to have depended to a fair extent upon the pastoralists of that area; even subsequently, when he was near the Salt Range, he ensured that the flocks of country people were not harmed.[38] During their early years in India the Mughals were probably better able to utilize the economies of pastoral societies. Apart from the fact that the extent of Babur's kingdom was much smaller than that of his descendants, the Mughal land-revenue system was yet to emerge in its fully institutionalized form. Quite possibly, then, the smaller size and the relative lack of organizational

[35] *Ain-i-Akbari*, p. 233. While the Kolis, Bhils and Gonds constituted the provincial military force of suba Khandesh, they do not seem to have been part of the peasantry in this otherwise well-cultivated suba. Manucci, *Storia*, II, p. 430, for Bhattis of Lakhi Jangal in suba Lahore entering the faujdar's service.

[36] See *Ain-i-Akbari*, I, p. 60, for large quantities of ghee from Hisar-Firoza used in Akbar's kitchen. Raibari herdsmen were also apparently employed to graze the royal camels; *Ain-i-Akbari*, I, pp. 155–6. Shiv Das Lakhnawi, *Shahnama Munnawar Kalam* (Patna, 1980), relates an incident where a caravan was plundered by Jats near Hodal during the time of Churaman Jat: the merchants were 'carrying with them 1300 carts of clarified butter' which were taken away by the robbers. Ghee in such huge quantities was very likely to have been procured from pastoralists. See also Chetan Singh, *Region and Empire: Panjab in the Seventeenth Century* (Delhi, 1991), pp. 266–70; Bayly, *Rulers, Townsmen and Bazaars*, p. 29.

[37] Singh, *Region and Empire*, pp. 269–70.

[38] *Baburnama*, pp. 380, 402.

rigidity of the state both required and facilitated the tapping of non-agrarian sources of income from scattered pastoral communities. After its establishment on firmer 'agrarian' foundations and subsequent expansion, however, the Mughal empire seems to have relied primarily upon land revenue from large agricultural expanses. With this shift in the scale and nature of the state's financial activity, extraction of economic surplus from scattered pastoral societies probably became a distracting task with unpredictable results. Despite these fundamental changes, however, the interaction between Mughal agrarian society and the pastoralists can hardly have ceased.

As suggested earlier, the relationship between the two was not simply one of outright confrontation. Apart from the apparent political and military dimensions of the relationship, its socio-economic content seems likely to have been far more substantial than has so far been recognized. In many parts of the Mughal empire the lives of peasants and pastoralists were inextricably entwined. Even while being involved in the mutual exchange of products, the two were simultaneously engaged in a silent and fluctuating struggle of encroachment upon and retreat from each other's living space. While agriculturists frequently intruded into areas where the herds of pastoralists grazed, it was equally common for abandoned fields and habitations to be reappropriated by herdsmen who wandered on the fringes of cultivated areas.[39]

The history of agriculture in Mughal India was not, therefore, a case of the unabated expansion of cultivation and the relentless destruction of forests. There were times and places where the forest reasserted itself; old clearings were abandoned and new ones made in different places. This is apparent from an observation during the reign of Akbar by Fath Ullah Shirazi regarding revenue matters: 'The fluctuations of civilization are apparent to everyone. If in a

[39] DeLaet, *Empire*, pp. 46–7, says, of Sikandarabad, near Bayana, that the place is in ruins and 'is inhabited only by a few shepherds called Goagers (Gujars)'. Even the 'vast ruins of the ancient city of Delhi' had become 'only an abode of shepherds'.

village some land falls out of cultivation one endeavours to increase cultivation elsewhere.'[40]

II

> It ought to be remembered that the whole of the merchandise which is exported from the Moghul kingdom, comes from four kinds of plants—that is to say, the shrub that produces the cotton from which a large quantity of cloth, coarse and fine, is made . . . The second is the plant which produces indigo. The third is the one from which comes opium, of which a large amount is used on the Java coast. The fourth is the mulberry tree, on which their silk-worms are fed, and, as it may be said, that commodity [silk] is grown on these trees.
>
> —Niccolao Manucci[41]

By stating matters in this way Manucci reduced the most commercialized sector of the Mughal economy to an essential dependence upon 'four kinds of plants'. In so doing he implicitly provided a partial explanation for the pronounced interest of the Mughals in fostering agriculture and championing the cause of the peasantry against more mobile social groups.

Since the primary objective of the state was, as we have seen, the extension of cultivation, the peasants were encouraged to break new land. Upon the inhospitable fringes of agricultural areas were probably to be found ploughmen who laboured to push back the forest. Certain land-revenue regulations were specifically formulated as an incentive for this purpose. That newly cultivated land was entitled to concessional rates of taxation is well known. In addition to the state, influential members of the village community played an important part in the granting of ownership rights on virgin land to those who had the capital resources to bring it under cultivation.[42] The village *muqaddams* were given the authority to

[40] *Akbarnama*, III, p. 690.

[41] Manucci, *Storia*, II, p. 393.

[42] Satish Chandra, 'Writings on the Social History of Medieval India: Trends

parcel out uncultivated village land to whoever offered to bring it under the plough.[43] In the case of *madad-i-maash* grants, too, half the land granted consisted of cultivable waste which the grantee was expected to bring under cultivation.[44] Given the incentives that were provided by the Mughals, it is very likely that many zamindaris emerged at the frontiers of cultivation as a result of the clearing of forests organized by entrepreneurs of this kind. The actual work of felling was done by groups of professional wood-cutters and there probably existed, in some regions, entire castes which specialized in this kind of work.[45]

*Bankatai* (the clearing of forests) and the subsequent settling of cultivators were adequate reasons for staking a claim to the zamindari of an area, a claim which imperial authorities readily recognized.[46] Adjacent to the core agricultural areas of the Mughal empire, therefore, was territory where a perpetual struggle went on between cultivators and forests. These were also areas where different socio-economic systems interacted with each other. They

---

and Prospects', p. 89, and 'Role of the Local Community, the Zamindars and the State in Providing Capital Inputs for the Improvement and Expansion of Cultivation', pp. 166–83, both in *Medieval India: Society, the Jagirdari Crisis and the Village* (New Delhi, 1982).

43 Habib, *Agrarian System*, p. 133; Ali Muhammad Khan, *Mirat-i-Ahmadi* (Baroda, 1965), p. 241. In the *farman* dealing in great detail with the matter of land revenue, it is stated that where 'land is not owned, the owner is unknown, it should be given to one who is able to reclaim it so that he reclaims it.' See Bayly, *Rulers, Townsmen and Bazaars*, p. 101, for certain castes of cultivators which were engaged in the extension of agriculture in the eighteenth century.

44 *Ain-i-Akbari*, I, p. 280; Habib, *Agrarian System*, pp. 302–3.

45 Chandra, 'Role of the Local Community', p. 175. John Francis Gemelli Careri, *A Voyage Round the World*, in J.P. Guha (ed.), *India in the Seventeenth Century* (New Delhi, 1979), II, p. 311: 'There are also two tribes of Sutars or timber-men; the one called Concanes, and the other Gujarati.'

46 Muzaffar Alam, 'Eastern India in the Early Eighteenth Century Crisis': Some Evidence from Bihar', *IESHR*, 28:1, 1991, pp. 65–6. In suba Bihar, ploughs were donated by the government to such people. 'Every *hal mir* (i.e. one who has four or five ploughs) was to be 'given a *dastar* [turban] so that he may clear forests and bring land under cultivation'.

were driven to this as much by the logic of an expanding agrarian economy as by the pastoralists' or forest-dwellers' need for essential commodities from settled agriculturists.

Even at the best of times, and in close proximity to many of the agriculturally developed territories, there existed only an uneasy balance between cultivated areas, cultivable village wasteland and forests. Whenever the struggle between agriculturists and the jungle intensified, or conversely when the husbandmen were forced to abandon cultivation, even this equilibrium was overthrown. It is quite likely that the oppressive demands of revenue officials occasionally compelled peasants to leave their homes and seek shelter in the forests.[47]

An ambivalence, therefore, seems to have marked the peasant's interaction with the jungles that were often adjacent to his fields. His hostility towards the untamed wilderness was tempered by a basic dependence upon its natural abundance. Timber for the construction of his hut[48] and implements obviously came from these forests, as did fuel and much of the cattle fodder.[49] Now and then, when wild animals were successfully hunted down, a little

[47] During the reign of Muhammad Tughlak, when taxation in the Doab became unbearable, the cultivators 'set fire to their houses, and retired to the woods with their families and cattle. Many populous towns were abandoned and remained so for several years.' Furthermore, certain tribes which 'inhabited the country about Soonam and Samana, unable to discharge their rents, fled to the woods.' Ferishta, *Mahomedan Power*, I, pp. 243–4.

[48] *Baburnama*, p. 428, about the nature of villages in Hindustan: 'they need not build houses or set up walls—*khas*-grass abounds, wood is unlimited, huts are made and straightway there is a village or town!'

[49] B. Ch. Chabra (ed.), *Antiquities of Chamba* (1957), II, p. 147. The Chamba plate of Balabhadra (dated 1641) refers to '*banj* trees used for fodder'. *Mirat-i-Ahmadi*, p. 256, refers to 'leaves of *dhakah*, *paliyah* and *babul* skin etc., brought from the jungle . . . ' Though the reference is to their sale in the city, it seems reasonable to assume that the villages, with easier access, would have utilized such forest resources quite freely. Moreland, *India at the Death of Akbar*, p. 144, argues that while the rural population enjoyed an 'unrestricted supply of such produce', this advantage was offset by 'the damage caused to their crops by the wild animals'.

extra food was obtained.[50] Interestingly, even salt was obtained, in Assam, by processing the large leaves of a 'fig-tree'.[51]

It was in times of dire need, however, that the importance of forests came to be fully realized. An early-eighteenth-century description of famines in the region of Palwal and Hodal brings out the crucial role of forests as a source of additional food. During the famine of 1713, we are told, 'Many repaired to jungles and collecting the leaves and blossoms of the *Karial* boiled them and subsisted on the same.'[52] In the following year the rains came rather too late to benefit cultivation, but were sufficient to rejuvenate the vegetation in the forests. We learn that 'In the forest a kind of wild millet (*shamakh*) shot up so profusely that the people of that region, big and small, went daily to the forest and collected as much as each of them could bring, and thus gave themselves some energy.'[53] Thus, as a last resort, the forest was often of critical importance to famine-stricken people, a resource that stood between life and death.[54]

Recognition of the value of forests and their usefulness to the rural economy is implied in the land grants made by Raja Balbhadra of Chamba in 1641. To his cook the raja gifted the village of Kuhmaro inclusive of the 'forest and the hill-slope . . .'[55] In

[50] *Ain-i-Akbari*, II, pp. 181–2, for wild buffaloes which were numerous in *suba* Awadh. Abul Fazl says that 'people find sport in hunting them'. Wild asses were found in some of the drier areas and were, according to Jahangir, 'lawful food': see *Akbarnama*, II, p. 522; *Tuzuk-i-Jahangiri*, I, pp. 83–4.

[51] Tavernier, *Travels*, pp. 221–2.

[52] Lakhnawi, *Shahnama Munnawar Kalam*, p. 22.

[53] Ibid.

[54] Armies that ran short of food supplies during military campaigns were forced to search for food in forests. See *Muntakhab-ut-Tawarikh*, II, p. 242. In a campaign against Mewar the Mughal army had to 'sustain life upon the flesh of animals and the mango fruit. This latter grew there in such abundance as defies description. The common soldiers used to make a meal of it . . . in default in bread.' Cf. *Akbarnama*, III, p. 682: when Muzaffar Gujarati fled Mughal forces in 1548 he went to the 'mountains of Barda' where the forests 'thirty *kos* long and ten broad, are well-watered, and produce abundance of wild fruit'.

[55] *Antiquities of Chamba*, II, p. 146.

another grant of the same year the village of Sarotha was gifted to a Brahmin along with a 'watermill as well as the *banj* [oak] trees used for fodder'.[56] The fact that forest land and trees were considered worthy of specific mention in land grants suggests that in certain areas various kinds of rights over them had crystallized. Some of these rights, indeed, appear to have taken the form of individual ownership.

Pastures were another very important natural resource for the peasantry. But because of variations in different areas and at different seasons, it would be inappropriate to make a definite statement about the amount of pastureland that was available. A stray remark by Abul Fazl, to the effect that the means of earning a livelihood were 'as abundant to the labourer as forage for his cattle', conveys the impression that there was no shortage of pasturage.[57] This impression is further reinforced by the fact that during four months of the rainy season, and also when the emperor was on the march, no fodder allowance was permitted for animals in the imperial stables.[58] Bernier, on the other hand, in a more detailed account, seems to contradict Abul Fazl by referring to a 'great deficiency of pasture land'. 'The heat', he noted, 'is so intense, and the ground so parched, during eight months of the year, that the beasts of the field, ready to die of hunger, feed on every kind of filth like so many swine'.[59] In his description of the countryside, perhaps around Surat, another European traveller similarly observed that as early as the month of March, while the leaves on the trees were green the grass was 'quite burnt up'. He goes on to add that though the plain areas were rich in all kinds of natural produce, the dry summers caused a shortage of pasturage.[60] For a large part of the year, therefore, the leaves procured from the neighbouring forests probably constituted a substantial portion of the cattle fodder.

56 Ibid., p. 149.

57 *Ain-i-Akbari*, II, p. 56.

58 Ibid., I, pp. 152, 160.

59 Bernier, *Travels*, p. 326.

60 Fryer, *New Account*, II, pp. 94–5.

With regard to pastures, however, it seems quite likely that the rights of different social groups were better defined than was the case with the forests. Control over pastureland was central to the economy of the tribes which were predominantly pastoral. In suba Kabul, for instance, where agriculture was not very productive,[61] the tribal economy apparently depended on pastoralism. Two of the most powerful tribes here were the Hazaras and the Afghans, and Abul Fazl makes a point of mentioning that 'the pasturage of the country is in the hands of these two clans'.[62] The grazing lands of the Hazaras were virtually treeless meadows, supporting grass particularly suitable for horses and for the large number of sheep they kept.[63] Nearer the town of Kabul it appears that the Mughals demarcated separate grazing areas for the animals of different sections of their army. A dispute arising from an infringement of these could escalate into a major confrontation.[64]

In well-cultivated villages the extent of pastureland was likely to have been relatively little. This is what seems to be implied by the statement in the *Ain-i-Akbari* that tax would have to be paid on cattle by 'whosoever does not cultivate land liable to taxation but encloses it for pasturage'.[65] The need to convert cultivated land to pasture indicates that grazing land used in common by the villages was not always adequate. The peasants were therefore particular about where the village livestock was permitted to browse. Grazing rights were perhaps fairly well developed, and the

61 *Ain-i-Akbari*, II, p. 405.

62 Ibid., II, p. 406. The Hazaras, in particular, were probably more dependent upon horses, sheep and goats.

63 *Baburnama*, pp. 222–3. Not all grassland in Afghanistan was suitable for rearing livestock. Babur points out areas where the grass, despite growing in abundance, was good neither for horses nor sheep.

64 Mutamad Khan, *Iqbalnama-i-Jahangiri*, Elliot and Dowson, *History of India*, VII, p. 428. 'A party of Rajputs turned out their horses to graze in the hunting ground near Kabul and a contention arose with the keepers, in which an *ahadi* was killed . . . the *ahadis* sought redress . . . and dissatisfied with the answer they received . . . attacked the Rajputs, and killed 600 or 700 of them.'

65 *Ain-i-Akbari*, II, p. 49.

ordinary cultivator was not entirely free to let his cattle roam all over the village commons.[66] Indeed, in certain areas individual usufructuary, if not proprietary, rights over clearly defined categories of uncultivated land had already emerged. The Himalayan state of Chamba was one such area, and numerous land grants dating from as early as the tenth century until Mughal times indicate this.

Many of these inscriptions specifically mention the inclusion of 'grass, grazing and pasture-ground' in the grant.[67] Furthermore, the officials within whose jurisdiction the land lay were ordered to desist from cutting the grantee's 'pasture whether green or ripe' or from seizing 'his wood, fuel, grass, chaff and so on'.[68] Apart from land that was thus donated by the raja, there appear to have existed larger stretches of fairly well-delineated pastureland. There were, in fact, some reserved pastures for which the term *ghali* was used and the extensive territory of Brahmaura (the homeland of the Gaddi shepherds) was referred to as a ghali.[69]

It was perhaps on the wastelands located at some distance from the carefully cultivated areas that large numbers of cattle were allowed easier access.[70] But with regard to such places, too, it might be erroneous to suggest that grazing rights were completely unrestricted. The existence of reserved pastures even in regions of

[66] DeLaet, *Empire*, p. 95: 'The condition of the peasants is such that they have to approach the chief man of their village (who is appointed by the king) and to declare to him what land, and how much they intend to sow, or where they will pasture their flocks and herds.'

[67] J. Ph. Vogel (ed.), *Antiquities of Chamba State* (Calcutta, 1911), I, pp. 168, 189, 196, 200; II, p. 69. See also Sharma, *Rajput Polity*, p. 86. Taxes on grazing (*ghasmari*), along with other agricultural cesses, were assigned to the grantee.

[68] Vogel, *Antiquities*, I, p. 169.

[69] Ibid., II, p. 126, Nagoda grant of Balbhadra, AD 1634. See also p. 183, for a glossary defining the word ghali. During the course of describing the boundaries of the land-grants, there are frequent references to such land bordering on the 'pasture-land' of particular areas; e.g., p. 38, the 'pasture-land of Mugala.'

[70] Fryer, *New Account*, I, p. 287, of the Surat region says, 'Here in the Marshes are brought up great store of cattle of all sorts . . . '

natural abundance, such as Chamba, shows that this was not the case. It suggests, furthermore, that the dangers of pasturelands becoming depleted were real even in medieval times.[71]

A question that arises in this context is whether the common cultivator in the Mughal period had a larger stock of cattle for carrying out his work than did the peasant of a later time. On account of the relatively greater extent of uncultivated land and forests, pastures and fodder were, it seems, more easily available to the Mughal peasant. The *Ain-i-Akbari* also states that while collecting tax on cattle an exemption of four oxen, two cows and one buffalo per plough should be allowed to the cultivator.[72] On the basis of this exemption it has been argued by some scholars that the peasant in the Mughal period maintained more cattle than his twentieth-century successor.[73] It may, however, be erroneous to arrive at such a conclusion. Among the primary objectives of the state was, as noted earlier, the extension of cultivation. The liberal tax exemption that the Mughals allowed on cattle is to be seen as an incentive in this direction and not as an indicator of the number of cattle that an ordinary peasant owned. For this reason the tax exemption was linked 'to each plough'.

Studies pertaining to eastern Rajasthan provide some interesting details in this regard.[74] While some of the prosperous landholders certainly owned numerous head of cattle, the large majority, lower down the social scale, were ordinary peasants who

[71] For a comparison with European areas similar in many ways to Chamba, see Georges Duby, *Rural Economy and Country Life in the Medieval West* (London, 1969), pp. 146–7: the 'opening of the "alps", and the meadows on the high mountains was organized' during the thirteenth century, and 'on the alpine slopes which had until then been uninhabited, the lords would install at great altitudes herds of 50 to 100 cattle . . . and entrust them to families of herdsmen.' By 1345 the high pastures on the Alps had been overgrazed and the village communities in the hills attempted to prevent the entry of outsiders.

[72] *Ain-i-Akbari*, II, p. 49.

[73] Moreland, *India at the Death of Akbar*, p. 106; Habib, *Agrarian System*, pp. 53–5; Moosvi, 'Ecology', p. 114.

[74] Chandra, 'Role of the Local Community', and 'Writings on Social History', in *Medieval India*.

possessed only one or two oxen.[75] Caste and other factors within the village community may have prevented the poorer sections from becoming landowners, and they would thus have maintained very few cattle of their own. Moreover, the wasteland available for supporting livestock in the immediate vicinity of well-cultivated villages in the agrarian areas was not inexhaustible. From available information it seems, therefore, that only a few rich peasants had four or more oxen and that the cattle population of the medieval agricultural village was not really as large as it has so far thought to have been.[76] Under the circumstances one is tempted to argue that if the number of cattle per capita during the Mughal period was, indeed, greater than what it was in the early twentieth century,[77] then it was not merely on account of the large number of livestock possessed by the peasantry. A very substantial part of it was owned by pastoralists whose huge herds grazed in the innumerable pastures or found abundant fodder amidst thickly forested tracts.

## III

The existence in many areas of an abundance of forests and pastureland should not convey the impression that Mughal society was unfamiliar with the scarcity of forest produce and fodder. Such an impression would be misleading, for in many cultivated

[75] In *qasba* Chatsu (AD 1606), for instance, 79 per cent of the cultivators had one or two oxen; in *mauza* Kotkhawda 68.7 per cent. Of 26 villages in *pargana* Chatsu, 68.7 per cent of the peasants had one or two oxen. The percentages for peasants in this category in the 94 villages of Chala Kalan (*sarkar Rewari*) and the 49 villages of Kotla (sarkar Tijara) were 79.65 and 58.74 respectively. In qasba Chala Kalan as a whole it was 45.8 per cent. See Chandra, 'Role of the Local Community', pp. 178–9, 182–3.

[76] Ibid., pp. 178, 182–3. In qasba Chatsu only 10 per cent of the peasants had four or more oxen, and in the 26 villages of pargana Chatsu an average 16.78 per cent of the peasants had four or more oxen.

[77] In *Agrarian System*, pp. 53–4, Habib argues that there was a 'larger number of working cattle per head of population'.

regions natural resources were already under stress. In some areas, for instance, fuel had to be transported over long distances. During the reign of Akbar, six hundred wagons were set aside for bringing 'in the space of ten months, 1,50,000 *mans* of fuel to the Imperial kitchen'.[78] Even in Kashmir, one of the obligations of the cultivator was to 'cut and bring some wood from a distance'.[79] The conveyance of firewood on boats in Kashmir, to which Jahangir refers, seems to indicate that the distances involved were considerable and that wood for fuel was not easily available in the vicinity of habitations.[80] Even in parts of Punjab 'firewood and grass' seem to have been similarly transported.[81] The scarcity of fuelwood is explicitly mentioned by Pelsaert when he writers that 'firewood is very dear and is sold by weight', and that the 'poor burn cow-dung mixed with straw dried in the sun . . . '[82] The latter, too, was sold!

Nor was the procuring of fodder for animals always a simple task. A large number of horses, camels and elephants were maintained by the Mughal emperor and the *mansabdars* who resided in the cities. At the imperial stables cash allowances were made for the purchase of hay, grass and oats, and it is also likely that land was set aside to provide fodder for these animals. The price of fodder was naturally higher in the cities compared to the countryside.[83] That a reasonable profit could be obtained by

[78] *Ain-i-Akbari*, I, p. 159. One Akbari *man* was equal to 55.32 lbs. Babur makes what seems a contradictory statement about Kabul. He notes that 'excellent firewood is had nearby' and then adds: 'Given one day to fetch it': *Baburnama*, p. 233.

[79] *Akbarnama*, III, p. 1088. For references to the transportation of firewood to cities, see *Mirat-i-Ahmadi*, pp. 148, 232, 256.

[80] *Tuzuk-i-Jahangiri*, II, p. 142.

[81] Ibid., I, p. 66. During his rebellion, Khusrau attempted to cross the Chenab at Sodharah. However, he could only lay his hands on two boats, one of which was 'full of firewood and grass'.

[82] Pelsaert, *Remonstrantie*, p. 48. The use of 'dried cowdung is further substantiated by DeLaet, *Empire*, p. 89, and by Bernier, *Travels*, p. 368. See Fryer, *New Account*, I, p. 111, for a toll levied on cow-dung by the English in Madras.

[83] *Ain-i-Akbari*, I, pp. 142–3, 152. We are informed that 'three *bighas* of land will yield sufficient fodder for a horse', and that 'in winter each horse gets

people dealing in this commodity is implied by references in our sources to professional grass-sellers.[84] Some of them were required to ensure its regular supply to the imperial army wherever it proceeded, and Bernier has provided an interesting description of how they went about it:

> These poor people are at great pains to procure forage: they roam about from village to village and what they succeed in purchasing, they endeavour to sell in the army at an advanced price. It is common practice with them to clear, with a sort of trowel, whole fields of a peculiar kind of grass, which having beaten and washed, they dispose of in the camp at a price sometimes very high and sometimes inadequately low.[85]

There were times when the shortage of fodder would become acute. This was particularly the case in the eighteenth century, when large armies moved through well-populated areas. We have the interesting example of the invading army of Nadir Shah which, after making numerous assaults on the Mughal encampment near Karnal, carried away 'corn, grass and wood'![86] During Ahmad Shah Abdali's confrontation with the Marathas at Kunjpura, the shortage of fodder became so severe that from time to time 'one or two thousand of the Maratha horse went out for grass and forage'.[87] Abdali was subsequently able to prevent such excursions;

---

a *bigha* of fresh oats'. Iraqi and Turki horses at the court were provided a daily allowance of two *dams*, and in the countryside one and a half dams. The price of oats also varied.

[84] *Tuzuk-i-Jahangiri*, I, p. 432. We come across a reference to a 'grass-seller' in Ahmadabad killed by a thief who had broken into his house. Lakhnawi, *Shahnama Munnawar Kalam*, p. 8: when ordered to capture some 'free-booters' who had been creating trouble near Araul (forty miles south-west of Patna) a Mughal official mistakenly arrested 'thirteen men, some of whom were vegetable and grass vendors'.

[85] Bernier, *Travels*, p. 381. Shops selling 'forage' were a regular part of the tent-bazaar which sprang up wherever the imperial army encamped.

[86] Rustam Ali, *Tarikh-i-Hindi*, in Elliot and Dowson, *History of India*, VIII, p. 61.

[87] Muhammad Jafar Shamlu, *Tarikh-i-Manazil ul Futuh* in Elliot and Dowson, *History of India*, VIII, p. 150.

matters reached such a state that the only people who ventured out of the Maratha camp were 'wretched naked labourers who, going by stealth into the open country, used to dig up grass from the ground with their *kharpas* and offer it for sale'.[88]

It seems that, in as early as the latter part of the sixteenth century, the cost of construction materials in urban areas was rising. Perhaps on this account Akbar was prompted to fix the prices of different materials.[89] Among these was wood. Abul Fazl provides a detailed price-list of eight kinds of wood, graded according to quality and size.[90] Some of the other materials included in this price regulation were bamboo, *khas*, reeds for thatching, *munj* and *san*.[91] Traders must have brought these materials into the larger towns and cities in huge quantities. From Bernier's description of Delhi we learn that even amongst the high Mughal officials, very few possessed houses 'built entirely of brick and stone'.[92] The city, in fact, consisted of an immense number of thatched cottages which gave Delhi the appearance of a 'collection of many villages'.[93] In one year, fire is said to have destroyed 60,000 thatched-roof cottages in Delhi. Considering that the materials mentioned above had already become items of commercial value, even constructing houses made of bamboo or wood was not always cheap.[94]

[88] Ibid., p. 151.

[89] *Ain-i-Akbari*, I, p. 232: 'Many people are desirous of building houses; but honesty and conscientiousness are rare, especially among traders. His Majesty has carefully inquired into their profits and losses, and fixed the prices of articles . . . '

[90] Ibid., p. 233.

[91] Ibid., p. 234. *Kah-i-chappar* (reeds for thatching) were sold in bundles. Munj was 'the bark of *galam* reeds and was used for making ropes to fasten the thatching'. San was mixed with quick-lime and ropes were also made of it.

[92] Bernier, *Travels*, p. 246.

[93] Ibid.

[94] *Ain-i-Akbari*, II, p. 134. In Bengal a single bamboo house could cost Rs 5000: *Muntakhab-ut-Tawarikh*, II, p. 185. In Bihar a type of house called '*chappar-band* could cost as much as '30,000 or 40,000 rupees each, although they are covered with wood'.

By the seventeenth century, at least, timber of good quality seems to have become a commodity which could not be obtained very easily. In Punjab, where it was used for boat-building as well as house construction, it had to be floated along rivers which issued out of the northern hills.[95] While clearing the thick jungles around Jasrota (near Jammu) during a campaign, the Mughal commander Shaikh Farid is said to have come across 'several old trees' which, being suitable for purposes of construction, 'were cut down and sent to Lahore for use in government buildings'.[96] The growing commercial value of timber led to its organized exploitation in forests that were easily accessible. Some of the Himalayan chieftaincies rich in this resource, too, seem to have benefited financially on this account.[97]

There had emerged, therefore, in certain parts of Mughal India, a profitable market for forest produce and other similar natural resources.[98] Some of these were transported over fairly long distances, suggesting thereby that they were not available everywhere, or not easily available in adequate quantities. In many of the typically 'Mughal' agrarian areas, growing commercialization and the extension of cultivation combined with the growth of urban centres to put a strain on locally accessible materials.

[95] Bhandari, *Khulasat-ut-Tawarikh*, p. 77; Habib, *Atlas of the Mughal Empire*, p. 32: Khizrabad, on the banks of the Yamuna, was a timber mart.

[96] Sirhindi, *Akbarnama*, in Elliot and Dowson, *History of India*, VI, p. 126. According to Babur, *mahuwa* wood was used most in the houses of Hindustan: *Baburnama*, p. 505.

[97] *Sirmur State Gazetteer, Part A, 1904* (Lahore, 1907), p 14. A farman (dated 1084 H) of Aurangzeb is quoted to the effect that the emperor asked Raja Budh Prakash of Sirmur to 'permit a contractor to take *sal* timber from the Kalakhar forest free of charge and to refund to him any due which had been levied. Timber worth Rs 8000 was, in consequence, taken for imperial use.' It is obvious, therefore, that forests had become a source of revenue for some chiefs and that contractors were engaged in the business of timber extraction.

[98] For the existence in medieval times of a market in Himalayan forest produce, see Chetan Singh, 'Humans and Forests: The Himalaya and the Terai During the Medieval Period', in A.S. Rawat (ed.), *History of Forestry in India* (New Delhi, 1991), pp. 171–2.

But there still remained the peripheral regions within the territorial bounds of the Mughal empire where such resources existed in plenty. It was into these areas that agrarian society steadily encroached, both pressurized and supported as it was by the Mughal state. The combined logic of military expansion, increased cultivation and the growing requirement of well-populated areas for natural resources[99] brought the Mughal state into even closer contact with societies residing in forested and relatively less cultivated areas.

Agrarian society was certainly not the sole beneficiary of this increased interaction. Many peripheral societies which had earlier been only marginally affected by the Mughal state were gradually drawn into playing an increasingly important role in its economy as well as its political fortunes. These societies were neither numerically nor militarily insignificant, and their active participation, either as fuller constituents of the empire or as its opponents, could hardly have been without consequence. It seems reasonable to suggest, all things considered, that the ecological diversity found within Mughal India enabled and encouraged the existence of a corresponding variety of socio-economic systems. Among these the most influential was an agrarian society based principally upon peasant production. Growing interaction between diverse social systems affected not only the peripheral areas and their people but also transformed the nature of agrarian society and the Mughal empire which was the latter's most powerful political expression in South Asia.

[99] Apart from the collection of wood, herbs, grass etc., cows and elephants were also captured from the forests: *Travels of Thevenot*, in Guha, *India in the Seventeenth Century*, II, pp. 66–7. 'The huntsmen of Agra go five days' journey from the town as far as a mountain called Narwar . . . their business in going so far is only to catch a kind of wild cow which they call *merous*, that are found in the wood round this hill, which is upon the road from Surat to Golconda; and these cows being commonly very lovely, they make great advantage of them.' For cultivators paying revenue in elephants, see *Ain-i-Akbari*, II, p. 207.

## Chapter Two

# Pastoralists in a Colonial World

NEELADRI BHATTACHARYA

This essay attempts to understand how the world of pastoralists in Punjab changed over the colonial period. I proceed with two assumptions. One: the specific experience of change was a function of the form of pastoralism. So it is important to look at the varieties of pastoralism which existed: the composition of the pastoral stock, the terrain over which pastoralists operated, the rhythms of their movements, the range of activities they combined. Two: pastoralists had to relate not only to their ecological surroundings but also to changing political, legal and cultural contexts. I begin with a discussion of the varieties of pastoralism in colonial Punjab, and then analyse how pastoralists found their relationship to the world redefined in legal and cultural ways.

### Long-distance Nomadism

Much before the nineteenth century, India was linked to Afghanistan through an important annual migratory flow between the two regions. *Powindah* was the term of reference for all the migratory Pathan tribes who came down to Punjab every year from their base in Central Asia. They came to India not only to trade, but in search of pasture, work, and a life away from the snowy uplands of Central Asia. Determined by geo-ecological conditions, their movements had a seasonal cycle. They assembled every autumn in the plains east of Ghazni with their families, flocks, herds and long strings of camels laden with the goods of Bokhara and Kandahar. The caravans traversed the Gakkar and Waziri country, crossed the Suleimans through the Gomal and Zhab passes, and entered Dera Ismail Khan. Here they left their families and flocks on the great grazing grounds on either side of the Indus. While some looked after the flocks and some wandered around in search of employment, others proceeded with the caravans and merchandise to Multan, Rajputana, Lahore, Amritsar, Delhi, Kanpur, Benaras, and sometimes up to Patna. In spring they gathered again and returned by the same route to the hills around Ghazni and Kelat-i-Ghilzai. As the summer approached, the men moved off to Kandahar, Herat and Bokhara with Indian and European goods acquired in 'Hindustan'. In October they would return and prepare once more to start their journey to India.

Militarization was essential for long-distance nomadism. Powindahs had to pass through regions settled by tribes for whom feuding and raiding were an integral part of life.[1] The persistent fear of attack and plunder necessitated the formation of *kafilas* (caravans) and arming of the people.[2] The daily march of the kafilas was 'like that of an army through an enemy's territory'. The main body of the kafila, the camels carrying families and merchandise, was continuously guarded from all sides:

> A few armed men with knife, sword and matchlock, guard the main portion, but a few hundred yards ahead may be seen a compact body of fighting men of the clan, mounted and dismounted, all armed to the teeth . . . On their flank, crowning the height with greatest care, and almost military exactitude, move a similar body of footmen, whilst in rear follows an equally strong party, all on the watch for their hereditary enemies, the Waziris.[3]

[1] Punjab Foreign Department Proceedings (Hereafter Punjab For.), February 1872, A 27; Punjab For., January 1872, A 7; Punjab For., April 1872, A 18; Punjab For., December 1872, A 28; Punjab For., March 1879, A 11.

[2] Punjab For. (Frontier), April 1894, A 114–19.

[3] William Patrick Andrew, cited in David Ross, *The Land of the Five Rivers and Sindh: Sketches Historical and Descriptive* (Lahore, 1883; Delhi 1970).

What we have here is not the movement of individuals and small groups, but the mass migrations of humans and animals. Powindahs moved with their families and children, with their herds and flocks, with arms and merchandise. In the cold weather of 1877–8 an estimated 78,000 powindahs crossed the passes. Two years later about 42,000 entered Dera Ismail Khan. Animals out numbered humans. Every year the powindahs were reportedly accompanied by about 70,000 camels laden with merchandise, and more than 100,000 sheep, besides other animals.[4]

The powindahs were not a homogeneous community. They combined various forms of economic activities. They were internally differentiated on the basis of property and wealth, occupation and function. Those who had fixed camping grounds known as *kirris* (camp village) could bring their families along to Derajat. The rights over the kirris were mutually recognized and the same camping ground was resorted to year after year.[5] Many powindahs had no fixed camping rights, and they came down without their families. Others, the *charra* folk, had no belongings and came as labourers, wandering about in search of work. Among the various powindah tribes (mostly Ghilzai and Lohani Pathans), Mian Khels were the richest, dealing with luxury commodities; Kharotis were the poorest, many of them were labourers; Suleiman Khels brought little merchandise to India, but acted as *dalals* between powindah traders and Indian merchants; Nasers, Dawtanis and Tarakis were primarily pastoralists.[6]

Within each group there was both a combination of different activities as well as sub-specializations. Nasers, for instance, were said to be the 'least settled of all powindahs'; they had no home of their own. While living primarily as pastoralists, they also

[4] *SR: Dera Ismail Khan 1883–84*, p. 76.

[5] Punjab For. (Frontier), August 1895, A 67–76.

[6] There was a relationship of intense conflict between the different groups of powindahs. For the conflict between the Kharotis and Suleiman Khels, see Punjab For., August 1873, A 1; Punjab For., August 1873, A 20; Punjab For., September 1873, A 21.

traded.[7] Their activities combined in a variety of ways. Among the Naser Ushwals (camel folk), the poorer faction brought salt from Kohat mines, Multani *matti* from the hills, and were employed in India at small jobs. The richer Ushwals brought grapes, madder and almonds for sale and had their own kirris. The Naser Gayewals (ox-folk), Kharwals (ass-folk) and Goshfandwals (sheep-folk) had no kirris and usually took up odd jobs in India—carrying earth or bricks.

How did this nomadism change over the colonial period? At one level, the colonial state attempted to encourage and sustain the trade which flowed through this network. It hoped to capture by this means the Central Asian market, displacing the Russian presence there. After the British annexation of Punjab, passes were opened, trade posts established at different points, and control over 'banditry' as well as the pacification of frontier tribes were taken up as serious projects.[8]

Yet British policies undermined the very basis of powindah nomadism. British intervention in the frontier created a prolonged crisis of tribal power relations, accentuating tribal feuds and banditry. High grazing taxes (*tirni*)—these trebled between 1870s and 1920s—adversely affected pastoralism, already under pressure from vanishing grazing grounds.[9] Collective tribal rights on camping grounds were disturbed in many areas when the British granted proprietary rights to loyal tribal groups. The disarming of powindahs on the British border exposed the camps (kirris) to Waziri raids, which the British border posts were incapable of resisting.[10]

Despite these pressures powindah nomadism continued. The

[7] H.A. Rose, *A Glossary of the Tribes and Castes of the Punjab and North-West Frontier Provinces* (1883: reprint, Languages Department Punjab, Patiala, 1970), vol. III, p. 244.

[8] Punjab For., April 1872, A 4; Punjab For. (Frontier), August 1890, A 97–100; Punjab For., October 1876, A 24; Punjab For., February 1877, A 5.

[9] Punjab For. (For.), October 1879, A 3; Punjab For. (For.), November 1877, A 20.

[10] Punjab For. (For.), February 1873, A 20; Punjab For., September 1879, 2a; Punjab For. (Frontier), March 1894, A 54.

powindahs regularly changed their migratory routes to avoid border posts; they resisted the collection of tirni tax; they forcibly recovered animals requisitioned by the colonial state. When railways and lorries threatened to displace their trading activity in India, powindahs sometimes combined caravan journeys up to the frontier with railway travel within India.

It was the combination of different forms of economic activity which allowed powindahs to survive the strains of changing times. In the long run, some forms of economic activity were more adversely affected than others. Powindah fortunes seem to have suffered more from the constraints on moneylending in India and from the decline of the Central Asian trade than from the problems of pastoral grazing. This was reflected in the composition of the migratory flow from Afghanistan. The Lohanis and Suleiman Khels, who were most actively involved in trade, stopped coming to India by the 1940s. Members of the Dawtani and Tarkai tribes, who were primarily pastoralists, continued their annual migration in large numbers. Indian markets were finally lost after the Partition of India in 1947, and the grazing grounds of Dera Ismail Khan were closed to powindahs after 1961.[11]

## Alpine Pastoralism

*Gaddis* were the shepherds of the hills, and *Ban-Gujars* were cowherds. In Kangra sheep and goats together numbered over six lakhs in the 1890s, constituting about half the animal population. On the hills, flocks of sheep and goats could be more easily maintained than cattle. Alpine pastoralism is usually sustained by a vertical movement between the summer pasture in the high mountains and the winter pasture in the low hills. Buffaloes—even hill buffaloes—found the climb to the high ranges difficult.

[11] D. Balland and C.M. Kieffer, 'Nomadisme et secheresse en Afghanistan: l'exemple des nomads Pastun du Dast-e Nawor', in *Pastoral Production and Society* (Cambridge, 1979); Balland, 'Nomadism and Politics: The Case of Afghan Nomads in the Indian Subcontinent,' *Studies in History*, 1991, vol. VII, no. 2.

By the 1880s, the gaddis and gujars of the hills felt the pressures of colonial change. They found their access to forests closed, their rights redefined, the rhythms of their movements controlled, their spatial mobility restricted. The relationship between pastoralists and their grazing runs, and the social relationships which sustained their herding activities, changed in complex ways. This was not a simple shift from a regime of unrestricted grazing rights to one in which such rights were denied.

In the period before colonial laws were enacted, access to grazing runs was regulated through a combination of collective and segmented rights. In Kangra, pastures in the low hills were all divided among the shepherds. Each division or circuit was called a *ban*, and each ban was claimed by some gaddi family as its *warisi.*[12] A prefix was attached to each ban to distinguish the warisi of one family from another. A warisi usually originated with a *pattah*, acquired from the raja by a gaddi family to graze in a particular run. The family which acquired the pattah jointly used the run with five or six other families. Usually a flock of 800 to 1200 grazed in one ban. The *waris* who held the pattah had some powers and functions. Grazing in the runs had to be managed and conflicts over rights resolved. 'The holder of the pattah directed the course of the flock, and acted as the spokesman and negotiator in the case of quarrels or dealings with the people along the line of the march.' He was recognized as the *mahlundi* or *malik kanda*, i.e. the master of the flock; the other shepherds were *assamis.* The relationship between the waris and the assamis was forged through reciprocal claims and obligations, and sustained through the collective use of bans. The waris held the pattah, but he could graze his sheep only with other families. They had to move together through the forests and up the high mountains, protecting their flock from attacks and accidents. So the waris charged no dues from assamis for their right to graze; he did at times claim the *mailani* paid by zamindars for sheep dung.

Summer pastures above the limit of forests in the high

[12] *SR: Kangra 1856–72*, paras 26–7.

mountains were similarly divided. Each run, a *dhar*, belonged to a waris with a pattah but was collectively used by a number of families. The association between families was said to be 'a brotherly one, no rent or fee being given or taken'.[13]

In Kulu, again, individual rights and collective rights co-existed. But here the nature of rights in the summer and winter pastures was different. Till spring, up to mid June, sheep grazed in *rirs*, the grazing areas near the hamlets. From here they first moved up to the *gahrs*, the forest grazing grounds just above the limits of cultivation, and then up to the *nigahrs* or grassy slopes above the limits of the forest. After two months at the nigahrs the flocks descended back to the gahrs, grazed there for six weeks, and then moved further down to the low hills.[14] In each nigahr a hereditary title was claimed by a *rasu*, the person who held the pattah. To each nigahr was attached a gahr. But exclusive rights of a flock to graze in the gahr operated only during the descent from the nigahr, not on the way up in spring. The rasu in Kulu, like the *malundhi* of Kangra, was a waris of a nigahr. In the lower hills, however, no warisi was claimed by anyone. There were no exclusive hereditary rights over the winter pastures.

Warisi thus marked and segregated the right of a group of gaddi families from that of others, but did not define any exclusive right of the waris within the ban or nigahr. The waris did enjoy some power and privileges, but his right to his ban was no different from that of the other families who formed a part of the group he led. His power was premised on the role he performed. He could even lose his power and rights if he was not in a position to lead the group. Segregation of rights between the bans restricted competition and conflict between pastoralists, while collective, non-individuated rights within the bans ensured co-operation among each herding group.

[13] Ibid., para 46.

[14] 'Report on Kulu Subdivision', *SR: Kangra 1856–72*. 'Kulu Forest Settlement Report', paras 126–27, *Selections from the Records of the Financial Commissioner of Punjab* (hereafter *SRFCP*), *NS 25*.

When the colonial state claimed forests and 'wastes' as state property, and prepared the record of rights, the framework of rights was redefined. Having appropriated the forests as state property, the state could see gaddis only as lessees. So assamis became tenants who could graze only on the payment of a fee to the proprietor—the state. The tax was to be collected by the *muqaddam*.

The right of the muqaddam was now premised on his role as a revenue collector of the state, not on his participation in the collective pastoral activity of a group.[15] This legal redefinition of rights led to a complete transformation of the relations between assamis and muqaddams. Many muqaddams began calling themselves maliks.[16] The assami now had to pay 4 annas to 1 rupee per hundred sheep to the muqaddam as his due. To increase his income, the muqaddam brought in 'outsiders' to graze in his run. As the flocks of the muqaddam expanded and the grazing area was restricted, assamis were dispossessed. At the end of the nineteenth century it was reported: 'in many areas there are no assamis, and the grazers are the descendants of the first mukaddams.'[17] This in turn sharpened competition and conflict among assamis, and between them and the muqaddams.

The grazing dues charged by the state increased rapidly. Very often, the tax had to be paid separately on each of the runs through which the gaddi flocks moved. Between the summer and winter runs there were many small patches of forest where the gaddis had to spend a few weeks. In each place they now had to pay a tax to the muqaddam.[18] The increasing shortage of pastures complicated

[15] Very often, the muqaddam was not a pastoralist. Of the eleven runs demarcated in Dehra tahsil, the Raja of Chamba was recorded as the muqaddam of two runs. 'Record of Sheep-grazing Runs in the Dehra Tahsil' appended to the 'Kangra Forest Record of Rights', *SRFCP, NS 26.*

[16] 'Kangra Valley Forest Settlement Report', para 82, *SRFCP, NS 26.*

[17] Ibid., para 82.

[18] No. 972, dated 8 July 1896, From A. Anderson, Deputy Commissioner of Kangra, to The Comm. and Superintendent, Jullundar Division, paras 12–15, *SRFCP, NS 26.*

the problem. Unable to find sufficient grass in one or two places, the shepherds had to move over a wider area, multiplying the number of times they were taxed.

The state sought to redefine the temporal rhythms of pastoral activity. While the gaddis could graze their flocks in the summer and winter pastures in which they paid grazing dues, they were allowed only a 'right of way' through the 'unassessed waste' which they had to pass on their way up and down. Dates for the arrival and departure of flocks in each place were specified. In Kulu the gaddis could not come in before 15 Jait (the beginning of June) on their way up, and they had to leave Kulu by 20 Assauj (the first week of October) on their way down to the low hills.[19] Fines were imposed if they arrived too soon or delayed their departure. This created problems for the gaddis. The temporal rhythms of their pastoral activities were defined by the seasons and were subject to seasonal fluctuations. Clock time and fixed calendars had no meaning for them. When the winter was severe the gaddis could not move to the high pastures in Lahul within the time fixed. They had to wait for the snow to clear.

Moreover, the gaddis needed time in Kulu if they were to sustain their relationship with the zamindars. Gaddi flocks manured the rice fields. So great was the demand for manure that the zamindars offered food, grain and even money to have sheep penned in their fields.[20] But in the official calendar there was no time for all this.

The reservation of forests, the restrictions on the lopping of tree branches—crucial for winter pasture when grasslands were dry—and the ban on the firing of grass, all added to the constraints within which the gaddis now had to operate. They protested against these new constraints, thus forcing changes in official policies. At the same time they altered their ways; they too adjusted to the changing times.[21]

[19] 'Kulu Forest SR'; chapter V, paras 174–77, *SRFCP, NS 25.*

[20] Ibid., paras, 127, 167, 171.

[21] Exasperated by the hostility of pastoralists to the closure of forest reserves, Robertson declared: 'they (the graziers) have been accustomed to graze absolutely

## Pastoralism on the Semi-arid Plains

The nature and rhythms of alpine pastoralism were very different from the form of pastoralism dominant in the semi-arid south-east of Punjab. This region was largely uninhabited in the early nineteenth century. When Karnal pargana was annexed in 1803, about four-fifths of it was estimated to be covered with forest.[22] Almost the whole of Sirsa was 'an uncultivated prairie with few permanent villages'[23] Here, in Sirsa, settled agriculture was unknown. Pastoralism coexisted with shifting cultivation.

> The pastoral Musalman tribes who were its only inhabitants drove their herds of cattle hither and thither in search of grass and water and had no fixed dwelling place. There were no boundaries and no defined rights. Some families of herdsmen had certain ponds and grazing grounds which they were in the habit of visiting in turn . . . Sometimes when grass was scarce, a family would roam long distances in search of pasture and settle down in some place far from their former haunt until grass or water failed them, or until they were driven from their encampment by some stronger family who coveted it.[24]

Over the nineteenth-century, the open fields in the region were colonized and the limits of cultivation extended. Yet pastoralism continued. Pastoral groups like the Bhattis, Joiyas, Wattus and Bodlas, who earlier grazed their large herds in this tract, felt the

---

without restriction of any kind up to now, and their real complaint is against any restriction of the privilege, however necessary and however innocuous to their real interests'. Note by F.A. Robertson on the Forest Settlement of Tahsils Muree and Kahuta, *SRFCP, 16.* And Baden Powell said: 'The people want nothing less than to have the *rakhs* given over to them absolutely, to graze everywhere . . . '. No. 14F, dated Camp Kaghan, 16 June 1876, Baden Powell, Conservator of Forests Punjab, to the Sec. to Financial Comm.) Punjab, *SRFCP, 16*, p. 1484.

22 No. 30, 14 February 1878, Denzil Ibbetson, Settlement Officer Karnal, to Comm. & Sup., Delhi Division Records, Series I, Basta no. 118, p. 81.

23 *SR: Sirsa 1879–83*, p. 311.

24 Ibid., p. 311.

pressures of nineteenth-century colonization. But the pioneer colonizers—the Sikh Jats from the north, the Bagri Jats from the south, and the Muslim Jats and Rajputs from the neighbourhood of Sutlej—had to operate against the ecological constraints of the region. They settled villages, cleared forests and ploughed the soil, but accepted pastoralism as an integral part of their economic activity. Agriculture could not displace pastoralism; they coexisted. The relationship between the two modes of life was both complementary and opposed. And this interrelationship defined the very nature of pastoralism in the region.

To understand the dynamic of pastoralism in this region, we need to look at another interrelationship: that between this semi-arid tract and the intensively cultivated tracts of Central Punjab. These two areas formed two distinct geo-ecological zones, intimately related in complex ways.

The soil over large areas of Central Punjab was fertile alluvial loam. As one moved south, the soil became lighter, the proportion of sand increased, and near the southern extreme of the province firm loam was not to be found. Central Punjab was intersected by numerous rivers—Sutlej, Beas, Ravi—and drainage lines. The south-east had fewer rivers. The Jamuna, which formed its eastern boundary, deposited more sand than fertile loam. Water supply in the two regions varied. The level of precipitation declined in relation to the distance from the Himalayan range in the north. In Central Punjab it was a good 20 to 30 inches; but in the south-east it fluctuated between 10 to 20 inches, falling to less than 10 inches in the southern extreme of Hissar and Ferozepur which bordered the deserts of Rajasthan. The concept of an average rainfall is therefore misleading. In the south-east a year of heavy rain was followed by a cycle of bad years. The few natural inundation canals which existed in the south-east flowed only during the monsoon, and their water flow was much less certain than the perennial canals of Central Punjab, which flowed with even speed and volume through the year. Central Punjab was also a region of well irrigation: the ground-water level was only 10–30 feet below the surface. Towards the south-east the water level sank in places to below 150 feet, making well irrigation difficult.[25]

The south-east was, in short, more sandy, arid and insecure than Central Punjab. Recurring cycles of famine were an integral part of the life of the region. In the nineteenth century, a series of fifteen famines culminated in the two major famines over the tragic closing years of the century.[26] Even after 1900, scarcities continued to plague the region, though the areas affected by distress contracted. The 1905–6 famine was immediately followed by one in 1907–8, and then after a long gap came the famine of 1920–1.[27] In Sirsa, five out of six harvests failed between 1919 and 1921; and in Gurgaon, Rohtak and Hissar most harvests between 1928 and 1935 failed partially or totally.[28]

Within this geo-ecological context, intensive agriculture could be sustained in Central Punjab, but not in the south-east. While double cropping (*dofasli harsala*) was common in places like Jullundar, it could not be practised in a region like Hissar. When there was rain, the semi-arid south-east could produce one crop a year (*ekfasli harsala*) or two consecutive harvests in two years (*dofasli dosala*). Here agricultural expansion could not easily displace pastoralism: the two activities did not always compete for the same land space or for the labour time of communities. Each activity supplemented the meagre and insecure income from the other, allowing a more optimal use of land and labour resources. In the language of political economy one might say that multi-

25 Information on nineteenth-century conditions of the different eco-zones of Punjab can be found in the numerous *Tahsil Assessment Reports, District Settlement Reports, District Gazetteers, Seasons and Crops Reports, and Land Revenue Administration Reports.*

26 Land Rev. and Agr. (Famine), April 1898, A 30–7; Land Rev. and Agr. (Famine), July 1901, A 7; *Report of the Famine in the Punjab in 1896–7* (1898); *Punjab Famine of 1899–1990* (1901), 7 vols.

27 Home Rev. & Agr. Fam., May 1907, A 5.

28 *Report of the Fodder Famine Operations in the Ambala Division* (1930); *Final Report of the Operations for the Relief of Distress in the Hissar District* (1932–33).

resource nomadism is a way of optimising resource use and spreading risks; except nomadic societies cannot be conceptualized through this language. The calculations of pastoralists and their notions of work and time are not necessarily determined by a desire to maximize utilities.

The pastoral and agrarian zones were tied through myriad structures of interdependence. The agrarian communities of Central Punjab, and later of the Canal Colonies, provided a market for cattle reared in Hissar, Rohtak, Karnal and Gurgaon. At the famous Hissar cattle fair, an average of 12,000 to 20,000 cattle were sold every year in the 1870s and 1880s, and the total value of annual sales was over three lakhs of rupees.[29] Buyers came from different districts of Punjab and beyond: from Lyallpur, Ludhiana, Ferozepur, Jullundar, Meerut, Aligarh, Muzaffarnagar, Farukhabad, Bijnaur, and from as far away as Kanpur.[30] Over 10,000 bullocks were annually imported into Jullundar. There was a reverse flow of foodgrain and fodder from the agricultural to the pastoral zones.

This relationship of interdependence is reflected in the composition of agricultural stock. In the agricultural districts, bullocks outnumbered cows and calves; whereas the pastoral tracts present a reversed picture (see Tables I and II). Agricultural zones required bullocks for ploughing and the working of wells, but they could not internally reproduce their agricultural stock. Pastoralists sold their bullocks but retained their cows for breeding, and for the supplies of milk and ghee which formed an important component of their family income. Young calves, carefully tended, were ultimately sold at cattle fairs. More than 90 per cent of the cattle sold at these fairs were bullocks.

The cycle of pastoral activities was structured by the seasons. But the nature of the cycle in the semi-arid plains was different

[29] 'Report on Cattle Fair at Sirsa: 1871–72, *SRFCP, No. 13; SR: Sirsa 1879–83*, pp. 296ff, Punjab Rev. (Rev.), March 1879, A 9; Punjab Rev. (Agr.), February 1884, A 6–7.

[30] 'Report on Cattle Fair at Sirsa: 1871–72', *SRFCP, NS 13*.

Table I
Variations in Cattle Population
(in thousands)

| *Years* | *Bulls & Bullocks* | *Cows* | *Buffaloes Male* | *Buffaloes Female* | *Young Stock* |
|---|---|---|---|---|---|
| *Pastoral Tracts* | | | | | |
| HISSAR | | | | | |
| 1893 | 137 | 180 | 5 | 65 | 164 |
| 1898 | 116 | 130 | 4 | 58 | 151 |
| 1904 | 85 | 79 | 5 | 59 | 132 |
| 1935 | 103 | 121 | 2 | 91 | 251 |
| ROHTAK | | | | | |
| 1893 | 131 | 119 | 2 | 60 | 163 |
| 1898 | 115 | 107 | 2 | 58 | 136 |
| 1904 | 88 | 63 | 1 | 54 | 127 |
| 1935 | 128 | 87 | 1 | 92 | 226 |
| *Agricultural Tracts* | | | | | |
| JULLUNDAR | | | | | |
| 1893 | 183 | 79 | 29 | 41 | 91 |
| 1898 | 175 | 76 | 32 | 47 | 108 |
| 1904 | 194 | 76 | 31 | 55 | 112 |
| 1935 | 152 | 48 | 27 | 94 | 163 |
| LUDHIANA | | | | | |
| 1893 | 142 | 73 | 4 | 48 | 73 |
| 1898 | 130 | 81 | 4 | 53 | 95 |
| 1904 | 131 | 55 | 3 | 55 | 95 |
| 1935 | 108 | 47 | 1 | 80 | 146 |

Source: Up to 1899 the statistics of Punjab cattle censuses are reported in *Punjab Administration Reports and Punjab Land Revenue Administration Reports.* The 1904 and 1909 Censuses are reported in *Punjab Seasons and Crops Reports.* Subsequently there were separate volumes of *Punjab Cattle Census.* Some of these census statistics are also reproduced in the *Agricultural Statistics of British India.*

Table II
Composition of Cattle Population
(percentage distribution)

| *Years* | *Bulls & Bullocks* | *Cows* | *Buffaloes Male* | *Buffaloes Female* | *Young Stock* |
|---|---|---|---|---|---|
| *Pastoral Tracts* | | | | | |
| HISSAR | | | | | |
| 1893 | 25 | 32 | 1 | 12 | 30 |
| 1898 | 25 | 28 | 1 | 12 | 33 |
| 1904 | 23 | 22 | 1 | 16 | 37 |
| 1935 | 18 | 21 | 1 | 16 | 44 |
| ROHTAK | | | | | |
| 1893 | 27 | 25 | 1 | 12 | 34 |
| 1898 | 27 | 25 | 1 | 14 | 32 |
| 1904 | 19 | 14 | 0 | 12 | 27 |
| 1935 | 24 | 16 | 0 | 17 | 42 |
| *Agricultural Tracts* | | | | | |
| JULLUNDAR | | | | | |
| 1893 | 43 | 19 | 7 | 10 | 21 |
| 1898 | 40 | 17 | 7 | 10 | 25 |
| 1904 | 41 | 16 | 6 | 11 | 24 |
| 1935 | 31 | 10 | 5 | 19 | 34 |
| LUDHIANA | | | | | |
| 1893 | 42 | 21 | 1 | 14 | 21 |
| 1898 | 36 | 22 | 1 | 14 | 26 |
| 1904 | 39 | 16 | 1 | 16 | 28 |
| 1935 | 28 | 12 | 0 | 21 | 38 |

from the one in the hills. As long as grass was available, village herds were sent out under the charge of a cowherd to graze in village commons. And where there was water in village ponds cattle were allowed to drink and wade about.[31] By the beginning

[31] *SR: Sirsa 1871–72*, p. 302.

of April the grass in the *barani* tracts withered, the pools in the jungles dried up. Then, pastoralists had to move in search of pasture and water. From the Karnal *nardak*, cattle were driven to the hills and riverine tracts. With the beginning of the monsoon the herds were back on their return journey.[32] But there were tracts where rainfall was always inadequate and grasslands rarely greened. In such tracts the monsoon did not bring the herds back home. In the rainy season, we are told, when the Bikaner grasslands were lush, cattle from the dry parts of Sirsa, Patiala and even Ludhiana were driven south to graze.[33] They returned north only after the grass there was exhausted.

These cyclical migrations were of two sorts. One: a regular annual movement between uplands and lowlands, between the dry tracts and the green. Two: a more irregular movement conditioned by cycles of good and bad years. In years of drought, migrants from barani tracts went to irrigated areas, within the district and outside, in search of pasture and work, returning home after the drought was over.[34] These migrations were 'in proportion to the dryness of the season amounting to an entire exodus in times of famine.'[35] Such movements set up relationships of interdependence between different regions and communities.

The history of droughts left a very deep mark on the life of

[32] No. 30, 14 February 1878, Ibbetson, Settlement Officer, Karnal to Davies, Comm. and Sup., Delhi Div., Delhi Division Records, Basta no. 118, Series I, p. 85.

[33] *SR: Sirsa 1871–72*, para 198.

[34] In the famine of 1896, pastoralists were seen migrating from all the *barani* tracts of the province. A report on Sharakpur, a cattle grazing tract in the Lahore district, tells us: 'When the people realized the impossibility of saving the cattle if they stayed at home, many families emigrated with their cattle and all their belongings to the Chenab Canal, the banks of the Ravi and Sutlej, and the submontane tracts of Sialkot and Gurdaspur. Many villages were left half empty and in two only one family remained. It is estimated that over 1700 families left the tehsil.' Land Rev. and Agr. (Famine), April 1898, A 30–5.

[35] No. 97, May 1885, Deputy Commissioner Karnal to Commissioner and Superintendent, Delhi Division, Land Rev. and Agr. (Famine), September 1885, A 3–4.

pastoralists who were affected. Cattle are a volatile resource: they perish in large number during times of famine. Enervated by hunger, they succumb to cattle disease and the winter frost.[36] The famous cattle breeds of Hissar were periodically decimated by fodder famines which recurred in the region with tragic regularity. When the rains failed in 1863–4 and the year after, large herds were driven towards Karnal. Only two-thirds of that number returned. Between 1866–7 and 1867–8 over half the cattle in the district perished. Those that survived were 'tottering and emaciated': they could not even be driven out to graze.[37] In 1868–9 both harvests failed again. Of the estimated 202,327 horned cattle in the district, only 53,737 survived. In the disastrous years of 1896–7 Hissar cattle-owners moved to the native states in the hope of fodder. When they returned after the kharif sowings were over, only a fifth of their stock was left. An estimated 77,000 cattle died.[38] After the famines, when bullocks were scarce, buffaloes were used to plough the fields and work the wells; at times women were to be seen pulling the plough.

Pastoral and agricultural zones experienced good and bad years in different ways. A look at Table II will show that when Hissar lost its herds, Jullundar did not. Between 1893 and 1904, a decade of acute scarcities, there was a sharp decline in the cattle stocks of Hissar: as much as 36 per cent in the case of bullocks and 56 per cent in the case of cows. Over the same years the cattle stock of Jullundar continued to increase. Peasants in Jullundar did not suffer scarcities.

In fact, a bad year for Hissar was a good year for Jullundar. When the pastoral zone was affected by famines, peasants in Central Punjab gained. The failure of local harvests forced the pastoralists of the south-east into a greater dependence on the market for fodder and grain. As the demand for grains and fodder increased, their prices soared, inflating the incomes of peasants in

36 This fact is authenticated in a large number of studies on ruminants.

37 *SR: Sirsa 1871–72*, para 189, p. 294.

38 Land Rev. & Agr. (Famine), 1898, A 30–5.

the agricultural zones and pushing up the expenses of pastoral and other buyers. When expenditure increased, income dipped. The volume of transaction in cattle fairs and the level of bullock prices depended on the seasons. The prospect of a drought led to a rush of anxious sellers.[39] While supplies increased, demand fell. Many cattle fairs could not be held in the famine years of the late nineteenth century for want of buyers. The price of bullocks therefore had a direct relationship to the harvest: it was low in years of drought and high in years of plenty. In 1895–6, when a dearth of fodder led to high rates of cattle mortality, bullocks which ordinarily cost Rs 60–80 could be purchased for Rs 25.[40] Cycles of bad years benefited nomadic cattle dealers, who bought their cattle cheap in the arid cattle-breeding zone and sold them dear in the agricultural tracts. A part of the benefit also went to those peasants who acquired agricultural stock in these years.

Within such structures of a skewed interdependence, impoverishment of pastoralists in the arid zone and peasant accumulation in the agrarian zone were tied processes. The symbiotic relationship between agriculture and pastoralism provided both the basis and the limits within which the pastoral economy could reproduce itself.

Different groups of pastoralists confronted these limits in different ways. Some effectively redefined the ecological constraints within which they had to operate, others could not. Mobility was a pastoral strategy to overcome seasonal scarcities of grass and fodder. But all groups could not be equally mobile. Mobility itself had to be sustained by other strategies. In Karnal, intermarriage between people of nardak (an upland) and the riverine tract provided a mutual guarantee of grazing rights: 'In years of drought they [the people of Nardak] seek pasture with riverine countries, and in years of flood and heavy rainfall, when the grass in the riverine countries is rank and of inferior quality, they allow their

39 Punjab Rev. and Agr., February 1878, A 10; Punjab Rev. (Rev.), March 1879, A 9; Ambala Division Records, Basta no XIII/28 (ii), Case 231, 16 March 1869.

40 Land Rev. and Agr. (Famine), April 1898, A 30–5.

relations to bring cattle into the grasslands of the Nardak.'[41] Not every one could establish such reciprocal relations of mutual rights and obligations.

Pastoralists had to live with high rates of cattle mortality during scarcities; but they sought to devise strategies of minimizing long-term losses.[42] When grass and fodder were scarce, supplies were reserved for calves. Older animals were allowed to die of starvation, or slaughtered if they could not be sold. Table I shows that during famine years the number of calves did not decline as rapidly as the number of cows and bullocks. This led to a change in the age structure of herds. After the famines, 'young stock' constituted a larger proportion of the cattle population (Table II).

In the longer term, the pastoral economy in the dry tracts did suffer a crisis. The extension of arable and the enclosure of forests meant an overgrazed, shrinking pastureland. This led to soil erosion and the deterioration of available grazing lands. Migration to wet tracts became difficult as pastures disappeared from there. Even the *shamilats* were partitioned by agriculturists. The pressure on pastures reflected itself in the decline of agricultural stock. After the sharp decline in the late nineteenth century there was a recovery, but not to earlier levels (Table I). This decline, in turn, affected agriculture. The supply of manure and plough cattle could not keep pace with the demand, creating barriers to agricultural expansion.

## The Discourse of Property

The colonial debate on the rights of pastoralists, forest dwellers

[41] No. 30, 14 February 1878, Ibbetson, Settlement Officer, Karnal to Davies, Comm. and Sup., Delhi Div., Delhi Division Records, Basta no. 118, Series I, p. 85.

[42] On the continuing problem of fodder scarcities in the twentieth century, see Land Rev. and Agr. (Famine), November 1911, A 8–42; Land Rev. and Agr. (Famine), April 1912, A 1–4; Land Rev. and Agr., January 1916, A 13; Land Rev. and Agr., February 1918, A 1; Land Rev. and Agr. (Famine), October 1920, A 1.

and peasants was framed within a specific discourse of property. This discourse celebrated proprietorship and viewed all forms of society through two important categories: proprietor and tenant. The framing question of this discourse was always the same: who has the right of property? The rights of all groups were conceived, classified and fixed in terms of such categories; they were defined in response to such questions. From this initial framing question, others followed: who owned the grazing runs? the uncultivated land? the open pastures? the forests? how were the rights to these lands to be defined?

Within the Punjab tradition, coparcenary village proprietors were seen as the core of the agrarian order. The proprietary body was linked together through ties of kinship and a claim to common descent. Within such a *pattidari* community, village land was to be divided among the proprietors according to ancestral shares. At the time of the settlement a part of the open grazing land was allocated to each village as *shamilat deh*. The ancestral shares of agricultural land were to determine each proprietor's claim to the shamilat. Only proprietors could have a right to graze their cattle in this common land. Within this framework, nomadic pastoralists—people without property—could have no access to the shamilat. The right to pasture was appended to the right to revenue-yielding agricultural land. Later, pastures claimed for the agricultural community were assimilated into agricultural land: they were partitioned and cultivated.

The logic was caught in the contradiction which it generated. Access to the shamilat was first made dependent on membership to the coparcenary proprietary community, but then the very identity of the pattidari community was defined in terms of its relationship to the shamilat. Revenue officials of the nineteenth century realized that the actual area of land held by proprietors had no relation to their notional ancestral shares. The size of holdings changed continuously through a complex process of land transfers. What then was the pattidari tenure? Having invented the tenurial term, officials now sought to save it by redefining its meaning. In a pattidari community, argued some officials, ancestral shares may not define rights in the village but were to be the absolute basis of rights on the shamilat. By a peculiar logic, rights to pastureland became the defining basis of the agricultural community.[43]

But grazing lands given over to village communities were for agricultural use, not pastoralism. The record of rights categorically stated that the rights to shamilat were to be 'exercised only for the bona-fide agricultural and domestic purposes of the *bartandars* (right holders in protected forests) and only on behalf of their own cattle, not for . . . purely pastoral as distinguished from agricultural purposes'.[44] Cattle could be kept for agricultural and domestic use, not for trade. It was repeatedly emphasized in official discussions: 'it is to be distinctly understood that the Government of India do not desire that grazing should be looked upon primarily as a source of income'.[45] Not only were the rights of nomadic pastoralists denied, but so were the rights of those who wished to practise agro-pastoralism. Within this regime of rights, proprietors could not allow pastoralists to graze in the shamilat. Orders specified that even 'lambardars and other influential villagers have no right to grant leases of the grazing'.[46] Only by becoming a proprietor and an agriculturist could a pastoralist graze his cattle on a village common.

[43] Douie, *Punjab Settlement Manual*, chapter VIII; *SR: Karnal 1872–80; SR: Ludhiana 1878–83*; C.L. Tupper, *Customary Law of the Punjab: Records of the Punjab Government* (1881), vols 1–3.

[44] 'Records of Rights: Kangra Forests', Section C para 11, *SRFCP, NS 26*.

[45] This statement applied to all pasture lands—the class four forests, as defined in the resolution on forest policy issued by the Government of India in 1894. *Punjab Land Administration Manual*, p. 485.

[46] 'Kangra Valley Forest Settlement Report', para 35, *SRFCP, NS 26*. See also 'Record of Rights of Villages in Kangra Proper Prepared for the Revenue Settlement of 1865–69', Section 18, *SRFCP, NS 26*; Lyall reported that 'the *Khewatdars* only have the right to graze their own cattle and sheep and goats, and they have never exercised any greater power since. . . . the owners of the soil have no right to allow other persons to graze . . .' Note by James Lyall, dated 19 February 1892 on Mr Anderson's Report of 20 August 1887 on Forest Settlement of Kangra Proper, *SRFCP, NS 26*.

This framework of thought could not tolerate open access to pastures and forests. Vast stretches of grazing tracts in West Punjab were taken over and partitioned, and property rights were given over to individuals for cultivation. It was officially stated that 'hopes should be held out to cultivators that if they fully cultivate the land (earlier used for grazing) they would be treated as proprietors, and that if they sank wells the land would be assessed at barani rates only.'[47] In many areas, permanent leases on grazing lands were given to individuals on the condition that the lessees cultivate the land instead of using it to graze their cattle.

The rights of gaddis were not linked to rights to agricultural land. But within colonial discourse, all rights were recast in the image of agricultural property rights. As regards the rights of gaddis, it was stated: 'their rights are personal and not attached to land; but they are hereditary and descend like property in land . . .'.[48] On the grazing runs of gaddis, colonial officials continued their search for assamis (tenants) and muqaddams (headmen). After claiming grazing runs as government property, the state classified shepherds as lessees who held their right direct from the government. Like village headmen who collected land revenue from villages, muqaddams were appointed from among pastoral gaddis to collect grazing dues. Landed tenures provided the frame through which the pastoral tenurial structure was conceived. Within this regime of property, all rights to land were segregated, fragmented, classified and fixed. Within it the rights claimed by nomadic pastoralists appeared unintelligible and illegitimate.

## Culture and Nature

In colonial descriptions, pastoralists were objects of contempt. They were inevitably represented as lazy, improvident, 'wretched' as cultivators, lawless, wild, and even mean and cowardly. They were

[47] Order issued around 1852 by the Commissioner of the Lahore division, *Punjab Land Administration Manual*, para 764.

[48] 'Kangra Valley Forest Settlement Report', para 30, *SRFCP, NS 26*.

associated with all that was considered evil, ugly and miserable.[49] Brandreth wrote of the Gujars, Dogars and Bhattis of Ferozepur:

> They are utterly devoid of energy and are the most apathetic, unsatisfactory race of people I ever had anything to do with. They will exert themselves occasionally to go on a cattle stealing expedition or to plunder some of the quite well-conducted Arains . . . but their exertions are seldom directed to a better end. They take not the slightest interest in any agricultural pursuit; their fields are cultivated in the most slovenly manner; you see none of the neatly kept houses, well-fenced fields, fat bullocks, and wells kept in good repair which distinguish the industrious castes; but the hovels in which they live are generally half in ruins; no fences ever protect their fields. Their cattle are half starved, and their walls often in the most dilapidated condition.[50]

This statement, made in the first decade of British rule in Punjab, was endorsed by Malcolm Darling in 1925.[51] Seventy-five years of *pax Britannica* had failed to transform the pastoralists. Embodied in such statements is a range of cultural notions about work and leisure, good and evil, order and beauty. The statements express a specific understanding of the relation between nature and culture.

The 'lazy' pastoralist was inevitably defined in opposition to the 'sturdy industrious' Sikh peasant, cultivating his field with care and yielding revenue to the British. Pastoralism was not a worthwhile enterprise, cultivation was. Lack of interest in cultivation was a sign of 'apathy'. Land that had not been cultivated was considered 'waste', 'barren', a 'wilderness'. Through cultivation, through human enterprise, barren land could be made productive

[49] The Gujars of Ferozepur were said to be 'unwilling cultivators and greatly addicted to thieving': Brandreth, *SR: Ferozepur*, the gaddis of Kangra were 'the most pernicious enemies of conservancy': Egerton; the graziers of the West Punjab *bar* were termed 'janglis' and stated to be 'wild' and 'lawless nomads' who held 'all peaceful pursuits in unaffected contempt'; Malcolm Lyall Darling, *The Punjab Peasant in Prosperity and Debt* (London, Oxford University Press, 1947), p. 123.

[50] *Ferozepur SR*, 1853, p. 4.

[51] Darling, *The Punjab Peasant in Prosperity and Debt*, p. 62.

and fertile. The labour involved in this project was 'productive', to be classed as more valuable than that which added nothing to the fertility of the soil. Those involved in this human endeavour were superior to those who did not participate in it. Nomadic activity, in fact, was not purposive action. Pastoral nomads were always described as roaming or wandering 'hither and thither'. So, pastoral activity was spurned and pastoralists stigmatized.

Like other natural resources, land was seen as scarce. Since its supply was limited, its use had to be ordered and controlled, its productive capacity augmented and reproduced. Proceeding from this perspective, pastoral practices were condemned. They used scarce resources indiscriminately, it was said, and contributed nothing to augment or regenerate the productive capacity of the soil.

The uncultivated countryside was not only barren and desolate but also dreary and ugly. Tamed, ordered, inhabited and productive landscape was beautiful. Shrubs were dreary, wheatfields were not. The 'well-fenced field' was a sign of industry and order, as also a picture pleasing to the eye. The clearance of 'wastes' and the colonization of land were therefore processes which transformed dreary landscapes into beautiful ones, activities by which 'wild' nature was tamed and ordered.

The extension of cultivation was synonymous with progress, and the 'reclamation of waste land' was a civilizing project. Uncultivated tracts where pastoralists grazed their cattle were outside the pale of culture: they had to be 'claimed' or 'reclaimed' for humanity through cultivation. Agricultural colonization, a metaphor for the expropriation of pastoralism, was represented as a process of civilization. Pastoral tracts, in fact, appeared physically segregated from the realm of culture. 'Cut off from the rest of the world by desert and hill, the people [the pastoralists of west Punjab] are caged in the surroundings, and like birds born in captivity, have small desire for anything else.'[52] Enclosed and trapped, these pastoral regions had no link with the wider, civilized

[52] Ibid., p. 94.

society. To be civilized, they had to be physically integrated with the peasant world.

In a way, this ideology of improvement was not specifically colonial: it was rooted in a long tradition of western thought. The drive to dominate nature began with the desacralization of the world and asserted itself with cold vigour in the post-Enlightenment Age of Reason. Christianity was deeply anthropocentric: the function of nature was to serve man's needs. Nature was seen as predatory and as a possible source of demonic threats.[53] Subsequently, rationalist post-enlightenment thought conceived of nature as a quantitative, mechanistic mass, a resource to be exploited. Its utility could be maximized through scientific, rational control, through productive labour. The concept of ordering, domination and the conquest of nature was integral to the ideology of improvement which developed in eighteenth-century Europe.[54]

In England, this ideology of conquest was questioned by the romantic tradition.[55] For the romantics, nature had an inner life, an organizing principle, an innate beauty. This natural order had to be discovered, and a communion with nature had to be re-established. India played upon this European romantic imagination.[56] Reacting against the monotony of ordered landscapes in the age of agricultural and industrial revolution, travellers voyaged to India in search of wild nature unspoilt by human intervention.[57] Through this communion with nature, travellers hoped to understand the 'true' meaning of life, in part via psychic experiences which their own country denied them.[58] This romantic spirit

[53] Lynn White Jr., 'The Historical Roots of Our Ecological Crisis', discussed in Donald Worster, *Nature's Economy: The Roots of Ecology* (New York, 1979).

[54] See Worster, *Nature's Economy*, and Keith Thomas, *Man and the Natural World: Changing Attitudes in England* (Harmondsworth, 1983).

[55] See Worster; also Thomas, *Man and the Natural World.*

[56] John Drew, *India and the Romantic Imagination* (New Delhi, 1987); Javed Majeed, *Ungoverned Imaginings: James Mill's The History of British India and Orientalism* (Oxford, 1992).

[57] Ibid.

[58] See the discussion of E.M. Forster's *A Passage to India* and 'The Road from Colonus' in Drew, *India and the Romantic Imagination.*

found expression in literary texts, sketches and paintings. Yet this romanticism did not throw overboard the official ideology of improvement: rather, it was wedded to this ideology.

The romantic generation of British Indian officials reacted against the flattening uniformity of western laws, against the impersonality of Cornwallis's system of government. They wanted indigenous systems to be preserved in all their variety.[59] They dreamt of a personalized, paternal rule over the countryside. But they were concerned primarily with peasant institutions and customs. And their filial care extended to peasants, not pastoralists. Lawrence's ideal was of a 'country thickly cultivated by a fat, contented yeomanry, each riding his own horse sitting under his own fig tree . . .'.[60] In this pastoral imagination, the pastoralists did not figure. Punjab was seen by officials as a land of peasant proprietors. The great debate in Punjab over protective measures concerned only the peasants.[61]

These notions inform even the most sensitive colonial accounts of rural Punjab. Consider Malcolm Darling's *The Punjab Peasant in Prosperity and Debt.* Perceptive and brilliant in many ways, the book is emphatic in its celebration of peasant culture in opposition to that of the pastoralist. And it is an account in which the story of colonization becomes a narrative of progress. In the Canal Colonies over twenty lakh acres of grazing lands were taken over by the state, pastoralists were expropriated, agricultural colonies were set up, canals were constructed, and blocks of land were granted to the 'sturdy peasants' of Central Punjab. Darling's chapter on the Canal Colonies is preceded by one on the pastoral tracts of West Punjab, a narrative strategy meant to heighten contrasts between the two regions. The arid pastoral region represented a picture of 'poverty, ignorance and oppression', a life 'dominated

59 Stokes, *The English Utilitarians and India* (Oxford, 1992).

60 R.N. Cust, *Pictures of Indian Life* (London, 1881), p. 255.

61 The shifting concerns within the debate over protection is studied by P.H.M. van den Dungen, *The Punjab Tradition: Influence and Authority in Nineteenth Century India* (London, 1972).

by relentless nature'. For Darling, life here was 'the immemorial life of India, primitive, isolated and fatalistic'; while that in the Canal Colonies was 'the new life brought in by *pax Britannica*, prosperous, progressive, and modern'. The colonization which modernized the region also transformed the landscape:

Ten years ago it was a country of rolling sand dunes patched with grass, and of hard, unfruitful plains glistening with salt. In the early nineties, a man journeying south from the Jhelum to the Sutlej would have had to traverse 150 miles of some of the ugliest and dreariest country in the world. Here and there round scattered wells . . . his eye might have been gladdened by a smiling oasis of wheat; . . . his way would have probably have lain through an endless waste of bush and scrub, with little sign of life beyond the uncertain footmark of camel, buffalo, and goat, and the moveable dwelling of the nomad grazer, with its roof of thatch propped upon wooden poles. . . . most people would have agreed with the deputy commissioner of Jhang who described it as 'unrivalled in the world for its combination of the most disagreeable features a landscape is capable of affording'.[62]

Darling could never forget the 'impression of desolation made upon his mind' when, 'fresh from the verdure and beauty of England', he found himself in this West Punjab scrubland. His description repeats all the stereotypes of colonial discourse. We have the contrast between pastoral land—subject to uncontrolled, untamed nature—and agricultural colonies where we 'feel everywhere the beneficent hand of man'. One region epitomized poverty, misery, ugliness, a primitive state of being; the other prosperity, well-being, beauty and progress. Darling reacted against the Utilitarian ethos, but his writings are saturated with much the same Utilitarian attitude to nature.[63]

Darling loved the Punjab countryside and hated the 'uncleanly

[62] Darling, *The Punjab Peasant*, p. 112.

[63] Dewey argues that Darling was influenced by the late-nineteenth-century idealist philosophy at Cambridge which reacted against traditional utilitarianism. See C.J. Dewey, '"Cambridge Idealism": Utilitarian Revisionists in Late Nineteenth Century', in the *Historical Journal*, XVII, 1974.

aroma of Indian city life'.[64] Yet he clearly did not discover any innate beauty in nature. During what he calls his 'rural rides', he was not in search of unspoilt nature or the beauty of the wilderness. Almost invariably, an ideology of improvement is woven into his lyrical descriptions of landscapes:

> the hills were veiled in the thick mist of a drying earth. But the earth itself could not have been lovelier—young wheat, ripening cane and dark mango grove all showing man's cunning hand in complete harmony with nature's, and not, as so often in India, struggling half heartedly against her callous caprices.

Only labour yields the desired harmony with nature. Beauty is a productive landscape marked with human toil.

From such a framework of thought flowed a specific measure of civilization. The level of control over nature and the level of efficiency in using natural resources here define the status of a society.[65] Those who master nature are advanced; those subject to the rhythms and dictates of nature are primitive. This argument legitimizes the power of the West and sanctions its 'civilizing' project. It sustains the critical attitude of officials towards nomadic pastoralism.[66]

The evolutionist ideas of the late nineteenth century

[64] Darling rode through the Punjab countryside and produced several volumes on his rural rides. See Darling, *Rusticus Loquitur* (London, 1930); *Wisdom and Waste in the Punjab Village* (London, 1934); *At Freedom's Door* (Oxford, 1949). The diaries and notes of these rural rides are available at the Library of the Centre for South Asian Studies, Cambridge. See Darling Papers, Boxes II, III, V, LVI, LIX, LX.

[65] See Michael Adas, *Machines as the Measure of Men: Science, Technology, and Ideologies of Western Dominance* (Cornell, 1989; rpt., New Delhi, 1990).

[66] Only beyond the agrarian frontier could the nomads capture the romantic official imagination. The Pathan nomads were troublesome, yet objects of fascination; the desire to subdue and control them went along with a respect for their masculine pride. Ibbetson wrote: 'The true Pathan is perhaps the most barbaric of all the races with which we are brought into contact in the Punjab . . . he is bloodthirsty, cruel, and vindictive in the highest degree; he does not know what truth or faith is.' Condemned as barbaric, the Pathan is immediately

strengthened this association between the pastoral nomad and the primitive. The evolutionist scheme saw the movement from savagery to civilization as an evolution from tribe to state. Family, property and territory were established at different stages of this unilinear movement. Once the signs of civilization were fixed, different groups could be ranked within a single evolutionary scale. Social groups such as the pastoral tribes—which were assumed to have no association with property, territory and state—appeared on the lower rungs of the scale. And once characterized as primitive, property, territory and state were always seen as alien implants on pastoral nomadic society.

## From Nomads to Vagrants

How were the pastoralist and the nomad perceived within popular culture?

There is no doubt that at one level the social and cultural world of nomads was opposed to that of settled peasants. Powindahs considered mobility as their defining characteristic: the very term powindah, as I said, means 'one who travels on foot'; the alternative Persian term 'kochi', used in Afghanistan, has a similar meaning: 'one who moves'. Powindahs saw nomadism not only as a legitimate way of life but as the very basis of their status and pride.[67] Those who settled, lost this identity. But the settled Pathans of the plains distanced themselves from the mobile hillmen. For them, 'a hill man is no man'. And they commonly said: 'don't class burrs as grass, or a hill man as a human being'.[68]

Each group, the settled and the mobile, looked down upon

---

rehabilitated as a masculine pastoral hero: 'there is a sort of charm about him . . . He leads a wild, free, active life in the rugged fastness of his mountains; and there is an air of masculine independence about him which is refreshing in a country like India.' Denzil Ibbetson, *Punjab Castes* (1916; reprinted, Lahore, 1986), p. 58.

67 Akbar Ahmad, 'Nomadism as Ideological Expression: The Case of the Gomal Nomads', *Contributions to Indian Sociology*, vol. 17, no. 1, 1983.

68 Ibbetson, *Punjab Castes*, p. 58.

the other. Pastoralists were frequently the subject of peasant ridicule. In the dry tracts of the south-east, a gujar was suspect as friend and neighbour. There was a common saying: 'befriend a gujar only when all other communities die' (*sabhi zat marjae jab, kar gujar se dosti*).[69] One could sleep with ease, it was said, only when dogs, cats, *ranghars* and gujars were not present (*kutta billi do; ranghar gujar dol ye charon na ho, to pair phelake so*).[70] Ahirs were similarly stigmatized: they were faithless (*ahir be-pir*); they were as ruthless as the Baniya, as treacherous as the jackal.[71] In their self-conception, represented in the myths of their origin, Ahirs contested such terms of censure.

The mobile and the settled, nomads and peasants, were thus locked in continuous conflict. But they also coexisted through conflict: nomadism was not yet repressed. Nomadic activity operated not merely within the pores and interstices of society but was an integral part of it. And social attitudes towards the wanderer, the outsider and the nomad were complex, contradictory, ambivalent.

The wanderer was not univocally or universally censured. The theme of travel or wandering appears insistently in Punjabi *kissas*. In the kissa of Raja Rasalu, for instance, the prince is banished from the kingdom for violating social propriety.[72] As Rasalu wanders from one region to another, he faces new problems, new tests. He confronts them all and in the process reveals himself—his valour, determination, intelligence, kindness. At the end, he returns to his kingdom.

This narrative structure recurs in other kissas. The prince becomes a commoner, wanders into unknown land, and later the commoner becomes the king. It is usually a journey which mediates

[69] R. Maconachie, ed., *Selected Agricultural Proverbs of the Punjab* (Delhi, 1890), p. 242.

[70] Ibid., p. 242.

[71] Rose, vol. II, p. 7.

[72] Several versions of the Raja Rasalu stories are recorded in Temple, *Punjab Legends*, vols I, II, III. See also Charles Swynnerton, *The Adventures of the Panjab Hero Raja Rasalu and Other Folktales of the Panjab* (Calcutta, 1884).

between the double transformation from king to commoner and back from commoner to king. In such popular narratives a life of wandering is seen in opposed ways: it is both a punishment for social transgression as well as a quest for knowledge, an act through which the norms of society are re-established. The journey reveals the innate nobility of the prince who is in commoner's clothes. The journey becomes a method of self-discovery, a process by which experience and knowledge are acquired, a passage through which the self is constituted in confrontation with the world. The individual moves out of society to demonstrate his right to be reintegrated within it.[73]

This notion of journey as a mode of self-realization and self-constitution was premised on a specific conception of knowledge and experience. It is implicit here that knowledge comes from experience, that experience is spatially limited, that a specific experience is contained within a particular space. So, spatial mobility is necessary for the expansion of experience and knowledge, for self-realization. The journey marked the movement from one enclosed world to another, one realm of experience to another.

In many popular Punjabi kissas the 'outsider' is romanticized. The hero is very often a *pardesi*. Izzatbeg, the hero of the kissa of Sohni-Mahiwal, is an *amirzada* from Bokhara who comes to India with a kafila of *saudagars*. Izzatbeg moves with the saudagars, helping them sell horses and spices, and falls in love with Sohni, the daughter of a potter. In the kissa of Hir–Ranjha, Hir's passionate romance unfolds with Ranjha, who comes from across Chenab. In the kissa of Sassi–Pannun, Sassi falls madly in love with a pardesi, a Biloch, whom she has never even met. When

[73] For a discussion of the theme of journey in the context of Bengali popular literature, see Roma Chatterji, 'The Voyage of the Hero: The Self and the Other in One Narrative Tradition in Purulia', *Contributions to Indian Sociology*, vol. 19, no. 1, 1985. On the theme of transformation, see Brenda Beck and A.K. Ramanujan, 'Social Categories and their Transformations in Indian Folktales', in D.P. Pattanayak and Peter Claus, eds. *Indian Folklore I* (Mysore, 1981).

Pannun comes to meet Sassi, he accompanies the saudagars from Afghanistan and is dressed as one of them.

Yet relationships with outsiders was in a sense problematic. A stranger could never be trusted. In the kissa of Sassi–Pannun, recorded in the early nineteenth century,[74] Sassi is fated to love a stranger who will desert her. Her love for Pannun ends in tragedy for both. This kissa powerfully expresses the popular fear of relating to outsiders. The stability and security of the knowable community appears in contrast with the instability of the outside world.

Pastoral themes recur in the kissas in a variety of ways, revealing a complex of a nbivalent and conflicting attitudes. In the kissa of Hir–Ranjha, Hir falls in love with a zamindar's son who becomes a cowherd.[75] In the kissa of Sohni–Mahiwal, an amirzada from Bokhara becomes first a traveller and later a *mahiwal*, the cowherd with whom Hir's passionate love develops. Both Ranjha and Izzatbeg have to renounce their material, social inheritance. Only as mahiwals can they act out their romantic roles. This transformation from a person of social standing to a wanderer and then a cowherd is not represented as a fall: social transgression does not produce a feeling of guilt among those who transgress.

The pastoral theme has a spatial imagery. Romance in these kissas usually develops on the grazing runs and in the forests. It is

[74] This kissa, originally from Sindh and southern Baluchistan, was popular all over Punjab. Hasham Shah transformed the folktale into a literary form. Bardic versions continued to differ from literary versions. For a bibliography on the kissa, see *Indian Antiquary*, vol. XI, p. 291. The bardic versions of Hir–Ranjha and Sassi–Pannun recorded by Temple in the late-nineteenth-century show the complex relationship between the bardic and literary versions of these kissas. They show how the bardic versions borrowed from, contested and transformed the classic literary renditions of folktales. See 'A Version of Sassi Pannun as Told by a Bard from the Hoshiarpur District', Temple, vol. III, and 'Qissa Hir Ranjha Musannifa Hafiz Ahmed Mutawattan-i-Jhang', Temple, vol. II.

[75] In some popular versions of the kissa, Ranjha claims to have been a cowherd since he was five. See 'The Marriage of Hir Ranjha as Related by Some Jatts from the Patiala State', Temple, vol. II.

in these open spaces that Hir–Ranjha and Sohni–Mahiwal meet each other. They move out of the village, away from the constraints of society, into a realm of freedom, a world of passion and dream.[76] Their return to the village marks a return to the sphere of constraints.

In these kissas the flute appears as a metaphor for romantic love and freedom from society's norms. In the popular imagery here, as in some of the pastoral forms which developed elsewhere, the flute is associated with the pastoral nomad. Ranjha as well as Mahiwal wander about in the grazing runs, playing the flute, much like their literary counterparts in British or Italian Pastoral poems and eclogues.[77]

The flute is in fact associated with an entire way of life. Ranjha and Izzatbeg delight in a life of ease, untroubled by work. Even when compelled to work, they only end up playing the flute and grazing cattle. The kissas set up a rhetoric of contrasts: a good life without work and pain is opposed with a life of toil and labour; nomadic life appears in opposition to the norms of settled society. Pastoral life appears, in the Indian context as in the Western, as the romantic other; and so the object of the romantic imagination comes into being coterminously with the social censure of a peasant society.

The kissas, it could be said, reveal a tension between the necessity of social codes and the urge to transgress them; between the conjugal norms of society and the dream of passionate extra-marital union. Norms are represented as constraints on freedom as well as the basis of order; transgression is celebrated as well as damned. The pardesi, the wanderer and the cowherd appear as romantic heroes, but they are also transgressors of norms. They

[76] '*Bela vich o maujan karde, koi no rokandar*' (They made love in the wilds, where no one was to restrain them) 'Qissa Hir Ranjha Musannifa Hafiz Ahmed Mutawattan-i-Jhang', in Temple, vol. II.

[77] In one version recorded in Temple, vol. II, Ranjha plays thirty-six beautiful tunes in the forest and makes all creatures dance. For the Renaissance Pastoral, see Sukanta Chaudhuri, *Renaissance Pastoral and Its English Developments* (Oxford, 1989).

enact their romance but, in the end, move out of society: they have to renounce the world or die. The lovers reunite through death: Ranjha enters Hir's grave and Pannun enters Sassi's.[78] And once dead they are deified: there is a shrine of Hir–Ranjha near Jhang where, in the late nineteenth century, a fair was held in February.

The pastoral heroes of the kissas are deified in a variety of ways. In the version of Hir–Ranjha's marriage narrated by the Patiala Jatts in the late nineteenth century, the character of Ranjha the cowherd fuses with that of a yogi with miraculous powers. Ranjha does not become a follower of Balnath after Hir is married to Khera. The powers of a yogi inhere in him.[79] In the kissa of Abdullah Shah of Samin narrated by Ghulam Muhammad Balachani Mazari, the story of Hir and Ranjha reappears, emplotted in a narrative which sanctifies Ranjha.[80] In this, Abdullah Shah sets off on a pilgrimage to Mecca. His ship having run aground, Abdullah disembarks to make the ship move. In the process, the ship sails off, leaving Abdullah upon a desolate shore. Abdullah then discovers Hir and Ranjha. Ranjha takes Abdullah to the Prophet and brings him back to earth. In this kissa Ranjha has

78 This plot structure is common in Punjabi kissas. See the kissa of 'Adam Khan and Dur Khanai' in W.L. Heston and Mumtaz Nasir, *The Bazaar of the Storytellers* (Lok Virsa Publishing House, n.d.). What is important is to see the way familiar plots are imbued with specific meaning: how the characters are actually defined and subplots worked into the general structure.

Through this plot, Waris Shah explores the relationship between earthly love and mystical love. Grewal has suggested that Waris Shah, who wrote *Hir-Waris* in 1766, was deeply influenced by Sufism. When Hir dies, Ranjha's soul departs from his body. Waris says that both Hir and Ranjha have left *dar-i-fana* and gone to *dar-i-baga*. In *Hir Waris*, true love on earth is like a Sufi's union with God. J.S. Grewal 'The World of Waris,' in Sudhir Chandra, ed., *Social Transformation and Creative Imagination* (New Delhi, 1984). For a reading of Hir, as a failed allegory within the framework of Sufi imagination, see Surjit Hans, 'Why the World of Waris Collapsed', *Journal of Regional History*, vol. IV, 1983.

79 Temple, vol. II.

80 'Kissa of Abdullah Shah of Samin' (recorded in the Biloch language from the narrative of Ghulam Muhammad Balachani Mazari), Temple, vol. II.

direct access to the Prophet, for he is the cowherd who supplies the Prophet with his daily requirement of milk. Hir and Ranjha inhabit a liminal space between the human and the divine: the seashore where Abdullah's ship is stuck, and where no other human lives, represents that liminal space. Ranjha, rather like Virgil in Dante's *Divine Comedy*, has the power to move between spaces, between different worlds. Abdullah's journey between the human and the divine world is made possible by Ranjha. Abdullah was a Sayyid and was known for his sanctity. But it is Ranjha the cowherd who has closer proximity to the Prophet.

Nomads, pedlars and pastoralists faced a more univocal opposition under the colonial regime as the state attempted to discipline and settle them, and as the institutions of disciplinary power crystallized over time. The conflicting images, with all their ambiguities and possible variations in meaning, fused into one stereotypical image of the nomad as vagrant. Watched, hounded, harassed and frequently prosecuted by the police, nomads henceforth lived a life of eternal persecution.

The Criminal Tribes Act of 1871 gave legal sanction to official actions against 'wanderers'. By the act of 1871, wandering became a crime. Tribes classed as 'habitual wanderers' were now expected to stay confined to their villages. Licences of leave were to be issued, but only to those who pursued an 'honest livelihood'. Anyone found wandering without a licence was to be prosecuted, fined and arrested. Pastoralists in the Canal Colonies ('*janglis*') were classified as criminal; in many districts gujars, *bhattis* and others pastoral groups appeared in the list of criminal tribes.

Through other acts, the state extended control over the pastoralist's animal stock. All animals—camels, ponies, horses, mules—were to be enumerated, registered and branded. In each district, the number of animals had to be ascertained, and in times of war they were pressed into the service of the state. These measures provoked continuous conflict as well as frequent confrontations between pastoralists and the state. When in 1878 powindah camels were forcibly requisitioned for military carriage, the powindahs rebelled. In a massive operation, celebrated later as the great rescue, armed bands of powindahs fought the police, stripped them naked, burnt several *thanas* and recovered their animals. Such confrontations were common. Yet the Punjab Military Transport Act of May 1903 was passed, legalizing government rights over all transport animals. To exercise more effective control over animals, nomadic pastoralism was discouraged in favour of settled animal husbandry. Willing breeders could get large land-grants in the Canal Colonies.

Nomads, vagabonds and wanderers were thus to be disciplined and settled. Their identities had to be fixed. They had to belong to a marked territory—a village, a district, a province. To exercise power the state *had* to know the identities of those over whom power was to be exercised, and confine them within controllable, delimited spaces. Nomads appeared elusive, unknowable, anonymous beings whose identities were difficult to ascertain. Their mobility was, to an extent, acceptable; their anonymity was not. Since the anonymity of the nomad threatened the very basis of power, their mobility had to be restricted and regulated.

## Conclusion

In conclusion I wish to draw out the implications of my general argument.

In an interesting essay, Chris Bayly has written about a general process of peasantization of nomads in the nineteenth century.[81] He counterpoises this process to the traditional thesis on the proletarianization of peasants. This counterposition is problematic: in a sense, Bayly shares the premises of the argument he opposes. This is because both these apparently opposed theses share the common assumption that vulnerable social groups invariably succumb to the irresistible and all-powerful forces of commercialization and agrarian expansion. Unable to resist, peasants, according to one thesis, become paupers; according to the other, nomads become peasants.

[81] C.A. Bayly, 'Creating a Colonial Peasantry: India and Java, *c.* 1820–1880,' *Itinerario*, vol. I, no. 1 (1987), pp. 93–106.

I would argue that a more complex process is at work. While pauperized, some nomads took to wage labour, earning small sums by digging canals or building roads. Some became part-time peasants or expanded their cultivation to supplement a declining income. Others concentrated on trading activities. And finally, there were those that continued their earlier pastoral activities even within the new regime where a legal order classed them as vagrants and criminals, forest acts appropriated their grazing grounds, and an expanding agrarian frontier colonized the tracts over which they earlier moved. At times, they silently defied the encroaching norms of the new order; at other times they rebelled more openly. Their conflicts with the state and agrarian society sharpened over time. Grazers set fire to reserved forests, defied restrictions on grazing rights, raided peasant communities, destroyed crops, and carried off peasant cattle.[82] The conflict with peasant society was perhaps most acute in the Canal Colonies, where pastoralists were expropriated on a grand scale. For a prolonged period, the 'janglis' carried on a war with the early peasant migrants from Central Punjab.[83]

There was thus both resistance and adaptation to change. I can see no simple, smooth process of displacement and dispossession; no uniform, unilinear development.

[82] On Grazing: no. 47, dated 16 October 1883, Report on Rohtak Birs, Delhi Division Records, Bundle 4, Memorandum on Grazing in Government Forests and Wastelands, Delhi Division Records, Bundle 4; on cattle lifting, see no. 260, dated 17 January 1907, from the Superintendent of Police, Lahore, to the Deputy Commissioner, Lahore, Punjab Home Police, September 1907, A 13.

[83] Peasant settlers found the pastoral scrubland hostile in every way, and the pastoralist ('janglis') appeared as their worst enemies. Malcolm Darling asked Maharaja Singh, one of the first 140 migrants to Lyallpur, about his initial impressions of the place. Singh recollected that the country was 'all waste but dotted with jand trees, snakes lifting angry heads, enormous scorpions, and not a bird to be seen'. Darling, *At Freedom's Door*, p. 79. In this description we have all the images of danger, fear, poison, death and desolation which recurred in other accounts that Darling heard from the colonists. All the colonists also complained of trouble created by the 'janglis'.

Chapter Three

# Whose Trees? Forest Practices and Local Communities in Andhra, 1600–1922*

ATLURI MURALI

In order to understand the depletion of forest resources under the colonial paradigm of 'scientific' management and exploitation, we have to start with the differences between traditional and colonial approaches to the use of forest resources, as well as the nature of the conflict arising over the use of these resources between local communities and the state.

To reconstruct the culture of the human–environment relationship—which is traditionally mediated by religion (i.e. beliefs, rituals and institutions)—we have to depend upon unconventional sources in the regional languages, in particular upon classical literature, *stalapuranas*, village *kaifiyats* (local chronicles) and oral traditions. Classical Telugu poetry is full of observations on the countryside, the landscape, the seasons, the fauna, the flora and the inhabitants of the region. Equally, a mapping of the environmental situation from the 1790s to the 1850s could be done by using travelogues and the sympathetic observations and notations of district-level colonial administrators. Finally, after the 1860s we have the records of the Forest Department.

* I am grateful to David Arnold and Ramachandra Guha for their support and keen interest in my work; also to Richard B. Barnett, University of Virginia, and V. Rajagopal, University of Hyderabad, for their comments.

By using classical literature, oral traditions and archaeological evidence, M.L.K. Murty and Gunther-Dietz Sontheimer reconstructed the history of pastoralism and pastoral communities in the Deccan region from prehistoric times.[1] Their studies pointed to the antiquity of a sedentary, village-based dairy-cum-agricultural system, and also the historical evolution of a complex relationship between agricultural, forest and pastoral regions. By tracing through religious legends the cultural history of Kuruvas living in Balapalapalle, a village seventy kilometers south-west of Kurnool town, Murty shows the 'acculturation of communities of different subsistence systems, who were drawn into the fold of each other in an ecosystem.'[2] Even though some pastoralists might, over a period of time and on account of ecological changes, have retreated to a life in the forest—thereby leaving space for others to become settled agriculturists—there were legends and oral traditions, like that of Mallikarjuna, which showed the 'permeation of pastoralism and agriculture.'[3] The legends associated with this pastoral god Mallikarjuna, endowed with two wives—one from the higher caste (or class?) and the other from the tribes—supports the argument for this process. The legend associated with a famous Siva shrine, Mallikarjuna, in Nandikotkur *taluqa*, Kurnool district, shows Siva meeting a beautiful Chenchu girl on one of his hunting expeditions and marrying her. He is worshiped both by the tribal Chenchus and the pastoralist Gollas.[4]

[1] M.L.K. Murty, 'Ethnoarchaeology of the Kurnool Cave Areas, South India', *World Archaeology*, 17; 2, 1985, pp. 192–205; and with G.D. Sontheimer, 'Prehistoric Background to Pastoralism in the Southern Deccan in the Light of Oral Traditions and Cults of Some Pastoral Communities', *Anthropos*, 75, 1980, pp. 163–84; G.D. Sontheimer, 'The *Vana* and the *Ksetra*: The Tribal Background of Some Famous Cults', in G.C. Tripathi and Hermann Kulke, eds, *Eschmann Memorial Lectures* (Bhubaneswar, 1987), pp. 117–64; and Sontheimer, *Pastoral Deities in Western India* (New York, 1989).

[2] Murty and Sontheimer, 'Prehistoric Background to Pastoralism', p. 165.

[3] Ibid.

[4] The story is taken from N. Ramesan, *Temples and Legends of Andhra Pradesh* (Bombay, 1962). For information on the legend of Mallikarjuna at Sri Sailam, see Murty and Sontheimer, 'Prehistoric Background to Pastoralism'.

Starting from the time of the Chalukya-Cholas and Kakatiyas (eleventh to fourteenth centuries AD), the inscriptional sources found on the walls of Draksharama, Srikurmam, Simhachalam and other temples clearly indicate the involvement of these temples in agriculture, irrigation, taxation and the land reclamation that followed the expansion of cultivation. All these aspects were directly related to the management of the ecosystem in medieval Andhra. The *pullary* (tax) on grazing lands seems to have been one of the main sources of income for the state. Temples were also involved in appropriating—via royal and private grants or donations—the income from grazing and from the businesses of cattle-breeding and rearing goats. Pastoralism therefore played an important role in social life. For instance, the inscription in the Draksharama temple (in East Godavari district) specifically recorded the role of *go-raksakas* (cowherds), *kiratas* (hunters) and *boyas* (tribals) in village life and temple functions. The support of these social groups—tribals, cowherds and hunters—along with the peasant and artisan classes was considered to be crucial for the political legitimacy of the rulers. From the fifteenth-century we have textual sources elaborating state policy towards these social groups and the ecosystems they were living in.[5]

The necessity for a well-defined policy towards agricultural and forest regions and its relevance for political stability drew the attention of Krishnadeva Raya, king of the Vijayanagara empire. A sixteenth-century classical literary text, *Aamuktamalyada*,[6] written

5 This account is based on M. Rama Rao, *Inscriptions of Andhradesa*, vol. II, part I (Tirupati, 1968); N. Narasimha Rao, *Corporate Life in Medieval Andhradesa* (New Delhi, 1967); *Draksharama Inscriptions* (Hyderabad, 1970); E. Hultzsch, ed., *South Indian Inscriptions*, vol. I (1870), vol. II (1892), vol. III, part i (1899) and part ii (1903), and later H. Krishna Sastri, ed., vol. III, part iii (1920) and part iv (1929); S. Subramanya Sastri, ed., *Tirumala-Tirupati Devasthanam Epigraphical Series*, 4 vols (Tirupati, 1930); V. Kamesvara Rao, *Temples in Rayalasima* (Telugu, Hyderabad, 1974); B.R. Subrahmanyam, 'Social and Economic Life in Ancient and Medieval Andhra', and A.V. Jevechandrun, 'Temples as Cultural Centres', in H.M. Nayak and B.R. Gopal, eds., *South Indian Studies* (Mysore, 1990), pp. 288–99, 310–23.

6 Krishnadeva Raya's *Aamuktamalyada alias Vishnu-Chittiyamu* was said to

by Krishnadeva Raya, spells out what ought to be the policy of the state towards forests and tribal groups. Though he recommends that the state should deliberately develop impenetrable forests on all the boundaries of its kingdom in order to protect people from thieves, he advises only a partial clearing of forests in the centre of the kingdom, not others.[7] The policy towards the people living in the forests, called *mannepu janulu*, was aimed at assimilation and not annihilation. One poem reads thus:

> The tribal people, who roam about in the forest and hill areas, possess several defects. Even by imposing severe punitive measures one cannot remove their defects, for it is like washing a mud wall to remove the mud. Instead, it is better to maintain friendship with them by a policy of truthfulness and offering gifts. By doing so the king can get their physical support during his expeditions against rival kings. Moreover, by using them, the king can get his enemy's lands looted . . .[8]

In the medieval period the maintenance of well-nourished forests, interwoven with hills, was helpful not only as an effective defence against the enemy, but also as a political boundary. In fact, Krishnadeva Raya is very specific in his policy about the need to avoid hills and forests during military expeditions against rival

---

have been written between AD 1515 and 1521 I have used the critical and explanatory edition of Sri Vedam Venkataraya Sastry, first published in 1927 (in Telugu, Madras, 2nd reprint, 1964).

[7] *Adavulu gadi desamulavi,*
*dadamuluga pempumu,*
*aatma dharanistalikin nadumalavi, pollupolluga,*
*podipimpumu dasyu badha pondaka yundan.*

Poem no. 256, ibid., pp. 459–60.

[8] *Kshama gurumannepum gahanachari janambeda doshadrusti Kudyamu gaduganga pooniki; tega dalgina sarvamu; baasa neegi Vasyamuga nonarpa daadikagu; now gadi Kollalakun; shataaparaa dhanunu sahasradandamu natarkyamu sarvamu neeluvanikin.*

This English translation is a free-style prose version of Poem no. 257, ibid., p. 460.

kingdoms.[9] He also evolved a well-defined policy to combine his own subjects in alliance with migrants from outside. He provided immigrants with cattle (apart from other items of wealth) whenever such people came on account of scarcity, drought, epidemics and other calamities.[10]

One important aspect of the Vijayanagara economy was the encouragement given to the spread of settled agriculture. The state was directly involved in developing irrigation systems and helped expand agricultural production with lower taxation on small farmers. But this thrust towards expanded irrigation does not seem to have depleted the forest cover. From the twelfth to the sixteenth centuries, the peasant-warrior migrant groups from coastal Andhra are said to have introduced tank irrigation technology into the dry upland zone, resulting in the development of cultivation on dry, fertile soils. How far these newly irrigated areas diverted pressure from the reclamation of forest lands to cultivation in the wet and the dry upland regions is a matter yet to be researched. For the purposes of our argument, we can safely presume that the spread of tank irrigation did engage the energies of peasant-warrior migrants from coastal Andhra by bringing the dry fertile zones under cultivation, not only in Telangana but also in Rayalaseema and some regions of Tamil Nadu.[11] Naturally the peasants, and even

[9] See Poem no. 268, ibid., p. 466.

[10] See Poem no. 245, ibid., p. 453.

[11] For details, see K.S. Shivanna, *The Agrarian System of Karnataka, 1336–1761* (Mysore, 1983); Gribble, *A History of the Deccan*, 2 vols (London, 1895–1924); T.V. Mahalingam, *Economic Life in the Vijayanagar Empire* (Madras, 1951); T.M. Srinivasan, *Irrigation And Water Supply: South India, 200 BC–AD 1600* (Madras, 1991); B. Muddachari, 'Economic Life in Vijayanagar', *Journal of Historical Studies* (University of Mysore, 1979), vol. 15, pp. 47–56; M.L. Saraswathi, 'Irrigation in Vijayanagar: Methods of Construction', ibid., vol. 16, pp. 77–89; 'The Irrigation System in Vijayanagar as Reflected in the Porumamilla Tank Inscription of AD 1369', ibid., vol. 17, 1983, pp. 15–19, and 'Irrigation System in Bellary during the Vijayanagara Period', ibid., vol. 18, pp. 16–20; M. Krishnamurthy, 'Vijayanagar Interest in Irrigation Facilities in Cuddapah District, Andhra Pradesh', in *Itihas* (Journal of the Andhra Pradesh State Archives, Hyderabad), IX and X, 1982; Burton Stein, 'The State, the Temple and

the state, did not put any pressure or, broadly speaking, evolve a 'commercial' attitude towards the forests. In reality the control of tribal groups over the forests was recognized by the state as an unquestionable natural right. By recognizing the natural rights of *mannepu janulu* over forests, and through its policy of friendship, the state tried to assimilate them into the empire.[12] In other words, during the sixteenth-century the well defined, mutually sustaining relationship between agriculture, forest and pastoral regions seems to have continued.

The antiquity of the cultural–economic and political construction of human–ecological relationships can also be discerned from the stalapuranas and village kaifiyats.[13] I attempt here to discuss the role of religious traditions in preserving virgin forest tracts around the sacred hills, pilgrim centres, temples and sacred springs which were associated with curative miracles.[14] I will also analyse some of the village kaifiyats in order to map out the character of the relationship between agriculture, pastoralism and village settlement patterns in the seventeenth and eighteenth centuries.

Colin Mackenzie, Surveyor-General of India, who arrived in India in 1783, was entrusted the task of surveying the villages of Andhra in 1790. With the help of Kavali Boraiah, Bhaskaraiah, Ramaswamy, Abdul Azees and Srinivasaiah, he compiled a series of descriptive histories of villages known as kaifiyats. They covered

---

Agricultural Development: A Study in Medieval South India', *Economic Weekly*, Annual Number, 1961; *Peasant State and Society in Medieval South India* (New Delhi, 1980), and *Vijayanagara* (Cambridge, 1990); David Ludden, *Peasant History in South India* (Princeton, 1985).

12 See poems in *Aamuktamalyada*, pp. 435–44, 447–9.

13 The important stalapuranas which I have looked at are related to Sri Kalahasthi, Sri Sailam, Tirupathi, Alampur, Annavaram, Draksharama, Simhachal Kshetram or Simhadri Kshetram and Annavaram.

14 I am making a detailed study of these aspects in my project, 'The Mediation of Religion in the Human-Ecological Relationship in Andhra, 1600–1900', which is part of an all India joint project on 'Socio-Religious Movements and Cultural Networks in Indian Civilization', Indian Institute of Advanced Study, Shimla, 1991 to 1995.

the origins—historical, but also as preserved in the social memory through legends and myths—of each village, its flora and fauna, people, religious and secular monuments, inscriptions, natural resources, religious customs, functions and practices.[15] These kaifiyats offer us very useful information about the geographical and topographical background of each village from the seventeenth-century through to the early twentieth centuries.

The histories of Anakapalli, Yalamanchali, Aarantlakota and other small villages in Doddugolla Seema in Visakhapatnam district illustrate an interesting pattern of harmonious relationship between pastoralism and the agricultural economy. Though most of the village settlements started with the clearing of small patches of virgin forest, initially the transition from pastoralism to settled agriculture converted some of the forest lands to agriculture. However, it was mainly the *gayalubhumi* (waste, uncultivated land) which was converted into pasturage and cultivated land. There seems to have been no particular pressure on forests once enough area for subsistence had been cleared.[16] One important feature of the ecology of all the villages was the widespread pattern of maintaining a variety of orchards, fruit gardens, tanks, and *topes* (orchards) especially of toddy trees, and some form of *mandabayalu* (open space).

For instance, Gopalapatnam village in Visakhapatnam district was started as a pastoral settlement, and its origins went back to myths of the Mahabharata period. One legend was associated with Sahadeva, the youngest of the Pandavas, who spent his time in hiding, looking after the cattle of the king of Virata. As with

[15] The origins and histories of villages were, quite often, converted into oral traditions. This kept the histories alive in social memory. The religious ceremonies and annual religious functions or rituals associated with temples constructed over a period of time also played an important role in the memorialization of these histories.

[16] Only fifteen village kaifiyats of Visakhapatnam district have so far been published; the rest are in manuscript form in the Andhra Pradesh State Archives, Hyderabad. See H. Rajendra Prasad, ed., *Grama (Village) Kaifiyats: Visakhapatnam District* (Telugu, A.P. State Archives, Hyderabad, 1990).

numerous settlements, the origins of this village are associated with a cowherd, a pond, a sweet mango tree, and pastoral lands on a distant hill covered by a dense forest. This legend also demonstrates that the traditional process of pastoralism coexisted with virgin forest zones. The pressure exerted on forests never seems to have been above the needs of the subsistence agrarian-cum-pastoral economy.[17] In the case of Namavaram village, it seems this was surrounded by five big as well as a few small water tanks on all sides, the existence of which went back to antiquity; however, four out of the five major tanks were dug in the mid-seventeenth-century. Because of the newly expanded tank irrigation, both the productivity and the value of the lands is said to have increased. One of the two mango groves was a hundred years old, established by a Vaishya (Komati) named Kandula Kanumanthu.[18] In Madugula taluqa, there were twenty-four *agraharas* with fertile lands brought into settled agriculture. The unique character of these agraharas was that they were full of well-nourished groves with many varieties of fruit-bearing trees. The whole area, before the establishment of East India Company rule, was controlled by the family of a Konda raja. Though the water was unhealthy, the hills were covered with *manchigandham* (sandalwood) trees and were rich in honeycombs. The hills and the surrounding dense forest areas were also full of different species of birds and wild animals.[19]

The story of Rapathinpatnam, written down by a Niyogi, Dinavali Krishnam Raju, is another example of ecological conditions decisively influencing the pattern of a village pastoral-cum-agricultural economy. This account describes, in considerable detail, hills covered with dense virgin forests as well as areas developed both for pastoral and agricultural needs—with irrigation from natural streams and waterfalls. One is reminded of Krishnadeva Raya's policy of integrating tribal areas as a natural protective political barrier against attack, for the whole settlement was protected

[17] For full details of the story, see ibid., pp. 10–11.
[18] Ibid., p. 12.
[19] Ibid., pp. 13–14.

on one side by hills covered with forest and on the other three sides by tribals (*kondavaandlu*) living in the forests. The natural ecology was thus exploited cleverly: the pastoral and agricultural needs of the community were met, and these served simultaneously as a natural protective barrier against external threat.[20]

The village kaifiyats in West Godavari district also show the tradition of clearing forests and *porambokes* (common wastelands) to construct village settlements; the development of tank irrigation; the conversion of *bidu* (wasteland) into cultivation, the paying of *shrotriem* (an estate on which the land revenue had been assigned to the holder), and the development of well-nourished topes.[21] The story of Aaginapalli village in Krishna district, written in 1815, is another fascinating example. The origin myth of this village was traced back to the legend of Sri Sobhanachala Swami *stala mahatyam*, narrated in the *Brahmanda Purana*, and the changes in the name of the hill in different *yugas*. Except for the temple of Sri Sobhanachala Swami, the other temples in use at the time (Malleshwara Swami and Shiva) were said to have been constructed around 1700. To support religious functions, rituals and temple institutions, elaborate arrangements were made in land grants. Apart from these land grants, various *totalu* (gardens) were cultivated and often dedicated to various gods: they played a very significant role in maintaining the ecology of village settlements. Even the temple *mantapas* were constructed on hilltops, integrating a wider ecological zone into the protective ring of temples.[22]

In Srikakulam district there is, among various histories—of Kalingapatnam, Kasipuram, Nagavalinadi, Tyadmanyam, Veera Ghottam, Rajam and Srikakulam—one particular narrative, by

[20] Ibid., pp. 17–26.

[21] For details, see H. Rajendra Prasad (ed.), *Grama (Village) Kaifiyats: West Godavari District* (Telugu, A.P. State Archives, Hyderabad, 1990). Only twelve *Kaifiyats* are published in this volume.

[22] So says the story of Aaginapalli, in H. Rajendra Prasad, ed., *Grama (Village) Kaifiyats: Krishna District* (Telugu, A.P. State Archives, Hyderabad, 1990), pp. 1–12.

Mokhalingam, which is very important.[23] It traces the antiquity of the settlement to the sage Agatsya in *Kritayuga*, and while doing so it depicts the taming of forests to create a settled agricultural area. Yet, in the process, on account of some natural calamity, the whole area is said to have been once again covered with dense forest. The reclamation process in the subsequent periods and also the entry of new tree species is explained in detail. The history of this reclamation process is preserved in a legend associated with *devatas* and kiratas, basically representing the penetration of social groups from settled agricultural areas (devatas) and their interaction with the people living in the forests.[24]

Even in Guntur district, now a completely settled agricultural area with well developed irrigation systems, the stories and histories are the same in character.[25] The origin myth of Amrithaluru runs thus:

> Previously the area was covered by a jungle in which a cowherd used to graze his cattle. A cow from the herd was giving milk daily over a Siva lingam hidden in an anthill. When the shepherd tried to milk her after returning home, he found her udders dry. Presuming that somebody was milking the cow stealthily, he waited in ambush in the branches of a tree and threw his axe over the lingam when the cow was milking. The cow jumped for her life and trampled over the lingam, and a chip of the lingam the size of the cow's hoof came off. During the night Lord Siva appeared in the cowherd's dream in a terrible form and informed him that he was the God Amriteswara who had been living in the anthill for a long time and consuming the milk, and he ordered the shepherd to expose the lingam from the anthill and construct a shrine. The cowherd brought his relatives and others to the anthill and found the lingam after excavation. Then he built a shrine, consecrated the lingam

[23] For details, see H. Rajendra Prasad (ed.), *Grama (Village) Kaifiyats: Sri Kakulam District* (Telugu, A.P. State Archives, Hyderabad, 1990).

[24] Ibid., pp. 22–30.

[25] All the village kaifiyats of Guntur district have been published. I have used the latest collection for the English summaries provided here. See V.V. Krishna Sastry, ed., *Grama (Village) Kaifiyats: Guntur District*, vol. 5 (A.P. State Archives, Hyderabad, 1990).

and named it Amriteswara. Then he built the village after clearing the jungle and gave it the name Amrithaluru.[26]

Though the origin of the village was related to a pastoral economy, over a period of time it expanded into a town, especially from the sixteenth-century. During the rule of Krishnadeva Raya, his *karyakartha* (regent) Nagappa Nayanimgaru allowed a remission of *sunkam* (tax) and gave donations for a period of three years; thereafter he regulated taxes and issued lease documents to weavers, servants, and merchants in the year 1526. The village is said to have declined under Mughal rule and passed into the hands of the East India Company in 1802. At the time of the writing of this kaifiyat (the date is given as 8 September 1811) by Karanam Mallayya, this village was in the hands of Raja Vasi Reddy Venkatadri Naidu. With the completion of the Krishna *anicut* the village, which by then was settled as a *ryotwari* area, was transformed into a fully developed agricultural area in Nizampatnam taluqa. As Sontheimer and Murty suggest, most of the origin stories of Andhra villages which are recounted in myths and oral traditions were closely related to the god Siva or Mallikarjuna, and to the spread of village settlements based on a bovine-cum-agricultural economy.[27] What is worth exploring is the close association of pastoralist groups and Brahman cultivators with temples and village settlements.

The ecological situation was not radically altered till the middle of the nineteenth-century, as shown by the travel accounts of Enugula Veeraswamy in *Kasiyatra Charitra* (1830–1)[28] and Kola Seshachalakavi in *Nilagiri Yatra* (1846).[29] In *Kasiyatra Charitra,*

[26] The story is taken from the English version, in ibid., pp. ii–iv.

[27] See footnote 1.

[28] Enugula Veeraswamy, *Kasiyatra Charitra,* Telugu original compiled by Komaleswarapuram Srinivasa Pillai, English translation by P. Sitapati and V. Purushottam (Hyderabad, 1973).

[29] Kola Seshachalakavi, *Nilagiri Yatra (Journey to the Nilgiris).* This is a prose work written in Telugu in 1846. The critical edition is published by the Madras Government Oriental Manuscript Library (Madras, 1950).

Enugula gives a detailed narrative of villages that were mixed with forest tracts, and shows the close relationship between settled agricultural regions, pastoral lands and natural forests. He also shows that hills and forest tracts were linked with famous temples of all faiths, pilgrim centres, sacred rivers and springs associated with curative miracles, fruit-bearing groves, ponds, and so on. There are interesting descriptions of virgin forests preserved around temple centres like Srisailam, and of tribal involvement in managing these ecological zones. The author records how in several places he was told about wild beasts, such as tigers, which roamed freely, and of the grazing available for goats and cattle in the villages. Even the urban business centres seem to have become integrated with agricultural regions and forest zones. The forests adjacent to village settlements appear to have been used for mango orchards and other fruit-bearing species.[30]

The description of the living environment in these travel accounts could also be collated with the observations made by Julia Thomas during 1836–9.[31] Like the author of *Kasiyatra Charitra*, Thomas depicts a close relationship between wild jungles, cultivated regions and village areas. Giving her impression of the journey by road from Vizagapatam to Rajahmundry, she says there was 'a great deal of pretty country and some notorious tiger-jungles.'[32] She also comments on the early clearing of forest tracts by the colonial administration to make roads. She describes in passing the beauty of the wildlife living close to inhabited areas, the ecology of towns and villages, the revolts by tribals and native rajas, and the raging of a cholera epidemic which took a heavy toll of the 'poor natives'.[33]

Between 1760 and 1800 the growing demand for teak was one of the matters which received attention from the colonial

30 *Kasiyatra Charitra*, pp. 1–29 and 198–232.

31 *Letters From Madras, During The Years 1836–1839*, by 'A Lady' (new edn, London, 1861).

32 Ibid., p. 41.

33 Ibid., pp. 39, 41–3, 66, 137–8.

rulers.[34] From 1800 the Madras government 'encouraged and supported' those who showed an interest in entering the teak trade in coastal Andhra, and the Revenue Department even started gathering information systematically, at least starting from 1800–2. The creation of a market for teak and the imposition of government control over forests were resented by the local communities because colonial needs cut into their customary subsistence needs. The administration, however, partially succeeded in reorienting local business through altered taxes and duties on the timber trade, and also by intervening in and manipulating local markets and bazaars for their needs.[35] By 1813, as is indicated in the Board of Revenue Proceedings, the colonial administration could easily find eager local merchants to cut, process and supply timber for export from places like the Raichotee and Chitwell taluqas. One contractor is said to have offered to pay three times the price offered by others to exploit forest timber for the market. The government, however, did not give total control over timber exploitation to private commercial interests, since sympathetic local administrators expressed concern about the displacement of people's interests in the forests by commercial middlemen.[36] In August 1838 G.A. Smith, Collector of Rajahmundry, in his report to the Board of Revenue on the state of forests in the region, expressed sadness at the decline in the supply of 'large timber'. Smith was of the opinion that supplies of such timber had fallen off since he first joined the district in 1822. He had seen an immense quantity of large timber, 'for the supply of which the forests had been severely taxed', so that now 'only small timber was to be observed, and complaints had been made about the failing supply'.[37]

[34] E.P. Stebbing, *The Forests of India*, 3 vols (London, 1922–7); see vol. I, part II, p. 63.

[35] Letter to Samuel Skinner, Collector of the 2nd Division of Masulipatam, from G. Garrez, Fort St George, 6 April 1802; and William Petrie to Board of Revenue, in *Godavary District Records*, vol. 944–8, pp. 395–412.

[36] See Cuddapah Collector, C.R. Ross, to the Board of Revenue, Madras, July 1813, and other correspondence, in ibid., vol. 904, pp. 177–237.

[37] Stebbing, *Forests of India*, vol. I, part II, p. 77.

Close scrutiny of the Board of Revenue Proceedings indicates that, at least till the 1850s, the old forest cover did not suffer much depletion despite the advent of private commercial interests. A speedy transformation occurred from the 1860s, with the completion of the Godavary and Krishna anicuts.[38] In a recent study, T. Vijay Kumar has argued that, as a consequence of this anicut system, coastal Andhra was rapidly transformed from subsistence to market-oriented or commercial agriculture.[39] The rapid strides in the development of canal irrigation in Godavary, Krishna and Guntur districts converted most of the *banjar* (wasteland), minor forests and even common porambokes into cultivated land producing mostly paddy and commercial crops.[40]

The pressure on forest resources on account of expanded cultivation was only a part of the story of the process of forest depletion after the 1860s.[41] Pressure was being exerted by the

[38] For details on the 'projected'/intended consequences of the anicuts, see *Reports on the Direct and Indirect Effects of the Godavary and Krishna Annicuts in Rajahmundry, Masulipatam, Guntoor, etc., and the Coleroon Annicuts in Tanjore and South Arcot* (Madras, 1858); A.T. Cotton, *Report on the Irrigation of Rajahmundry and the Deltas of Godavary* (Madras, 1844).

[39] See T. Vijay Kumar, 'Agrarian Conditions in Andhra Under the British Rule: 1858–1900', unpublished Ph.D thesis, Department of History, Osmania University, Hyderabad, 1992; also G.N. Rao, 'Agrarian Relations in Coastal Andhra Under Early British Rule', in *Social Scientist*, 61, 1977, pp. 19–29; Rao, 'Transition from Subsistence to Commercialised Agriculture: A Study of Krishna District of Andhra, c. 1850–1900', *Economic and Political Weekly*, XX, nos 25–26; 'Review of Agriculture', June 1985, and Rao, 'Canal Irrigation and Agrarian Change in Colonial Andhra: A Study of Godavary District, c. 1850–1890', *Indian Economic and Social History Review*, XXV; 1, 1988, pp. 25–60.

[40] See, *Madras Irrigation: Reports for Years 1876–77 to 1916–17* and *1925–26*. The land reserved by the state for public purposes—village sites, roads, tankbeds, etc.—is called a poramboke.

[41] Several new cattle diseases also seem to have appeared with the anicuts and their numerous canals, such as Jalaga disease. Cattle mortality, the appearance of new diseases, and the shrinking pasturage were closely related. H. Morris, Acting Collector of the Godavary, to Wudleston, Sec., Board of Rev., 28 September 1863, no. 314, in *Board of Revenue Proceedings*, 1 December 1863, pp. 6991–2.

Government of India on Fort St George for effective control and management of forests, obviously for the benefit of the state and state-aided commercial interests.[42] Early Conservators of Forests, such as Cleghorn and H.R. Morgan, did respond critically, though without much effect, to pressure from the Government of India.[43] The discourse of a 'scientific' conservation of forests, both at the all-India level and in the Madras Presidency, sought to make a clear demarcation between the state and private commercial needs on the one hand and the customary rights of local communities on the other.[44] On 17 September 1875 the Government of Madras appointed a committee to prepare a draft Forest Bill which would apply to state forests, communal forests and proprietary forests. As early as 5 August 1871, the Board of Revenue wrote endorsing traditional community rights over the forests:

> There is scarcely a forest in the whole of the Presidency of Madras which is not within the limits of some village, and there is not one in which, so far as the Board can ascertain, the State asserted any rights of property —unless royalties in teak, sandalwood, cardamom, and the like can be considered as such—until very recently. ***All of them, without exception, are subject to tribal or communal rights which have existed from time immemorial and which are as difficult to define and value as they are necessary to the rural population . . . Here the forests are, and always have been, a common property*** [emphasis added].

But by 1882, 'circumstances' seemed to 'have changed', and, as Brandis put it, 'It is now recognized that there are no communal forests as distinct from state forests in the Presidency of Madras.' In fact Brandis's report on the need for effective state control over the forests epitomizes the logic of the ultimate denial of the needs of agricultural and tribal communities in the Madras Presidency,[45]

42 See Stebbing, *Forests of India.*

43 Ibid. See the sections on Madras Presidency.

44 The *Board of Revenue Proceedings, 1862–97*, contains several interesting observations by district administrators on the conflict between the Revenue and Forest Departments over the issue of controlling wasteland, porambokes and minor forest areas.

45 D. Brandis, *Suggestions Regarding Forest Administration in the Madras*

for his views were immediately transformed into the Madras Forest Act of 1882.[46]

This colonial 'scientific' conservation policy denied the needs of local communities at two levels. At one level, it denied the tribals their traditional subsistence living by banning both *podu* (shifting cultivation) and the collection of minor forest produce.[47] This created the basis for a series of tribal revolts after the mid-nineteenth century.[48] At a second level, the peasantry in the settled agricultural regions—both in the wet and the dry ecological zones—were deprived of their traditional grazing facilities and their customary rights to fuelwood, manure leaves and wood for agricultural implements.[49] The consequences of this policy could be seen during the 1920–2 no-tax movements and forest satyagrahas.[50]

## Peasant Perceptions of Colonial Intrusions

By encroaching on small forests, the government stripped many peasants of their grazing facilities.[51] Once the forests, porambokes and *dharmakhandams* (community common lands) were declared

---

*Presidency* (Madras, 1883), p. 20.

46 For the text of The Madras Forest Act, 1882, see *The Madras Code*, vol. I, pp. 368–97.

47 See Atluri Murali, 'Alluri Sitarama Raju and the Manyam Rebellion of 1922–24', in *Social Scientist*, 131, April 1984.

48 Ibid.; and David Arnold, 'Rebellious Hillmen: The Gudem-Rampa Raisings, 1893–1924', in Ranajit Guha, ed., *Subaltern Studies I* (Delhi, 1982).

49 See the last section of this essay.

50 See Atluri Murali, 'Civil Disobedience Movement in Andhra, 1920–22: The Nature of Peasant Protest and the Methods of Congress Political Mobilization', in Kapil Kumar, ed., *Congress and Class: Nationalism, Workers and Peasants* (New Delhi, 1988).

51 *Report of the Forest Committee, Appointed in G.O. No. 1677, Revenue, 5 June 1912* (Madras, 1913), vol. II (hereafter *RFC*); D. Brandis, *Suggestions Regarding Forest Administration*, p. 61; C.H. Benson, *An Account of the Kurnool District Based on Analysis of Statistical Information Relating Thereto, and on Personal Observation* (Madras, 1899), pp. 5–7; F.R. Hemingway, *Godavari Gazetteer* (Madras, 1907), pp. 95–102.

reserved areas, people were not only deprived of grazing facilities for their cattle, but their animals were also impounded whenever they trespassed into adjacent areas.[52] As Dunda Nagireddi, a peasant from Guntur district, observed before the Forest Committee:

The reserve (formed around 1900) is not even one furlong from the village. There is no vacant place where we can let our cattle stand in groups and there is no ground for men to ease themselves. The forest people [officials] are putting us to many troubles [sic] that we should not even enter the reserves. When we go to our *patta* lands for cultivation purposes they say that we have no right of way. On the sides of the reserve lie our *patta* lands. The reserve runs midway between the *patta* lands, and to the east and west of our lands we have reserves. We pay them [the officials] a bribe and go.[53]

In other words, the main cause of friction between the Forest Department and the peasants was the question of control on 'public grazing . . . rural needs for fuel, and small timber for agricultural [purposes]'. This friction surfaced as an anti-imperialist consciousness by 1920, for the exploitative and oppressive 'interference of the low-paid [forest] subordinates in the daily life of the villager was great'.[54]

There were several sore points associated with the government's control of forest resources. The Forest Department's monopoly of fodder extraction and the sale of it with the help of forest subordinates was one area of conflict, for this adversely affected peasants' grazing needs.[55] One peasant complained in

[52] *RFC*, II, pp. 3, 7, 13, 22–3, 39, 64, 71, 82, 177–8, 230, 256–7, 451.

[53] Ibid., pp. 177–8; also pp. 230, 451. A patta is a memorandum of the particulars of a holding and land assessment, given by the state to the landholder, usually considered as constituting a title to the land. A pattadar is a holder of a patta.

[54] *Annual Administrative Report of the Forest Department of the Madras Presidency, 1912–13* (Madras, 1914), p. 13. (Hereafter *ARFD*.).

[55] Ibid., *1904–05* (Madras, 1906), pp. 26–7; also see *Reports* for *1902–3 to 1922–3*.

1912 that the 'Kondavidu reserve [was] . . . closed for the last 5 or 6 years. It is cut for hay . . . [After the grass has dried] it is cut and removed by the Forest Department. They keep it in a depot to sell and the ryots buy it at 6 annas a bandy [cart-load] . . .'[56]

The colonial government also extended its control over activities like the collection of fuel, leaf manure and wood for agricultural implements. For centuries, villagers had depended on small forests and porambokes for the free supply of firewood and fuel. In the words of Kalavai village ryots in Nellore district, paying for permits to get firewood 'has not been the custom up till now. There are only three or four rich ryots and all the rest are poor and cannot pay for fuel.' But they had to pay: there were no free permits to be had. Moreover, there was 'no fuel on *patta* lands;'[57] and if people brought fuel from unreserved forests, they were caught for having brought it from reserved forests by corrupt forest officials who extracted *mamuls* (bribes).[58] All this naturally fuelled peasant resentment against the government's monopoly on the sale of firewood.

Another vexed question was the peasant's right to collect manure leaves, such as *bandaru*, from the forests. Before the government's control, villagers below the hill ghats or nearer the forest never lacked leaves for manure: they had access to forests without payment. But from the beginning of the nineteenth century this collecting of manure leaves was barred by the Forest Department.[59] Moreover, the Madras government increased the price of leaf manure in those areas where peasants were allowed to collect it on payment of a fee, from 5–6 annas to Re 1 per bandy. This meant the cost of manure increased by nearly 125

[56] See the evidence by Indupalli Veeriah of Prattipadu, Guntur district, *RFC*, II, pp. 200–3.

[57] Ibid., p. 64.

[58] Evidence by R. Duraiswami Aiyar, Nellore tahsildar, ibid., p. 5. For evidence from other parts of Andhra see, pp. 13–22, 143, 215–17, 259; also *ARFD, 1902* (Madras, 1903), pp. 23–30; *1912–13* (Madras, 1913), pp. 13–14; Govt. of Madras, Revenue, G.O. 141 (Revenue), 3 February 1901, p. 3.

[59] *RFC*, II, pp. 34–6; also pp. 58, 64–5, 134, 138–9, 422–3 and 446–50.

per cent, even without the transport charge.[60] It was observed by one ryot:

> I got a license for one rupee. The cost of bringing one cartload of leaves will be Rs 3.50 because they have to pass the ghats. Seven or eight cartloads are required for one acre of wet land. Rs 24 or 25 worth of leaves is required. More money is required for other manure. We have to pay for fuel, and thus poor people suffer. It costs much to maintain cattle for manuring purposes.[61]

Free access to timber in the forests for agricultural implements had also been the traditional peasant practice. Here again, the Forest Department's monopoly on forest timber came in the way. The permit system allowed peasants to take wood from unreserved porambokes which lay adjacent to the villages, but the inconveniences involved in getting permits or licences caused them to wait for months to make a plough. The area under unreserved porambokes had, by the second decade of the twentieth-century, been slowly swallowed up by 'reserves'. Consequently, the peasants had to pay private agencies high prices for wood to make their agricultural implements. Waiting for permits would have meant getting their tools much after they needed them.[62]

Traditionally, the organization of living space in the villages, both public and private, was organically linked with the total ecological space. Colonialism, in its bid to extend control over forest resources, destroyed this traditional organization resulting in a shifting of the boundaries of public space (forest reserves) closer to private space, especially to houses and cultivated lands. The slightest violation of this, by beast or human, was seen by the colonial administration as a 'crime', whereas the peasants perceived this reordering of geography and space as 'illegal'. It is this dimension of peasant consciousness or 'social memory' which I propose to illustrate through the use of oral evidence as narrative texts.[63]

60 Ibid., p. 71.

61 Ibid., p. 513.

62 Evidence by R. Subbarayadu, Nellore, ibid., pp. 6–7; also pp. 3, 82.

63 For an interesting analysis of 'social memory' as a cultural faculty, see Paul

Raghava Reddy, a landlord of Chennagiripaliam village in Gudur taluqa, Nellore district, narrated that the reserve

> is only 4 or 5 yards from my house. I am 45 years old, and the reserve was constituted 25 years ago and the house was built by my ancestors. The boundary of the *patta* lands is the reserve itself. If the bullocks in ploughing put a foot within the reserve land, then fees are collected.[64]

It was this proximity of the boundary of the forest reserves, and the consequent official harassment, which was most resented.

> If a reserve is near, cattle generally go there . . . Immediately, they are impounded, whether there is a permit or not [and] . . . charged compounding fees in addition to the permit fees; they cannot get inside the forest for fuel and to bring *jala* sticks for protecting fields; even if one cow goes there [to the forest], all the cattle are taken to the pound by the Forest Guards and Watchers.[65]

Thus runs the narrative of one marginal peasant.

The peasants' other grievances were integral to their understanding of the new colonial control over space. The traditional system of manuring cultivated lands depended upon leaves from the forests and porambokes. Biradavolu Venkataraghavayya, the village *munsif* and a middle-class peasant, said that from time immemorial peasants had gathered manure leaves from the forest, 'but not now, because we have to pay for permits and it is very difficult to get them. Paying fees and bringing manure leaves "is not an advantage to us".'[66] The evidence of the ryots of Kalavai further illustrates this interesting process of the appropriation and

---

Connerton, *How Societies Remember* (Cambridge, 1989).

64 He had '2000 cattle before the reserves' were constituted 'ten or twelve years ago' but their strength had been reduced to 100—fifty bullocks and fifty cows. Even though he grazed the cattle on his own lands (340 acres including 40 acres wet), Reddi took permits for 50 cattle for Sriharikota reserve, for 'he has to go through the reserve lands to his patta lands through a narrow path of 3/4 of a mile. Even if they touch the margin they are impounded'. *RFC*, II, p. 22; also see pp. 26–30.

65 Ibid., p. 13; also see pp. 4–5, 39.

66 Ibid., p. 58.

reconstruction of tradition in social memory when confronting contemporary issues.[67]

| | |
|---|---|
| *Committee*: | What is your next grievance? |
| *Ryots*: | We have no firewood; and are not given permits for them. |
| *Committee*: | Are you willing to pay for permits for firewood? |
| *Ryots*: | No; it has not been the custom up till now. There are only three or four rich ryots and all the rest are poor and cannot pay for fuel. We pray that we may be given the grants. |
| *Committee*: | At present what do you burn? |
| *Ryots*: | We use cow-dung cakes. No fuel on *patta* lands. We want more manure leaves. |
| *Committee*: | Do you always use them? |
| *Ryots*: | When the land was a *shekada*, we used to get leaves for manure, sixteen years ago. |
| *Committee*: | You do not get them now? |
| *Ryots*: | Occasionally one or two men who can afford it send their men to distant places and get leaves from there. By the time we return to Kalavai time is lost; and only one or two get permits, and the rest cannot go. Our cattle also suffer much for want of grazing, and we are obliged to send them to Cuddapah district. |

Invoking tradition was not, however, the exclusive preserve of the peasantry. The colonial interrogation of 'tradition in history',[68] and the particular construction of social memory in support of the existing system can also be discerned. It was this contradictory process of the recovery of historical tradition which is a useful pointer to the emerging social and political crisis. At one end of the spectrum, the peasant's narrative of tradition implicitly sought to undermine the colonial hegemony over community space—porambokes, shekadas and dharmakhandams—and forests. The evidence of P. Seshagiri Rao of Penumaka village near Mangalagiri, Guntur district, indicates this:

We want Penumaka hill—Tadepalli reserve. We want the whole reserve

[67] Ibid., pp. 64–5. For another example, see pp. 65–6, 69–78.

[68] See Edward Shils, *Traditions* (Chicago, 1981).

to be open to grazing. Since 1879, it has been closed. During the time of floods it was open for grazing. At other times it is not open . . . There are some charitable [grazing] tanks close to our village and between our village and the Kistna river and if cattle go, they are impounded by the forest people . . . I was fined Rs 3 . . . prior to 1879, the whole was *dharmakhandam* [for three villages—Penumaka, Yerrapaliam and Gundavalli]; no pullary [grazing tax] . . . each ryot had sixty or seventy cattle.[69]

The 'substantive economy' in peasant societies has a physical and ecological dimension.[70] Since the physical basis of a peasant economy was subject to the vicissitudes of the natural environment, there evolved a specified way of adapting to natural ecosystems. This 'harmonization', in turn, was sustained through a network of community-based customary rights and cultural systems. Since colonialism basically operated within the ideological logic of the 'capitalist law of nature', it came into conflict with the traditional customary rights of peasants in forests.[71] Through intermediaries (private contractors) the logic of the colonial money economy was ordained upon the peasant's life-world.[72] A

69 *RFC*, II, pp. 200–1.

70 Karl Polanyi defines the substantive economy as having a physical base in nature: 'The substantive meaning of economic derives from man's dependence for his living upon nature and his fellows. It refers to the interchange with his natural and social environment, in so far as this results in supplying him with the material means of want satisfaction.' See his essay, 'The Economy as Instituted Process', in Conrad Arensberg and Harry Pearson, eds, *Trade and Market in Early Empires* (Glencoe, 1957), p. 243. For an elaboration of the implication of Polanyi's ideas, see Rhoda Halperin and James Dow, eds, *Peasant Livelihood: Studies in Economic Anthropology and Cultural Ecology* (New York, 1977). And for a Marxist critique, see Maurice Godelier, *The Mental and the Material* (London, 1986), pp. 179–207.

71 One finds a striking similarity between eighteenth-century Britain and nineteenth-century colonial India in so far as conflict over forest resources was concerned. See E.P. Thompson, *Whigs and Hunters: The Origin of The Black Act* (Harmondsworth, 1977).

72 For colonial and neo-colonial interventions in African societies, with disastrous consequences on their ecosystems, see David Anderson and Richard

realization of this conflict was at this level very much part of peasant consciousness. Two memorials sent to the Forest Committee by peasants of Nizampatam and the surrounding villages of Guntur district expressed this consciousness:

'We have considerable difficulty about grazing leaves. Our cattle graze on *mudda* leaves and *kadu* grass and they cannot live upon grass. Others' cattle do live without *mudda* leaves or *kadu* grass. They are not used to it from time immemorial. The *mudda* leaves which are necessary to our cattle will kill other cattle . . . Now we are prohibited from getting *mudda* leaves and *kadu* grass —from some 10 years ago. We aren't allowed to go to the forest and cut grass. There is a contractor who demands payment, who changes every year and who gives permits on a monthly basis. It is not the contractor who oppresses the people. It is the forest officials . . . From time immemorial we have been grazing our cattle free . . . The *mudda* leaves are also sometimes used to build houses.'[73]

There was also a witness who pinpointed the magnitude of the crisis. Before it was closed, 'some 20 villages were grazing' in Kondavidu reserve: 'with hardship they are now sending cattle to Palnad or Gurupala taluqas or Nizam's Dominions'.[74]

How did colonial discourse seek to address this issue? To deny legitimacy to peasant demands, administrators, in their turn, invoked the tradition of customary practices and by this means sought to justify their control over forest resources as well as their commodification as well. There is an interesting interrogation of a witness by the Forest Committee which shows these conflicting invocations of tradition to legitimize both sides of the struggle in

Grove, eds, *Conservation in Africa: People, Policies and Practice* (Cambridge, 1989).

[73] *RFC*, II, pp. 185–6.

[74] Ibid., pp. 202–3. According to one Lambadi, Nilanayakudu of Birijepallipad: 'Before the reserves were constituted they were not levied grazing fees . . . In the initial stages (of the formation of reserves) the Rangers took As. 3, and even As. 8 in khaṇḍams, but at that time they were allowed to take cattle wherever they like in the forest'. Ibid., pp. 242–5.

Madras Presidency. The witness was C. Rama Rao, a landowner of 200 acres and a retired district munsif of Ongole in Guntur district.

*Committee*: You say that the payment of fees in lieu of free-grazing which was enjoyed until the enactment of the forest laws was a grievance. Is that a grievance?

*C.R. Rao*: It is not so in the big jungles, but in the scrub jungles it was so.

*Committee*: I am inclined to think you are mistaken. Records show that 120 years ago, there was a charge called *pullary* levied on cattle whether on forest or village lands. They all paid *pullary*?

*C.R. Rao*: Yes. That was an old custom. At the same time, a tax called *moturpha* was levied on every sheep and goat even if it is grazing in the backyard.

*Committee*: In view of these facts, are you able to say that it was free?

*C.R. Rao*: At all events *it was not considered to be a charge and not complained against.*

*Committee*: Did you not say that there were village commons? [called *mandabayalu* in Telugu].

*C.R. Rao*: Yes. The village cattle used to lie freely there. There were village commons where the cattle used to graze and lie down there.[75]

What was left out, perhaps deliberately, by the administrators when they called upon tradition was the fact that under the old system cattle 'had their belly-full of pasture from all the open area', and this with 'no fee' being 'levied on cultivators'.[76] Not surprisingly, they showed a one-sided eagerness in pointing out the practice of paying pullary under the traditional system.

At the heart of this legitimization struggle was also the issue of access to temples located on hills within the forests, another traditional cultural practice. For instance, here is the narrative of Timma Reddy of Yerrabommanahalli, Anantapur district.

[75] Ibid., pp. 132–5 (emphasis added).

[76] Ibid., narrative of a seventy-five-year-old big landlord, Dodla Bera Reddy, p. 129.

*Committee*: What are your difficulties about the forests?

*Timma Reddy*: There are two temples on the top of the hill, the Anjaneyaswami and Lakshmidevi temples. There is worship there every week. There are many devotees. If ryots go there, the forest subordinates trouble them and they do not go even to the temple. *If we do not worship in any year, tanks will not get supply of water.*

*Committee*: Did you worship this year?

*Timma Reddy*: Yes. A case was also made against us. While the God was being taken along the path, some trees were said to have been injured and the District Forest Officer inquired and let us off. The Ranger took an explanation and the case was dismissed. We worship the God every year. *Instead of worshipping the God there, the ryots have to worship the forest subordinates* . . .

*Committee*: Did you not represent to the District Forest Officer?

*Timma Reddy*: Once we went to worship the God and a case was made against my brother that he went for hunting. The District Forest Officer charged us for trial in the Taluk Magistrate's Court. There we were acquitted. Even if we go to the D.F.O., we thought we will not have justice. So we do not go to him . . . There is a *right of way* (to the temple). But the branches of trees obstruct the path. We represented the matter to the Ranger [but in vain]. The District Forest Officer has permitted us to worship four or five times a year and to take Gods there [in a ceremonial procession] and worship. But Ranger does not permit us to take them there. [They were worshiping for 'all these 30 years in the reserve.']

Timma Reddy's narrative ends with his demand for 'free grazing' and 'free worship'. Why the peasants had chosen to link their worship with the water supply in the tanks—and build around it an elaborate system of cultural practice—is a question which cannot be answered here. But what is important is the fact that their livelihood was rooted in these cultural practices. Therefore, when their right of way to their temples and traditional practices of worship in order to get water in their tanks were replaced by a 'worship [of] forest subordinates', it caused a huge resentment among peasants.[77]

In sum, the forest conflict was, to borrow the words of E.P. Thompson, 'a conflict between users and exploiters'.[78] This evolved into a conflict between two different cultural systems under colonialism in the Madras Presidency. While the colonized people looked 'upon the forests as their own',[79] the colonizers' monopolistic interests sought to close them off. These monopolistic interests were camouflaged in an ideological discourse: the conservation of forests was for the 'good of all'.[80] This 'good of all'[81] meant curtailing peasants' customary rights and conserving forests for colonial commercial needs.[82] As S. Eardley Wilmot observed:

> If the Forest Reserves in the Presidency will not yield produce in grazing or other material enough to satisfy the desires of the population in grazing and other forest produce, only two courses appear to be available, the area of Reserves must be increased and the unreserved lands more stringently protected or the demands of the people reduced . . . I cannot but recommend that [the latter] be followed here . . . .[83]

Before going into factors which catalysed peasant protests, it is interesting to note conflicting class interests among the peasantry and the expression of these in their demands.

[77] Ibid., pp. 451–3 (emphasis added). He had 30 acres of wet and 112 acres of dry land; 8 cows, 14 bulls and 6 she-buffaloes, 150 sheep and 10 or 12 goats.

[78] *Whigs and Hunters*, p. 245.

[79] *RFC*, II, p. 152.

[80] See D. Brandis, 'Memorandum on the Demarcation of the Public Forests: *The Indian Forester*, December 1901, pp. 618–22.

[81] In the process of establishing social hegemony the ruling class has first of all to persuade those it rules that the norms and sanctions of society, especially the laws and acts which in reality benefit only the privileged few, are devised for the good of all. See Antonio Gramsci, *Selections from the Prison Notebooks* (New York, 1971); Joseph V. Femia, *Gramsci's Political Thought: Hegemony, Consciousness, and the Revolutionary Process* (Oxford, 1981), pp. 23–60.

[82] For a similar construction of logic in Africa, see Anderson and Grove, eds, *Conservation in Africa*.

[83] *Notes On An Inspection Of Some Forests In The Madras Presidency 1907–1908* (Calcutta, 1908), p. 26.

Before going into factors which catalysed peasant protests, it is interesting to note conflicting class interests among the peasantry and the expression of these in their demands. I hasten to add that these class perceptions and interests were articulated within a nationalist ideological discourse. The rich peasantry demanded 'more freedom' and 'less fees', not the free grazing and traditional system of community management of forests. 'All the cattle should be allowed to graze *with a lower fee*. If all cattle are allowed the grass will be exhausted. There should be differentiation in the reserves', argued one contractor and landholder.[84] An educated and professional non-cultivating rich landlord, H. Narayana Rao, a pleader, was pragmatic (as was the Gandhian nationalist leadership). He merged the demands of the rich and the poor peasantry in a bid to reconcile different class interests, at least at the level of articulation. By arguing that the existing 'grazing fee is not heavy' on the rich, he advocated 'free grazing for poor people, since the poorer class of people find it difficult to pay.'[85] Sanjiva Reddi of Somandepalli, Anantapur district, who had 200 acres of wet and 1,000 acres of dry land, told the Forest Committee: 'We are ready to pay for permits. We wish to have free permits . . . It is because of the trouble of the Forest subordinates that we are ready to pay permit fees . . . We will be freed of the trouble if the minor subordinates are removed.'[86] The rich peasant class thus shifted the conflict from 'the burden of fees' to freedom from forest subordinates.

For this poor peasant class, the conflict was obviously located in their inability to pay. R. Subbarayadu, pleader from Nellore, summed it up: 'even though the amount may be small it presses rather heavily on the poor ryots, and works a hardship on them, especially when they happen to have dependents . . . '[87] On several occasions the system of imposing a compounding fee had ruinous

84 *RFC*, II, p. 39 (emphasis added). Also pp. 132–5.

85 Ibid., pp. 421–2. Also pp. 35–6, 446–50.

86 Ibid., pp. 424–5.

87 Ibid., p. 5.

consequences for poor and marginal landholders.[88] As S.P. Rice, I.C.S., Acting Collector of Anantapur, remarked:

I am told that in a reserve close to Anantapur and adjoining the public road, straying cattle have been impounded and one Anke Yengadu, a Boya Ryot of Anantapur had to pay Rs 300 which reduced him to beggary. Another man named Bandar Ahmed had to pay Rs 15 which cost him his only cow. He sold it for Rs 8 and borrowed the rest.[89]

Under this system the main victims were the poor, as they were also the main offenders of fuelwood lifting, etc. It is not surprising that the major grievance of villages like Penubarti, with a predominantly poor peasant population, had been 'disafforestation.'[90]

There were other causes equally, if not more compelling, which prompted the peasantry to take to forest satyagrahas. One cause was the enhancement of rates charged for grazing in the Andhra districts after 1915. The enhancement in Kurnool, for example, for ordinary cattle was from 3 annas to 8 annas per cow; in Vizagapatnam it was increased from 4 to 8 annas per cow.[91] To reduce heavy grazing in Chittoor reserve, a higher grazing fee was charged from 1 July 1920.[92] Higher grazing taxes were charged in other areas as well: the rates of grazing fees fixed for reserves situated in the plains were, for a cow 8 annas, for a sheep 4 annas, and for a buffalo Re 1.[93]

As noted earlier, the pressure of this enhanced grazing fees was felt more by poor and middle-class peasants, not so much by the rich, for it was the former classes who depended most on government grazing grounds. Oral evidence in Volume Two of the *Report of the Forest Committee* of 1913 shows that almost all the rich ryots

[88] Ibid., p. 508.

[89] Ibid., p. 71.

[90] *ARFD, 1919–20* (Madras, 1921), p. 4.

[91] Ibid., p. 17.

[92] R. Dis. no. 6065/30, A4, 29 September 1931, Visakhapatnam district, Dept. of Revenue, Collectorate Records, Visakhapatnam, p. 55.

[93] *RFC*, II, p. 152; Proceedings of the Chief Conservator of Forests, Mis. 579, 7 December 1920, Govt. of Madras.

sent their valuable cattle to private grazing grounds, even though the fees there were higher than government rates, whereas poor and middle-class ryots invariably sent their cattle to government grazing grounds, even when these were nearly bereft of grass, for they could not afford to pay the higher fee. This perhaps explains the militancy of forest protests: their origin lay in a poor peasant subsistence economy. Leadership, however, was provided by the rich peasant class, which had links with the Congress organization, ideology, programme and politics.

The intrusion of corrupt forest officers, especially subordinates, and of the oppressive colonial judiciary in the day-to-day existence of the peasantry was also an important catalyst in transforming peasant discontent into organized protest. The peasants along with the Lambadis—traditional graziers who took cattle into the forest for grazing—were subjected by subordinate officials to endless demands for bribes, or to 'what they [officials] consider their due'. These illegal exactions by forest officials were almost twice as much the actual government fees paid by the peasants and Lambadis.[94] This apart, if the ryots or Lambadis failed to strike a bargain with forest officers to get grazing permission, their cattle were likely to be impounded on the pretext of some offence or other, and they themselves subjected to other 'petty annoyance'.[95]

Forest Department employees were notorious for corrupt practices in many other ways. For instance, they often drove away cattle grazing near forest reserves and extracted 'from the ryots pound fees as well as compounding fees, or else prosecuted'.[96] If the matter led to prosecution, peasants were either charged exorbitant fines or set free only after parting with heavy sums as

[94] Ibid. For numerous instances, see narratives of different witnesses from various districts of Andhra, pp. 1–3, 13, 17, 22–3, 28, 36–9, 58, 69–71, 149–54, 177–9, 231, 242–3, 258–9, 424–5, 434, 476–7, 508–9. Also see *ARFD*, 1902–3 to 1923–24. In each year's report the subject of increasing corruption among the forest officials was discussed in detail under the head, 'Conduct of Establishment'.

[95] *RFC*, II, p. 1.

[96] See for instances, ibid., pp. 23, 36–7, 57–8, 159–64, 434, 476–7.

bribes.[97] For such peasants, justice was no easy matter: there was an unwritten understanding between lower forest employees, forest officers and village munsifs.[98] In one case, 'the Munsif and the Forest Officer brought a charge that 30 cattle grazed in the reserve, but they caught hold of 12. We paid poundage for 30, but payment for 18 was divided among the subordinates themselves, and Government got only for 12.'[99]

Thus, nefarious extractions like 'yearly mamools',[100] heavy compounding fees,[101] and bribes to overcome false charges and prosecutions left peasants and Lambadis open to full exploitation by forest officials and subordinates.[102]

The peasantry saw the British judicial system as the epitome of coercion. The experience of a rich landlord, Vema Reddi Rama Reddi of Varapali in Nellore district, revealed to him the excessive nature of colonial retributive justice. In 1901, Reddi took a permit for forty cattle and once, when he failed to carry this permit with

97 Ibid., p. 23.

98 Evidence by the ryots of Kotagunta and Lingampalam village, ibid., p. 69.

99 Ibid., p. 3.

100 In his evidence, B. Narasinga Rao, Vice-President, Taluqa Board of Narasaraopet, Guntur district, quoted a classic case where he personally appeared. He said that 'In a case in which 4 annas worth of grazing implements were taken by a ryot in Madalapad, the composition fee fixed by the District Forest Officer was Rs 100.' When an appeal was made 'he was fined by the Magistrate Rs 125, at the rate of 4 annas per rupee above the composition fee. I had some talk with some magistrates, and they told that there was a circular that fine should be heavier than the fee'. Ibid., p. 258.

101 For instance, one witness, Venkataraghavayya, a village munsif of Nellore district, observed that the forest officers 'say they will impound the cattle and ask money for leaving off. They sometimes ask Rs 50 to Rs 60. They threaten to impound the cattle and make out a case against us. I'm also told that they take 3 pies per permit issued over and above the permit fee. The ryots are afraid of cases and try to give money to them, and they are demanded Rs 2 per head of cattle (whereas the pound fee per head of cattle was 4 annas).' Ibid., p. 58; also see pp. 64, 164, 172, 434.

102 The evidence of the previous five instances is from ibid., pp. 31–2, 69, 232, 476–7.

him, the Forest Ranger impounded the cattle. The magistrate is said to have 'believed the evidence of the Forest people and fined Rs 60.' He said the peasants were not against the law as such, but 'the way in which the rules [were] being carried out by the forest subordinates . . . To begin with there [was] the infliction of two sets of punishments for one offence. Compounding fee itself [was] higher than the usual impounding fee.' The enormity of the miscarriage of justice was such that even the Forest Ranger on Special Duty in Nellore district, Seshagiri Rao, had to admit before the Forest Committee that 'the percentage of cases in which the District Forest Officer has made any enquiry when reported by Guard before fixing the compounding fee was 3 or 4 in a 100.' The best illustration is the evidence of the ryots of Kotagunta and Lingampalem villages, Nellore district:

*Ryots*: The elders were not at home. The cattle were sent and brought half-way. Boys were in charge. Rupees 10 were demanded [by] the Watchers. The boys said they will bring their father, and settle the matter. He was two miles off. He threatened us by saying that if we did not compound the case, we would be charged Rs 10 per head.

*Committee*: If you said in the Magistrate's Court that it was your own *kancha*, and it was your own cattle, you would not have paid fines?

*Ryots*: But we have paid fines already to the extent of Rs 300.

*Committee*: Why were you fined Rs 300?

*Ryots*: There was a Supervisor in our beat. He asked us for a bribe for allowing our cattle in the reserve. Our villagers were afraid that something will happen if the goats go into the reserve. Therefore they did not pay anything. So he collected a large number of Watchers of Gundagolu and other villages, and said that permits are to be checked. So they drove all the cattle to a place called Jangambavi where the Supervisor said the Ranger was. They cheated the boys and drove the cattle to Jangambavi. Then the forest people took all the permits. The boys asked where the Ranger was. They said he was somewhere further off, and they must go there. So they went to the boundary of Chagaram. The

Ranger was not there. But some had their own suspicions, and they returned to the village. Then all the villagers went to the place. In the meantime, they drove the cattle to the pound, and they were handed over to the Chagaram Munsif. The permits were shown to the Village Munsif. He wanted to know why they should be caught when they had permits. 'We do not care for them. Will you take the cattle and give us the receipt or not?' was the question put to the Munsif by the Watchers. The village Munsif would not give the receipt for a long time, since he has seen the permits. We put in a petition to the Collector, and the District Forest Officer and told all our difficulties. The Magistrate fined us Rs 300—Rs 50 each man.

*Committee*: What was the offence?

*Ryots*: The offence was that we grazed in the closed *kanchas*. It happened two years ago.

*Committee*: Did you make an appeal?

*Ryots*: We made appeals in two previous cases without success. So we did not make an appeal. It is for fear that we paid compound fees.[103]

So much for the colonial legal permit. One is reminded of Marx on the juridical illusion 'that a man may have a legal title to a thing without really having the thing.'[104] The theory and practice of colonial forest laws were light-years apart. There was not only no proper administrative check on official misuse of power, the retribution did not fit the 'crime' either.[105] Poor peasants' customary rights were not recognized, nor were they

103 *RFC*, II, pp. 69–71. Kancha is a Government wasteland let out for grazing.

104 'Theses on Feuerbach', in Marx and Engels, *Selected Works* (Moscow, 1969), p. 79.

105 The colonial situation was in conformity with the legal discourse and practice in Britain from the seventeenth-century. See David Lieberman, *The Province of Legislation Determined: Legal Theory in Eighteenth Century Britain* (Cambridge, 1989); J.S. Cockburn, ed., *Crime in England, 1550–1800* (London, 1977); Thompson, *Whigs and Hunters*. For an interesting analysis of the operations of the Waltham Black Act in eighteenth-century England, see Frank McLynn, *Crime and Punishment in Eighteenth-Century England* (London, 1989).

compensated for the loss of their old 'life world'. To borrow from Marx again: 'the right of human beings give way to that of young trees.'[106]

These ruinous day-to-day experiences and their consequent 'hatred'[107] of British rule not only strengthened anti-colonial consciousness over time, it also took the form of a movement which expressed itself in a spontaneous peasant protest. This eventually linked up with the national liberation struggle of 1920–2, via the local Congress leadership.

Officially, it was conceived that 'an important branch of forest work consists in the protection of the forests from damage at the hands of the people or by forest fires.' It was 'the people' who seemed to have hunted the colonial forest administrators, for the 'usual course of operations' of the Forest Department were 'with regard to the detection and punishment of arson, theft and encroachment in the forests.'[108] In the first two decades of the twentieth century, one notices a shift in the nature of 'punishment' meted out to such people, who now turn out to be simple 'offenders' of forest regulations. In the Madras Presidency, while the number of cases disposed off by the courts decreased from 7082 in 1901–2 to 5363 in 1911–12, the number of cases compounded increased from 13,827 in 1901–2 to 19,456 in 1911–12. Legalistic forms of punishment were slowly being overshadowed by arbitrary punishments meted out on the spot. This shift in the

106 'Debates on the Law on Thefts of Wood', in Marx and Engels, *Collected Works*, I (Moscow, 1975), p. 226.

107 The cause for this 'hatred' was summed up by G.N. Thomassen of the American Baptist Telugu Mission, Bapatla, Guntur district, in his evidence before the Forest Committee: 'I presume that it is [hatred] because people look upon the forest as their own. They cannot get firewood and cannot take a single stick without being handed over to the Magistrate. The Forest Department has interfered with their liberty. This is reason for complaining against the Forest department . . . again and again that they pay *mamul* and yet they have no surety their cattle will not be impounded.' *RFC*, II, p. 152.

108 *Statement Exhibiting the Moral and Material Progress and Condition of India 1901–2* (London, 1903), p. 222.

punishment of 'forest offenders' should be seen in relation to the steady increase of pressure for grazing rights in the forests. For example, the total number of buffaloes, cows and bullocks grazed during 1899–1900 in the Madras Presidency was 1,441,000; in 1901–2 it was 1,487,000, and in 1911–12 it rose to 1,858,135.[109] The result was a clash between forest law-enforcement officials and peasants—'the infringers of forest regulations'.

The first and spontaneous individual peasant protest against forest regulations took the form of a violation of government restrictions. Illegal grazing and the resulting impounding of animals had become perennial problems, despite strict supervision by forest subordinates.[110] There was an increase in cases of unauthorized grazing and the removal of grass and other forest produce. Unauthorized felling was the biggest forest offence in the eyes of the state in Guntur, Nellore, Chittoor and Anantapur.[111] In 1919–20 as many as 8900 cases of forest 'crimes' were reported. Of these, '2434 relate to Guntur and this district probably tops the Presidency as regards forest offences.' In fact, 'protection from man and beast become the chief problem in Guntur district.'[112] These perennial forest 'offences', the symbols of peasant protest against the removal of customary rights, were considered by the colonial state as 'crimes', and the peasants and the villages that harboured these offenders were 'dens'.[113] This transformation of forest 'offences' into 'crimes' which invoked severe punishments undermined the legitimacy of the colonial state:

> In short, if popular customary rights are suppressed, the attempt to exercise them can only be treated as the simple contravention of a police regulation, but never punished as a crime . . . The punishment must not inspire more repugnance than the offence, the ignominy of crime must not be turned into the ignominy of law; the basis of the state is

[109] These statistics are from ibid., pp. 221–2; for *1911–12*, pp. 260–1.

[110] See tables on 'Comparative Statement of Impounded Cattle' in *AFRD*, for *1910 to 1924*.

[111] Ibid., for *1905–6*, *1918–19*.

[112] Ibid., *1919–20*, p. 17.

[113] Ibid., p. 29.

undermined if misfortune becomes a crime or crime becomes a misfortune.[114]

How appropriate these words are to our situation!

Protests against such definitions of forest 'offences' consolidated into a coherent movement in 1920–2 not only because of this ignominious situation but also, as was observed by the District Collector, due to '(a) unfavorable season, (b) great short-age of fodder and water, (c) the recent more vigorous enforcement of the Forest Rules, and (d) non-co-operation agitation.'[115] When the unfavourable season and the consequent famines added further misery to peasant lives, the Non-Co-operation Movement started by Gandhi gave a political character to social protest.[116] The nationalist intelligentsia articulated peasant perceptions of an immoral colonial monopoly over forest resources and mobilized the peasants to join the Gandhian movement. This can be illustrated with a famous nationalist song sung in the villages and at political meetings.[117]

Three hundred years back *Bharatamata,*
Company man descended *Bharatamata,*
You have kept quiet *Bharatamata,*
He robbed the whole nation *Bharatamata,*
He claims all forests are his *Bharatamata,*
Did his father come and plant? *Bharatamata.*

[114] Marx, 'Debates on the Law on Thefts of Wood', p. 235.

[115] Confidential letter from F.W.R. Robertson, to Marjoribanks, Chief Sec., Govt. of Madras, 17 July 1921, in G.O. 483, Ordinary Series, 30 July 1921.

[116] For details, see Murali, 'Civil Disobedience Movement in Andhra', *Andhra Patrika*, 21 January, 3 February, 25 March, 22 July, 8–9 September 1920; *Anasuya* (Telugu monthly, Kakinda), July–August 1919; *Report on Native Newspapers* (Madras, 1921), pp. 843, 1235–6; Madala Veerabhadra Rao, *Deshabhakta Jeevita Charitramu* (Masulipatnam, 1966), pp. 81–3; *Nyaya Dipika* (Madras), 4 October 1921; *AFRD, 1919–20*, p. 17, *1920–21*, pp. 14–15.

[117] 'Dandalu Dandalu Bharatamata' by Vaddadi Sitaramanjaneyulu, in Sarojini Regani and Devulapalli Ramanuja Rao, eds, *Deesam Pilupu* ('Call of the Nation') (Hyderabad, 1972), pp. 19–22 (translated from Telugu).

## Conclusion

In the pre-colonial period, people in the Deccan region lived in an ecosystem which had evolved historically with a complex but mutually sustaining relationship between agricultural, forest and pastoral zones. We have seen the antiquity of the cultural, economic and political contours of this interface after the sixteenth century, especially through Telugu literary texts and kaifiyats. An important point is that peasants and pre-colonial rulers did not develop a 'commercial' attitude towards forests; the control of tribal groups over forests was recognized by the rulers as their unquestionable natural right. The forest cover in Andhra districts was not altered radically until about the mid-nineteenth century: only from the 1850s did the deliberate policy of the Madras government—to develop both private and state commercial interests in teak and other varieties of timber—begin the depletion of forest resources.

Simultaneously, during this period, the systematic extension of colonial juridical control over the entire minor and major forests—porambokes, village wastelands, etc.—as well as the emergence of market-oriented agricultural production, brought new pressures on the forests. In other words, the entire ecosystem was transformed under the influence of the colonial model of 'private property' in land, water and other natural resources. The custom of cultivating wastelands by villagers 'without authority' was banned by converting wastelands into 'reserved lands'. This extension of colonial law to wastelands meant the exclusion of the poor. The state claimed a monopolistic right to alienate these lands, 'under the wasteland sale rules', basically to the propertied classes. The same was true for trees: these were converted into 'reserved' trees; the right to fell them was entrusted to the Forest Department, which in turn sold them 'at higher rates than those charged for unreserved trees.'[118] In 1862, the 'use of teak or Satinwood for ploughs' by the ryots was declared 'clearly an abuse

[118] Brandis, 'Suggestions Regarding Forest Administration', pp. 27–8.

which should be checked.'[119] But this did not restrict the colonial state from selling this same wood to the same ryots on payment of *seigniorage.*[120] The pre-colonial method of a collective village regulation of grazing lands was banned; the state now introduced a uniform tax on all kinds of grazing lands.[121] The most crucial change, however, was the conversion of all the major and minor forests into government reserved forests, with boundaries drawn on the land conspicuously. This 'skilfull demarcation' of the boundaries of reserved forests and the 'settlement of rights'[122] had, by the 1910s, become the visible space for the execution of colonial laws. 'The world condition of unfreedom', said Marx in the context of a debate on the law on the theft of wood in Germany, 'required laws expressing this unfreedom.'[123] It was this colonial juridical and socio-economic context which shaped popular perceptions of colonial rule as unjust, alien and immoral. Such perceptions and their context were the ultimate basis for radical agrarian and tribal movements in Andhra during 1920–4. A quotation from the report of a correspondent, published in *Swadesamitran* on 18 July 1893, may serve as a conclusion:

> [I regret] to see that there is no space left for cattle-grazing in the North Arcot and Ceded Districts; all the wastelands, including even village sites and porambokes, having been brought under reservation by the Forest Department . . . that this procedure on the part of the Forest Department is due to ignorance prevailing among the ryots, whose sole kingdom is their village, of which the village *monigar* is the sovereign . . . that reservations of this nature are not in the least felt by officials and traders, but fail with great severity on the poor ryots, whose stock of cattle dwindles into nothing day after day.[124]

119 Board of Revenue Proceedings, Govt. of Madras, 19 December 1862, 8284, pp. 3946–7.

120 Ibid., 3 February 1864, 733, pp. 552–3.

121 Ibid., 24 June 1867, 3885, pp. 3777–8; C.F. Brackenbury, *Cuddapah District Gazetter*, p. 105.

122 Brandis, 'Suggestions', p. 16.

123 Marx, 'Debates on the Law on Thefts of Wood', p. 230.

124 *Report on the Native Newspapers, Madras*, July 1893, p. 179.

## Chapter Four

# British Attitudes Towards Shifting Cultivation in Colonial South India: A Case Study of South Canara District 1800–1920

JACQUES POUCHEPADASS

There is a subject of much interest and importance and which is deserving of the attentive consideration of Government, not so much perhaps with reference to the immediate or future supply of timber for public purposes as in the general bearing which it cannot fail to have at no distant period upon the welfare and condition of the Province. I allude to the rapid destruction which is going on amongst the forests along the whole length of the district by the process of Coomeri cultivation.[1]

These are the introductory words of the section on shifting cultivation in a report sent by the Collector of Canara to the Madras Board of Revenue in 1847, when the preservation of the Canara forests began to assume in the eyes of the colonial authorities a character of primary importance. The problem, in this opening sentence, is at once set in very general terms, in accordance with the tendency of the time: shifting cultivation, locally known as *kumri* (literally 'hilly land') cultivation, is deprecated not merely

[1] Collector of Canara to Board of Revenue, Fort St George, 31 August 1847, in Madras Board of Revenue Proceedings (hereafter BRP), 8 November 1847.

as a waste of forest resources, but also as a persistent threat to the general well-being of the region and, as we shall see, to its progressive march towards civilization. This old question had in fact been raised afresh in all the districts along the Western Ghats, and indeed in all the main forest areas of the Indian empire, at about the same time. It will be studied here in some detail within the framework of one particular area, the South Canara district of Madras Presidency, in which two juridically distinct forms of shifting cultivation were found, namely *sarkar kumri* (practised by itinerant cultivators in forests not claimed by owners of estates) and *warg kumri* (practised by tenants in the holdings—called *wargs*—of the local proprietors or *wargdars*). The comparison between the different policies followed by the colonial government regarding these two forms of kumri cultivation will throw some light on the ideological foundations of official attitudes towards shifting cultivation. It must be emphasized that the shifting cultivators and their practices will only be seen here through the eyes of the administrators. As is well known, the subalterns of the past—here peasants and tribals—were mostly unable to write, and left no accounts of themselves. The agents of the modern state considered them only as consumers of natural resources, as actual or potential tax- or rent-payers, and from the point of view of law and order. Thus, while the records provide interesting insights into the ideology and worldview of the British state and its agents, they give only fragmentary or oblique evidence about the people and practices with which they explicitly deal. The present essay then, is primarily a study of British attitudes and policy.

### Shifting Cultivation in Nineteenth-Century South Canara

South Canara as a distinct administrative entity came into being only in 1862, when the old Canara district of Madras Presidency was divided into two districts, North Canara and South Canara, the former being transferred to Bombay Presidency. During the British period, South Canara included the present-day districts of Dakshin Kannada (Karnataka) and Kasargod, now the northernmost district of Kerala, which then formed its southern *taluk*. The country was described as follows by B.H. Baden-Powell in 1892:

The whole district lies along the coast between the sea and the lofty Ghats clothed with evergreen forest. This country is undulating, composed of laterite ridges intersected by the deep-soiled valleys of the streams coming down from the hills, and by estuaries running in from the sea: cultivation is here very rich. Beyond this, there are valleys running farther into the hills, and a tract of table-land above . . . Above, rise the main slopes of the Ghats with dense evergreen forest on the ridge.[2]

The district was still characterized at that time by one of its former collectors as 'essentially a forest district,' where heavy forest approached within a few miles of the sea to the north (the northern part of Coondapur taluk) and south (the southern portion of Kasargod taluk), though it generally began from twenty to thirty miles from the coast. Cultivation was confined mainly to the coastal plains and to the bottoms of the valleys of the numerous streams which wound their way from the Ghats to the sea. Most of the forest below the Ghats was however already highly degraded, 'varying from moderate forest to mere scrub,' with occasional bare spots which produced nothing but thatching grass, having been 'recklessly denuded for the supply of fuel and manure'.[3]

Kumri cultivation was mainly practised in the extreme north and south of the district (Coondapur and Kasargod taluks), where the Ghats came close to the sea and the breadth of dense forest was widest. Some shifting cultivation was also met with in the eastern Uppinangadi (later Puttur) taluk, which at the end of the last century was still largely covered with heavy forest. There is no place here for a detailed description of the techniques used by the local 'kumri cutters,' but a good account given by the District

[2] B.H. Baden-Powell, *The Land Systems of British India* (Oxford, 1892), vol. 3, p. 146.

[3] J. Sturrock, *South Canara* (Madras, 1894) (*Madras District Manual* series), p. 15.

Collector in 1858 is appended to this paper.[4] In the warg kumri area of Kasargod, the crop raised was usually paddy mixed with gram and cotton. Elsewhere, *ragi* and gram were the principal crops. Castor, gingelly, chillies and vegetables of different sorts were also mixed with the main crops in small quantities.[5] This form of cultivation was both strenuous and uncertain: '[It] requires great toil and is very fluctuating in its success, depending entirely on a favourable monsoon. From the necessity of being carried on in dense jungle, it requires constant exertions both by night and day and constant exposure to the inclemency of the weather to defend the crop from the attack of bison, elk and hog to which they are liable'.[6]

It is impossible to estimate the area of kumri cultivation in Canara in the nineteenth century with any accuracy, as the district remained unsurveyed until 1896, when this practice was decidedly on the wane. The district accounts for the year 1856 gave the area under kumri at 17,084 acres for North Canara and South Canara together, of which roughly one third (5983 acres) were within the limits of Kasargod taluk (this was mainly warg kumri). But it was well-known that the actual quantity of kumri cut every year was related more to the capacity and means of the cultivators than to the official figures found in government accounts. Large areas of forest were and had long been under untaxed kumri. In such cases, the local authorities had no means to assert the rights of the government, because the taluk employees were unable to investigate the situation in a mountainous jungle country where they

[4] See Appendix. This is taken from the report sent by W. Fisher, Collector of Canara, to the Board of Revenue, Fort St George, 30 August 1858, in BRP, 13 October 1858, 91 (hereafter Fisher's Report). Fisher's description partly draws on earlier reports devoted to the same question. One of the first accounts is that of F. Buchanan, *A Journey from Madras through Mysore, Canara and Malabar* (London, 1807), vol. 3, p. 72.

[5] Sturrock, *South Canara*, p. 209; *Statistical Atlas of the Madras Province* (Madras, rev. ed., 1949), p. 938.

[6] BRP, 4 April 1850, 2370. 'Bison, elk and hog' most probably refer to the Indian wild buffalo (*gaur*), sambhar and wild pig respectively.

could only travel on foot.[7] In any case, as kumri was at that time repeated on the same ground only once every twelve years on the average—though the lapse of years was more in some localities and less in others—the real extent of forest land subjected to slash-and-burn amounted to more than 200,000 acres (70,000 in Kasargod).[8] This official kumri area probably started decreasing in South Canara from 1860 on account of the gradual enforcement of the restrictive orders issued by the Madras Board of Revenue in Coondapur and Kasargod taluks. Cases in which kumri was cleared in excess of the extent allowed or cultivated contrary to existing orders were then punished either by the collection of double assessment or by confiscating the produce and punishing the offender under the Penal Code. The actual decrease of kumri in Kasargod was slow because the ryots, at least in the beginning, were quite successful in resisting the orders. It was thought to be somewhat quicker in Coondapur, where officially not more than 803 acres of kumri were actually cut in 1865. In Puttur only 156 acres were cut in that year. Even in Kasargod, however, the assessed area under kumri in 1868 had shrunk to 35,000 acres.[9] But these figures were only approximations of the truth, which was almost impossible to ascertain in a district which remained unsurveyed. The Revenue Survey conducted from 1889 to 1896 placed the kumri area of South Canara at the much more realistic figure of 140,000 acres.[10]

In all likelihood, kumri cultivation in Canara during the first

[7] Fisher's Report.

[8] Government Order 830, 23 May 1860, in Madras Government, Revenue Department Proceedings (hereafter RDP), May 1860, 33.

[9] Land Revenue Settlement Report of South Canara for 1861–62, 825; *idem* for 1862–63, para. 8–III; Collector of South Canara to Madras Board of Revenue, 180, 22 September 1866, in BRP, 24 June 1868, 4664; Sub-Secretary to Secretary, Board of Revenue, Madras, 24 June 1868, *ibid.*; 'Statement of kumaries in the talook of Kasargod' in BRP, 21 March 1871.

[10] K.N. Krishnaswami Ayyar and J.F. Hall, *Statistical Appendix, together with a Supplement, to the two District Manuals for South Kanara District* (Madras, 1938), p. 29.

half of the nineteenth century had been in a phase of expansion. 'It was formerly confined entirely,' the Collector wrote in 1847,

> to the race of wild and uncivilized people who dwelt habitually in the jungle, but others have since taken it up and many of the ryots from the plains and others who have come from the Mysore and the Mahratta country have adopted it as a means of livelihood. There is little doubt that the prohibition of this practice in the Mysore country will drive a great many of those who have carried on their operations in the forests of that country into Canara, and the destruction will be carried on more rapidly than ever until the woods are finally exhausted.[11]

As the old forest gradually decreased along the coast, the cultivators resorted to jungles in the interior which were formerly left alone because of their remoteness. And since firewood was becoming increasingly scarce in the coastal zone, the peasants began practising kumri cultivation in the forest areas adjoining the numerous streams issuing from the Ghats. This provided them with both ragi and firewood, which they floated down in large quantities.[12] There is, moreover, evidence that in Kasargod, where land suitable to garden and rice cultivation had become insufficient for the support of a growing population, and where kumri cultivation had assumed the character of regular cultivation, the length of the fallow period tended to decline from the original ten or twelve years to eight and even, at times, six years.[13] The Collector of South Canara in 1860 was of the opinion that while the area of kumri cultivation in Kasargod, according to accounts furnished by the ryots themselves, had trebled since the British annexation, it was in reality probably quadruple or quintuple of what it was then.[14] The rate of forest destruction was accelerated, as foreseen

[11] Collector of Canara to Board of Revenue, Fort St George, 109, 13 July 1860, in BRP, 4 August 1860, 3595.

[12] Sub-collector Hall to Collector of Canara, 22 March 1849, in BRP, 4 April 1850, 2370.

[13] Fisher's Report; Board's letter to Collector of South Canara, BRP, 4 August 1860, 3595.

[14] Collector, South Canara, to Board of Revenue, Fort St George, 109, 13 July 1860, in BRP, 4 August 1860, 3595.

by the Collector in 1847, by the influx of Marathas from above the Ghats following the prohibition of kumri in Mysore.[15]

During the period of expansion of kumri cultivation, its social base grew more complex. 'It was formerly carried on almost exclusively by a wild and little civilized class of people who had no fixed habitation, but built temporary huts on the spot which they occupied for the year, and shifted their place of residence with their cultivation,' the Collector wrote in 1850. But it was now pursued to a considerable extent by more 'civilized' and settled cultivators who had begun to resort every year to the forests to carry on this cultivation. This, however, was actively discouraged in the 1850s, as it was increasingly felt that only the forest tribes should be allowed to continue practising kumri. In the warg kumri areas of Kasargod and elsewhere, kumri cultivation was part of the regular business of every ryot. But in this case also, the actual kumri cutters were mostly forest dwellers who cultivated the forest as tenants-at-will or labourers of substantial and influential raiyats, whose oppressive terms they had no means to resist. In South Canara, they were either local forest tribes (Malai Kudigals) or Maratha Kudubis. These two categories together, according to an early census, represented about one sixth of the population of Kasargod in the late 1850s (59,500 persons).[16] The Malai Kudigals ('inhabitants of the hills') were described by the Collector in 1820 as 'a miserable class of human beings' who were rarely seen in the villages below the Ghats, and whose 'wretched and only means of support' was kumri cultivation. 'They are a people,' he added, 'with whom (compared with their present state of incivilization) the slave on a Champagne estate is an enviable creature. No melioration can be attempted with a prospect of good resulting therefrom'.[17] There were more than 10,000 Kudubis in 1891,

[15] Ayyar and Hall, *Statistical Appendix*, p. 159.

[16] Collector of Canara to Board of Revenue, Fort St George, in BRP, 4 April 1850, 2370; Sub-Collector Hall to Collector of Canara, 22 March 1849, in BRP, 4 April 1850, 2370; Fisher's Report.

[17] Collector of Canara to Govt. of Madras, 13 September 1820, quoted in BRP, 21 March 1871, p. 1958.

mainly in Coondapur taluk, into which they had migrated two centuries earlier from the Maratha country. Unlike the Goa Kudubis, who had taken to settled cultivation in the plains, they were almost exclusively itinerant forest dwellers living on kumri cultivation.[18]

Kumri was not considered an unprofitable cultivation in money terms, though it was not as remunerative as *punam* cultivation in Malabar was generally believed to be.[19] An Assistant Conservator of Forests conducted an enquiry on this point among kumri cutters in 1859, and gave the following details of the cost and profit of 1½ acres of kumri:[20]

| *Expenditure* | | *Rs* | *As* | *P* |
|---|---|---|---|---|
| | Assessment per 1½ acre | 1 | 8 | 0 |
| | Two men cutting for ten days | 3 | 0 | 0 |
| | *Ragi* seed (9 *seers*) | 0 | 4 | 0 |
| | Clearing grass for 1 month (1 man) | 4 | 0 | 0 |
| | Watching 3 months (at Rs 2 per month) | 6 | 0 | 0 |
| | Gathering crop | 4 | 0 | 0 |
| | | 18 | 12 | 0 |
| Receipts | *Ragi*, 28 *modas* at 1 Re. | 28 | 0 | 0 |
| Profit | | 9 | 4 | 0 |

Of course the problem with such computations is that they evaluate in money terms factors of production and agricultural products which belong largely to a non-market economy, or, if commercialized, are subject to forced instead of free commercialization, and thus are not in fact as remunerative as they seem

[18] Sturrock, *South Canara*, p. 178.

[19] Punam lands were the wooded highlands of the Northern Division of Malabar district on which shifting cultivation was practised. The lands were cultivated every six years. The main crops were 'jungle rice,' millet and pulses. Cotton was also grown occasionally: see W. Logan, *Malabar* (Madras, 1887, repr. 1951), vol. 1, p. 630, and vol. 2, p. ccvi.

[20] Conservator of Forests, Madras, to Secretary to Govt., Revenue Dept., Fort St George, 755, 17 August 1859, in RDP, May 1860, 32.

to be. In point of fact, the kumri cutter did all the work himself with the help of his family, and the assessment, in remote forest areas, was often evaded. Thus the real profit was probably higher than estimated. But a large part of it went to the moneylenders of the coastal zone who gave advances to the kumri cultivators, and that part of the crop which had to be marketed in order to meet their demands fetched a very poor price, being sold in times of seasonal price depression, and to all-powerful intermediaries who were in a position to dictate their own terms. It was well known that kumri cutters, whatever the 'profits' they were supposed to make, lived in wretched temporary huts, were kept in abject poverty by their masters or moneylenders, and hardly earned or produced enough to survive—in complete contrast to the generally substantial raiyats of coastal Canara.[21] Their lot improved somewhat in the warg kumri areas of Kasargod after the 1860s. In those areas, although land was ostensibly taken up for the purpose of kumri cultivation, and partial burning did still take place here and there, the main object of the raiyats was to cut and sell the firewood growing on the lands in question. Large quantities of firewood were exported annually from that part of South Kanara both for the Mangalore and Bombay markets, and it is the kumri cutters who were employed in cutting this firewood, a rather more lucrative pursuit than their original occupation.[22] As far as the wargdars were concerned, this new dimension of kumri cultivation on their forest lands of course increased their profits substantially.[23]

[21] *Ibid.*; Collector of Malabar to Conservator of Forests, Madras, I–663, 5 July 1869, in RDP, May 1860, 32; Govt. Order 830, 23 May 1860, in RDP, May 1860, 33.

[22] Collector of South Kanara to Board of Revenue, 180, 22 September 1866, in BRP, 24 June 1868; Acting Collector of South Kanara, to Board of Revenue, 126, 17 July 1867, *ibid.* The riverside *kumri wargdars* of Kasargod taluk supplied a very large proportion of the firewood used in Mangalore in the 1880s: *cf.* Acting Collector of South Canara to Board of Revenue, Madras, 512, 6 March 1883, in RDP, 29 August 1883, 1050.

[23] Madras Board of Revenue Resolution, 1760, 19 June 1883, in RDP, 29 August 1883, 1554.

## Ideological Foundations of British Attitudes

The principal reason put forward by the colonial foresters to justify the restriction of kumri cultivation was, of course, its destructive character. Commenting upon the rapid shrinkage of the forest cover in Canara since the beginning of the nineteenth century, the Collector in 1847, Mr Blane, singled out the kumri cutter as the main culprit who 'recklessly felled and burned [the forest] for the purpose of obtaining one or two scanty crops of dry grain'. 'The practice of kumri cultivation,' he added, 'is one of so wasteful and improvident a nature that it appears to me it ought not to be tolerated except in a very wild and unpeopled country, and the time seems to have arrived when it would be most advisable to place it under considerable check and regulation, if not entirely to prohibit it'—as had recently been the case in the neighbouring Mysore state. The one objection to total prohibition which he saw was that the clearing of jungles, according to all reports he had received, tended to diminish the prevalence of fever. This had been particularly evident in the Mangalore region, where kumri cultivation had been carried on with great activity in the preceding years.[24]

The question of the effect of forest clearance on climate and soil fertility was very much on the agenda at that time, as the Court of Directors had raised the question in a despatch to the Madras Board of Revenue, and all the Collectors of the Presidency had consequently been asked to report on the subject.[25] Shifting cultivation was at first severely condemned on this account. Indictments became less radical thereafter. W. Fisher, the Collector of Canara in the late 1850s, doubted whether kumri had any strong adverse effect on climate, as it was only rarely carried on in the forest at the crest of the hills, which, he thought, had a greater effect on the passing clouds than those beneath them, while providing the seed for resowing the clearings made below. He also

24 Blane's Report.

25 Board of Rev., Fort St George, to Chief Secretary to Government, 8 November 1847, *ibid.*

observed that forest regeneration was not jeopardized even after two or three successive episodes of slash-and-burn, as was sometimes believed. Nothing of the sort ever happened in Kasargod, where kumri cultivation was practised in a systematic way.[26] As against such pleas in partial defence of kumri, H. Cleghorn, the influential Conservator of Forests of Madras Presidency, when asked by government to state his views on shifting cultivation in Canara, declared that this practice, which he described as 'a rude system of culture' and 'a wasteful and barbarous system,' had serious disruptive effects on climate, and, moreover, had none of the alleged beneficial effects on public health. While permanent clearings brought about a distinct improvement in this regard, he said, the dense thorny scrub which succeeded slash-and-burn was more unhealthy than open high forest. Cleghorn also deplored the destruction of valuable timber which was urgently required for shipbuilding and railways. This, incidentally, was an old official complaint: the Bombay Government had already addressed the Madras Government in 1820 on the report by the Marine Board of Bombay of 'instances of the devastation by the owners of land of teak trees growing in that Province, the property of Government,' for shifting cultivation.[27] For all these reasons, kumri cultivation in Canara, in his opinion, had to be done away with. It could at best be tolerated on poor soils where trees did not attain a great size, or in areas where the timber could not be transported to a road or river due to physical obstacles, or in jungles where bamboo growth was extensive.[28]

These views, which became the official view regarding kumri in Canara, were fraught with moral overtones. This system of cultivation, the Collector wrote in 1847, 'has no doubt some attraction for those who are impatient of control, and are fond of a wild roving life, but it leads to unsettled habits,' and every step

[26] Fisher's Report.

[27] Quoted in BRP, 21 March 1871, p. 1957.

[28] Conservator of Forests, Madras, to Revenue Dept., Fort St George, 755, 17 August 1859, in RDP, May 1860, 32.

should be taken to discourage a pursuit which 'takes many away from the regular cultivation of a fixed spot'. In 1855, his successor added that 'this must not be done too suddenly. The habits of a people cannot be changed at once,' and too sudden a prohibition can be 'the cause of severe suffering to a people who have so long subsisted by this species of cultivation'. W. Fisher concurred in this view three years later:

> Want of capital, and the ease with which a man who possesses nothing but a good knife and a strong arm can obtain a living by labour which habit has rendered more congenial to him than that which falls to the lot of the common cultivators of the soil, will prevent anything but a gradual change. But I am satisfied that that change has already commenced, and that a more settled mode of life and more regular habits will spring from it, and in the end benefit this class, and make them both more useful and more independent members of society . . . Regular cultivation [he added] is not palatable to these people, who are accustomed to migrate from one position to another among the hills, but the restrictions placed on kumri have I think already had some effect in inducing them to follow more regular pursuits, and will eventually lead to their becoming tenants or labourers on the regular estates, and to the improvement of their position in the social scale.[29]

This discourse on the social dangers implicit in 'wild roving habits,' on the necessity of social 'control,' on the desirability of 'regular pursuits' and 'settled habits,' belongs to the normative Victorian social ideology which was to lead a little later to the legal definition and arbitrary repression of the so-called 'Criminal Tribes'.[30] The cliché of the 'lazy native' occasionally showed up in these statements. The Revenue Surveyor of Dharwar and Belgaum wrote to Cleghorn in 1859 that people resorted to kumri because 'it requires no stock or agricultural capital' and 'it requires less labour than any other description of cultivation' (a quite unfounded statement, as we have seen). 'The habits of the people

[29] Blane's Report; Collector of Canara to Board of Revenue, Fort St George, 1664, 12 June 1855, in BRP, 7 August 1855; W. Fisher's Report.

[30] Cf. J. Pouchepadass, 'The "Criminal Tribes" of British India: A repressive concept in theory and practice', *International Journal of Asian Studies*, 2:1, 1982.

in kumri districts,' he added, 'are even for natives idle in the last degree. They detest work . . . The easy subsistence afforded by kumaring [*sic*] appears to be somewhat similar in its effects on the habits of people to that of the potato (before the disease was known) on the Irish.'[31] Thus, shifting cultivation was regarded as a social evil, the eradication of which would be a civilizing measure and would benefit the shifting cultivators themselves (much as the British empire in general was believed to promote the well being of the Indian people without their being conscious of it or even against their will). The Order (830 of 23 May 1860) passed by the Government of Madras on the subject stated explicitly: 'Sarkar kumri . . . seems to be a great evil even as respects the interests of the cultivators themselves. It appears certainly to retard the improvement of the forest races, and tends to keep them in their present degraded condition'. Thus *sarkar kumri* without previous permission was prohibited in Canara.[32] It was decided twenty-five years later that permits would only be granted to those applicants who were willing to undertake some settled cultivation along with their kumri, 'with the view of gradually accustoming these men to do with smaller amount of kumri and at the same time contract the habits of a settled life'.[33]

Finally, the British attitude towards shifting cultivation was dictated in part by the concerns of the colonial state regarding the ownership of land and the taxation of its produce. Modern ideas on property in land and on the land revenue implied, as is well known, that every piece of land should have a recognized (individual or collective) owner for the payment of a determined land tax, itself calculated on the basis of a systematic assessment of the productive capacities of the land concerned. Shifting cultivation, of course, fitted rather badly with these conceptions, as it was practised on lands whose ownership was open to question, which

[31] Superintendent of the Revenue Survey, Southern Mahratta Country, to Conservator of Forests, Madras, 26 July 1859, in RDP, May 1860, 32.

[32] RDP, May 1860, 32.

[33] *Settlement Report of South Canara for the Year 1884–85*, 18(3).

were difficult of access, and on ever-changing patches of forest, by people who escaped 'control'. In the more accessible forest areas of Canara, however, kumri cultivators were taxed directly by the local government officers. 'They cut and cultivate [the jungle] as they please,' the Head Sheristadar of the district wrote in 1830:

> After they have cleared a spot and sown it, the Tahsildar collects from them the tax payable according to the custom of the village. In some places this tax is fixed at so much for a couple (man and woman) or so much for a man alone. In others it is fixed according to the number of bill-hooks, or hatchets they make use of in clearing the jungle, there being a fixed rate of payment on each bill-hook, and another on each hatchet.[34]

In more remote areas, the collection of the kumri dues was initially farmed out to substantial peasants of the neighbouring villages, who made their own terms with the kumri cutters, usually on a non-monetary basis. The assessment was similarly fixed in relation to the number of cultivators or implements concerned and not to the area of forest to be burnt.[35] The Collector of Canara in 1822 described the system in these terms:

> [The *kumri* cutters] inhabit the Ghats and never descend into the low country. They depute a headman to the renter on the part of the sarkar annually to arrange their barter of hill produce such as cassia, pepper, cardamoms, ragi and wax. The renter gives them dal, rice, tobacco, and arms in return. For this permission, he enters into contract with the sarkar.[36]

[34] Quoted in BRP, 21 March 1871, p. 1969. It was similarly common until the end of the nineteenth century, in unsurveyed pioneer areas such as the Himalayan terai, to tax cultivators according to number of ploughs without reference to the actual area cultivated. Because of the same problems of estimating acreage, shifting cultivators in some other parts (e.g. Bastar) would be taxed according to the number of 'able bodied men' (information communicated by R. Guha).

[35] BRP, 4 April 1850, 2370, pp. 4878, 4890; BRP, 21 March 1871, pp. 1968–9.

[36] Collector of Canara to Board of Revenue, 20 August 1822, in BRP, 10 June 1822, quoted in BRP, 21 March 1871, p. 1962.

Until 1822, the kumri due owed by the village contractor was actually entered in his account under the head of *motarfa* (i.e. miscellaneous revenue, such as fisheries, honey, etc.), and not as an item of land revenue. In 1822, however, the Board of Revenue directed that this due, being a revenue from the land, should figure in the accounts of the estate holders as an item of land revenue.[37] This being done, the kumri assessment gradually came to be mixed up with the regular land revenue levied on the raiyat's private permanently cultivated lands. The kumri cultivation even became the subject of transfer by sale, suits, attachment for decrees of court, thus ceasing to be merely a right involved in a lease, but apparently incorporating a proprietary right.[38]

At this stage, there were two distinct juridical forms of kumri cultivation:

(i) sarkar kumri, under which an individual settlement was made with each *kumri* cutter who paid his due directly to the government;

(ii) warg kumri, under which the raiyats (wargdars) collected the kumri due from shifting cultivators who cultivated portions of their land or were otherwise under their influence, subject to payment by these raiyats of a specified sum as part of the revenue demand on their estates.[39]

Warg kumri posed a problem to the government from the 1840s, when the restriction of kumri cultivation became the order of the day. If the proprietary right of the wargdars in the forest tracts from which they were levying kumri dues was given general recognition, the government would cease to have any kind of control over such tracts. In a period when kumri cultivation was clearly on the rise, every settler would simply become their tenant. It was moreover the interest of the wargdars along the Ghats to encourage kumri. By so doing, they increased their local influence and could command the additional labour force they needed to

[37] Ibid., p. 1969.

[38] BRP, 4 April 1850, 2370, pp. 4881–2.

[39] Fisher's Report, para. 44, 63.

bring waste lands into cultivation, for which they would be otherwise unable to find tenants from the plains, due to the inferior quality of the lands or to the unhealthiness of the climate.[40] Against the claims of the wargdars to the ownership of the kumri tracts, the government asserted its rights with increasing rigour from the 1840s onwards. Private proprietary rights in forest lands which were deemed to have been formerly public were gradually extinguished. When the various categories of peasant proprietors had been initially created in south India for the establishment of the colonial land-revenue system, the non-existence of property rights in the modern sense, before the advent of the British, had been overlooked. Ironically, it was now upheld in order to justify the government take-over of the forests claimed by these proprietors. 'As under native Government,' Fisher wrote, 'all cultivation was taxed according to description and value of its produce, the government having a recognized right to a certain share in that produce whatever it might be, there is good reason to suppose that this kumri tax was but a rent for certain forest privileges, and did not confer [on the wargdars] any proprietary right in the soil'.[41]

The claims of the wargdars on kumri lands were, however, exceptionally recognized in Kasargod the southernmost taluk of South Canara district. The rights which these wargdars claimed on the forests attached to their estates were held to be of a different nature, superior to those which were denied to the wargdars of other parts. Kasargod had initially been part of Malabar, and the wargdars there were Nairs. The government had never questioned the rights of property enjoyed by the Nair chiefs on the forests of Malabar. It was only logical that the same course should be adopted regarding the wargdars of Kasargod.[42] Kumri cultivation,

[40] BRP, 4 April 1850, 2370, pp. 4891–2; Fisher's Report, para. 20.

[41] Fisher's Report, para. 61.

[42] India, Home, Revenue and Agriculture (Forests Branch) Proceedings, June 1880, part B, 112: 'Papers relating to state rights in the forests of South Canara'. Baden-Powell questioned, however, the idea that private property in land existed in South Canara or Malabar while it did not elsewhere: *cf.* Baden-Powell, *Land Systems*, vol. 3, pp. 144–5.

as the Government Order of 23 May 1860 said, was carried on by the resident wargdars of Kasargod 'as a regular part of their farming, and not by wandering tribes unconnected with the soil,' as in the northern parts. Two-thirds of the warg kumri area of Canara was located in Kasargod in 1859, in a total of 147 estates.[43] These forest areas thus escaped reservation during the forest settlement operations at the end of the century. Though some of these warg kumris were subsequently converted to permanent wet or dry agriculture, kumris still existed in twenty-one villages of Kasargod at the resettlement of 1932–4.[44]

## The Stages of Government Repression of Kumri Cultivation

Very little is known about the status of shifting cultivation in Canara before the advent of the British. The Collector reported in 1820: 'There is no subject on which so little information is to be gathered as on the "forests of Canara." I have searched the records of my office in vain; my people are unacquainted with the subject.' He attributed this state of things to the fact that control over forests was not in the hands of the Collector but of the Conservator, whose establishment and powers were limited, and who usually lacked local experience and knowledge. Regarding shifting cultivation in particular, Fisher similarly reported in 1858: 'No researches that I have been able to make enable me to place the question before the Board in other than [a] very general way.'[45] It was, however, known that in this part of India prior to British rule, under the Nagar kings for instance, or in the Coorg kingdom, the government exercised close control over the forests, and that certain kinds of trees were preserved for its use. The forests, moreover, were often strictly preserved from destruction on account of the security which

[43] BRP, 16 April 1859, 1350, pp. 337–8; Collector of South Canara to Board of Revenue, Madras, 512, 6 March 1883, in RDP, 29 August 1883, 1054, p. 595.

[44] Ayyar and Hall, *Statistical Appendix*, pp. 160, 189.

[45] Collector of Canara to Board of Revenue, 13 September 1820, quoted in BRP, 21 March 1871, p. 1953; Fisher's Report, para. 104.

they were supposed to afford against invasion. In Mysore, kumri was believed to have always been treated as a temporary rent, and as such was abolished in 1848 on account of the rapid destruction which the forests were undergoing because of the increase of this form of cultivation.[46]

In Canara the official policy was relatively lenient until 1847. Replying to the already mentioned complaint by the Marine Board of Bombay that teak trees belonging to government were being 'devastated' in Canara by kumri cultivators, the Collector wrote in 1820 that the cases alluded to were mostly trivial, and that to prohibit kumri would 'in a great measure interfere with the actual welfare of the most abject race of our subjects equally deserving of our protection as the highest.'[47] His successor, Mr Thackeray, impressed upon the Board in 1822 that it was in fact highly desirable to clear jungles from which in any case it was impossible to extract teak for naval purposes on account of natural obstacles or distance from the sea, while both revenue and health purposes would be served. Thackeray's report was fully endorsed by Thomas Munro, then Governor of Madras Presidency, in his minute dated 16 November 1822.[48] This policy remained by and large unchanged for a quarter of a century. The Court of Directors wrote to Madras in 1846:

> The forests of Canara are represented as being less unhealthy and more easy of access than those of Malabar, and it may therefore be advisable to reserve some of them to meet the requirements of Government. But when those best adapted for the purpose have been selected and placed under proper management, there seems to be no reason why the natives should be excluded from the others or subjected to new restrictions in the felling of trees in them excepting teak and sissoo. On the contrary, it seems rather desirable to encourage them to clear away the jungles by which so large a portion of the province is covered.[49]

[46] BRP, 4 April 1850, 2370, pp. 4883–4.

[47] Quoted in BRP, 21 March 1871, pp. 1957, 1962.

[48] Quoted in BRP, 21 March 1871, pp. 1957, 1962.

[49] Letter from the Court of Director, 28 November 1846, quoted in Minutes of Consultation, 518, 17 December 1847, in BRP, 3 February 1848.

The problem, of course, was that while the burning for cultivation of forests containing trees required for state use was prohibited, the prohibition was not strictly enforced because of lack of surveillance.[50] With the increase of population and the imposition of restrictive regulations in neighbouring regions, this problem began to assume serious proportions, as the report by Dr Gibson, the Conservator of Forests of Bombay, showed in 1847. However, in consideration of the fact that forest clearance was believed to diminish the prevalence of fever, the recommendation of the Collector of Canara (Mr Blane) went no further than the renewal of the former rule prohibiting the cutting of the better kinds of timber, and the entire preservation of the forest in spots near the rivers or the sea coast, where timber extraction was easy and where ordinary wood could be cut as firewood for export.[51] The government thereafter simply decided to authorize the Collector to restrict the cultivation 'to such places and to such an extent as he might deem expedient'.[52]

Explicit official restrictions were first imposed in 1849, when it was decided that the felling of jungle for kumri would be prohibited within nine miles of the sea, and within three miles of rivers capable of floating timber or high roads. It was also prohibited in sites favourable to teak and in virgin forests. The Collector in 1855 was, however, of the opinion that the time had not yet come for the stopping of the clearing of forests and of the extension of agriculture. Gibson, he said, had received a false impression regarding the state of kumri cultivation in Canara from the fact that clearings, for accidental reasons, were particularly extensive along the high road which he had taken. Kumri in this district was the only means of subsistence of the population in a large part of the district. Thus it was quite out of the question to prohibit it entirely, as had been done in Dharwar district, and the

[50] See for instance A. Gibson's 'Report on the Forests of North Canara,' in BRP, 19 July 1847.

[51] Blane's Report.

[52] Government Order, 3 December 1847, in BRP, 16 December 1847, 3226.

existing restrictions, which were almost identical to those imposed in Belgaum district, had already been carried as far as practicable. The rules, however, had failed to have full effect because of the prevailing system of assessing kumri by the bill-hook. The money-lenders were always ready to give advances to the kumri cutters once they had been registered, so that they might call in relatives to cultivate with them. For two or three bill-hooks officially taxed, areas of up to forty or fifty acres were consequently burnt for cultivation. The Collector for this reason changed the system entirely in 1852, and assessed the land by the acre. This brought about an immediate decline in the area of kumri. 'I cannot say,' he added, 'that in a country so wild and extensive the rules have never been broken, but in each year additional knowledge is gained and the system gains ground.'[53] While the rate for sarkar kumri per bill-hook had been around Rs 2, the rate per acre was Re 1 in North Canara, and As 8 in the South, where the assessment had always been low. People not belonging to the 'jungle tribes' were forbidden to practise kumri, and three acres per year was the maximum area of forest allowed to one kumri cutter. When this limit was found to have been exceeded, the offender was fined or a double tax levied on the excess area. In extreme cases, the crop raised was sometimes confiscated. The extent of kumri allowed to each individual was subsequently reduced gradually. By 1858 it had shrunk to 1.5 acres in North Canara.

These restrictions were considered sufficient by Fisher in 1858. Both Revenue Officers and Conservators were, he says, 'unanimous of opinion that, under proper restrictions, large, and as far as procuring timber goes inaccessible, jungles may be submitted in rotation to the knife of the kumri cutter and be made to contribute to the resources of the people and the revenues of the State.' He added: 'I am far from wishing to see a complete prohibition except as regards tracts producing the more valuable kinds of timber, and such positions on the banks of our numerous

[53] Collector of Canara (F.N. Maltby) to Board of Revenue, Fort St George, 12 June 1855, in BRP, 7 August 1855.

rivers as would under proper care produce valuable plantations of timber suited to shipbuilding and domestic purposes.' The Board found it wise to follow the recommendation of the successive Collectors of Canara (Blane, Maltby and Fisher), who concurred in the view that kumri should not be prohibited altogether: 'It has been shown to have diminished the prevalence of fever, and the grain thus raised is said to be necessary for the subsistence of the population, while the species of cultivation affords a means of livelihood to wild races who, in all probability, can only be gradually brought to settle down to a more regular kind of agriculture.' However, in accordance with the suggestions of Fisher, it was proposed that warg kumri in South Canara as a whole should be confined to certain patches of forest, 'portions of which the cultivators must cut periodically if they cut at all.' This was already the case in the warg kumri areas of Kasargod. The assessment of As 8 per acre of kumri was to be continued. As far as sarkar kumri was concerned, it was to remain prohibited within nine miles of the sea and three miles of a river, as warg kumri had been since 1847. This last rule was to be relaxed at the Collector's discretion in Kasargod, as it appeared to be harsh in a country intersected by rivers and which did not contain 'valuable' timber. All these recommendations of the Board were sanctioned by Government Order 830 of 23 May 1860. The Government added that sarkar kumri, meaning kumri cultivation in government forests, was prohibited from then on without special permission, and that permission 'should be given sparingly, and never for spots in timber forests'.[54] The demand assessed on kumri lands (both warg and sarkar) was raised by the Board from As 8 to Re 1 per acre towards the end of 1860, as the Collector considered the former rate to be excessively moderate.[55]

The sweeping orders of 1860 amounted in fact to a virtual prohibition of kumri, both warg and sarkar, except in Kasargod taluk, where private property in forest land was recognized.

[54] Fisher's Report, para. 26–32, 83–85, 96.

[55] See correspondence in BRP, 21 September 1860, 4297.

Though these orders were not strictly obeyed at once, they did bring about a decrease in the area of kumri during the following year.[56] The roles regarding sarkar kumri had however to be subsequently relaxed in order to meet the needs of the tribals in the forests of Coondapur and Uppinangadi (later Puttur) taluks, who had no other means of livelihood than shifting cultivation. Moreover, the total prohibition of kumri might have depopulated the forests of these areas to such an extent that labourers would have become difficult to find to collect minor forest produce and carry on other operations on behalf of the Forest Department.[57]

It was warg kumri in Kasargod which proved most difficult to restrict. A set of 'subordinate' rules was drawn up for the taluk by the Assistant Collector and put into force in 1865, without success.[58] According to these rules, each wargdar carrying on kumri cultivation was allotted a block of forest eight times as large as the annual clearing allowed, a special permit being issued to him to this effect. The kumri assessment was Re 1 per acre. Kumri was forbidden in virgin forest or in forest that had remained uncut for more than nine years. In addition, the wargdars were requested to cut a path or ditch around the year's clearing. Each year's block was to be contiguous to that of the preceding year, so as to ensure that after eight years, the kumri holding of each wargdar would be entirely demarcated on the ground. The wargdars almost unanimously refused to comply with this requirement, ostensibly on account of the labour and expense involved, but more probably because they were unwilling to have any restrictions at all. They claimed an absolute property right to the forests and waste lands

56 See the Settlement Reports of South Canara in *Report on the Settlement of the Land Revenue of the Provinces under the Madras Presidency for the Years 1861–62* (para. 25), and *1862–63* (para. 8).

57 Sturrock, *South Canara*, pp. 17, 210; Sub-secretary to Secretary, Board of Revenue, Madras, 24 June 1868, in BRP, 24 June 1868. According to the settlement Report of South Canara for 1865–66, 803 acres of sarkar kumri were cut in Coondapur and 156 in Puttur, which corresponds, in the case of a kumri rotation of twelve years, to a maximum kumri area of 11,500 acres.

58 See text of the rules in BRP, 21 March 1871, pp. 1917–19.

of their villages, and consequently held that they could not be legally forbidden to cultivate kumri to whatever extent they wished within the limits of what they considered their estates. The government, on the other hand, did not admit this claim to property in forests and waste lands, but conceded that the right to kumri had gained some degree of validity by long prescription, and thus allowed warg kumri to continue while sarkar kumri was virtually stopped.[59]

In order to ensure that only the permitted amount of kumri was cut, permits were given annually, and the cultivation measured every year, all excess over 10 per cent of the permitted area being charged with a penal assessment of Rs 8 per acre. But it proved difficult to implement the annual measurement of steep and impracticable hillsides by low-paid subordinates:

The accurate survey of hilly forest land is difficult under any circumstances . . . The wargdars who cut under the permits can only guess at the extent they are cutting, and the untrained men who are told to measure it up without either adequate time or knowledge or appliances, and with every man's hand against them trying alternately to cheat, to intimidate and to bribe, are just as likely to come to grief when they work honestly as when they do the reverse.

After various attempts at reform, the government eventually gave up the measurements in 1883, and decided that instead of paying Re 1 per acre actually felled, each wargdar would pay annually a fixed standard assessment based on the average of the kumri charges he had paid the preceding years. Pending the carrying out

[59] Collector of Canara to Board of Revenue, 180, 22 June 1866, and Sub-Secretary to Secretary, Board of Revenue, 24 June 1868, in BRP, 24 June 1868; Sub-Secretary, Revenue Department, Madras Government, to Secretary to Chief Commissioner, Mysore, 1240, 5 May 1869, in BRP, 12 June 1869, 4225. A wealth of information regarding the functioning of *warg kumri* in the adjoining North Kanara district can be found in the proceedings of the 'Kanara Forest Case', which have been reprinted in the *Indian Law Reports, Bombay Series*, vol. III (Bombay, 1979); see M. Buchy, 'Colonial forest exploitation in the Western Ghats of India: A case study of North Kanara district,' *Pondy Papers in Social Sciences*, 7, Pondicherry, French Institute, September 1990, pp. 6–7.

of the regular survey and settlement of the district, 'a register should be prepared recording as accurately as possible the boundaries and descriptive particulars of the tract within which each wargdar is allowed to cut kumri; and during the felling season, the revenue and forest subordinates should be on the alert to prevent felling outside the authorized limits, in virgin forests and in jungle of twelve years' growth.' In fact, the total amount of the kumri revenue being inconsiderable, the government was not prepared to take more expensive measures (such as the appointment of a special establishment) to improve the system. The new system was also more willingly accepted by the wargdars concerned: 'A little grumbling still continues that the government won't admit absolute property right to the whole of the forest of the [villages], but there is no doubt that the present arrangements give very much more satisfaction than those which preceded them,' the Collector wrote in 1885.[60]

Warg kumri was thus allowed to continue under strict restrictions. As regards sarkar kumri, the prohibition was not rigidly enforced, and it was still being practised in a few areas towards the end of the century, both in the north and south of the district. It remained permitted in Coondapur in the case of tribals who were shifting cultivators by tradition; but with a view to accustom them to settled life it was decided in the early 1880s that, along with their kumri, they must undertake either to cultivate waste lands in the estates of the neighbouring wargdars, or to gather forest products for the government against payment at the depot rates. Similar arrangements were made with the Kudubis of northern Kasargod, and in a few scattered areas elsewhere in the district where cultivated estates were reverting to forest or where valuable minor forest products were unutilized for want of labourers to gather them.[61] As a result of this policy, the plea of the tribals that

[60] Collector of South Canara to Board of Revenue, Madras, 512, 6 March 1883, and Government Order, 1054; Sturrock, *South Canara*, p. 124; 'Settlement Report of South Canara for 1884–85', para. 18(3), in BRP, 16 August 1886, 1837.

[61] 'Settlement Report of South Canara for 1884–85'.

they were ignorant of the methods of settled cultivation gradually lost weight in the eyes of the foresters.

With the progress of forest settlement and reservation at the turn of the century, sarkar kumri was thus increasingly curtailed, and the Kudubis were often forced 'to live by cultivation or coolie work like other people' (as the authors of the revised *District Gazetteer* wrote in 1938). Many of them took to paddy cultivation under the local landlords. They usually took advances from these landlords, and thus became permanently attached to them, as they could never repay the money. 'Some of them,' the District Forest Officer of Mangalore said in 1916,

> who happen to live near the locality where the Forest Department permits kumri cultivation, take to kumri cultivation, but their number is few. In return for kumri cultivation, the kumridars are bound to supply labour on payment whenever wanted by the Department, and the works on which they are employed are creeper cutting, fire protection works and catechu manufacture . . . But it is very difficult to attract them to work. They are a class without ambition and extremely lethargic and ignorant. They do not want money but generally yield to pressure . . . The only way of attracting them to labour is by permitting shifting cultivation on a greater scale. This is against the interest of reserved forests and cannot be permitted. Kudubi labour is thus becoming scarce year after year.

Sarkar kumri was stopped altogether in 1920, but it did not die out completely even then. The Forest Department initiated a policy in 1898 which allotted limited areas of forest to the Kudubis for kumri cultivation combined with the raising of crops of teak. This lasted until 1915, and scattered patches of teak were already noticeable at that time among the re-growth on old kumri areas in north Kasargoḍ. In the 1920s the plight of the Kudubis prompted the Forest Department to revive the system. They were given kumri work to do on condition that they raised a forest crop under the supervision of the Department in conjunction with their field crop. Thus a satisfactory solution had, it was felt, at last been found to what was now largely a humanitarian problem: 'The experiment has proved successful, as it not only provided congenial work for the Kudubis, but greatly improved the existing forest, which was the result of the old unregulated kumri . . . .'[62]

## Conclusion

The imposition of state control over the forests of India during the second half of the nineteenth century, which included the restriction or suppression of shifting cultivation in the more threatened forest areas, was only one aspect of the all-round expansion of the modern state which characterized the post-Mutiny period of Indian history. Modernizing legislation was then being passed in the domains of social and economic life which the state needed to regulate; the peoples of the subcontinent were being systematically counted, described and classified by state statisticians and ethnographers; the integral surveying and mapping of the Indian territory at the cadastral scale had begun; rights in land were everywhere being recorded and customs were codified; the network of administrative divisions and jurisdictions was being slowly tightened and brought closer to the people; road and railway communications were being developed. (To what extent this resulted in a parallel progression of effective state control over Indian society at the local level remains, however, an open question.) While the instrument of state control in the rural areas was the Revenue Department, the implementation of forest legislation was the responsibility of the Forest Department. In the countryside, one of the characteristics of the new age was the regression of nomadic lifestyles, which had been so prevalent all over India until the beginning of the nineteenth century. In the forest, the shifting cultivator similarly came to appear as the last remnant of an uncivilized past. Shifting cultivation was not banned everywhere in India. But as far as the central Western Ghats were concerned, it was eventually allowed to survive only in very strictly

[62] Indian Industrial Commission, *Minutes of Evidence, 1916–17*, vol. III, Madras and Bangalore (Calcutta, 1918), p. 366; Ayyar and Hall, *Statistical Appendix*, pp. 159–60, 302.

circumscribed areas, mainly for humanitarian reasons, or within the settled limits of the wargs, in domesticated form, so to say.

It has been contended that shifting cultivation, though it is commonly equated with primitive forms of social life, has in fact been able to sustain in the past stratified societies and centralized states, as long as increasing population densities did not impose the adoption of more intensive forms of agriculture.[63] This contention necessarily implies that this type of cultivation could be a surplus-producing activity. The evidence from the central Western Ghats in the early nineteenth century, as we have seen, seems to point to the same conclusion. It proves that shifting cultivation was not inconsistent with market exchange, that it could bear taxation, and that it was not incompatible with property in land. It also shows that the shifting cultivators of the hills in that region maintained regular contacts with the population of the plains. There existed in fact a complementary and even (in the case of warg kumri) symbiotic relationship between shifting cultivation and sedentary agriculture, which formed one aspect of the diversified pattern of interaction between the settled peasantry of the countryside and the forest people. In the colonial situation, the combination of population growth and the rise of the modern state transformed this stable system into a lopsided relationship between an expanding centralized space and a residual periphery. This evolution was helped by the dominant ecological preconceptions of the authorities, who tended to view the domestication of nature and the artificial, specialized ecosystems of settled agriculture as one of the distinguishing features of civilization.

[63] See for instance D.E. Dumond, 'Swidden agriculture and the rise of Maya civilization,' *Southwestern Journal of Anthropology*, 17(1961), repr. in A.P. Vayda (ed.), *Environment and Cultural Behaviour* (New York, 1969).

## APPENDIX*
## Kumri Cultivation in Nineteenth-Century Canara

Level ground is not suitable to this kind of cultivation and a hill side is always selected on the slopes of which a space is cleared during November, December and January.

The fallen timber is then left to dry until March and April, by which time the action of the sun and of the dry easterly winds which prevail at that season have rendered the dead branches and brushwood highly combustible.

The largest trees, it must be observed, are usually left standing, their arms and branches only being removed, and this mass of comparatively dry wood generates a fierce fire, the effect of which are visible in the soil to a depth varying from three to six inches.

In most localities, the seed is sown in the ashes on the fall of the first rains, the soil having been left untouched by implements of any kind. In Bekul [later Kasargod] however, the ground is ploughed before the bed is sown.

When the young plants begin to appear, the coomery is fenced in by a kind of wattle where its place is not supplied by fallen trees, and the chief labour afterwards is weeding. The whole process, it will be observed, is one requiring little skill and less capital, but long continued and hard labour on the part of the cultivator, who must moreover watch his clearing day and night until harvest time in order to protect his crop from the ravages of elk, bison and other wild animals with which the forests abound.

In the South (Bekul) the grain raised in coomeries is chiefly paddy but in other parts of the District ragee takes its place. The shares of the different cultivators are marked off in the South by cotton and castor oil plants, whilst in the North the latter only is common. The cotton grown in these clearings is of course small in quantity, but is highly esteemed by the people, though its value in the English market as estimated by the Bombay Chamber of Commerce would be small and much better prices can be obtained for it here than could be obtained in the Bombay market.

* From Fisher's report.

In the North the crops are reaped in November and December, and in the South in October and November, and the produce is said to be at least double that which could be obtained from the same extent of ground under the ordinary mode of culture.

A small crop is taken off the ground in the second year, and in Soopah (North Canara) I have heard that a scanty produce is sometimes reaped in the third, after which the spot is deserted until the jungle is sufficiently high to tempt the coomery cutter to renew the process.

In the South, where ground suited to regular cultivation is comparatively scarce and the population is more dense them in other talooks, coomery has long been carried on in a systematic way unknown in the North. The forest is regularly worked, and a man goes over his holding once in 12, 10 or 7 years as the case may be, whereas in North Canara virgin forest often falls before the coomery knife and the people select at pleasure (or rather have done so) old coomeries or jungles which in the memory of man have never been subjected to the process.

Chapter Five

# Maps as Markers of Ecological Change: A Case Study of the Nilgiri Hills of Southern India*

R. PRABHAKAR AND MADHAV GADGIL

> To do science is to search for repeated patterns, not simply to accumulate facts, and to do the science of geographical ecology is to search for patterns of plant and animal life that can be put on a map.[1]
>
> Robert H. MacArthur

## I. Introduction

Human societies have had a significant impact on the patterns of distribution of plants and animals on the earth's surface. Especially over the last two hundred years, human societies have expanded to every corner of the world and have transformed landscapes in significant and irreversible ways. Our area of study, the Nilgiri hills of southern India, has been colonized by people at least from the second century BC. These communities, mainly pastoralists, hunter-gatherers and

* We wish to thank Dr Anindya Sinha for his editorial help, and the Ministry of Environment and Forests, Government of India, for partial financial support.

[1] Robert H. MacArthur, *Geographical Ecology* (Princeton, 1972), p. 1.

shifting cultivators, have interacted closely with the environment. Although there have been debates on the impact of these communities on the vegetation of the Nilgiris, recent research has shown that the Nilgiri *shola* (thicket) and grassland vegetation complex has not changed significantly for the last 30,000 years. Settled agriculture is supposed to have come into the hills during the fifteenth and sixteenth centuries. This was brought in by the immigrant Badaga community.[2] With this, a wide variety of crops like *ragi*, wheat and barley were introduced into the hills. Major and significant changes in the environment and ecology of the Nilgiri hills were brought about in the colonial period, after 1800. This essay concerns itself with ecological changes in the Nilgiri area from the colonial period to the present, as discerned in maps of the area.

Maps are a graphic representation of selected natural and man-made features of a geographical area at a particular point in time and at a particular scale. For ecological studies, where the interest lies in analysing the spatial and temporal distribution of biological communities, maps form an important data source. For historical studies as well, they provide information that has hitherto lain unused among historians of modern India. They provide quantitative, location-specific information on different aspects or 'layers' of land use, topography, vegetation, communications, settlements, etc.; all this can be used for a formal analysis of landscape. In addition, the graphic representation of time series over the maps yield visual impressions and inferences that provide significant clues on the process of ecological change.

## II. The Nilgiri Area and its Cartographic Data Base

> The historical value of these maps [of the Survey of India] is considerable, though uneven. Many of them make definite reference to interesting historical events, persons and dates . . . Generally speaking, these maps may be taken as good evidence

[2] Paul Hockings, *Ancient Hindu Refugees* (New Delhi, 1980), p. 12.

as to the face of the country at the actual time of survey, especially as to roads, towns and villages and boundaries also where they are definitely indicated.[3]

Colonel R.H. Phillimore

The Nilgiri area, lying between 11°N to 12°N and 76°E to 77°15′E, forms a part of the Western Ghats chain of mountains in southern India. The area is constituted by an upper plateau, with an average elevation of over 1800m, the surrounding plains tapering off in the south to the Palghat gap. Our study area stretches about 80 km east to west and about 50 km north to south (see Map 1). Geologically, the entire area belongs to the continental block of peninsular India made up of metamorphic Archaean rocks.[4] The fault plains in the Nilgiri area suggest considerable tectonic activity causing block upliftment of the Nilgiri massif from the surrounding plains during the late Jurassic period, which is about 160–210 million years ago.

Our cartographic data base of the area starts when it came into the possession of the East India Company after the fall of Tipu Sultan in 1799. The first efforts of the British in the area were to consolidate their position and to gain control over the western and northern portions of the hills. In 1802 Colonel Colin Mackenzie was deputed to survey these hills. He does not seem to have ascended the Nilgiris but his report refers to an account and a map of the hills drawn by his surveyors. These could not be found.[5] Other colonial officers from the collectorate of Coimbatore did discover routes of access to the hills, but there were no detailed maps prepared until 1822. A map and a brief report were prepared by Captain B.S. Ward, showing the early routes to the hills and the progress of European settlements in the Nilgiris.

The next detailed map that forms an important data base for

[3] Quoted in S.N. Prasad (ed.), *Catalogue of Historical Maps of the Survey of India (1700–1900)* (New Delhi, 1989), p. 1.

[4] Hans J. Von Lengerke, *The Nilgiris* (Berlin, 1977), p. 8.

[5] W. Francis, *The Nilgiris* (Madras, 1905), p. 106.

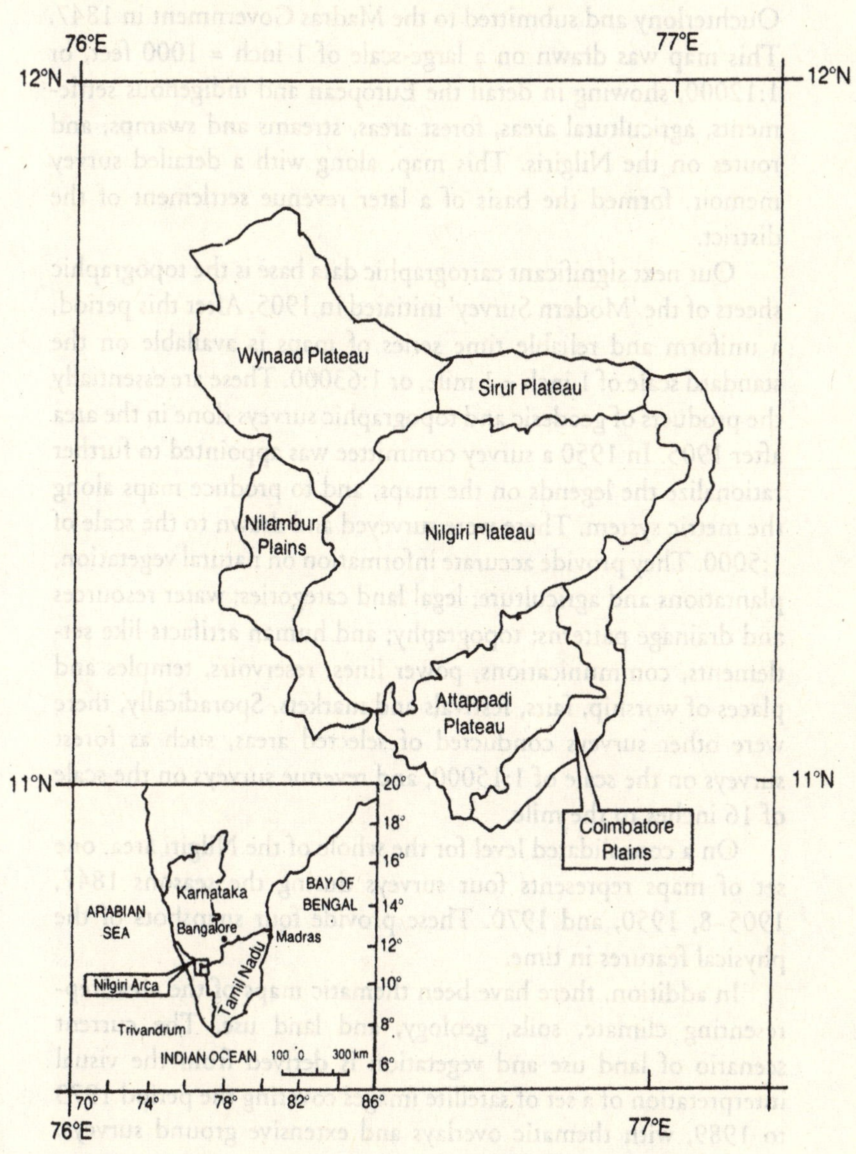


Map 1. Biophysical Zones of the Nilgiri Area.

our study was a consequence of a survey done by Captain Ouchterlony and submitted to the Madras Government in 1847. This map was drawn on a large-scale of 1 inch = 1000 feet, or 1:12000, showing in detail the European and indigenous settlements, agricultural areas, forest areas, streams and swamps, and routes on the Nilgiris. This map, along with a detailed survey memoir, formed the basis of a later revenue settlement of the district.

Our next significant cartographic data base is the topographic sheets of the 'Modern Survey' initiated in 1905. After this period, a uniform and reliable time series of maps is available on the standard scale of 1 inch = 1 mile, or 1:63000. These are essentially the products of geodesic and topographic surveys done in the area after 1905. In 1950 a survey committee was appointed to further rationalize the legends on the maps, and to produce maps along the metric system. These were surveyed and drawn to the scale of 1:5000. They provide accurate information on natural vegetation, plantations and agriculture; legal land categories; water resources and drainage patterns; topography; and human artifacts like settlements, communications, power lines, reservoirs, temples and places of worship, fairs, festivals and markets. Sporadically, there were other surveys conducted of selected areas, such as forest surveys on the scale of 1:15000, and revenue surveys on the scale of 16 inches to the mile.

On a consolidated level for the whole of the Nilgiri area, one set of maps represents four surveys during the seasons 1847, 1905–8, 1950, and 1970. These provide four snapshots of the physical features in time.

In addition, there have been thematic maps of the area, representing climate, soils, geology, and land use. The current scenario of land use and vegetation is derived from the visual interpretation of a set of satellite images covering the period 1973 to 1989, with thematic overlays and extensive ground surveys. These are listed in the Appendix.

For a historical analysis with maps, some features such as topography, climate and geology are invariant over the period in question, i.e. over the two hundred year period. These features, then, form the basis of the biophysical zones of the Nilgiris.

## III. Methodology

We divide the Nilgiri area into six biophysical zones, based on topography and climate. These form an independent variable on which the ecological history of the area is constructed (see Map 1).

1. *The Nilgiri plateau and slopes*: This is formed by the triangular mountain block rising steeply from the surrounding plains with an average elevation of 1800 m. The physiographic and orographic effects combine to give the area a cooler climate than the surrounding plains, and expose the western portions of the plateau to monsoon fury. Thus, it has a rainfall ranging from 1000 mm to 5000 mm. Its natural vegetation is the shola grassland system on the upper plateau, with dense forests on the outer slopes.

2. *The Sigur plateau*: This stretches on the northern side of the Nilgiri hills and forms a part of the Mysore plateau. However, it is separated from the latter by a chasm 300 m deep, known as the Moyar gorge. The Sigur plateau itself is at an elevation of 1000 m. Being on the leeward side of monsoon winds, it receives a very scanty annual rainfall of 500 mm to 1000 mm, but is fed by many streams originating in the Nilgiri plateau. The natural vegetation is mainly dry deciduous, with pockets of scrub in drier places and riverine evergreen vegetation along the perennial streams.

3. *The Coimbatore plains*: These plains stretch on the eastern side of the Nilgiri plateau and are contiguous with the Tamil-nadu plains. The area has an average elevation of 300 m, and receives sporadic rainfall of 1000 mm to 1500 mm, in the winter months, from the north-east monsoon. The area is mainly agricultural, with a few patches of natural vegetation of dry deciduous forests and scrub. There are a few perennial streams and the tract is well endowed with subsoil water.

4. *The Attappadi plateau*: This is a narrow plateau of undulating hills, stretching from the south of the Nilgiri hills to the

Palghat gap, with an average elevation of 800 m. The western portions of the plateau receive heavy monsoon rains, amounting to 2500 mm a year. The annual rainfall declines eastward towards the Coimbatore plains, to 800 mm. The natural vegetation, consequently, ranges from dense evergreen forests in the western portions to dry deciduous and scrub jungle in the eastern parts.

5. *The Nilambur plains*: On the western side of the Nilgiri plateau lies the Chaliyar valley and the Nilambur plains, with an elevation of about 80 m. From here the Nilgiri massif rises steeply to over 2000 m, forming deep and highly eroded escarpments. Open to the western seaboard of the Arabian Sea, it receives a very high rainfall of 2500 mm to 5000 mm. The natural vegetation is dense evergreen forests, with all the altitudinal variations.

6. *The Wynaad plateau*: This is a flat tableland with an average elevation of 800 m. It lies to the west of the Nilgiri hills, forming the south-western extremity of the Mysore plateau. It contains low rounded hills with large swampy valleys. It has a monsoonal climate and receives an annual rainfall of 1500 mm to 2500 mm. The natural vegetation consists of swampy grasslands in the valleys, with dense moist deciduous and evergreen forests on the hill slopes. The area is currently under intensive plantation cropping.

We analyse the ecological changes in these six zones with respect to each of the following parameters:

1. *Land use*: This is represented in the available maps as a colour wash, giving details of agricultural lands, natural forests, commercial plantations, forest plantations and settlement areas. In addition, the survey memoirs give information on agricultural areas and agricultural practices.

2. *Legal and administrative categories of land*: These are marked on the maps and represent revenue lands under the control of the Revenue Department. Such lands are used for agriculture, and for various other purposes which come under open access to local communities. Also represented on these maps are reserved forests under the control of the Forest Department, where local communities have restricted access.

3. *Communications and settlement patterns*: The opening up of hinterlands by communication networks have helped the spread of commercialization and the market economy into remote areas. These have been conduits for resource extraction, leading in many cases to ecological change. The progress of communication networks, faithfully represented on the maps, thus reveals the integration of areas into the market economy.

4. *Water resources*: The utilization and distribution of water resources have played a significant role in agricultural and urban communities. Further, the availability of water, whether seasonal or perennial, is significantly linked to the rainfall and land use patterns in catchment areas. Human artifacts like dams, reservoirs, canals and wells, which have altered the water regime in significant ways, have had consequences for the ecology of many areas. These water resources have been well represented in historical maps of the Nilgiri area.

## IV. Analysis and Results

Based upon our cartographic data base and survey memoirs, we analyse each of the biophysical zones and draw inferences on the process of ecological change. Further, we attempt a more formal quantitative analysis for the Attappadi biophysical zone.

1. *The Nilgiri plateau and slopes*: The Nilgiri plateau, with an area of 1686.44 $km^2$ was considered an isolated tribal enclave of peninsular India during the pre-colonial period. However, the evidence of routes suggests that the Nilgiri plateau had regular contact with the northern areas of Devarayapatna in Mysore, and with the Kongu region, stretching to the Coimbatore plains. The area seems to have been administered from a place called Denaikenkotai in the north-eastern tip of the plateau. The presence of many antiquities and forts on the northern prominences of the Nilgiri plateau suggests that the area was in regular contact with the surrounding country. Early surveys of 1812 record three routes to the plateau, one from the north-east, one from the north, and the other from the south-west. None of these was suitable for

wheeled traffic and thus most of the communication and trade was on foot, although it is asserted that Tipu Sultan carried up some cannons and horses to the forts on the northern prominences overlooking Mysore territory.[6] The settled villages were confined to the eastern and northern portions of the plateau, and so was agriculture.[7] The western portions of the plateau were mainly pastoral. Locally by custom, the area was divided into three territories: Porunganad to the east, Maikanad to the south, and Todanad to the west. William Keys notes that there were 41 principal and 119 subordinate villages. However reliable or unreliable the actual numbers may be, most of the agricultural villages were small, consisting of about four to six houses in a row, surrounded by agricultural fields.[8] Village hamlets were often in clusters of three or four within one kilometre of each other.[9] The only large and well-settled villages were the Kota villages, distributed evenly all over the plateau. Their main activity, in addition to subsistence agriculture, was to provide artisanal services to the agriculturist Badagas on the plateau. Each village had forty to fifty houses, arranged in neat rows.[10] On the north-eastern and south-eastern slopes, in the flat portions of the steep valleys, there were a few Irula and Kurumba villages that subsisted with some shifting cultivation in the fertile valleys, augmented by the gathering of numerous sorts of forest produce for both subsistence and trade.[11]

The soils of the cultivated areas were very fertile and well looked after.[12] On the flat upper plateau, cultivation was done with the use of the plough, and with two cropping seasons each

[6] Letter from William Keys, Assistant Surveyor, to W. Garrow, Collector of Coimbatore, 1812, in 'A Topographical Description of the Neelaghery Mountains', in H.B. Grigg, *A Manual of the Nilagiri District in the Madras Presidency* (Madras, 1880), Appendix 17, pp. xlvii–li.

[7] B.S. Ward, 'Geographical and Statistical Survey of the Nealgherry Mountains' 1822, in Grigg, *Manual of the Nilagiri District*, Appendix 20, pp. lx–lxxviii.

[8] Keys, 1812.

[9] Ward, 1822.

[10] Ibid.

[11] Ibid.

[12] Ibid.

year. Early estimates of the total agricultural lands on the plateau were fixed at about fourteen square miles or 3625.2 ha, i.e. 2.25 per cent of the total land area.[13]

The western portions of the plateau were largely uncultivated. They were used as seasonal grazing grounds by Toda buffalo keepers during the dry months of January to March. There were no permanent habitations in the area, only several seasonally-used buffalo penning sites.[14] There were brooks and streams on the plateau but practically no irrigation.

It was upon this scene that the Europeans descended in the first half of the nineteenth century. Discovering the cool environment of the hills, they established many routes to the upper plateau. By 1850 they had set up townships, municipalities and sanatoriums at Kotagiri, Wellington and Coonoor on the eastern side of the hills, and Ootacamund towards the west.[15] These townships and municipalities became centres of immigration, drawing a large number of people from the plains of Coimbatore and Mysore. By 1847, at the time of the Ouchterlony Survey, the immigrant population was 8887, slightly higher than the indigenous population of 7704 persons.[16]

The agricultural area expanded fourfold during this period, to 12718 ha, and many marginal lands were put under shifting cultivation. All this expansion was still confined to the northern and eastern parts of the plateau. The western parts were relatively untouched by all this activity, although two routes had been established westwards, one via the Sispara pass and Silent Valley to the Nilambur plains, the other via Gudalur towards Mysore.[17] There were some experiments with tea and coffee on the hills.[18]

[13] Keys, 1812.

[14] Ibid.

[15] Major J. Ouchterlony's, *Map of the Neilgherry Mountains upon a scale of 1000 ft. = 1 inch or 1:12000*, 1847.

[16] J. Ouchterlony, 'Geographical and Statistical Memoir of the Neilgherry Mountains, under the Superintendence of Captain J. Ouchterlony', *Madras Journal of Literature and Science*, 15 January–December 1848, pp. 1–138.

[17] Ouchterlony, 1847.

[18] Ouchterlony, 1847, and 'Statistical Memoir', 1848.

Europeans and immigrants from the plains had already begun to see the brooks and streams as a resource. They had plans for the utilization of water for agricultural expansion, and by 1847 they had built the Ooty lake, with plans for harnessing other streams in the Nilgiris.

By the beginning of the twentieth century, communications were well established all over the Nilgiri hills. The main route to the plains was via Coonoor, the railway route having already been laid from Mettupalayam to Ootacamund. The centre of trade and commercial activity shifted from Kotagiri to Coonoor. On the western side, the route over Kundahs was abandoned and a new route to the Kerala plains opened via Gudalur. A network of roads opened out southwards from Coonoor, bringing the southern fringes of the Nilgiri hills in proximity to markets. Plantation crops like tea and coffee, first experimented with on the northern slopes, spread to the southern side. These areas, with an altitude of 1200 m to 1800 m, were ideally suited for plantation crops. These occupied 18.75 $km^2$ as one continuous patch.[19]

The western side of the plateau was still unpopulated. By this period the European elite, concerned with the destruction of the sholas, introduced many exotic plantation crops to meet the fuelwood requirements of the population, and they reserved uninhabited areas and remaining sholas all over the plateau. Thus, by 1905, eighty per cent of the lands of Ootacamund taluk and forty per cent of Coonoor taluk were declared as reserved in over 400 small and large patches under the Madras Forest Act of 1882.

By the 1950s the road communication networks had further expanded into the western portions of the hills. Tea plantations were experimented with in these inhospitable areas. In the southern fringes, many forested tracts were converted into coffee estates, utilizing virgin soils in the area, under the micro-climate provided by natural forest vegetation. Tea and coffee estates expanded

[19] Survey of India, 58A, 1922, Survey Year 1905–8.

during this period from 18.75 $km^2$ to 47 $km^2$, mainly in the southern portion of the hills.

It was also during this period that water resources in the area began to be harnessed to generate electricity. A series of dams and reservoirs was built, which significantly altered the water regimes. This was to have important consequences for the ecology of the lower hills. On the Nilgiri hills themselves, most of this activity was confined to the western portion. The reservoir and dam-construction activity itself had major ecological consequences. These areas had been relatively undisturbed and were the only remnants of the original vegetation within the Nilgiri hills. They were penetrated with a network of roads, and the influx of a large labour force led to the destruction of sholas around the reservoirs. The Pykara Reservoir, built in 1932, had a waterspread of 4 $km^2$ and a catchment area of 185 $km^2$. This scheme linked up the northern streams of the Moyar catchment; these had consequences for the Sigur plateau which will be discussed later.

The modern period is marked by a massive growth in communication networks; the growth of non-agricultural labour settlements; the large-scale conversion of reserve forest areas into forest plantations; a massive manipulation of the water regime by dams and reservoirs; the conversion of agricultural and degraded lands into tea plantations; and the degradation of the Nilgiri slopes into scrub vegetation.[20]

The Kundah range, the last hinterland area without communication networks, was suddenly opened up by roads for the development of hydro-electric schemes. Over 90 per cent of the catchment of the Bhavani was bound with a network of reservoirs to generate power.[21] With it came settlements to provide labour and other services for their construction and maintenance.[22] The series of dams built did not essentially change the land use patterns on the hills, but they made many of the streams flowing southward

20 Satellite Image Interpretation of LANDSAT TM, 6 February 1989.

21 Survey of India, 58A, 1981, Survey Year 1974.

22 Ibid.

and eastward seasonal, which had consequences for land use on the lower hills.

With the impetus given by the National Forest Policy of 1952, large areas under the control of the Forest Department were converted to plantations to provide raw material to industry. Attempts were made to covert over 90 per cent of the grasslands into wattle and eucalyptus plantations. These failed on the western fringes of the plateau because of frost and the fury of the monsoon. In other areas, plantations became an industry and supported a large immigrant labour force that encroached on government lands. Agriculture witnessed a marginal expansion with attempts to settle Toda graziers. Because of the loss of tree cover in the southern portions, soil fertility and the micro-climate had changed. Consequently, many coffee plantations were replaced by the hardier tea plantations. Other areas degraded into scrubland.

Table I summarizes the ecological changes on the Nilgiri plateau; Map 2 shows important landscape changes during the period.

*The Sigur plateau*: This plateau, with an area of 281.25 km$^2$, had been a major population centre during the pre-colonial period, being at the tri-junction of the Tamil plains, the Mysore plateau and the Wynaad area. It had many settled agricultural villages along the perennial streams and was a major communications route. The many ruins of forts, as well as indications of bridle tracks criss-crossing the area, reveal that Tipu Sultan had significant control over the area on account of its strategic importance in his fight against the British. Thus, when it came into the possession of the British after the fall of Tipu in 1799, early surveyors set down much detail on this area, as revealed in Ward's map of 1822.[23] Ward's map shows the area thickly forested by teak trees in the western portions, with sandal trees towards the east. It shows roads through the area leading to Wynaad in the west and Devarayapatna in the north. All the routes to the Nilgiri plateau were from this area. There were three perennial streams,

23 B.S. Ward, *Map of the Neelgherry Mountains*, 1822.

Table I
Ecological Changes on the Nilgiri Plateau

| *Year* | *Land use* | *Communications and Settlements* | *Legal Categories* | *Water Resources* |
|---|---|---|---|---|
| 1847 | Subsistence agriculture in north and east. Seasonal grazing in west. Tea, coffee and fuelwood plantations | Agricultural settlements in north and east. Three urban settlements. Routes to the plains through the north | Land controlled by local communities and Europeans | Many streams and springs. One water body at Ooty |
| 1905 | Tea and coffee plantations in the south (18.75 $km^2$) Forest plantations (6 $km^2$) | Urban settlements larger. Main road and railway through Coonoor. Roads into southern portions. Routes towards the west | Revenue and forest settlement. 55 per cent of area reserved as forests | Increase in irrigated agriculture. One more water body in the east |
| 1950 | Coffee and tea plantations in south (47 $km^2$). Forest plantations (18 $km^2$) | All settlements larger. Labour settlements in interior areas. Communication networks into south-west | Forest land leased to Electricity Board | Pykara hydro-electric scheme executed with catchment of 185 $km^2$ |
| 1990 | Commercial agriculture in north and east. Conversion of coffee and agriculture to tea. Increase in scrublands on outer slopes | Urban settlements larger. Permanent settlements on encroached lands. Routes to all parts of the hills | Encroachments on revenue and leased lands | Kundah hydro-electric scheme executed. High siltation into reservoirs |

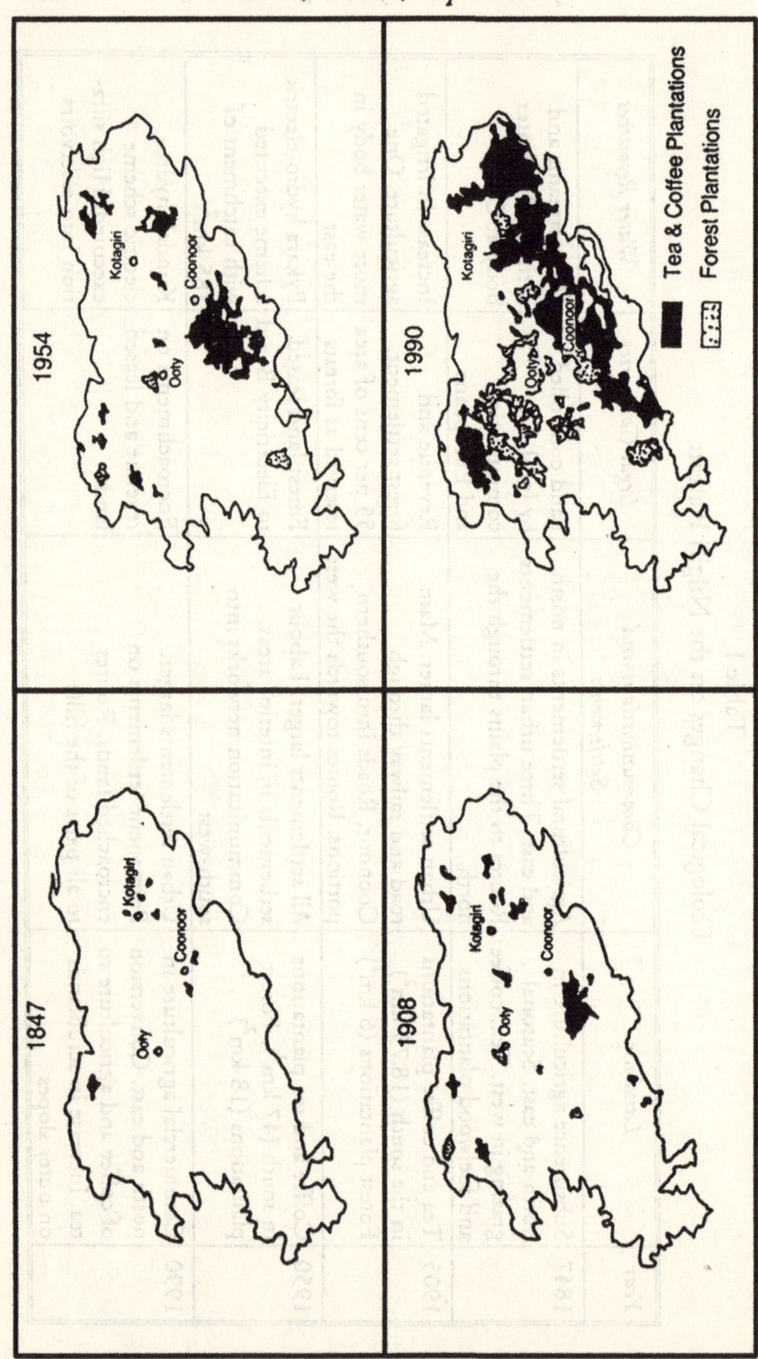


Map 2. Landscape Changes on the Nilgiri Plateau.

along which were settlements. Some of these streams had canals branching off for the irrigation of paddy lands.[24]

The map notes eight inhabited villages, seven abandoned villages and a couple of temples in the area. 'It is plain that it had been more largely cultivated some years back, and had likewise some paddy fields; but the depredations of wild elephants of late and the diminution of hands have almost laid it desolate'.[25]

The British considered the plateau highly malarial and did not venture there in the wet season. Early attempts to expand agriculture into the area with commercial crops like cotton failed. But during the second half of the nineteenth century they extracted valuable timber, which was used as building material for townships in the Nilgiris. The Sigur ghat was also opened up and formed the main route into the Nilgiris from Mysore.[26]

At the beginning of the nineteenth century the agricultural area constituted 4.2 km$^2$, i.e. 1.4 per cent of the total. This was not much more than existed in 1822. But in forest clearings, coffee plantations were tried. They constituted about 1 km$^2$ in the western portions. By this period the whole area was reserved under forest reservation laws, and commercial timber removed. There were many seasonal cattle-penning sites in the reserved forests which were frequented by Badaga agriculturists of the Nilgiri plateau. Along the Mysore route, a new township had come up at Masinagudi. It provided trade and services to coffee plantations and travellers.

There were no major changes till the 1950s, when hydro-electric projects were established on the Sigur plateau. This was a part of the Pykara hydroelectric system that diverted the Pykara's westward-flowing water onto the Sigur plateau. Construction activity further increased the township of Masinagudi. It was during this time that malaria was eradicated, and this too contributed to immigration.

[24] Keys, 1812.
[25] Ibid.
[26] Survey of India, 58A, 1922.

The modern period has been marked by a decrease in agriculture, declaration of forest lands as a wildlife sanctuary, water shortage due to the seasonality of two of the earlier perennial streams, and increased scrubland in the area.[27]

As a consequence of the increased utilization of water in the upper plateau for intensive agriculture, two of the major streams watering the Sigur plateau have become seasonal. Agricultural areas have thus shrunk to less than 200 ha.[28] Further, because of overgrazing by an increased cattle and buffalo population concentrated near water-holes and milk-collection centres, areas around them have degenerated into thorny scrub.[29] The declaration of 60 km$^2$ of the plateau as part of a wildlife sanctuary brought increased tourism alongside the growth of the Masinagudi township. Coffee estates have deteriorated as a consequence of changes in the micro-climate, brought about by a decrease in forest cover, and many have since been abandoned.

Table II summarizes the ecological changes on the Sigur plateau; Map 3 shows important landscape changes during the period.

3. *The Wynaad plateau*: Little is known of the Wynaad plateau, with an area of 1048 km$^2$, during the pre-colonial period. Even after the fall of Tipu there was independent resistance in this area. It is first mentioned in the Ouchterlony survey memoir of 1847.[30] Detailed maps of the area are available only from the 1900s. From these, inferences are drawn to indicate that during the pre-colonial period the area was thickly forested with evergreen and moist deciduous trees. Major portions of it did not contain permanent settlements but were, all the same, used by tribal communities for hunting and gathering. Permanent settlements with settled agriculture existed only in a few swampy lands where paddy was cultivated.

By 1847 a rough track was established from the Nilgiri hills through Gudalur to Sultan's Battery in the Wynaad. The area was

27 LANDSAT TM, 1989 and Survey of India, 58A, 1981.

28 Survey of India, 58A, 1981, *ibid.*

29 LANDSAT TM, 1989.

30 Ouchterlony, 1848.

Table II
Ecological Changes on the Sigur Plateau

| *Year* | *Land use* | *Communications and Settlements* | *Legal Categories* | *Water Resources* |
|---|---|---|---|---|
| 1812 | Six patches of dryland agriculture. Teak forests in west and sandal trees in east | Few settled villages. Many abandoned villages. Routes to Wynaad, Mysore, Coimbatore and Nilgiris | Lands under local control | Perennial streams: Minor irrigation works in disuse |
| 1905 | Coffee estates towards the west | One trade and communication settlement | Most of the plateau as reserved forest | Few perennial streams |
| 1950 | Increase in grazing | Interior areas opened up by game roads. Trade and communication centre larger | No change | Hydroelectric schemes initiated |
| 1990 | Decrease in agricultural area. Increase in scrubland | Unprecedented growth of township | Wildlife sanctuary declared (60 $km^2$) | Two perennial streams become seasonal |

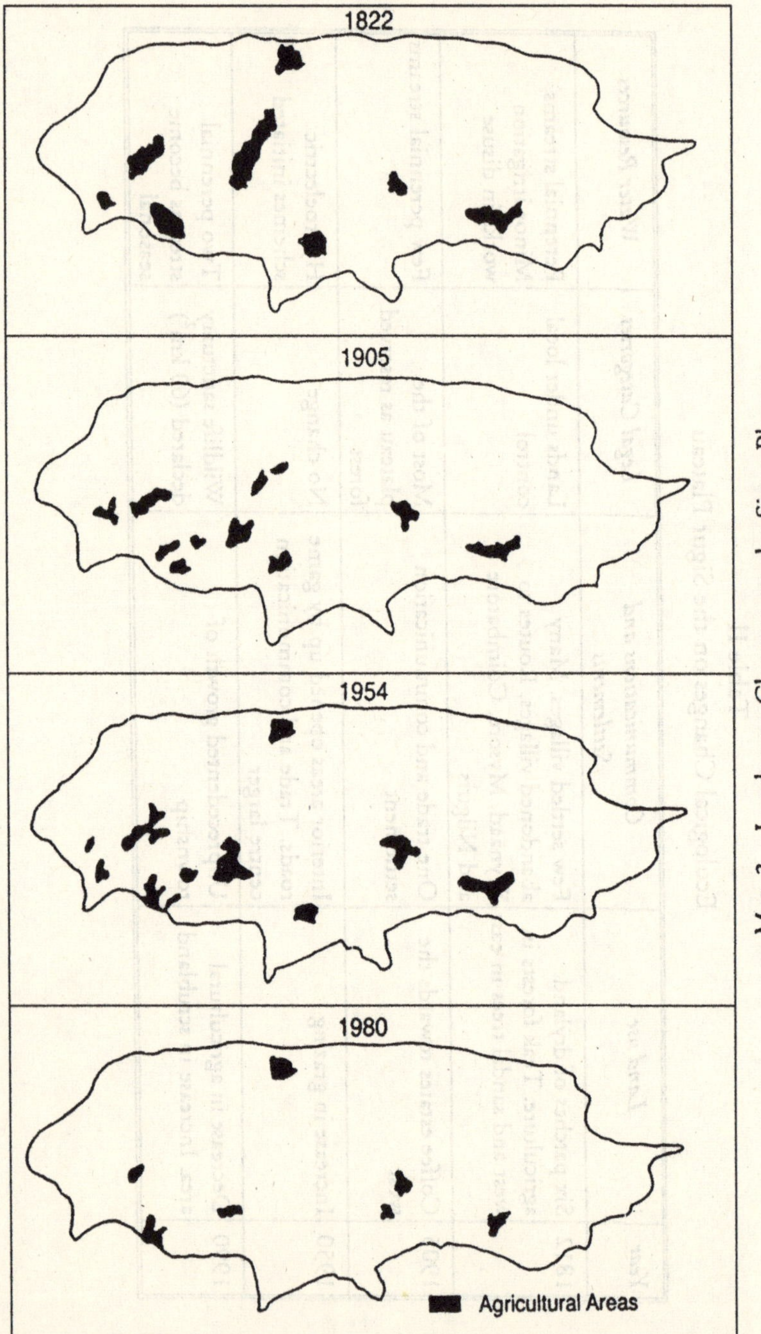


Map 3. Landscape Changes on the Sigur Plateau.

surveyed in 1847 and pronounced very suitable for coffee plantations.[31] By 1905 regular communication routes for wheeled traffic were established, and coffee estates had spread to cover an area of about 25 km$^2$. There was a well-established European community in the plantation area with its own settlements and recreation centres. The northern portions of the Wynaad, rich in teak trees, were constituted into reserved forests by 1905 under the Forest Act of 1882, with an area of 281 km$^2$. These forests were regularly worked and teak trees harvested to build townships on the Nilgiri plateau.

By 1950 Gudalur had become a trade and communications centre, with roads leading to Mysore, the Kerala plains and the Nilgiris. With the eradication of malaria, the area drew immigrants from Kerala and Mysore, and Gudalur became the most important town in Wynaad. Tea and coffee estates spread in the area occupying a total of 130 km$^2$ by the end of this period.

In recent times the area has seen an unprecedented growth of settlements. Ambiguous legal land categorization and political reorganization of the linguistic states brought waves of immigrants from Kerala. Forested areas were cleared for agriculture and cultivation, and the government took over 800 ha, converting them to tea estates to settle refugees from Sri Lanka. While lands were under litigation between the Forest Department and immigrants, forested areas were being clear-felled and cultivation expanded. Thus, at the end of this period, except for the reserve forest of 281 km$^2$ and 1200 ha of other forest,[32] all the other areas were converted to intensive agriculture and plantation crops. About 260 km$^2$ of forest lands in the northern portion were declared a sanctuary and forest workings in them were minimized.

Table III summarizes the ecological change in the Wynaad area.

4. *The Nilambur plains*: The first detailed map of the Nilambur area of 265 km$^2$ was after the 1905–8 survey of the area.

[31] Ibid.

[32] Survey of India, 58A, 1974, Survey Years 1954–1955.

Table III
Ecological Changes on the Wynaad Plateau

| *Year* | *Land use* | *Communications and Settlements* | *Legal Categories* | *Water Resources* |
|---|---|---|---|---|
| 1800 | Agriculture limited to few swamps. Other areas thickly forested | No major communication links | Lands held by chieftains and temple | Many perennial streams |
| 1905 | Coffee estates in forest clearings (25 $km^2$). Forests worked | European settlements around estates. Routes to Nilgiri, Sultan's Battery and Kerala plains | Northern portions reserved. Other areas leased from chieftain | No change |
| 1950 | Agriculture expands. Tea and coffee plantations larger (130 $km^2$) | Gudalur settlement as trade and communications centre. Routes to Nilgiri, Kerala and Mysore. Game roads in forested areas | No change | No change |
| 1990 | Forests cleared for agriculture and plantations | Increased communication in south and west | Change in land categories. Reserved forests declared a sanctuary | No change |

In the pre-colonial period parts of the Nilambur plains adjacent to the Nilgiri hills were densely covered with lowland evergreen forests, inhabited by a few hunter-gatherer tribal societies. The flatlands of the Nilambur plains were cultivated. By tradition, the forested areas were called temple lands and were held with the temple of the area. On the periphery of the forest there were a few teak and other commercial timber trees.

By 1905 Nilambur had become an important trade, communications and administrative settlement. It was on the main route connecting the Kerala plains with Mysore and the Nilgiris. Realizing the importance of teak, efforts were made to raise plantations of this species. This, the first attempt by the British to grow teak artificially in India, proved successful on the Nilambur plains. Rubber was also experimented with as a plantation crop during this period. The thickly-forested hill areas were reserved under the Forest Act of 1882 and many of the accessible areas worked for timber.

By 1950 the railway line was extended to Nilambur with the sole purpose of exporting sleeper timber for railway expansion from the evergreen forest around the Nilambur area, and on the slopes of the Nilgiri hills. The rubber plantations had established themselves in the Nilambur plains, where the climate was most appropriate. They were confined to an area of about 12 $km^2$ on the forest fringe at the edge of the plains.

During the recent period, large areas of the plains have been converted to rubber plantations. On forest department lands, about 25 $km^2$ of forests were clear-felled and converted to teak and other timber plantations.[33] On the fringes of the forests, new settlements were established which provided labour for rubber plantations and forest work.

Table IV summarizes ecological change in the Nilambur plains.

5. *The Attappadi plateau*: We attempt a quantitative analysis for the landscape changes in the Attappadi plateau with an area of 806.25 $km^2$ during the historical period. The earliest

[33] Survey of India, 58A, 1981, ibid.

Table IV
Ecological Changes on the Nilambur Plains

| *Year* | *Land use* | *Communications and Settlements* | *Legal Categories* | *Water Resources* |
|---|---|---|---|---|
| 1800 | Densely forested hills. Flat lands under cultivation | Few permanent settlements | Forested lands under traditional temple control | Many perennial streams |
| 1905 | Teak and rubber plantations on the forest fringes | Nilambur town becomes a trade, communication and administrative centre. Routes to Kerala, Mysore and Nilgiris | Forested areas reserved | No change |
| 1950 | Rubber plantations in the plains | No change | No change | No change |
| 1990 | Timber and rubber plantations increase. Agriculture expands | Nilambur town expands. New labour settlements in forest fringes | No change | No change |

maps of the area date from 1905; and we have four data points for the landscape from that time to the present.

In the pre-colonial period the Attappadi area was mainly inhabited by tribal communities growing a variety of crops by shifting cultivation, along the perennial streams and water courses. The area was watered by two perennial streams from the south and three from the north, joining into the main Bhavani river that flows eastward through the plateau. This thickly-forested area was an important source of minor forest produce in the form of roots and herbs collected and traded for medicinal use.

The first available maps, those of 1905, show 89 km$^2$ of the Silent Valley designated as reserved forest, and the remaining land under local control. Minor routes extended towards the Coimbatore plains in the east and Mannarkad in the west. Agriculture was limited to about 22.5 km$^2$ in thirty-six patches all over the northern portions of the plateau. These were mainly small patches of shifting cultivation used with an intervening fallow period.

By 1954 communications into the plateau were opened up from the Coimbatore plains, bringing in agricultural immigrants who occupied the flat valley bottoms on the banks of the Bhavani river. A large patch of about 60 km$^2$ thus came under annual cultivation. Shifting cultivation tribals were displaced to the slopes of the hills. The total agricultural area of about 109 km$^2$ increased to about 171 km$^2$ by 1975. Smaller patches along the slopes were completely inadequate for rotation, and much of this area degraded into scrub. A series of dams, built on the upper plateau in the 1970s, made the two perennial streams on the northern side of the plateau seasonal. This transformed these regions of the plateau into dry scrubland too, and much of the agriculture now shifted southward.

During this period communication links were established with the Kerala plains in the west. A wave of colonizers from the west occupied the south-western portions of the plateau, converting the forests into a variety of garden and plantation crops. By 1989 this had come to occupy about 66 km$^2$.[34]

[34] LANDSAT TM, 1989, *ibid.*

Table V
Patch Size Distribution of Agriculture on the Attappadi Plateau

| *Patch Size* * $6.25\ km^2$ | *1908* | | *1954* | | *1974* | | *1989* | |
|---|---|---|---|---|---|---|---|---|
| | *No.* | *Area* | *No.* | *Area* | *No.* | *Area* | *No.* | *Area* |
| < 0.1 | 27 | 1.51 | 15 | 0.8 | 1 | 0.05 | 4 | 0.24 |
| 0.1 – 1.0 | 9 | 2.09 | 9 | 2.13 | 7 | 2.65 | 5 | 0.85 |
| 1.0 – 5.0 | 0 | 0 | 3 | 4.9 | 1 | 1.45 | 0 | 0 |
| 5.0 – 10.0 | 0 | 0 | 1 | 9.59 | 1 | 8.15 | 1 | 5.25 |
| > 10.0 | 0 | 0 | 0 | 0 | 1 | 15.12 | 1 | 17.83 |
| Total | 32 | * | 28 | * | 11 | * | 11 | * |
| Total agricultural area | 3.60 | | 17.37 | | 27.4 | | 24.17 | |

For a formal analysis of the landscape, we calculate the area of each agricultural patch for each of the years 1903, 1954, 1974, and 1989. Their patch size distribution is shown in Table V. In 1908, all the agriculture was in shifting cultivation patches of below 6 km², distributed along the perennial streams of the area. These patches were rotated around favourable sites which were numerous in the Attappadi area. By 1954 immigrant agriculturists from the Coimbatore plains had settled permanently in the Bhavani Valley and 55 per cent of the agricultural land was aggregated into one large patch of 65 km². By 1989, with immigration from the surrounding areas, 73.8 per cent of the land was aggregated into one large area of permanently used agricultural land, marginalizing the small shifting cultivation plots to just 1 per cent of the total agricultural area.

Table VI summarizes the ecological changes on the Attappadi plains; Map 4 shows changes in the landscape during this period.

6. *The Coimbatore plains*: With an area of 750 km², the Coimbatore plains were a major agricultural area during the pre-colonial period. They had agricultural settlements typical of the Tamilnadu plains, formed by both agricultural and artisanal com-

Table VI
Ecological Changes on the Attappadi Plateau

| *Year* | *Land use* | *Communications and Settlements* | *Legal Categories* | *Water Resources* |
|---|---|---|---|---|
| 1800 | Densely forested. Shifting cultivation in patches | Paths towards east: to the Coimbatore plains | Local chieftain control | Many perennial streams |
| 1905 | No change | Paths towards east and west | Small forested areas reserved | No change |
| 1954 | Settled agriculture. Forest degraded and reduced | Road linked to Coimbatore plains. New settlements along the river | Immigration and Encroachments | No change |
| 1975 | No shifting cultivation. Settled agriculture shifting southward. Forest degraded to scrub | Road linked to Coimbatore and Kerala. New settlements in the south-west | No change | Perennial streams in northern parts become seasonal |
| 1989 | Garden and plantation agriculture in the south-west | Settlements in the south-west increase | No change | Perennial streams in southern parts become seasonal |

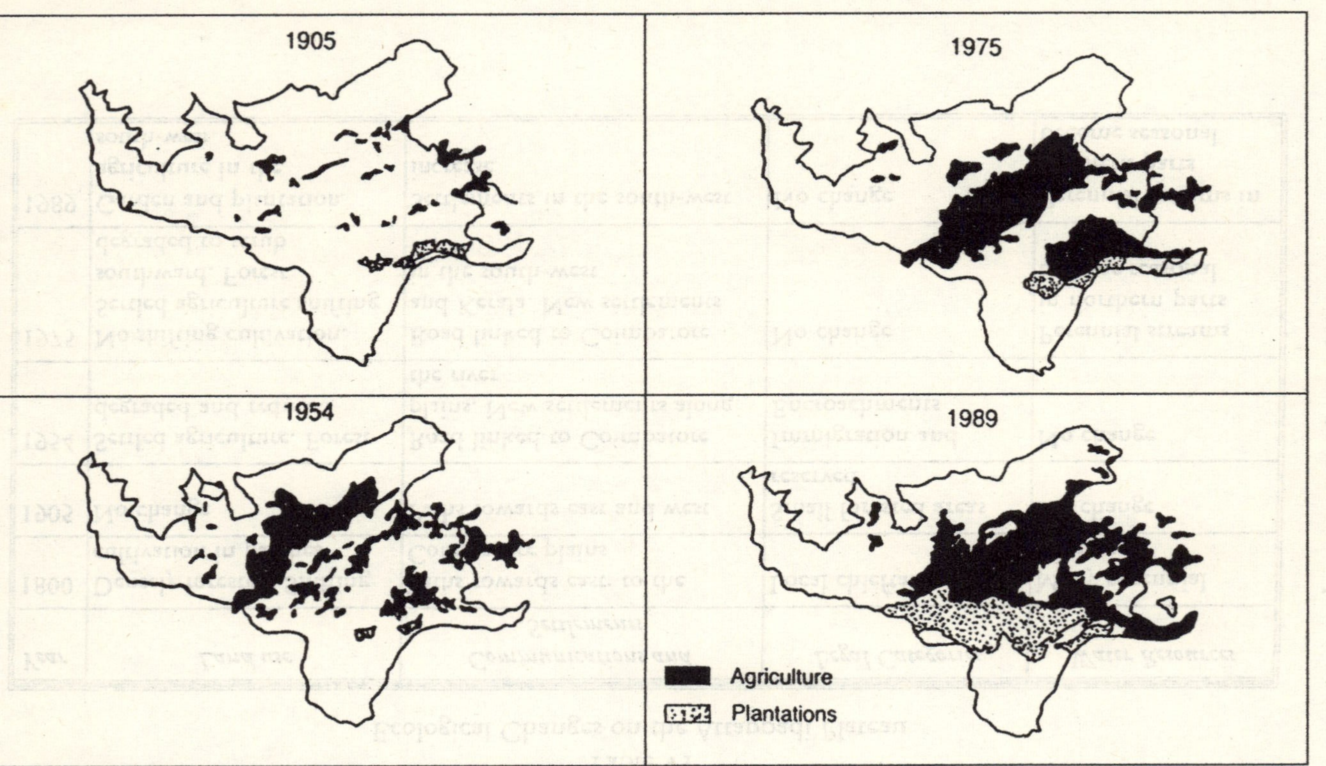


Map 4. Landscape Changes on the Attapadi Plateau.

munities. Wells and lift irrigation were prevalent in this area. To the east and north were the hills of the Nilgiri and Mysore plateau respectively. These were thickly forested and inhabited by tribal communities practising shifting cultivation and collecting forest produce for barter with the agricultural communities of the plains. Many routes passed through the area, connecting Mysore, Wynaad, the Kerala plains and the Tamilnadu plains.[35] The Coimbatore plains came into the possession of the British after the defeat of Tipu Sultan in 1799. The British established their administrative centre at Coimbatore, and soon it became an important trade and communication centre.

By 1850 routes to Mysore and the Nilgiris passed through Coimbatore. The forested tracts adjoining the hills were thus opened up for exploitation. Agriculture had spread to the foot of these hills and tribal communities inhabiting the area were pushed further up the hill slopes of the Nilgiris.

The 1905 map shows patches of cultivation all along the slopes of the hills: permanent cultivation had spread along the streams and communication routes of the Coimbatore plains. The remaining forests adjoining the hills towards the west and north were reserved, limiting the further spread of agricultural areas. The 1905 map shows some of the agricultural settlements on the hills as being abandoned, possibly as a consequence of the famine of 1876–8.[36] In addition to being an important administrative and trade centre, Coimbatore became an important railway junction, with tracks leading to Kerala in the west and Mettupalayam and the Nilgiri hills to the north.

By the 1950s Coimbatore had grown in size and stature to become an industrial town, drawing in waves of immigrants. In the perennial river valleys some plantations had spread and many dry agricultural areas were irrigated by means of wells. The Noyil river basin was one such region where lift irrigation was practised. During this period roads were laid into the hill slopes and into

[35] Ward, 1822.

[36] Survey of India, 58E/3, 1927, Survey Years 1905–8.

the Attappadi plateau, which opened up areas for the emigration of agriculturists from the Coimbatore plains.

During the recent period the increase in lift irrigation by deep borewells has significantly lowered the water table in the area, leading to the abandoning of cultivation in large tracts. This has also led to an increase in scrub vegetation on the hillsides and the foothills of the region. With a fall in agriculture and an increase in efficient communication networks, many small industrial townships have sprung up over the entire area.

Table VII summarizes ecological changes in the Coimbatore plains.

## V. Summary and Conclusions

A study of the time series of maps for the Nilgiri yield a history of the landscape of the area which has implications for changes in resource use patterns. In the pre-colonial period resource flows were localized in each of the bio-physical zones. The area supported a wide spectrum of communities from hunting-gathering and pastoral communities to subsistence agriculture and artisanal communities. These communities interacted among themselves in the exchange of goods and services. The area also had cultural links with the larger south Indian civilization. There were many trade and communication routes passing through the lower plateau, some of which led up to the northern ridges of the higher plateau. However, there was no large-scale export of resources from the area, other than certain special forest products like medicines and honey.

The British gained control of the area after the defeat of Tipu in 1799. Their earliest efforts were to consolidate their control over the area. They discovered the cool climate of the Nilgiri plateau and concerted attempts were made to establish a European colony in the hills. Townships and cantonments were established; routes were laid to the hills from the surrounding plains; agricultural stations were set up to experiment with and acclimatize temperate plants; and the immigration of people from surrounding areas was

Table VII
Ecological Changes in the Coimbatore Plains

| *Year* | *Land use* | *Communications and Settlements* | *Legal Categories* | *Water Resources* |
|---|---|---|---|---|
| 1800 | Mainly agricultural. Hill slopes thickly forested, also under shifting cultivation | Agricultural settlements. Routes to Kerala plains, Mysore, and Tamil plains | Lands under local control | Some perennial streams, well and lift irrigation |
| 1905 | Agriculture spread to foot-hills. Forest workings | Coimbatore a trade, communication and administrative centre. Routes to Nilgiris, Mysore, Kerala and Tamil plains. Railway lines to Kerala and Nilgiris | Forested areas in the hills reserved | No change |
| 1950 | Hill slopes degraded into scrub | Coimbatore township larger and becomes industrial. Communications extended into hills | No change | Well and lift irrigation increased |
| 1990 | Increase in scrubland. Reduction in agricultural area | Coimbatore township larger. Growth of small industrial towns | No change | Depletion of subsoil water |

encouraged to provide the necessary services. Consequently, agriculture expanded in the Nilgiri hills. The surrounding plateaus and plains were relatively undisturbed during this first phase of colonial rule. But during this period an infrastructure was created and commercial experiments, such as tea plantations and mining for gold, were tried. However, major resource flows were still confined within the area, and there was an inflow of resources in the nature of immigration, infrastructure and biota from outside.

By 1905 coffee and tea had established themselves as significant commercial crops. Large areas on the Nilgiri and Wynaad plateaus were cleared of natural vegetation and commercially exploited with tea and coffee plantations, integrating the area with the global market. The remaining natural forests on the Nilgiri plateau were legally 'reserved' for their aesthetic and recreational appeal to the colonists, whereas forests with valuable timber species in the Wynaad and Sigur plateau were reserved for commercial exploitation, to the exclusion of the rights of local inhabitants. The pauperization of the surrounding areas in the Coimbatore plains and Mysore provided the much needed immigrant labour force for a commercialization of the Nilgiri plateau. Thus, but for the plantation crops and the expansion of agriculture to meet the requirements of the towns and settlements in and around the area, resource flows were still confined to the local area.

By the 1950s the favourable areas in the Nilgiri plateau had been completely converted to commercial tea and coffee plantations. Along with this, communication networks and settlements expanded in these areas. In the lower plateau a network of roads was selectively built to penetrate into areas that had commercial timber. In other areas subsistence and commercial mixed agriculture expanded with the entry of immigrants from the surrounding areas.

In the recent period the landscape of the Nilgiris has been significantly altered. With the encouragement of government policies, the natural resources of the area have been exploited for the larger 'national' interest. Thus, with the new forest policy of 1952, commercial forest plantations expanded to provide raw materials at highly subsidized rates to forest-based industries. Plantations of wattle and eucalyptus were established in remote areas. Under the 'grow more food' campaign of the agriculture department, the expansion, intensification and commercialization of agriculture were encouraged. The water resources of the area were extensively tapped by setting up a series of dams and reservoirs for the generation of power. These activities were accompanied by a network of communication routes in hitherto inaccessible areas. Settlements sprang up all over, and the natural vegetation was confined to limited areas where the government had established national parks and sanctuaries. The borders between such areas and the transformed areas became very sharp, bringing conservation objectives in direct conflict with the people. Now resource flows reached an unprecedented scale. A wide variety of agricultural and natural products were brought into the market economy. The indigenous inhabitants, mainly forest dwellers and hunting and gathering communities, were completely marginalized, with much reduced access to their subsistence resources. They had to depend mainly on labour for their livelihood. Agriculturists were at the mercy of market forces to provide inputs for their agriculture and markets for their produce, leaving small patches of subsistence agriculture in areas that were not suitable for commercial crop production and were inaccessible to markets.

The following conclusions are drawn from this study of the Nilgiri hills.

1. During the period 1800–1990, human activity has been the most significant force in transforming the landscape.
2. Each bio-physical zone has imposed its own range of possibilities and constraints in determining human activity.
3. Over the period in question, there has been a differentiation of access to natural resources with an increasing role for the state and corporate sectors.
4. There has been an increasing influx of market forces mediated by the spread of communications and labour settlements across the entire landscape.
5. During the period there has been a sequential exploitation of

resources: from more accessible areas to less accessible areas; and from a limited range of exploitable and marketable resources to a more diverse set of resources. These have been mediated by the development of infrastructure, communications and technologies.

6. There has been an increase in the scale of resource flows, from being confined within the geographical area to expanding into larger and larger domains.

7. These have caused large-scale transformations of the landscape from natural vegetation to man-made vegetation. Natural areas have been confined to state-protected areas such as national parks and sanctuaries.

8. Time series maps, representing selected landscape features at the time of the survey, are efficient markers of ecological change. However, they do not contain information on cropping patterns, forest types, or the socio-economic and cultural characteristics of the population which comprises the principal actors in the process of ecological change. This information needs to be added to the historical maps in order to create a comprehensive account of the ecological history of the Nilgiris.

## APPENDIX: Thematic Maps and Satellite Images Used

1. J.P. Pascal, *Bioclimates of the Western Ghats* (Pondicherry, 1974).
2. M.F. Bellan, *Nilgiri Hills (India)*, Map of the Main Vegetation Types from LANDSAT Imagery, Institut de la Catre Internationals du Tapis Vegetal (Toulouse, 1985).
3. SPOT Satellite Image, 4 February 1989.
4. SPOT Satellite Image, 23 November 1989.
5. LANDSAT TM Satellite Image, 6 February 1989.
6. LANDSAT Satellite Image, 31 December 1987.
7. LANDSAT Satellite Image, 21 January 1982.
8. LANDSAT Satellite Image, 27 February 1973.
9. LANDSAT Satellite Image, 10 February 1973.

Chapter Six

# Small-Dam Systems of the Sahyadris

DAVID HARDIMAN

One of the criticisms made today of large dam projects in India is that irrigation needs are served better and more equitably by a large number of small dams rather than by a few big dams. Small dams, it is argued, change the environment less drastically and encourage more sustainable and environmentally friendly forms of agriculture. The systems are more under the control of local people, are used more efficiently, and serve local needs better.[1] However, although it is clear that systems of irrigation based on small dams were important for agriculture in many parts of India in the past, very little is known about the extent of such systems, the manner in which they were organized, or the reasons why they often declined. Were they found only in a few limited areas where the terrain was suitable? Were they organized by autocratic rulers who deprived the cultivators of most of the fruits of their labour? Did they die out because they had become an anachronism? Answers to questions such as these could help us to evolve better strategies for the sustenance or revival of such systems today.

The existing literature provides no clear answers. Irfan Habib, in his comprehensive study of the agrarian system of Mughal India, has a lot to say about the major state-sponsored canal systems of the plains regions, and about tanks and wells, but very little about

[1] E.g., see Claude Alvares and Ramesh Billorey, *Damming the Narmada: India's Greatest Planned Environmental Disaster* (Penang, 1988), pp. 56, 157–61.

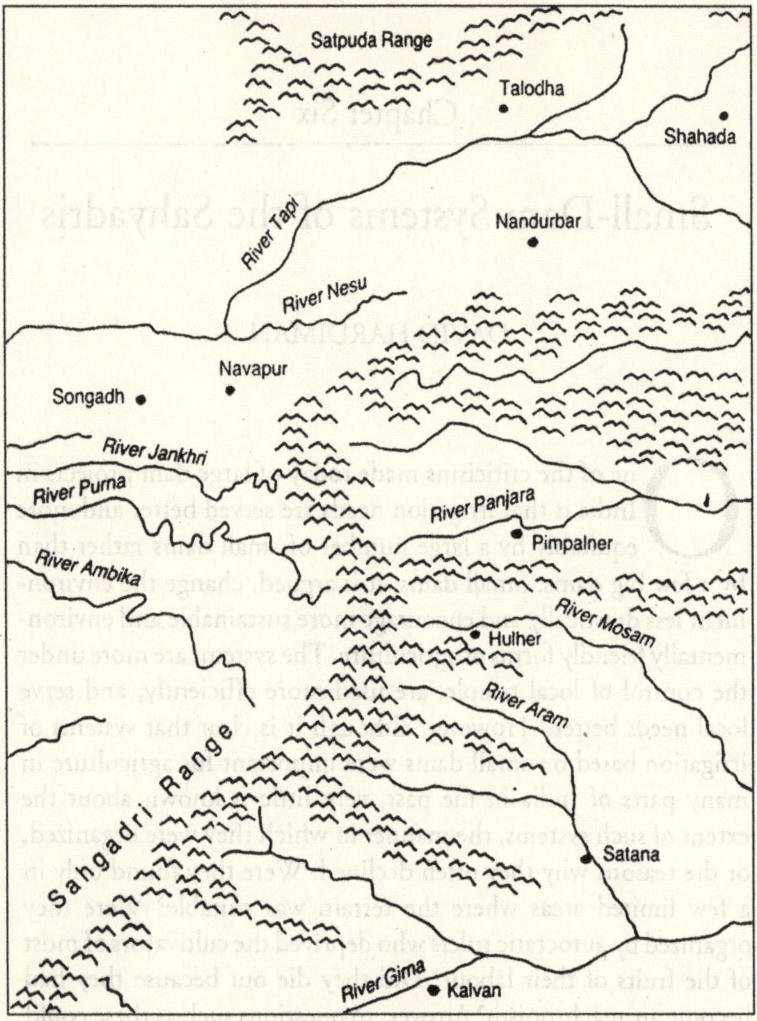

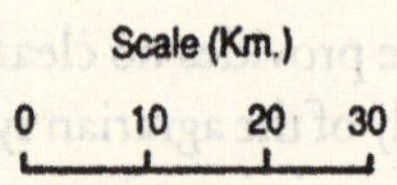


**The Baglan Region.**

small-dam systems. He has, however, one short paragraph which is of relevance.

In the Dakhin the practice of leading small canals from rivers and streams was, like that of storage, an ancient one. We are told, for example, that in Baglana 'they have brought into every town and village thousands of canals, cut from the river for the benefit of cultivation,' and these were managed, probably, according to the co-operative *phad* system, which still survives in that area.[2]

Baglan was a region in the Sahyadri mountains, with fertile river valleys. Although dams are not mentioned in this source, evidence which will be set out later in this essay shows that small dams were central to the irrigation system of Baglan. Such locations seem to have been particularly suited to small-dam-based agriculture. In South Bihar, where many small rivers run off the central Indian plateau towards the basin of the Gauges, there was similarly widespread irrigation using small dams. Water was diverted by the dams to the fields by channels. Rice could thus be grown in an area without very high rainfall. Nirmal Sengupta, who has studied these systems, believes that they date back to 700 BC and that they provided a surplus sufficient to allow major civilizations to flourish in the region.[3] Similar small dams feeding water via channels to rice fields were found in the southern tip of India, in what is now Tamilnadu. Again, the dams were on rivers running from mountain ranges, and they allowed rice to be grown in areas where otherwise the rainfall was inadequate. These systems date back about a thousand years.[4] In many Himalayan valleys agriculture depended on the use of irrigation channels. Small dams were not

[2] Irfan Habib, *The Agrarian System of Mughal India (1556–1707)* (London, 1963), p. 31. The quote within the quote is from Sadiq Khan, *Shahjahannama* (mid-seventeenth century).

[3] Nirmal Sengupta, 'The Indigenous Irrigation Organization of South Bihar', *Indian Economic and Social History Review*, 17:2, 1980, pp. 157–89.

[4] M.S.S. Pandian, *The Political Economy of Agrarian Change: Nanchilnadu 1880–1939* (New Delhi, 1990) pp. 27–8, 33–6; David Ludden, *Peasant History in South India* (Princeton, 1985), pp. 21–2.

needed, however, as water could be merely diverted from the rapid-flowing and perennial rivers. Small dams would not have withstood the constant pounding of these torrents.[5] It seems, therefore, that small-dam systems flourished mainly in piedmont areas where rainfall was less and the rivers often dried up or dwindled to a trickle during the dry season. The dams not only fed canals but also created reservoirs in which water could be stored during the dry months of the year.

How was all this organized? There are conflicting schools of thought in this respect. According to one school, irrigation systems of all sorts have in the past required highly centralized forms of organization. According to Wittfogel, they have provided the chief basis for despotism.[6] This has been disputed by Robert and Eva Hunt, who, in a comparative study of traditional systems of irrigation throughout the world, have argued that while such systems have normally been created by a ruling class—which has then exercised an overall responsibility for their continuation—organization and maintenance have been carried out at the local level most commonly by local collectivities.[7] This has been borne out in studies by Edmund Leach (Sri Lanka),[8] Clifford Geertz (Bali),[9] and others.[10] For India there appear to be no studies of similar quality on the organization of such systems, and it is hard to come to any definite conclusions. Nirmal Sengupta admits that little is known about the organization of the small-dam systems

[5] Jogishwar Singh, *Banks, Gods and Government: Institutional and Informal Credit Structure in a Remote and Tribal Indian District (Kinnaur, Himachal Pradesh) 1960–1985* (Stuttgart, 1989), p. 80.

[6] Karl Wittfogel, *Oriental Despotism: A Comparative Study of Total Power* (New Haven, 1957).

[7] Robert C. Hunt and Eva Hunt, 'Canal Irrigation and Local Social Organisation', *Current Anthropology*, 17: 3, 1976, p. 395.

[8] Edmund Leach, *Pul Eliya: A Village in Ceylon* (Cambridge, 1961), pp. 28–47.

[9] Clifford Geertz, 'Organisation of the Balinese *Subak*', in Walter Coward (ed.), *Irrigation and Agricultural Development in Asia* (Ithaca, 1980), pp. 72–84.

[10] See chapters by Beardsley, Hall, Ward, Lewis, Bacdayan, Roberts and Coward in ibid.

of South Bihar in earlier times, but during the colonial period they were maintained largely by zamindars. Peasants were required to carry out maintenance work—if they refused they were likely to be coerced by the zamindars. Gyan Prakash, in his study of agrarian labour in this region, has used oral tradition to argue that the dams were built and canals dug by low-caste labourers under the supervision of members of the gentry.[11] The small-dam system of South Bihar seems, therefore, to have involved highly exploitative relationships of production, but not a highly centralized autocratic state. The small-dam systems of southern Tamilnadu, on the other hand, appear to have been built by kings but managed subsequently by others. David Ludden argues that the maintenance was carried out initially by local chiefs, later, in some cases, by temples, and then by powerful peasants, and never by the peasant community as a whole.[12] M.S.S. Pandian shows that during the early nineteenth century the rulers—in this case the kings of Travancore—made it a legal requirement that the peasants carry out community labour to maintain the central canal in the Nanchilnadu region. Smaller channels were, however, the responsibility of local communities. At the village level the dominant peasantry, as a corporate group, employed workers to maintain the channels, and open and close the sluices. The workers were paid with a share of the crops, which helped to ensure that they were diligent in their work.[13] Pandian's evidence shows that community-based systems of irrigation did exist in India, as in Sri Lanka, Bali and elsewhere.

These systems all seem to have declined badly over the past two centuries. Why did this happen? Sengupta argues that the decline set in after the British took over the management of the systems of South Bihar from the zamindars in the 1930s.[14] Ludden believes that the British were interested only in large-scale

[11] Gyan Prakash, *Bonded Histories: Genealogies of Labour Servitude in Colonial India* (Cambridge, 1990), pp. 50, 73–8.

[12] Ludden, *Peasant History*, pp. 30, 90.

[13] Pandian, *Political Economy of Agrarian Change*, pp. 33–41.

[14] Sengupta, 'Indigenous Irrigation', pp. 171–2.

irrigation works which could be controlled by the government and which would provide a high revenue. The state, therefore neglected the small systems of southern Tamilnadu. High taxes on irrigated land and the loss of power by the local gentry also played a role.[15] Pandian likewise holds that the state—in this case Travancore—ruined the indigenous system of irrigation. The state asserted its control more tightly in the late nineteenth century and then neglected the infrastructure. In the 1920s it superseded the existing managing collectivities by Irrigation Boards. These proved inappropriate and they were moribund from the start. Without proper attention, the canal systems disintegrated quickly.[16] Over-centralization of management, introduced during the colonial period, is therefore blamed for the decline of these small-dam systems.

In this essay I want to explore some of these points, taking as my focus the area mentioned by Irfan Habib—the Baglan region. While travelling in the valleys of this part of the Sahyadri range in the 1980s I came across the remnants of ancient dams on small rivers running off the mountains. The dams were mostly broken and out of use. However, in the valley of the Mosam river I found the dams still in use. The peasants had dug small channels to carry water from these dams to their fields. This was organized by the people—there were no landlords or dominant peasants castes in the valley controlling these systems. I shall examine the small-dam systems of Baglan, using what written sources are available to me. I have not carried out any systematic mapping of the old dams or sought other archaeological evidence, or explored oral traditions in this respect. This would be a highly worthwhile task for the future.

## II

The kingdom of Baglan was situated in the northern reach of the Sahyadri range of the Western Ghats, in the area running from

[15] Ludden, *Peasant History*, p. 145.

[16] Pandian, *Political Economy of Agrarian Change*, pp. 105–13.

the north of Nasik to the Tapi river. The Kings, who were of the Rathod clan, at times controlled parts of the adjoining regions of Khandesh, the Deccan and South Gujarat. Their base was at Mulher—a strongly fortified hill commanding the valley of the Mosam. This river rises at Salher, the second highest mountain of the entire Sahyadri range. Salher and other mountains were also fortified. These strongholds were extremely hard to reduce. They helped to ensure that the kingdom maintained its independence until the mid-seventeenth century. The Baglan kings normally accepted the overall paramountcy of more powerful rulers, paying tribute to them. Between 1317 and 1347 they were under the paramountcy of the rulers of Daulatabad. After a period of independence, in 1370, they were again obliged to pay tribute, this time to the Rajas of Khandesh. In the fifteenth century they were tributaries of the Sultans of Gujarat. When Akbar conquered Gujarat in 1573, they transferred their allegiance to the Mughals.[17] At that time Abul Fazl described Baglan as being a country one hundred *kos* long and thirty kos broad (one kos was equivalent to about two kilometres). The ruler commanded 16,000 infantry and 2000 horse and the revenue was six and a half crores of *dams* (at that time a dam was worth between Rs 35 and Rs 40[18]).[19] The kingdom therefore represented a rich prize, and in 1599 Akbar attacked it. Akbar failed, however, to reduce the hill forts, and the two rulers eventually came to an agreement in which certain territory was ceded to Baglan.[20] In 1638 the future emperor, Aurangzeb, finally conquered the kingdom for the Mughals. The king of Baglan appears to have been allowed to continue to rule

[17] *Gazetteer of the Bombay Presidency*, vol. XVI, *Nasik* (Bombay, 1883), pp. 187–8 (hereafter *Nasik Gazetteer*); Abul Fazl, *The Akbar Nama* (reprint, Delhi, 1973), p. 41.

[18] Habib, *Agrarian System*, p. 388.

[19] *Akbar Nama*, p. 43. The revenue was surely exaggerated; what is important is that the Mughals believed it was very high.

[20] William Finch, in W. Foster (ed.), *Early Travels in India* (Oxford, 1921), pp. 136–7.

under the paramountcy of the Mughals for a time, but around 1658 the kingdom merged into the province of Khandesh.[21]

Accounts of the mid-seventeenth century talk of the great agricultural prosperity of the region. Jean Baptiste Tavernier travelled through this area on more than one occasion between 1640 and 1667. Writing of Navapur, which was in the Baglan kingdom, he said:

> Nawapura is a large village full of weavers, but rice constitutes the principal article of commerce in the place. A river passes by it, which makes the soil excellent, and irrigates the rice, which requires water. All the rice which grows in this country possesses a particular quality, causing it to be much esteemed. Its grain is half as small again as that of common rice, and, when it is cooked, snow is not whiter than it is, besides which, it smells like musk, and all the nobles of India eat no other. When you wish to make an acceptable present to any one in Persia, you take him a sack of rice.[22]

This description was echoed by Jean de Thevenot, who passed through the Baglan region in 1666 and wrote later: 'the rice (wherewith the fields are covered) is the best in all the *Indies*, especially towards Naopura, where it has an odiferous taste, which that of other countries has not'.[23]

According to Irfan Habib, this famous variety of rice was known as *kamod*.[24] Other agrarian products for which the region was famous were sugarcane, grapes, pineapples, pomegranates and citrus fruits.[25] Pineapples had been introduced to India by the Portuguese only in the sixteenth century, which shows that the farmers of Baglan had been quick to cultivate the new crop.[26]

Unfortunately, little is said as to how these crops were grown. Irrigation from the rivers running off the hills was clearly very

21 Habib, *Agrarian System*, p. 9; *Nasik Gazetteer*, pp. 403–4.

22 Jean Baptiste Tavernier, *Travels in India*, vol. I (London, 1889), pp. 49–50.

23 S. Sen (ed.), *Indian Travels of Thevenot and Careri* (New Delhi, 1949), p. 102.

24 Irfan Habib, *An Atlas of the Mughal Empire* (New Delhi, 1982), p. 26.

25 Ibid.

26 Habib, *Agrarian System*, p. 50.

important—going by the account of Tavernier. Sadiq Khan's statement, quoted earlier, that 'they have brought into every town and village thousands of canals cut from the river for the benefit of cultivation', bears this out.[27] Nothing is said, however, about small dams.

The Baglan region was conquered by the Marathas in 1670. Between 1723 and 1795 the area around the old capital of Mulher was controlled by the Nizam of Hyderabad. Between 1750 and 1753 there was a fierce battle for control of the region between the Nizam, the Peshwa, and the Maratha families of the Bandes and the Gaikwads. The latter two families, who were allied, looted the villages to prevent the Nizam or Peshwa from realizing taxes. The Bhils of the adjoining forest tracts took advantage of the disorder to carry out their own looting. In the process, many dams (this is the first clear reference we have to their existence) were destroyed and the region became depopulated. The Peshwa's army gained control over the area in 1753, and in 1754 the Peshwa ordered that Rs 5000 be paid annually for five years to repair the dams which had been broken.[28] The tract remained under the rule of the Peshwas until 1818, when it came under the British. A sub-division of Khandesh was formed which was called Baglan. In 1869 this taluka was transferred to Nasik district, with the headquarters at Satana. This arrangement continues to this day.

The British found a whole network of dams in the area. They were known locally as *bandharas*. In 1857 an anonymous officer of the Bombay Government gave a detailed description of them.[29] They were, where still erect, solidly constructed of blocks of black basalt stone bound together with coarse concrete mixed with small pieces of brick and pointed up with high quality cement. They

[27] Ibid., p. 31.

[28] Stewart Gordon, 'Recovery from Adversity in Eighteenth-Century India: Rethinking Villages, Peasants, and Politics in Pre-Modern Kingdoms', *Peasant Studies*, 8: 4 (1979), pp. 67–71. I am grateful to Mahesh Rangarajan for this reference.

[29] 'The Dams and Rivers of Khandesh', *The Bombay Quarterly Review*, vol. V, January–April 1857, pp. 48–73.

were thick at the base, tapering to the top. They were kept in place by foundation stones which were set in holes cut in the bed-rock of the rivers. If a firm rock-base could be found stretching straight across a river, the dams were straight, otherwise they were bent in an irregular manner, following the line of available rock. In this respect they were built to be practical, not to look good. The dams raised the height of the water in the river (making it resemble a weir). Channels were constructed on one side, taking water to subsidiary channels, and thence to the fields. These channels were excavated from the earth, with earth banks.[30] They followed the contours of the land so as to avoid a fast flow of water, which would have eroded or broken the banks. The channels needed constant maintenance, with silt having to be cleared from their bed and heaped on their banks or adjoining fields. Many of the dams were still in use in 1857, though some were abandoned—due to lack of water or because they had become silted up–and others were dilapidated or in ruins. In some places the only evidence revealing the existence of a former dam was a row of foundation holes cut in the bed-rock of the river. The official who wrote the description believed that 'the dams of this Province must have been very numerous in former times; for one scarcely crosses a nullah of any size, on which remains of them are not distinctly visible'.[31]

The largest number of dams were found closest to the western border of Khandesh. The border ran south to north along the high escarpment of the Sahyadri range, with, on the west, a precipitous drop towards Gujarat. To the east, running into Khandesh, there was a series of subsidiary ranges running parallel to each other. In the valleys between these ranges there were rivers running east. These were the rivers on which most of the dams had been constructed. Most important was the Mosam river, which rose on

[30] In the Mosam valley I have myself observed that the channels are carried over small gulleys in hollowed out tree-trunks. Otherwise, they are all dug from the earth, meandering around the sides of the hills.

[31] 'Dams and Rivers of Khandesh', p. 50.

the northern flank of Salher mountain and flowed down a valley past Mulher. For the first ten miles of this river there were a series of dams still intact with reservoirs stretching up-river from them.[32] Other such rivers were the Aram, rising on the southern flank of Salher and flowing down a valley towards Satana; and the Panjara, which rose west of Pimpalner. These river-valleys formed the heartland of the old Baglan kingdom. In 1857, of all the talukas of Khandesh, Baglan had the most dams which were still intact–97 in all. Of the other areas which had been a part of the kingdom, Nandurbar had 60 dams and Pimpalner (which then included Navapur) 56 dams. As one went east into the flatter plains of Khandesh (an area outside the sway of the Baglan kings), the number of dams became fewer and fewer. Dhulia taluka had 18, Malegaon 12 and Amalner 10. North of the Tapi river, where there was a plain bordered on the north by the dramatic escarpment of the Satpura mountains, there was only one dam, near Sultanpur. Here, it seems that the fall of the rivers off the mountains was so steep as to make construction impractical.

The report of 1857 covered only Khandesh district. Parts of the Baglan kingdom had, however, lain outside the boundaries of the British district. For instance, the upper valley of the Jankhri river, which ran west towards Surat from near Pimpalner, had once been a part of Baglan. There the anthropologist B.H. Mehta, who carried out fieldwork in the area in 1929-30, found the remains of 187 substantial masonry dams.[33] In Kalvan taluka, to the south of Baglan taluka and also once a part of the old kingdom, there were 59 dams on the Girna and other rivers.[34] In all these areas the landscape was well suited to dam building, with rivers running off the mountains down long valleys. The gradient allowed a good flow of water in the monsoon, but not a torrent.

[32] *Nasik Gazetteer*, p. 400.

[33] B.H. Mehta, 'Social and Economic Condition of the Chodhras, an Aboriginal Tribe of Gujarat', unpublished M.A. thesis, University of Bombay, 1933, p. 576.

[34] *Nasik Gazetteer*, p. 396.

The mountains attracted high rainfall, which was then carried by the rivers to areas with less rain.

The report of 1857 said that according to local tradition the bandharas were built by 'the Mohamedans', and that it was not unlikely that this vast system of irrigation had been constructed when Khandesh was ruled by the Mughal minister Malik Amber (1610–30).[35] This was felt to be likely because 'the Mohamedans' were great builders of canal systems, while Hindu kings were better at constructing vast tanks. This argument seems wide of the mark, for the Mughals did not at the time of Malik Amber control the Hindu-ruled Kingdom of Baglan, where most of the dams were located. The *Khandesh Gazetteer*, on the other hand, felt that it was probable that many of the dams 'date from the time of the late Faruki kings.'[36] The Faruki kings ruled Khandesh from 1295 to 1600. Again, they were not rulers of Baglan, so it is hard to see what connection there could be between them and the majority of the dams. Local people to whom I spoke in the 1980s told me that the bandharas had been built at the time of 'Gaoli Raj'. This is the name commonly given in the region for the Yadav dynasty of Devgiri (later Daulatabad, near Aurangabad), which controlled Khandesh in the thirteenth century. Many old temples, ponds and wells of Khandesh are said to have been built by an officer called Hemadpant, who was in charge of the region during the reign of Mahadev Yadav (1260-71).[37] At that time Baglan came under the overall paramountcy of the Solankis of Gujarat, rather than the Yadav kingdom,[38] so it is unlikely that Hemadpant and the Yadav Kings were responsible for the bandharas. The popular tradition about the Gaoli Raj might, if nothing else, be a means of indicating that the dams are extremely old. It is possible, however, that the idea reflects a fairly accurate understanding of the antiquity of the dams.

35 'Dams and Rivers of Khandesh', pp. 50–1.

36 *Gazetteer of the Bombay Presidency, Khandesh*, vol. XII (Bombay, 1880), p. 139 (hereafter *Khandesh Gazetteer*).

37 *Khandesh Gazetteer*, p. 242.

38 *Nasik Gazetteer*, p. 401.

This is possible because at the end of the thirteenth century there was a period of great social disruption in the region, brought about by the terrible Durga Devi famine, which continued from 1396 to 1408. This devastated the area, wiping out much of the population.[39] The chief peasant community of Baglan–the Konkanas—have a tradition that they came to the area at that time, themselves escaping from the effects of the famine.[40] They came from the Konkan region.[41] It is probable that they brought with them certain skills of agricultural engineering. The Konkan consists of a series of valleys running down to the Arabian Sea. The peasants had made fields by terracing the sides of the valleys. Water from the many small rivers and streams flowing off the mountains was diverted to the fields by dams and channels. A lot of land had, moreover, been reclaimed from the sea with the help of long embankments.[42] The Konkanas who migrated north to Baglan are likely to have brought with them the skill of building strong embankments, a skill used now to dam rivers rather than keep out the sea, and knowledge about how to construct systems of channels to convey water to terraced fields. If this was so, then it suggests that a peasant community was responsible for the construction and maintenance of the bandhara system of Baglan, rather than some centralized authority—such as a king or minister—as the British assumed (with a characteristic bias) must have been the case.

It is in fact difficult to know who was responsible for building and maintaining these dams. The Maratha evidence for the mid-eighteenth century shows that the state played an active role in

[39] *Khandesh Gazetteer*, p. 40.

[40] R.E. Enthoven, *Tribes and Castes of the Bombay Presidency*, vol. 2 (Bombay, 1922), p. 265.

[41] In his linguistic survey of India, Grierson reported that this tradition is supported by the fact that the Konkanas' language continued to have in it many elements of northern Konkani. G.A. Grierson, *Linguistic Survey of India*, vol. IX (Calcutta, 1907), p. 130.

[42] *Gazetteer of the Bombay Presidency; Thana*, vol. XII, part I (Bombay, 1882), pp. 281–4 (hereafter *Thana Gazetteer*).

encouraging the rebuilding of dams, after they were broken during disturbances, by providing grants. We do not know, however, whether the state took such work in hand itself or provided the means for the peasants to carry out the work. The official who wrote the report of 1857 felt that the dams had been built by the state, for they were large and solid and would have required much labour and organization to construct. The report also says that the state appointed certain people to maintain the dams and remunerated them with grants of tax-free land. The villagers were then required to dig and maintain the channels themselves. Because of this, the channels were less substantial in construction.[43] The Khandesh Gazetteer said that the channels were maintained by channel-keepers called *patkaris*, who were endowed with considerable grants of land.[44] A report of 1928 stated, however, that maintenance of the dams and water-channels, and access to the water, was controlled by the peasant community as a whole—a system known as *phad*. This was defined as: 'A system of irrigation under which a number of small holders join together for the economic use of the water supply available, for the growing of irrigated crops on a regular plan.'[45] When I visited the upper reaches of the Mosam valley in 1982, I was told that the system was organized on a co-operative basis, with the fields being distributed so that each household had a share of the irrigated land. Maintenance of the channels was carried out by the people themselves.

There is no technical reason why the people themselves could not have organized the construction of a large majority of the dams. The stone was available locally, and in the dry weather the rivers declined to a trickle, making construction work possible without the need for any diversion of the water. The dams were built in a rough and ready manner—not with the style associated with state-built dams, designed to enhance the prestige of the ruler.

43 'Dams and Rivers of Khandesh', p. 57.

44 *Khandesh Gazetteer*, p. 140.

45 *Report of the Royal Commission on Agriculture in India* (London, 1928), pp. 325, 755.

The only outside material used was the high quality cement with which the work was finished off. This could have been obtained outside and carried in the peasants' own bullock carts to the site of the dam. It is, however, likely that the state took an active interest in the construction of the dams. The wealth of the kings of Baglan—and thus their power in the region—seems to have rested largely on the agriculture made possible by these dams. The Peshwas, likewise, understood the importance of these dams for the prosperity—and thus the revenue—of the area, and provided grants for their reconstruction. It should also be noted that these dams needed the military protection of the state, for they could be broken fairly easily by enemies, as happened during the disturbances of 1750–3.

It seems unlikely that these systems were operated at the village level by a dominant class, such as the gentry of South Bihar. The inhabitants of the villages of these valleys tended to be overwhelmingly of one community, without any very great internal stratification and without any class of dominant peasants or gentry. There is no evidence that any such classes ever dominated these villages in the past. With each dam serving only a fairly limited area, extra-local organization was not in any case required. The state may well have appointed people to look after some of the bigger dams and their channels, while leaving the maintenance of the large majority of smaller dams to the people themselves. Such a division of responsibility has been found to exist generally in small-dam irrigation systems in pre-capitalist societies all over the world.[46]

In all, it seems probable that these small-dam systems were constructed as a result of co-operation between the state and peasant cultivators skilled in the use of such systems. The peasants were probably involved in the building of the actual dams, with some aid from the state. They are likely to have taken the initiative in constructing water-channels and terraced fields. A village council representing the cultivating households appears to have been responsible for the maintenance of the systems.

[46] R. and E. Hunt, 'Canal Irrigation and Local Social Organisation', p. 395.

Little is said in the land settlement reports for Nasik district or Khandesh district about the manner in which crops were cultivated in these villages. The settlement report for Songadh taluka (under Baroda State) describes rice cultivation using the method known as *rab.* This involved selecting a piece of ground for a seed-bed and then fertilizing it by burning tree-loppings and other vegetation before the seeds were planted. Once the rains had set in, the seedlings were transplanted in the fields. This was considered by many officials of the day to be a 'primitive' form of agriculture. The settlement report in question described the peasants as 'slothful and averse to hard work', and thus inefficient. This ignored the fact that a lot of labour would have been required to transplant the seedlings and then irrigate and weed the fields.[47]

A report for the Dangs of 1902 provides a more detailed account of rab. The Dangs was the region lying due west of Baglan. In the past it had been under the overall paramountcy of the kings of Baglan, though local Bhil chiefs had considerable independence. In the nineteenth century the population was divided almost equally between Bhils and Konkanas. According to the report of 1902, during winter time branches were lopped from trees and bamboos were cut and arranged in a square on the ground. This was burnt in the summer, after the wood had dried out. Seeds were sown in the ashes. The adjoining land was ploughed with a bullock-drawn plough, and when the seedlings were large enough they were transplanted. This form of agriculture was practised in river valleys on more level ground, largely by peasants of the Konkana community rather than by people of other communities —such as the Bhils.[48]

Although we are not told in the reports whether rab was used in cultivation in the valleys which formed the core of the old Baglan kingdom, it seems probable that it was. Rab is a method

[47] *Jamabandi Settlement Report of the Songadh Taluka of the Navsari Division 1902–03* (Baroda, 1902), p. 14.

[48] Report by E.M. Hodgson, 29 August 1902, Maharashtra State Archives, Bombay (hereafter BA), Revenue Department (hereafter R.D.), 1902, 107/949, part II.

practised all over Maharashtra, both in the Deccan and Konkan.[49] There are good accounts of the methods for the latter region, and, as the Konkanas came from there originally, it is worth describing them here. During the dry weather each year, bits of wood and other vegetation were gathered from the hills above the terraced rice-fields. Layers of cow-dung, tree-loppings, shrubs, leaves and grass were piled up on a field selected as a seed-bed. Earth was piled on top to keep it all in place, until it was set on fire just before the monsoon. Once the rain came, rice was sown and allowed to grow a few inches high. The seed-beds were always on ground slightly higher than the main body of the fields, as rice seedlings rotted if allowed to become too wet. Once they had grown sufficiently, they were transplanted on to land which had been ploughed up in the previous weeks. Transplanted rice gave a far higher yield than broadcast rice. Rab provided a particularly good medium for rice seeds. Cow-dung manure retained too much water, whereas rab allowed for a drier and more porous soil. Burning also destroyed any weeds in the soil before the rice-seeds were sown. It was calculated that for every acre of rice grown in this way, about three acres of forested upland were required to provide the rab. Valleys with such uplands were therefore ideal for such agriculture.[50]

It is therefore likely that rab cultivation was used in Baglan to grow its famous rice and other commercial crops such as sugarcane. These crops did not, however, cover most of the cultivated area. In 1880-1 only 0.95 per cent of the cultivated land of Baglan taluka was under sugarcane, and 0.71 per cent under rice. The chief crops were the millets *bajra* (56.47 per cent), and *juvar* (10.38 per cent).[51] In Pimpalner taluka in 1878-79, bajra

[49] D.D. Kosambi, *The Culture and Civilization of Ancient India in Historical Outline* (London, 1965), pp. 44–5.

[50] *Thana Gazetteer*, p. 284; J.A. Voelcker, *Report on the Improvement of Indian Agriculture* (London, 1893), pp. 109–10. See also Indra Munshi Saldanha, 'The Political Ecology of Traditional Farming Practices in Thana District Maharashtra (India)', *The Journal of Peasant Studies*, 17:3, 1990.

[51] *Nasik Gazetteer*, p. 406.

was grown on 37.29 per cent of the cultivated land; rice on 12.76 per cent. Sugarcane took up only 0.35 per cent of the land.[52] Even though it is likely that the area under rice and sugarcane had declined considerably since the seventeenth century,[53] it is likely also that bajra, and to a lesser extent juvar, had even then been the staple foodcrop of the peasants. These crops required far less water than rice or sugarcane, and, although they were to some extent grown on irrigated land, they were for the most part grown higher up the sides of the valleys, beyond the reach of the water channels. In the villages of Baglan as a whole, only a small area was irrigated by water channels. In 1867–8 only 2,908 acres fell in this category, out of a total cultivated acreage of 91,132 acres (3.19 per cent). Although the system of bandhara irrigation was by then in a state of decay, it is unlikely that the extent of land irrigated by water channels had ever been anything more than a fairly small fraction of the total land which was cultivated. What this meant was that the fine varieties for which this region was so famed in the seventeenth century were grown on only a limited irrigated part of the land, with many other crops being grown on the rest of the irrigated land as well as on the unirrigated land on the sides of the valleys.

It is probable, going by evidence from a part of the Sahyadri range lying to the south of Baglan, that the peasants sold the crops which had a high marketable value, retaining crops with a lower value for their own consumption. A report on the Mahadev Kolis, the chief inhabitants of this southerly region, written in the 1830s, mentions ten varieties of rice grown by methods very similar to those found in Baglan. These varieties ranged from very fine to very coarse. The best were much prized by the Brahmans and other moneyed people of Maharashtra. Most of the better rice was sold to local traders, who in turn sold it in the towns and cities. The villagers kept only a small amount for themselves, to be eaten when festivals were celebrated. They also sold the coarser varieties

52 *Khandesh Gazetteer*, p. 400.

53 The reason for this will be discussed later.

of rice. They grew the local staple foodgrain, *nagli*, on their poorer, unirrigated land. Besides this, they grew some wheat, maize, pulses, vegetables and sugarcane of a low quality, mostly for their own consumption.[54] It is likely that the peasants of Baglan did the same, selling much of their high quality rice and sugarcane to earn money to pay taxes to the state, while keeping the less marketable produce for their own consumption.

## III

The heyday of this system of agriculture was from the sixteenth to the eighteenth centuries, with the decline coming in the early nineteenth century. A report written in 1839, mentioning this development, said that the dams were not so far gone as to be unrepairable, and that timely maintenance would allow large areas to be irrigated once more.[55] The 1857 report revealed a system in a state of collapse, with dams and water-channels being allowed to silt up, and peasants carelessly damaging the sides of channels by driving their carts or cattle over them.[56] Figures for the number of working dams in Baglan Taluka show a continuing decline in subsequent years. In 1857 there were in Baglan 97 bandharas, in 1881–2 49, in 1902–3 31.[57] In West Khandesh as a whole (excluding Baglan, which came under Nasik district in 1869), there were, in 1857, 157 working bandharas, in 1911–12 80, in 1922–3 only 3.[58] The system therefore disintegrated under British rule.

Why was this allowed to happen? At the advent of British rule, the system was not in a healthy state, as a result of a profound

[54] A. Mackintosh, 'An Account of the Tribe of Mhadeo Kolis', *Transactions of the Bombay Geographical Society*, vol. 1, 1836–8, pp. 211–16.

[55] Dallas to Blane, 23 March 1839, BA, Political Department 1839, 15/1011.

[56] 'Dams and Rivers of Khandesh', p. 55.

[57] Ibid., p. 51; *Nasik Gazetteer*, p. 401; *Nasik Gazetteer*, B vol. (Bombay, 1903), p. 12.

[58] 'Dams and Rivers of Khandesh', pp. 51–3; *Khandesh Gazetteer*, B vol. (Bombay, 1926), p. 70. In the latter reference the figures are for sources of irrigation other than wells or tanks—which meant in that region bandharas.

social crisis which occurred in the region towards the end of the Maratha period. In 1802–3 civil war amongst the Marathas led to ruthless looting of the peasants to pay and feed the warring troops. This led to a devastating famine, with large number of peasants either dying of starvation or having to desert their villages, never to return.[59] Many villages were left with no population, and the land soon became covered in scrub, then trees.

There had, however, been earlier crises, as in 1750–3, and the systems had been repaired with state support. Why did this not happen again after the crisis of 1802–4? The Peshwas were still the rulers in the region, but now they lacked the resources, power and will to organize such work. The British, who replaced them in 1818, could, however, have done this. Briggs, the first Collector of Khandesh, commented on the subject:

> In many instances I met with the most importunate petitions for repairs of the numerous fine dams in Candeish which will at some future period so naturally tend to the increase of the land revenue, but I invariably told them it must depend on the expected increase of revenue desirable from those repairs whether or not Govt. would undertake to sink so much money. . .[60]

As a result he turned down all such requests for grants. The reaction was short-sighted in the extreme, for, without the restoration of the systems, the prosperity of the region could not be restored. As Stewart Gordon remarks, his attitude contrasted strongly with that of the Peshwas in 1754, who were quick to provide immediate aid for such rebuilding. Because of this, resettlement in the region was patchy and slow.

Although the British claimed frequently that they wished to preserve these irrigation systems, in practice they did little to encourage them. Generally, they placed a low value on any irrigation system which the peasantry themselves were responsible for. Even the otherwise sympathetic report on the bandharas of 1857

[59] *Khandesh Gazetteer*, pp. 182–3.

[60] Quoted in S. Gordon, 'Recovery from adversity in eighteenth-century India', p. 76.

was very critical about the way in which the water channels meandered around the contours of the slopes without any masonry lining to prevent the water from being absorbed by the soil. It was argued that the channels needed to be improved by the Public Works Department, with cuttings to straighten the line of the channels, and the use of more masonry.[61] This was never done, due to lack of funds for a department which was responsible also for road construction and official buildings. Whatever little money was available for irrigation works tended to be spent on new projects, laid out according to plans drawn up by the Civil Engineer, and which were subsequently under the complete control of the department. It was considered that the peasants were incapable of maintaining sustainable systems of irrigation by themselves. Maintenance of existing bandharas was hampered, furthermore, by the fact that permission for all PWD projects had to be obtained from Bombay. In some cases this meant that the file had to pass though the hands of nine different officials (not including the Civil Engineer himself) before work on a bandhara could go ahead.[62] This hampered any attempts at regular maintenance of the bandharas.

Official neglect is not, however, the only reason for the decay of the small-dam systems. In many cases the peasants themselves contributed to the decay. This was most obviously the case in the areas which were resettled after the crisis of the early years of the nineteenth century by members of the Bhil and Maochi communities, who practised slash-and-burn agriculture in an area which had reverted to forest.[63] A field was cut from the forest, the

[61] 'Dams and Rivers of Khandesh', pp. 49–50.

[62] Ibid., pp. 60, 65–6.

[63] *Papers Relating to the Original Survey Settlement of 148 villages of Nandurbar Taluka (including Navapur Petha), 17 Government Villages of the Shirpur Taluka, and 11 Government Villages of the Shahada Taluka of the Khandesh Collectorate. Selection from the Records of the Bombay Government,* No. CCCCXXIV—New Series (Bombay, 1904), pp. 2, 5. This report says that many of the Bhils and Maochis who practised slash and burn cultivation in Navapur Taluka had been in the area only since the last years of Maratha rule.

cut vegetation was burnt, and seeds were planted in the ashes. After two or three years of cultivation, the peasants selected a fresh plot in the forest. One such area was Navapur—formerly famed for its fine agriculture and prized rice—which was described in 1864 by the Collector of Khandesh as a 'vast jungle tract . . . The present inhabitants are mostly Bhils, with a few Konkanis, almost as wild as their country . . .'[64] Shifting cultivation did not require dams, water-channels and terraced fields, and without maintenance the systems quickly disintegrated. They have never been revived to this day.

In some areas small-dam based agriculture seems to have survived the crisis of the early years of the nineteenth century, only to have decayed later on. The report of 1857 found that many peasants who should have been capable of running such systems were failing to do so. One reason—advanced in a report on Nandurbar taluka of 1862—was that many of the rivers were no longer supplying adequate amount of water to fill the dams and feed the channels. Because of this, of the 69 dams found in the taluka, only 9 were still in use by 1862. The local people attributed the drying up of the rivers to British rule—though they could not explain why this was so beyond advancing what the official called 'superstitious reasons'. This official provided his own scientific explanation, arguing that the felling of trees in the adjacent hills during the early nineteenth century now caused the monsoon rain to run off the slopes so fast that very little water was absorbed by the ground. In the process much soil was washed down, leading to the rapid silting-up of the dams and water channels, making them almost useless. On top of that, lack of trees had led to a decline in rainfall.[65] The people of the area said that the hills had

[64] Quoted in *Papers Relating to the Revision Survey Settlement of the Nandurbar Taluka of the Khandesh Collectorate, Selections from the Records of the Bombay Government*, No. CCCXLIX—New Series (Bombay, 1896), p. 4.

[65] 'Report on Nandurbar Taluka, 25 January 1865', in *Papers Relating to the Introduction of Revised Rates of Assessment into Eight Talookas and Two Pethas of the Khandeish Collectorate, Selections from the Records of the Bombay Government*, No. XCIII—New Series (Bombay, 1865), p. 471.

been well wooded not long ago.[66] Deforestation therefore appears to have been an important cause of the decay of the bandharas and their channels in many part of Nandurbar.

This does not explain the decay of the small-dam systems in the valleys in which there was no radical change of population or deforestation during the nineteenth century. Baglan and Pimpalner talukas came into this category. There the cause appears to have been a combination of high taxes and growing indebtedness which made irrigated agriculture uneconomic.

When the British conquered the region they found a system of taxation in the channel-watered villages in which the rate of tax depended on the value of a crop grown in a field. Sugarcane paid the highest rate, normally over Rs 30 per bigha (in that area, one bigha was ¾ of an acre). Rice paid Rs 15 or more per bigha. Other crops paid less.[67] Rates in different channel-irrigated villages ranged from Rs 2 ½ to Rs 70 per bigha, according to crop grown.[68] The rates reflected the amount of water needed for each type of crop, and they helped to ensure that crops which used most water were grown in only a limited way, so that no excessive strain was placed on the irrigation systems. After 1818 the British imposed a uniform tax per unit of irrigated land. The rate was fixed high—the aim being to encourage the peasants to concentrate on growing the most valuable crops, so as to maximize the tax revenue.[69] The average rate per bigha in Baglan taluka was fixed at about Rs 12.[70] Although lower than the rates levied previously on rice and sugarcane, it was much higher than the rates paid for the less valuable crops which covered a good part of the irrigated land. To pay the new high rates, peasants were forced to take credit from moneylenders. By manipulating the books, these moneylenders soon had the peasants deep in debt. Using the civil courts established by the British, they could threaten to have the peasants'

66 Ibid., p. 469.

67 'Dams and Rivers of Khandesh', p. 62.

68 *Khandesh Gazetteer*, p. 279.

69 'Dams and Rivers of Khandesh', pp. 59–60.

70 *Nasik Gazetteer*, p. 253.

property and even land confiscated unless they handed over a larger and larger proportion of their crops at each harvest. By the 1860s it was being reported of Baglan that: 'Even the best channel-watered villages had few signs of wealth. Most of the people were forced to seek the moneylender's help and were in debt.[71]

Increasingly, peasants found that the only way they could survive was to abandon the high-taxed irrigated fields and concentrate on low-taxed unirrigated cultivation. In this way they ceased to have any interest in maintaining the bandharas and waterchannels. They allowed the sides of the channel to disintegrate, so that the fields below became swamped. Once such decay set in, a whole system could become useless in very little time.[72] In the end, bandhara-based irrigation survived in only a few pockets, such as the more remote reaches of the mountain valleys, where tax was paid according to the number of ploughs used rather than area cultivated.

The decay of the small-dam systems of the Baglan region was, therefore, brought about by a combination of causes, the most important of which were colonial disinterest, resettlement of certain regions by shifting cultivators who had no interest in the dams, deforestation, and the decay in the old system of community-based control as a result of colonial taxation and policies which gave rise to ruinous forms of usury. The forest policy pursued by the British at the end of the nineteenth century made the situation still worse. The hilltops were demarcated as reserved forests under government control and the peasants were prevented from gathering material for rab for their seed-beds. This caused great resentment, with protests against the forest laws culminating in forest satyagrahas in the 1930s.[73]

Nowadays this region is considered to be a backward one, inhabited by 'primitives', classified now as 'scheduled tribes'. Development projects in the area concentrate on building large dams

[71] *Nasik Gazetteer*, p. 251.

[72] 'Dams and Rivers of Khandesh', pp. 55–6.

[73] Interview with Madav Joshi, Mulher, 6 January 1982.

—such as the Haranbari dam on the Mosam river—which flood a huge area of what were once fertile fields irrigated by small bhandaras and their channels. Revival of small-dam systems is not a programme high on the agenda of the Irrigation Department—though a few small steps have been taken in this direction.

## IV

The evidence in this essay shows that small-dam systems of irrigation existed in the past which were sustained over long periods of time. Although they depended on state support, at the village level they were controlled and managed by village communities. Although the pre-colonial state derived a substantial surplus from this agriculture, there does not appear to have been severe exploitation of one class by another within the villages, as was the case with many small-dam systems studied in other parts of India.

Whether or not such a form of agriculture can be revived or extended today on a large scale in areas with a suitable terrain is problematic. The problem is not merely a technical one, depending on the policy of the Irrigation Department, but also a social one. Rural society has become so polarized over the past two centuries that it is hard to see how a genuinely co-operative system of management and resource allocation could be established. Nowadays access to any system of irrigation reflects the inequalities of the society.

If nothing else, however, a general policy in favour of small-dam systems would be far less damaging to the environment. Also, with small-dam systems in operation the conditions for more co-operative and environmentally friendly forms of agriculture would at least exist. With a certain amount of state support, the struggle to achieves this could be carried through. With large-dam systems, these conditions do not exist.

## Chapter Seven

# Models of the Hydraulic Environment: Colonial Irrigation, State Power and Community in the Indus Basin

DAVID GILMARTIN

As natural orders defined in relationship to particular human communities, 'environments' exist only insofar as human communities are defined. 'Environments' are in essence models of the relationship between communities and the natural world around them, and as such, they are, like all models, 'made by humans for specific communities'.[1] The environmental history of India under British colonial rule is thus bound closely to an analysis of the historical structuring of communities in colonial India.

British colonial rule shared in many respects the ethos of domination over nature that marked the emergence of 'middle-class' government in Britain. Shaped by the increasing influence of capitalist modes of thinking, many British leaders saw domination of nature, and its commodification, as both a critical measure of class power and a legitimizer of the British in India as a ruling community. As Michael Adas argues, Europeans often looked to their own 'vastly superior understanding of the workings of nature'

[1] Stephen Gudeman, *Economics as Culture: Models and Metaphors of Livelihood* (London, 1986) p. 37.

—and their ability to turn nature to human use—as among the most powerful justifications for 'their monopolization of leadership and managerial roles in colonized societies'.[2] Though it is doubtless a mistake to stress a single mode of thinking as a central explanation for a phenomenon as complex as the expansion of colonialism, the definition of the environment as a natural field to be dominated for productive use, and the definition of the British as a distinctive colonial ruling class over alien peoples, went hand in hand.

Expansion of irrigation represented one extremely important arena in which this ethos was reflected. Though nineteenth-century colonial irrigation policy reflected a variety of financial and political influences, it increasingly drew on an international discourse of water engineering that colonial engineers and irrigation administrators shared with entrepreneurs and water engineers in much of the world. As Donald Worster describes it, this ethos was rooted in the transformation of water itself into a commodity: 'All mystery disappears from its depths, all gods depart, all contemplation of its flow ceases. It becomes so many 'acre-feet' banked in an account, so many 'kilowatt-hours' of generating capacity to be spent, so many bales of cotton or carloads of oranges to be traded around the globe'.[3] Few British irrigation engineers in India, of course, held such a single-mindedly commercial view of the control of water. But the underlying engineering vision of environmental domination was widely held in India, and nowhere more so than in the Indus Basin, where British irrigation engineers sought in the late-nineteenth and early-twentieth centuries to bring the land under the 'command' of a massive system of irrigation. By transforming the region from 'an arid waste', fringed with narrow strips of cultivated area extending from the Jumna . . . to the mountains of the Suleiman Range', they defined both

[2] Michael Adas, *Machines as the Measure of Men: Science, Technology and Ideologies of Western Dominance* (Ithaca, 1989), pp. 205, 210–21.

[3] Donald Worster, *Rivers of Empire: Water, Aridity and the Growth of the American West* (New York, 1985), p. 52.

their power over the environment and the British right to dominate the region.[4]

The distinctive character of the engineering vision of domination derived also from the distinctive manner in which British irrigation engineers came to conceive of the environment—as a mathematically modelled system. With irrigation engineering only in the process of development, nineteenth-century British Indian irrigation by no means depended entirely on mathematical models. But as engineers increasingly came to dominate canal construction, they sought to control water and apply it to maximum areas of land by mathematically modelling its flow, distribution and use. In doing so, they defined a conception of the hydraulic environment as a system of discrete and interlocking parts, knowable (and potentially controllable) by 'objective' observers and by the state. As modelling conveyed to the concept of the 'environment' an increasingly 'scientific' definition as a bounded and knowable system, it thus underscored also the particular form of the state's power over nature. Indeed, it underscored the separation of the state (and the ruling British community) from its field of domination; 'scientists', as Michael Adas remarks, 'set nature apart as an object of dispassionate inquiry'.[5] As mathematical modelling set the observer apart from the system being modelled, it thus also carried implications for the conceptual separation of the state from the ruled that took on distinctive meaning within the colonial context.

The importance of models, or frames, in defining the character of colonial power more generally has recently been discussed by Timothy Mitchell for Egypt. Mitchell has stressed the significance of 'enframing' for the overall project of colonialism, the importance for the colonial power of forcing colonized societies into an

[4] The area 'commanded' by a canal referred, in technical jargon, to the area capable of being reached by its irrigation water. The quotation is from Punjab Public Works Department, Irrigation Branch, *A Manual of Irrigation Practice* (Lahore, 1943), section 3.0.

[5] Adas, *Machines as the Measure of Men*, p. 211.

encompassing structure of order that was continuous, 'forming a unity or whole whose parts were in mechanical and geometric co-ordination'.[6] Mitchell thus stresses not only the conceptual separation of the state from the ruled, but the disciplining of colonial society that was also inherent in the colonial process of 'enframing' or modelling.

Such a view only partially captures the political significance of the mathematical modelling of the environment. On one level, of course, turning the environment to productive use implied the discipline of water users. But in abstract terms the international ethos of irrigation science that shaped hydraulic modelling depended upon the distinctive social discipline provided by a middle-class partnership between state science and the maximizing capitalist water user. As Donald Worster has written of water development in the United States, the state and the individual, though potentially (and at times actually) at odds, each required the other for nature's conquest to be actualized. While 'science and technology are given a place of honour in the capitalist state and put to work devising ways to extract from every river whatever cash it can produce', the transformation of water into a commodity also required an 'aggregating [of] individual drives to maximize personal acquisitiveness'. The resulting 'drive to make the bleakest, most sterile desert produce more and more of everything' provided 'an ideology shared wholeheartedly by agriculturists and water bureaucrats, providing the bond that unites their potentially rival centers of power into a formidable alliance'.[7]

In colonial India, however, the mathematical creation of an integrated hydraulic environment took on a distinctive colonial colour. The political imperatives of colonial domination largely precluded the concept of a partnership between maximizing water users and the state. Colonial political authority required the conceptual separation of the state not only from the natural environment, but also from Indian society, a separation implicit in the

[6] Timothy Mitchell, *Colonising Egypt* (Cambridge, 1988) p. 38.

[7] Worster, *Rivers of Empire*, pp. 52–3.

definition of the British as a ruling community. Pulled in conflicting directions, British policy thus tended to focus on a vision of Indian society as composed of indigenous communities whose local water use could be adapted to the requirements of larger hydraulic models. Hardly partners with the state, these communities remained culturally alien even as they were pulled into the state's projects of environmental transformation. The British, in fact, grounded these communities in a language of 'naturalism' that defined them as parts of the 'natural' environment to be modelled and controlled. From the beginning, the processes of environmental modelling and change were thus tied to the larger political processes of colonial control.

By examining the history of irrigation in the Indus Basin during the British colonial period, this essay will focus on the relationship between environmental modelling, state power and the meaning of community. The history of British irrigation expansion was linked closely to the self-definition of the British as a community empowered to rule India. But it is a story marked by considerable ambiguity as the British sought to define their notions of the environment and of their relations with communities of Indians they ruled. This essay will examine the politics of irrigation in the Indus Basin on two levels. First were the problems intrinsic to the development by the British of a technology and a scientific state apparatus that could control an environment modelled as a broad system of interlocking parts. This involved both the development of state-controlled technology and the definition of state power. Second, and more critical in terms of the long-term relationship between environment and the structuring of political power in India, were the relationships implied by this environmental modelling between the state and the communities of Indians who inhabited the Indus Basin. By examining British irrigation systems in Punjab and Sind from the perspective of environmental history, the aim is thus to gain insight into the structurings of community that shaped British colonial rule.

## State Power and the Modelling of the Hydraulic Environment

The importance of the modelling of the environment as a system of discrete interlocking parts became evident in the development of Indus Basin irrigation in the last decades of the nineteenth century. The British, of course, were not the first to develop irrigation in the Indus Basin; large numbers of wells and many inundation canals off the Indus and its tributaries shaped patterns of agriculture and pastoralism long before the British arrival. In fact, the years before the British annexation of the Indus Basin region were years of considerable expansion in irrigation, under the auspices of the regional Indus Basin states that preceded the British, including the Sikhs, the Nawabs of Bahawalpur and the Amirs of Sind. All these states had used localized inundation canal construction to expand state revenue and to control elites by tying them to the land. The British were not the first to link investment in irrigation with the structuring of political power.

In the early years of their control in the region, the British, drawing on their experience elsewhere in the subcontinent and on the policies of earlier Indus Basin states, sought to develop irrigation works in part to encourage agricultural settlement and political stability, in part to expand production and stabilize state revenue. Though British administrators at the all-India level were increasingly moving in the mid-nineteenth century toward a more rationalized and coordinated irrigation policy,[8] early British irrigation development in the Indus Basin tended nevertheless to be piecemeal, focused largely on the repair and expansion of existing canals, including the Bari Doab canal in central Punjab and inundation canals in Sind and south-west Punjab. Local circumstances significantly shaped decisions on particular canal projects, and

[8] For a history of irrigation in colonial India, see the article by Elizabeth Whitcombe in Dharma Kumar (ed.), *The Cambridge Economic History of India*, vol. II (Cambridge, 1982) pp. 677–737. For a good account of British canal development in the Ganges Basin, see also Ian Stone, *Canal Irrigation in British India: Perspectives on Technological Change in a Peasant Economy* (Cambridge, 1984).

British policy tended to stress local initiative as much as overall state control. British irrigation policy in the 1860s and 1870s, for example, though influenced by larger strategic, financial and political concerns, frequently encouraged local initiative in private (or semi-private) canal building by local landlords or tribal chiefs.

By the late nineteenth century, however, Indus Basin irrigation disclosed an increasing concern with a view of the Indus Basin environment as an integrated network. In some respects, this reflected the more co-ordinated financial and investment policies of the Government of India emanating from Calcutta. But the development of Indus Basin irrigation also manifested a new ideology of state power fuelled by efforts to extend co-ordinated state control over the environment.

In some ways this began with transformations in the British view of the Indus River itself. Though long concerned with water control along the river, the British increasingly approached the river in the late nineteenth century as the central spine of a single water environment. One dramatic instance of this was the growing criticism by engineers, particularly in Sind, of the historically haphazard approach to the embanking of the river. As the Acting Superintending Engineer wrote in 1890, local embanking of the river to protect crops and local irrigation works had proceeded apace in the previous decades. But it had often shown so little attention to the 'natural ways' of the river that it had created the potential for devastating floods by creating linked embankments that were disastrously raising the river's bed above the surrounding countryside. 'Other nations', he said, alluding among others to China and its Yellow River, 'have learnt to their grief and cost a bitter lesson from interfering, for the sake of gain, with the natural laws of . . . large rivers'. But the answer to this was not an end to interference; the answer was greater attention to an understanding of the larger processes of the river as a whole—and the appointment of a larger engineering staff in the province for adapting the irrigation system to a scientific understanding of water's ways.[9]

[9] R.B. Joyner, Acting Superintending Engineer in Sind to Sec. to Govt.,

Collection of statistics that would facilitate the overall modelling of the Indus and its tributaries accelerated, and this led to the creation of an Indus River Commission in 1901 charged not only with the management of embankments and canal heads along the river, but also with the scientific collection of statistics for the study of the river and its capacities.

More important, however, was the increasing integration of irrigation works. This began with the decision in the 1880s to transform the Chenab Canal in Punjab (a project originally developed as an inundation canal) into a perennial canal and to open large tracts of 'wasteland' in the Rechna Doab for settlement. As the first of the successful 'canal colonies', the opening of the Chenab Colony marked a new era in irrigation development. Indeed, with the Chenab Colony recognized in the early years of the twentieth century as an overwhelming financial and technical success—'one of the finest properties of the greatest Government in the world', as a 1904 irrigation report declared—new proposals for large projects in the Indus Basin attracted widespread attention.[10] Since the opening of new canal colonies required perennial water supplies for new settlers, this also required increased attention to the overall availability of water within the Indus network. The increasing water demands of the canal colonies thus dictated an increasing concern for approaching the Indus Basin as an integrated hydraulic environment.

The debate in the early twentieth century that preceded the launching of the Triple Canal project in western Punjab made this clear. With inadequate supplies in the Ravi and Sutlej to open a new canal colony in the Lower Bari Doab and meet the existing and potential demands for water downstream, Punjab irrigation engineers decided to move water from the Jhelum River across to

Public Works Dept. (PWD), Bombay, 1 Nov. 1890, 105 of 1891, pt. I; Bombay PWD (Irrigation), vol. 349 of 1890–8, Maharashtra State Archives, Bombay.

[10] Technically, it was not the Chenab colony but the Sidhnai that was the first of the Indus Basin canal colonies, importing agricultural colonists from central Punjab. But the Chenab colony was the first great financial success. Punjab PWD, Irrigation, 355, 1904, p. 17.

the Lower Bari Doab, first carrying it to the Chenab via the Upper Jhelum Canal, then across the Rechna Doab via the Upper Chenab Canal to the Ravi, and finally into the Lower Bari Doab canal to water the new colony. For the first time, water was thus carried on a vast scale from one river to another, each now treated as part of a broader environmental system defined by state science and state control. The opening of the Triple Canal project meant that water supplies delivered to the canal commands on the Jhelum, Chenab and Ravi rivers were now all administratively and scientifically interrelated. Beginning in 1915, the Superintending Engineers of the five 'linked canals' (Upper Jhelum, Lower Jhelum, Upper Chenab, Lower Chenab, Lower Bari Doab), which watered the major canal colonies of the Punjab, met annually to discuss forecasts of needs and supplies, based largely on the expanding collection of hydrological and crop statistics. This allowed them to attempt (not always with success) to match water availability to water needs, often by mandating rotational closures of canals.[11] Perhaps most significantly, the opening and operation of the system also signified a new claim to state power—a power achieved by modelling the Indus Basin as an integrated, interlocking hydraulic environment that allowed the British to move water freely to maximize the environment's productive potential.

This is not to say, of course, that this vision of the environment was achieved without conflict. On the contrary, the structuring of the Indus Basin as an interlocking network of discrete parts also

[11] Punjab PWD, Irrigation, 122, 1914 ('Distributing the supplies of the Rivers Jhelum, Chenab and Ravi between the five canals'). Irrigators and officials complained at times of the 'expert' manner in which supplies were distributed, but engineers defended their right to make these 'technical' decisions. As one wrote of a request from another official to open these meetings: he 'can hardly be aware of the implications of his suggestion regarding throwing open our water meetings to officials and representatives of the interested public. With our Superintending Engineers fighting like tigers for optimum supplies for their own canal, to increase the personnel of the meeting would be to render it unworkable.' Note by Under-Secretary, Irrigation (29 Nov. 1934), Punjab Board of Revenue (BOR), file 251/46/00/2.

created greater potential for conflict among hydraulic segments in a single system. Old inundation canals, for example, which had long functioned under largely local control and which still provided a significant portion of Indus Basin irrigation in Sind, Bahawalpur and southern Punjab, now found their interests often in conflict with those of water planners who sought to distribute water to the new canal colonies. Particular attention had now to be paid to the effects of *rabi* withdrawals in the canal colonies on the critical opening and closing dates of irrigation on all inundation canals downstream, where the success of local cash cropping often depended less now on the effectiveness of local canal management than on upriver withdrawals. Perhaps most importantly, hydraulic integration also created the framework for increasing debate between Sind, Punjab, and Bahawalpur, which all sought to protect their existing irrigation while at the same time putting forward plans for large-scale perennial canal expansion. For many years Punjab's Sutlej Valley Project, for example, was pitted against Sind's attempts to finalize its long-debated project for a high-level perennial canal at Rohri, a project that developed eventually into the massive Sukkur Barrage scheme. But the long and convoluted debate over these large projects, which ultimately required the intervention of the central government, also illustrated the trend toward centralization of irrigation decision-making that marked the growing integration of irrigation development throughout the Indus Basin.[12] And the success of these increasingly large and 'scientific' projects served to define the colonial state's distinctive

[12] It also illustrated the need for the constant evaluation of the system to determine the relationship of the parts. For an overview of the history of disputes over the Indus network, see Aloys A. Michel, *The Indus Rivers: A Study of the Effects of Partition* (New Haven, 1967) pp. 99–133. Committees and commissions were repeatedly set up in the period between 1919 and 1947 to provide data on Indus flow and to evaluate the relationship of the interests of Sind, Punjab, Bahawalpur, etc. See, in particular, *Report of a Committee of the Central Board of Irrigation on Distribution of the Waters of the Indus and its Tributaries*, 1935 (Anderson Committee) and *Report of the Indus Commission*. 1942 (Rau Commission).

identity and its power. As H.T. Sorley wrote of the Sukkur Barrage (Lloyd Barrage), opened in 1932: 'Until the nineteen twenties Sind lay at the mercy of the Indus . . . But with the coming of the Lloyd Barrage the river was made to surrender its power before the largest ever irrigation system of the world . . .'[13] This was a product not only of the technology of canal construction, but also of the creation by the British of the concept of an integrated Indus Basin hydraulic environment. Defining an integrated model of the environment empowered the central state to control it, just as the state's power authorized the conceptual creation of an environment of discrete but interrelated parts.

However, British success in modelling the hydraulic environment depended not just on the definition of an environment of broad geographic scope, but also on an integrated understanding of the micro-constraints on optimum, productive local water use.[14] The British effort to explain the spread of waterlogging and salinity within the Indus Basin irrigating network provides a striking example, illustrating how the effective modelling of the overall system involved more than extensive, macro-level networking. British concern with rising water tables as a central aspect of expanding canal irrigation dated back to the mid-nineteenth century, and problems

[13] The project covered '1,028 miles of main canals, 1,071 miles of canal distributaries and 5,196 miles of watercourses. Old and new watercourses run for over 50,000 miles, enough to circle the globe twice . . . ' H.T. Sorley, *Gazetteer of the Former Province of Sind* (Lahore, 1968), p. 458.

[14] There were also some efforts to incorporate broader climatic and ecological concerns into hydraulic models, but this had little impact. Inquiries by the Secretary of State in 1907 prompted the Punjab Irrigation Department to evaluate whether the loss of forest cover in the Himalayas might have increased the seasonal variability of river flow, which in turn might have affected 'the utility of the canals' that depended on an adequate year-round supply of water. But when the first inquiries were undertaken along these lines in 1909, the Chief Engineer of the Punjab reported that there were inadequate data to reach any conclusions on the issue. Further inquiries were undertaken in the 1930s, but again no statistically significant results were reported. Punjab PWD, Irrigation, 349, 1908 ('Relation between forests and the retention of atmospheric moisture and soil moisture').

of waterlogging and salinity had caused difficulties even on some inundation canals.[15] But these problems became more marked as irrigation policy stressed the large-scale building of perennial canals. Already by the time of the planning of the Triple Canal project, engineers had begun to systematically monitor and map the level of the water table in the already opened Lower Chenab and Lower Jhelum colonies, and to incorporate data on ground water levels in modeling water requirements and water availability on the 'linked canals'.[16] Early proposed solutions to the problem thus focused on broad processes of canal construction and operation, including the lining of channels (which was expensive), the construction of drains, and particularly, the restriction of supplies in areas in which the water table had risen too close to the surface. This last approach tended to be favoured in the years before 1930, and led to the designation of certain new canals as *kharif* channels, which were not supplied with water during the cold weather.

But by no means all irrigation engineers agreed on the efficacy of this expedient, particularly since it created broader problems of water scheduling that undercut efforts to define other productive water needs as a foundation for distributing water within the broader irrigation system. Further, debate on these issues suggested that engineers (as many themselves realized) possessed inadequate data and understanding of the interrelations between ground and

[15] See, for example, the discussion of waterlogging in the Sanawan Tehsil of Muzaffargarh District, an area served by inundation canals. Punjab PWD, Irrigation, 55, 1899.

[16] In 1901, the Punjab Chief Engineer had issued instructions that for the prevention of waterlogging in the Khadir (low-lying) tracts of the Lower Chenab and Lower Jhelum colonies, the percentage of the gross areas of villages that could be supplied with water for irrigation would be based on a scale ranging from 50 per cent (when the spring water-level was 40 feet or more deep) to 25 per cent (when the spring water-level reached a level of less than 25 feet). Note by H.F.B. Frost, Superintending Engineer, LJC, 6 Feb. 1911. *Punjab Waterlogging Note*, pt. III, p. 12. The difficult relationship between waterlogging and the problem of distribution of supplies between the 'linked canals' is dealt with more generally in Punjab PWD, Irrigation, 12, 1909 ('Reduction of Rabi supplies and remodelling of the Lower Jhelum Canal').

surface water, and micro-level processes, to model them together effectively within a broader environmental system.[17] The appointment of a Waterlogging Enquiry Committee in the mid 1920s was intended to address the problem and led to the establishment in 1930 of an Irrigation Research Institute at Lahore, which undertook scientific experiments to explain (among other things) the processes within the soil responsible for the level of ground water and the movement of salts to the surface. Subsequently, the results of experimentation in Lahore and in the field were reported annually to a provincial Waterlogging Broad, and, despite continuing controversy about the causes and solutions for waterlogging and salinity in the years before Partition, scientific research on the interaction between ground water and surface supplies became a central part of attempts to model the hydraulic environment.[18] Though lack of consensus (and resources) prevented any concerted, large-scale effort to deal with waterlogging and salinity until well after Partition (when the massive projects of integrated canal and tubewell development under SCARP began), the history of the debate on waterlogging showed that the modelling of an environment that would define the state's ability to control nature for productive purposes required, ultimately, an integration of both macro-level and micro-level scientific concerns.

But the most critical difficulty in defining such an environment and in exerting state power over it lay in the incorporation into such a model of the role of the local producer, or the local community of producers, a problem that the emphasis on the micro-level processes involved in waterlogging reinforced. As a Punjab Conference on Waterlogging concluded in 1917, the need

[17] See, for example, the proceedings of the Conference on Waterlogging held at Lahore in 1917. *Punjab Waterlogging Note*, pt. III, pp. 95–103. This conference offered no comprehensive approach, though it found the earlier rules of 1901 entirely unworkable and inadequate.

[18] For an indication of the situation with respect to waterlogging at the time of partition in Punjab, see *Proceedings of the Waterlogging Conference, 1946*. For Sind, see *Report of the Sub-Committee of the Central Board of Irrigation Appointed to Enquire into the Question of Waterlogging in Sind* (1936).

for 'economical' use of water by cultivators played as important a part in the problem as other technical micro-processes, and itself required careful integrated research by the Agricultural Department.[19] In fact, the integration of the local irrigator into models of the hydraulic environment dated back to the earliest efforts to produce such models in the late-nineteenth century. As J.S. Beresford had written of the Ganges Canal in 1875 (in a memorandum reprinted in a Punjab Irrigation Branch Paper in 1905), an irrigating 'machine' consists of four separate parts: 'the main canal, the distributaries, the village watercourses, and the cultivators who apply water to their fields'.[20] As engineers realized, incorporating the 'losses' of water in village watercourses and in the cultivators' fields into their models was as important as the understanding of the movement of water in the main and distributary channels.[21] The search for a mathematical means to do this had, in fact, led early on to an emphasis on assessing the 'duty' of irrigation water within irrigation systems, a statistical measure of the cropped area that a specific quantity of water could be expected to bring to maturity. As an overall measure of the 'efficient' use and distribution of water within a system, this was an aggregate statistic that was yet sensitive to the theoretical impact of cultivator practices on a system's operation.

Such a measure also justified state intervention on the most local level in irrigator practices in order to control the wider hydraulic environment. But the modelling of human behaviour necessary to include irrigator practices in the larger hydraulic

[19] *Punjab Waterlogging Note*, pt. III, p. 103.

[20] Memo. of J.S. Beresford, Aug. 1875. Punjab Irrigation Branch Papers, 10 ('Remodelling of distributaries in old canals'), 1905.

[21] The importance of 'losses' in village watercourses was rediscovered in the 1960s and 1970s as a central problem of Indus Basin irrigation, but an awareness of the importance of this element in hydraulic models dates well back into the nineteenth century. R.G. Kennedy estimated in 1883, for example, that out of every 100 cu. ft. entering the Bari Doab canal system, 20 cu. ft. were 'lost' in the main channel, 6 cu. ft. in the *rajbahas* (distributaries) and 21 cu. ft. in village watercourses. Punjab Irrigation Branch Paper, 10.

environment represented a more fundamental challenge to both science and state power. For some engineers (and other administrators), the effective control of the state over the larger environment simply empowered the state to frame rules of proper irrigator behaviour that would allow them to control people as canals controlled water. Rules were thus issued on most canals to define correct irrigating practice and to punish breaches. These included rules for the proper application of water to the fields (including the mandated use in many cases of *kiaris,* or enclosed beds), rules against 'wastage' of water, rules requiring proper construction and clearance of village watercourses, rules prohibiting the growth of certain crops (such as rice) in certain areas, etc. These rules were laid out in Irrigation Department manuals and were enforced (theoretically) by a system of monitoring and the levying of fines by the Irrigation Department bureaucracies. At times, the bureaucracy seemed simply to become an instrument whereby irrigator behaviour was moulded by surveillance and punishment to fit into the scientifically modelled contours of the larger system. In practice, of course, the colonial bureaucracy—itself only partially under state control—proved entirely inadequate to this task.

Far more important for many engineers, therefore, were attempts to use a market model of human behaviour to define for it conceptually a more effective place within this system as yet another discrete, interrelated element in the larger structure of state environmental control. The British needed a framework in which both lower-level irrigation bureaucrats and irrigators would play their parts. And on one level this came from the framework of market thinking that had shaped the emergence of irrigation engineering as a discipline. Running through much of the discussion of local water 'use' (and problems of rule enforcement) in the nineteenth and twentieth centuries was an awareness of the ideal that 'efficient' use of water could be achieved only if irrigators were given choices allowing them to maximize their own productive return. By modelling irrigator behaviour mathematically in terms of market rationality, many irrigation engineers glimpsed a theoretical framework linking their larger vision of integrated environmental control to the effective micro-control of water in the fields. Though such a framework did not obviate the need for irrigation rules, it held the power to transform the meaning of these rules and thus also transform the theoretical function of the irrigation bureaucracy. It suggested the importance in environmental control of an alliance of large-scale state-controlled technology and administration with the small-scale action of maximizing individual actors to define and control the environment around them.

But significantly, in spite of considerable concern for these issues, the full British acceptance of this model of Indus Basin environmental control proved impossible. In matters of water pricing, for example, engineers discussed endlessly the sacrifice in 'efficiency' of water use caused by the official policy of taking canal rates based on the crop return from irrigated land, rather than as a market charge on the actual quantities of water delivered. But, in practice, technical and political pressures kept in place throughout the colonial era (and beyond) a system of water delivery in which charges for water reflected neither the constraints of demand or supply.[22] In part this resulted from the seemingly insurmountable technical problems of delivering water in such a manner as to make market pricing and individual maximizing behaviour possible. Technical problems of developing tamper-proof canal gauges (or modules) capable of delivering measured amounts of water to outlets (in the face of changing canal levels) preoccupied engineers for decades. Along with this engineers faced administrative problems in marking off the precise areas attached to each outlet so that the measure of water to fields could be calculated. These and other problems virtually stymied the few Punjab Irrigation Department experiments undertaken to deliver water to farmers on contract demand. After touring irrigation works in Spain and France in 1913, for example, F.W. Schonemann proposed that the British hold water auctions modelled on the system

22 For a discussion of British water pricing, see Ian Stone, *Canal Irrigation in British India*, pp. 159–94.

he found in operation in Lorca, Spain, in which the government auctioned water on contracts to syndicates of irrigators.[23] But the problems of delivering precise quantities and of defining the nature of the local 'syndicates' of irrigators that would contract for this water proved fatal to all experiments aimed at making such a system a reality.[24]

## Environmental Modelling and Indigenous Community

Perhaps most important of all, the establishment of a market model for irrigation raised larger questions about the political relationship between state environmental control and the nature of British rule in India. If the model of market rationality promised theoretically to integrate irrigators on a micro-level into a system of colonial environmental control, it also threatened to undercut the theoretical separation of the British, both from the environment *and* from Indian society, that was so central to their position as a ruling community. Indeed, the alliance between large-scale government control of the environment and profit-maximizing individuals held the potential to define political foundations for a community *linking* the state and society, a community forged through a common relationship to the environment. But this was not a vision of community for which colonial rule provided a structural foundation. For the British, the scientific definition of the environment served to legitimize the state's separation not only from the natural world that it sought to control, but also from the customary, community-based structure of Indian society.

British canal administration was therefore marked by a strong tendency to view the canal outlet as the great theoretical divider

[23] F.W. Schonemann, *Report on a Tour of Inspection of Certain Engineering Works in Spain and France* (Lahore, 1914).

[24] Problems of effectively fixing the amount of water delivered to individual outlets ruined even experiments aimed at fixing revenue assessments in the canal colonies over long periods of time, quite apart from the problem of adjusting supply to market demand. Imran Ali, *The Punjab Under Imperialism, 1885–1947* (Princeton, 1988), pp. 169–77.

of the irrigation system, with a system of rational environmental control operating on one side, and a world of indigenous, customary and kin-based community organization operating on the other. Even as indigenous communities were rigidly excluded from influence over the main, scientific irrigating system, their domination over the disposal of water 'beyond the outlet' was largely accepted as an inevitable fact of colonial irrigation. Indeed, such communities came to be viewed as part of the 'natural' environment, to be 'controlled and guided, led and regulated', like Punjab's rivers, by 'scientific' administration, rather than as allies of government in a common project of rational environmental domination.

Engineers were often well aware of the potential price paid for this division in terms of measurable irrigating 'efficiency', and they not infrequently pointed this out. But it became, nevertheless, a vision that dominated British conceptions of the system (and influenced irrigation administration well after Partition). The tensions that this created were indicated, for example, in the operation of the *warabandi* system, which was the closest that British engineers came to devising (or adapting) a technical structure for incorporating local communities of irrigators into the system at each outlet. On one level, warabandis, or registers of timed water turns for the irrigators on each outlet, defined the position of every individual irrigator with respect to the irrigation system, as each register specified the quantity of water (or, more accurately, the time of water use) to which each irrigator was entitled. But in practice warabandis were viewed more as efforts to energize local communities 'beyond the outlet' in water distribution than to extend a unifying system of rational irrigation control into the villages. Official intervention in the preparation and enforcement of warabandis thus depended, according to dominant engineering doctrine, not directly on the state but on the initiative of local irrigators. As Irrigation Department correspondence indicated in 1940, departmentally framed warabandis existed only for those outlets that had specifically requested them—at that time on less than half the watercourses in the Punjab. And perhaps more importantly, the effective working of warabandis depended critically—at least in British eyes—on the bonds of local community operating in the villages. *Warashikni,* or the violation of warabandis, was common. But as one engineer noted, unless canal officers were to be given magisterial powers to interfere widely in the village (which was a bureaucratic nightmare), the best hope for improvement would be 'to leave the present system alone and try and strengthen the village panchayat or public opinion'.[25] Though the meaning of village 'public opinion' in this context is less than clear, the implication was that only the strengthening and manipulating of the existing, indigenous community 'beyond the outlet' would make effective water distribution a reality.

But the contradictions that this engendered were considerable, and were reflected in continual complaining by irrigation officials about the failure of villagers to co-operate—as they were expected to—for the purposes necessary to make the overall system efficient. Central among these, for example, was the clearance and maintenance of village watercourses. Inadequate upkeep of village watercourses was an important cause of the seepage of water that contributed to waterlogging, as engineers well knew, and yet officials could only bemoan the lack of effective local combination in watercourse maintenance (and direct the bulk of their scientific concern with waterlogging elsewhere). Limited efforts were made before Partition to empower the formation of local silt clearance societies under the working of the Punjab Cooperative Societies Act 'with powers to allot work and get it done either by the member or at his cost', or to authorize panchayats to control watercourses in the villages (to prepare warabandis and repair watercourses). But these efforts had an extremely limited impact,

[25] Punjab PWD, Irrigation, 124, 1908. It is significant also that irrigators could be held collectively responsible for violations of *warabandis*, unauthorized irrigation, outlet tampering, etc. 'because', as one official wrote, 'the irrigators are in a position of trust, so to speak, being responsible for the maintenance of the watercourse and the due application of the water therein to purposes authorized and non-wasteful . . .' Note by M.W. Fenton, Commissioner, Multan (4 Dec. 1908). Punjab BOR, file 251/423.

and manifested the same problems that bedeviled government efforts under the Act to organize local societies and panchayats more generally: they encountered continual problems with internal disputes or domination by a few leading local landowners.[26] This is not to say, of course, that villages were without organization for watercourse clearance—or without relatively effective mechanisms for internal water distribution either according to warabandis or otherwise—but that these rarely operated without serious internal conflicts (and rarely according to an idealized vision of 'natural' community organization shaping irrigation 'beyond the outlet'). In fact, local conditions, and the nature of local water distribution, meant that structures of local organization varied enormously within the Indus Basin. And the structure of the colonial irrigation system thus guaranteed an ongoing tension between this variation and the British vision of an efficient, mathematically modelled system, combining rational networking and customary community along a vast chain of uniform outlets.

The irony in the whole structure becomes clear when it is viewed in terms of the relationship between environment and community. The moving force behind British irrigation expansion lay in the fact that the definition of the large, integrated, scientifically-defined (and potentially controllable) hydraulic environment helped to empower the colonial state and define the British as a distinctive, scientific ruling community. But insofar as local conceptions of the environment also helped to define the 'natural' communities 'beyond the outlet' that were supposed to fit into this system, British irrigation works were in many respects them-

[26] In 1923 there were only 18 cooperative silt clearance societies in Punjab; *Report on the Working of Cooperative Societies in the Punjab for the Year Ending 31 July 1923*, p. 31. Panchayats in Punjab were authorized under the 1921 Village Panchayat Act to prepare *warabandis*, but this power was withdrawn by the Punjab Panchayat Act of 1939. The reason, wrote one irrigation official, was that 'panchayats had made a mess of the warabandi cases during the years 1921 to 1938 when they had the necessary powers to frame or modify *warabandis*'. Punjab PWD, Irrigation, 115, 1932 ('Miscellaneous petitions-Lower Jhelum Canal').

selves responsible for undercutting the very vision of local community that the system relied on. In fact, the increasing dependence on relations with an irrigation bureaucracy for securing the most critical of productive resources for the local environment—water—guaranteed that a meaningful definition of the environment that was purely local was impossible, as was, therefore, a structure of encapsulated, 'natural', local communities operating in their outlet-defined spaces. By trying to incorporate indigenous 'natural' communities into a larger hydraulic model, the colonial state thus undercut the local environmental foundations for the very local communities that it professed to rely on.

An examination of the various local responses to these policies is beyond the scope of this discussion. But the implications of the colonial irrigation structure are evident in the recent work of Douglas Merrey. Merrey has used long-term data from one village in western Punjab to demonstrate the ways in which competition in the villages for *izzat* (honour) among leaders of local *biradaris* (extended kinship groups) undercut the development of local irrigation efficiency. Merrey describes in detail how kin-based concepts of honour and status created endemic conflicts beyond the outlet, which undermined government efforts to encourage co-operation and efficiency, as, for example, during a 1970s government-sponsored watercourse improvement programme. Though potentially benefiting the village as a whole, this project failed, in Merrey's view, largely as a result of a prevailing 'Punjabi culture' which inhibited the co-operation (or 'civic' sense, as Merrey puts it) that irrigation planners had sought to encourage in the village to improve distribution and efficiency. Merrey's analysis highlights the frustrations of irrigation officials and aid experts with the fact that the most powerful bonds of local community solidarity, based on kinship, made problematic the effective integration of villages into the larger hydraulic environment.[27]

[27] Douglas J. Merrey, 'Irrigation and Honor: Cultural Impediments to the Improvement of Local Level Water Management in Punjab, Pakistan', Colorado State University, Water Management Technical Report, 53 (Dec. 1979) p. 3.

But Merrey's descriptions also suggest the degree to which the bonds of biradari, however divisive, served ironically for many local irrigators as a means to counter the cleavages built into the colonial irrigation system by the state itself. Far from completely undercutting integration, the mobilization of biradari ties represented in some respects a form of both adaptation and resistance to a structure of environmental modelling that sought to separate a realm of mathematical modelling (and state control) from a realm of local community entirely encapsulated by the outlet. In fact, there is considerable evidence to suggest that kin-based biradari networks provided a mechanism through which some local irrigators were able to influence both local politics and the larger irrigation bureaucracy to exert control over the flow of water reaching their outlets from the outside. Frequently, powerful local leaders mobilized their clients and biradaris to stabilize their own water supply (and that of their followers) at the expense of opposing neighbours and factions, often by defying Irrigation Department regulations (by creating breaches, taking excessive water, putting dams in watercourses, etc.) and/or by allying themselves with Irrigation Department officials (through bribes or kinship ties) to protect their local position. Department engineers responded officially by fining offenders, but as the noting on petitions to the department indicates, it was often difficult to disentangle the networks of clientage and kinship relations penetrating across the outlet into the Irrigation Department bureaucracy itself.[28] In a world in which the colonial state sought simultaneously

---

Merrey has also written the most important, long-term historical case study of the influence of British irrigation on an Indus Basin village: Douglas James Merrey, 'Irrigation, Poverty and Social Change in a Village of Pakistani Punjab: An Historical and Cultural Ecological Analysis', University of Pennsylvania Ph.D. dissertation, 1983.

[28] Petitions against the actions of lower-level irrigation staff were common. As one engineer put it, 'it is not infrequent on the part of clever Zilladars [low-level irrigation officials] to join hands with clever Zamindars in order to hoodwink the simple share-holders in the matter of distribution of canal supplies'. Punjab PWD, Irrigation, 1, 1914 ('Petitions from and against Zilladars').

to include local irrigators within a larger hydraulic environment, and yet, at the same time, to separate them from the culture of scientific modelling that defined the larger hydraulic system (and the ruling community), the manipulation of biradari and clientage represented in some respects a rational response to the system—a mechanism for influential irrigators to mobilize forms of local solidarity and patronage to define and control their own hydraulic environment.

Even so, the price, in terms of poverty and the lack of effective mobilization for efficient productive control of the larger, modelled environment was, as Merrey's work shows, high. But this was not the only mechanism of cultural adaptation to the colonial structuring of the hydraulic environment. Many movements of rural cultural and political reform in the Indus Basin reflected more co-ordinated efforts, on a large scale, to come to terms simultaneously with the realities of colonial environmental transformation and colonial state structure. Rural movements of religious reform in part fit into this pattern; the gurdwara reform movement of the 1920s and the rise of the Akalis among the Sikhs, for example, represented at least in part a movement linking locally based communities that were increasingly tied into larger environmental and economic networks into correspondingly large community structures (and community conceptions) capable of exerting greater influence over integrated networks of environmental control. Sikh religious ideas were in many instances linked to local community control of irrigation in Punjab,[29] and it seems

Equally noticeable was the mobilization by powerful landholders of large followings in disputes for years. Departmental petitions chronicle, for example, a dispute over the local control of water between Gardezi and Tragger zamindars in Multan district that lasted a decade as each side appealed to connections at different levels of the official hierarchy. Punjab PWD, Irrigation, 115, 1932 ('Miscellaneous petitions-Haveli Canal Circle').

[29] The relationship between Jat Sikh religious identity and irrigation is suggested in Murray J. Leaf, *Information and Behavior in a Sikh Village* (Berkeley, 1972) pp. 163–4. In a village in Lyallpur with a departmental *warabandi*, for example, zamindars 'arranged 'arranged for a watch and a bell to be kept with

no accident in this connection that it was Akalis in the 1930s (with their notions of a *panth* composed of many smaller, linked communities) who took the lead in organizing co-ordinated village closures of outlets in the canal colonies to protest against the policies of the Punjab Irrigation Department (while most Muslim villages, in spite of similar local grievances, but without these forms of reformist religious organization, failed to participate effectively).[30] These were efforts, in essence, to define new indigenous models of community coterminous with new state models of the environment.

## Post-colonial Legacies

Ultimately, of course, the emergence of nationalist movements in both India and Pakistan created large conceptions of community capable of constraining bureaucratic and scientific control of the hydraulic environment. These movements challenged the British as a ruling community by establishing their own claims to rule—defined not only by their command of the language of science, but also by their assertion of the existence of national communities incorporating people on both sides of the outlet. But with ideologies developed in large part from above (by urban elites), these movements faced their own serious limitations in integrating large-scale scientific modelling of the environment in the Indus Basin

---

the Gurdwara priest who announces by the bell when the turn of one zemindar ceases and that of another begins'. Randhir Singh, *An Economic Survey of Kala Gaddi Thamman*, Board of Economic Inquiry, Punjab, 27 (1932), p. 47.

30 Protests were organized in 1938, for example, by Moga Committees ('Outlet Committees') on particular distributaries against canal department charges, enforcement of rules and, in particular, the reduction of water supply on the occasion of the engineering remodelling of channels. These were not exclusive Akali organizations, but government officials noted that there was a strong correlation between Akali strength on outlets and the co-ordinated closing of outlets as a protest. (Although the Punjab Congress took up these issues to attack the government at the provincial level.) See, for example, *The Tribune* (Lahore), 1–29 July 1938.

with the political mobilization of a large indigenous community. Indeed, these problems were evident in post-Partition efforts in both India and Pakistan to remake the environment (in both reality and in conception) and so to legitimize new conceptions of ruling community as the British departed.

This was clearest in the moves by both the new states after Partition to break the Indus Basin hydraulic environment in two so that the hydraulic environment would match (and legitimize) the claims of the two competing national ruling communities to rule separately. With a large investment from the World Bank, the rivers of Punjab were literally severed by the Indus Waters Treaty of 1960 along the Partition line; the waters of the Ravi and Sutlej that had flowed into the Indus were diverted into East Punjab and Rajasthan, while Pakistan constructed a new canal sweeping along the Pakistani side of the Indian border, intercepting and feeding the canals that had previously come from East Punjab with water brought from the Chenab and carried in a syphon under the bed of the Ravi (Bambanwala-Ravi-Bed Canal). Pakistan's water losses to India were retrieved with the construction of large storage dams on the Jhelum and Indus, in a process that allowed state control of the environment to proceed on both sides of the border with minimal reference to each other. Scientific modelling of the Indus Basin hydraulic environment thus matched (in each case) the state's claim to define and control its environment as a ruling community, perpetuating (at least in significant part) the relationship between environmental modelling and community definition and control established by the British.[31]

But the emergence of national states and the signing of the Indus Waters Treaty did not end political tensions in these Indus Basin environmental systems. The linking of environmental modelling and control with the political structuring of broad new

[31] The Indus Waters Treaty in part authorized the works that split the Indus Basin, and in part confirmed the developments that had already occurred since 1947 (including the Pakistani construction of the BRBD Canal). For a full account, see Michel, *The Indus Rivers*.

communities also empowered new elites to assert their own environmentally defined claims to power within environmental systems on both sides of the border. The definition of distinctive provincial water environments (linked to distinctive provincial elites), and the rhetoric of their appeals, like appeals to nationalism, demonstrated the continuing importance of environmental control as a charter for community. One urban Punjabi writer illustrated this in complaining about Pakistan's decision in the 1970s temporarily to close a critical Indus Basin link canal (to divert more water down the Indus to Sind): 'The closing of the Chashma Jhelum Link Canal created a Karbala in the Punjab', he wrote. 'After every Karbala Islam lives'. In the same way this canal closing gave life to the sleeping Punjabiness (*Punjabiyat*) in Punjabis'. A distinctive claim to provincial community identity thus emerged here from the fusing of Islamic imagery with the struggle to control the hydraulic environment—and in a way that defined an awakening Punjabi identity in opposition, not only to that of Sind, but also to that of Pakistan as a whole. Similar appeals to environment and community were increasingly used in the 1970s and 1980s by elites in Sind on the Pakistan side, and in Punjab and Haryana on the Indian side of the border as well.[32]

But the most severe tensions in the structuring of hydraulic environments in the Indus Basin continued to be those associated with the relationship of the 'communities' of irrigators beyond the outlets to the larger scientific system. Though developments in India and Pakistan have diverged considerably, the relationship between definitions and models of the environment and the definition and political structuring of local communities continues to shape irrigation development. In Pakistan at least, in spite of the

[32] Muhammad Hanif Rame, *Panjab ka Muqaddama* (Lahore, 1985), p. 149. The reference to Karbala is to the suffering and martyrdom of Husain, due to human oppression and lack of water, a moment which has often served in Islamic imagery as a charter of commitment to community. Provincial control over water has also been a major issue in Sikh separatist rhetoric and in Punjabi conflict with Rajasthan and Haryana.

acceleration of integrated irrigation development, and the massive mathematical modelling—now with computers—not only of canal flow but of conjunctive groundwater and canal development, the system still, in critical respects, continues to hinge at the outlet, and in ways that have helped to support a particular kind of state authority inherited from British colonial tradition. In spite of recent efforts to develop local water-users' associations, corruption and biradari patronage networks continue to shape the hydraulic system. Irrigation experts have hardly been oblivious to the problem—and the environmental degradation—that this has helped to cause. But the roots of the system are to be found in the political implications of the relationship between environment and community established in the colonial era.

## Chapter Eight

# The Environmental Costs of Irrigation in British India: Waterlogging, Salinity, Malaria

ELIZABETH WHITCOMBE

### Immense Canal System: Achievement in India

Today Sir Malcolm Hailey, Governor of the United Provinces, formally opens the Sarda Canal, and the day will be memorable even in the wonderful history of irrigation in India . . . [There are] 4000 miles of main canal and distributaries . . . commanding over 7,000,000 acres, a region as large as all the fertile land of Egypt . . . The country which will receive water is already highly cultivated, but the introduction of the canal, besides relieving distress and obviating heavy expenditure on relief work in famine years, will lead to a better class of crops being grown . . . It is anticipated that the project will yield to the State a net annual return of 7 per cent on the capital outlay of about 7.5 million.

*The Times*, 11 December 1928

The Sarda Canal, the last of the great systems constructed by the British Government of India, symbolized British Indian irrigation enterprise. The scale of the work was matched by the ingenuity of its engineering: an advanced technology devised by the government's engineers for Indian conditions;

a radical departure from precedent, Indian and European, it became the model for developing agriculture in the Middle East, western America and Australia. Sarda epitomized irrigation policy; unchanged in principle in the century since large-scale irrigation had begun, this policy was directed towards the rationalization of two aims: (a) to protect against famine; and (b) to produce a profitable return on investment by giving priority to works designed to enhance the productivity of the most highly cultivated regions.

Most of the works were financed by loan capital. Hence, in the sanctioning of constructions the emphasis was necessarily placed on the prospect of their remunerativeness. The procedure, however, failed to guarantee financial success. The canals as a whole did not pay until the hugely profitable Punjab systems were completed by the early 1920s.[1]

Table 1
British India Public Irrigation Works: Financial Results, 1937–8

| *Province* | *Works* | *Mileage* | *Acreage Irrigated* | *Total Capital Outlay (Rs '000,000)* | *Net Revenue (per cent)* |
|---|---|---|---|---|---|
| Uttar Pradesh | Productive (13) | 14,000 | 4,800,000 | 257 | 5.3 |
| | Protective | 2,000 | 427,000 | 36.7 | 1.0 |
| Madras | Productive (26) | 14,000 | 2,500,000 | 155 | 6.4 |
| | Protective | 1,500 | 190,000 | 38.6 | 1.2 |
| Bombay: | | | | | |
| Sind | Productive (16) | 9,000 | 4,000,000 | 297 | 2.6 |
| | Protective | 370 | 100,000 | 2.8 | – |
| Punjab | Productive (13) | 17,000 | 12,200,000 | 345 | 15.0 |

[1] For a summary of the economic history of large scale irrigation, see E. Whitcombe, 'Irrigation', in D. Kumar, (ed.), *The Cambridge Economic History of India*, 2 (Cambridge, 1983), pp. 677–737.

The huge investment entailed huge costs. The financial costs were accounted for in the dismal balance sheets presented annually by the Government of India. Other costs eluded the account books but were registered in the official records early in the history of the canals: water-loss from evaporation and seepage, aside from disrepair, was estimated to compromise the canals' efficiency by 60 to 70 per cent: 'deleterious effects', seepage, waterlogging, salinity and malaria were described repeatedly in association with extensive reaches of all the major systems within a decade of their opening.

To a detached observer, such as the American W.C. Sweet, seconded from the Rockefeller Foundation in 1936–7 to report on the association of malaria with perennial irrigation, such costs were the price of government policy:

> Just why an extensive irrigation system should be expected to repay its capital cost in a minimum number of years (at the expense of the efficiency of its operation and the health of its people) and in addition give government a handsome return on its money, is one of those mysteries which ordinary mortals may not fathom.[2]

Policy, dictated so largely by remunerativeness, determined that the engineers should concentrate their attention on the aspects of irrigation which paid: the calculation of the water requirement of crops and the devising of means by which it could be delivered as quickly and cheaply as possible. Drainage, in contrast, was neglected. But there was more to it. Official confidence that the vagaries of nature could be controlled and the physiography of the subcontinent amended to economic advantage was misplaced. The canals which were designed to remedy the imbalances of the environment in effect compounded them. Irrigation succeeded—profiting agriculture and thereby government—where natural conditions of adequate drainage permitted it: but where natural conditions did not permit it the costs of irrigation were written on the landscape and in the records of public health: waterlogging,

[2] W.C. Sweet, 'Irrigation and Malaria', *Proceedings of the National Institute of Sciences of India*, 4, 1938, pp. 185–9

salinity and malaria. The incomparable documentation of India's irrigation history makes it possible to demonstrate where, when and why these costs were incurred.

British-Indian irrigation began in the south, with the restoration of the Grand Anicut (barrage) on the Cauvery and Coleroon rivers. By the late-eighteenth century the Anicut had fallen into

### Construction of Principal Irrigation Works, *c.* 1800–1940

#### *I. South: Madras*

Table 2

Madras. Irrigation Works, 1820–46

| | | |
|---|---|---|
| *Cauvery—Coleroon Delta* | | |
| Grand anicut, Trichinopoly, with subsystems | | |
| ? 2nd century AD | Constructed (Raja Veeraman) | |
| . . . | | |
| 18th century AD | Gross disrepair | |
| 1804 | Survey, first repairs—reconstruction (Caldwell) | |
| 1820—1838 | Definitive reconstruction, extension (Cotton) | |
| 1840 | Further expansion | |
| *Kistna, Godavery Deltas* | | |
| 1830 | Reconstruction, extension of existing works | |
| *Madras Irrigation System, by 1846* | | |
| Number of major works | | 36 |
| Capital outlay (including repairs) | | Rs 6,000,000 |
| Annual irrigated area | | *c.* 781,306 acres |
| Percentage total gross profit/ outlay | | 69.5 |
| | 7 works | > 100 |
| | 6 works | 50–100 |
| | 10 works | 20–50 |

gross disrepair and hence failed to control the silting of the rivers. Silt choked the channels over a large part of the Cauvery basin, depriving the once highly productive land of its regular water-supply. The distress of the agricultural population and a concomitant falling-off of revenue prompted the government to repair the Anicut. The costs were low, which enhanced the work's attractiveness. No radical departure from the ancient design was needed to restore efficient sluicing of silt to the southern delta. The Anicut itself, acquired free of charge by conquest and cession, while never precisely valued, nonetheless accounted for a substantial proportion of the capital invested. The restoration was a huge success: agriculturally, since drainage of the delta was restored; and financially, since the capital investment was underestimated and revenue overestimated, the entire increment to land revenue being entered to the irrigation account. The huge profits proved a potent stimulus to expand the irrigation system into the northern deltas of the Kistna and Godavari, with something of the same success, discounted by the greater costs incurred in having to construct the barrages *ab initio.* The control of silting had felicitous effects on the environment, stabilizing the delta and enhancing the natural drainage. There was little or no waterlogging and irrigation did not complicate the natural endemicity or periodic epidemics of malaria in this region. Upcountry, however, where the abortive scheme of the Kurnool canal was constructed by private enterprise, the heavy black cotton soil proved, predictably, prone to waterlogging, and an intensification of malaria added to the costs of the scheme, bought by government to relieve the shareholders within a decade of its opening.[3]

## *II. North: The United Provinces and Punjab*

As with its first works in Madras, the government acquired a large part of the investment in the Jumna canals free of cost. The revenue was, as predicted, substantial and in the north entered

[3] 'Report on the Madras Irrigation Company's Canal to the end 1881', in *India, Public Works Department, Irrigation Proceedings,* July 1882, 13–14.

Table 3
Public Irrigation Works, Jumna Canals 1820–46

| *Jumna Canals* | | |
|---|---|---|
| *I. West* | | |
| 1358 AD | Initial works completed | |
| *c.* 1568 (Akbar) | Restoration and extension | |
| Mid-17th century (Shahjehan) | Extension to Delhi | |
| 1780 (Zabita Khan Rohilla) | Restoration | |
| 1807 | First survey, East India Company | |
| 1817 (Moira) | Restoration sanctioned | |
| 1820 | First line opened: 185 miles | |
| 1825 | Second, branch line, opened | |
| 1830 | Extensions | |
| *II. East* | | |
| Mid-17th century (Shahjehan) | Initial works | |
| 1780 (Rohilla) | Restoration | |
| 1807 | First survey, East India Company | |
| 1830 | First line opened<br>Extensions | |
| *Jumna System, by 1846* | | |
| | West | East |
| Mileage | 445 | |
| Command area (acres) | 800,000 | *c.* 300,000 |
| Capital outlay (Rs) | 1,200,000 | *c.* 2,000,000 |
| Net return/outlay (per cent) | 119 | 63 |

under two heads of account: the direct water-rate, collected by the Canal department, and the indirect increment to the land revenue from the enhanced value of irrigated land. But unlike the barrages of the Madras deltas, the Jumna canals were a great departure from precedent: a huge expansion of the ruined Mughal systems, more than twice the mileage and from three to four times the capacity. For two-thirds of their course, through low-lying country, the main canals were necessarily constructed at a high level to ensure gravitational flow. Costs, much in excess of the sanctioned estimates, were cut where possible. The new canals followed the old and tortuous Mughal alignment wherever practicable, which led rapidly to problems of silting and erosion, and therefore water-loss. Lining, even of a fraction of the mileage, was prohibitive, and seepage from the high-level sections went unchecked. The responsibility for the construction and maintenance of distributaries was made the responsibility of the zamindars: there was no system to it, and much abuse. The result was a greatly compromised efficiency and the ominous appearance of persistent waterlogging along the central and lower reaches of both the western and eastern systems reported on at length from the early 1840s.

The financial results, however, inspired confidence: that the faults in alignment could be corrected and the problems of distribution solved by replacing the zamindars' control by public administration. The revised irrigation policy was implemented in the Ganges Canal, an entirely new work, opened in 1854: 900 miles in length—more than twice the combined mileage of the Jumna canals, with no private watercourses and the first of the great canals to be financed by loan capital, on the government's confident estimate that the deficit would be converted into a comfortable surplus within ten years of the canal's opening. P.T. Cautley, its great engineer, was himself confident that the problems of the terrain could be conquered: the watercourses crisscrossing the upper reaches, the poorly drained basins of the middle and especially the lower reaches of the western doab, where his meticulous survey preparatory to the construction of the Kanpur and Etawah branches had demarcated large tracts of waterlogged and saline land.

With the accession of Crown government in 1857–8, the Company's irrigation policy was systematized. Public works were accounted as non-remunerative and remunerative, respectively: strict rules were drawn up for the regulation of expenditure.

Table 4
Imperial Irrigation, 1858–99

*Systematization of Policy: Classification of Public Works Heads of Account*

*I. State Works: Non-Remunerative*

Barracks, law courts, schools, dispensaries, etc.

*II. Works of Internal Improvement: Remunerative*

Including 'all engineering operations directed to the agricultural wants of the community'

*Programme of Works, 1868–99*

Projected command area = 'Half France + All Italy'

| | | |
|---|---|---|
| I | NWP | Lower Ganges canal opened 1877<br>Upper Ganges canal remodelling |
| II | Punjab | Bari Doab canals |
| III | Sind | Conversion of Inundation (Seasonal) Canals to Perennial System |

Capital outlay sanctioned, 1869–80

£ 30,000,000 Repayable over 10 years

'State works', according to Richard Strachey, the author of the rules, were not expected to be remunerative: here 'prudence will dictate the necessity for economy in such expenditure'. But the government's obligation for the construction of

> works of internal improvement is essentially based on the idea of their being profitable in a pecuniary point of view . . . to the Government and community, as partners. If it cannot reasonably be predicted that such a work will be profitable in this sense, it should not be undertaken.

An ambitious programme of works, inspired by the grandeur of the Ganges Canal, was launched on the expectation that expenditure on projects could be strictly controlled according to this clearly enunciated policy. But the prospect of the remunerativeness of the new systems proved an illusion. The annual return on investment on the Ganges Canal in 1874, twenty years after its opening, was a mere 3 per cent. Cautley's skill had not been sufficient to solve the problems of alignment in the central and lower reaches where silting, seepage and waterlogging compounded the natural disadvantages of drainage and already necessitated extensive remodelling in excess of estimated costs. Government, however, defended its policy: 'irrigation might not necessarily pay quickly, but that was not to be expected . . . people have to be educated in the use of water . . . there was no doubt that irrigation would pay'. But by 1876—7 the return on all irrigation works came to a net 4 per cent; of the forty-four 'remunerative works' only seven—the 'ancient restorations'—showed, in Lord Salisbury's words, 'the desirable result of a clean balance-sheet'.

The government pressed on with the expansion of irrigation, its expectations undimmed by the realities of its account books and the accumulating reports of 'deleterious effects' in the low-lying reaches of all systems so far constructed. By 1900–1 the return on the whole system had reached the minimum 7 per cent. From 1901–3 the Irrigation Commission met to advise on policy for what was to be the last chapter in British India's irrigation history. The Commission recommended a stricter definition of criteria: it devised a stricter, mathematical method of estimating the value of irrigation: it proposed a strictly limited programme of further works. (See Table 5)

Table 5
Indian Irrigation Commission: Public Irrigation, 1900–1901

| | |
|---|---|
| Total cultivated area (acres) | 226,000,000 |
| Total irrigated area (acres) | 44,000,000 |
| By public works | 19,100,000 |
| Total return on capital outlay (per cent) | 7.1 |

Official belief in 'protective' works was waning: the costs reclaiming what was at best marginal land indifferently deterred such investment. Profitability took on an even greater significance.

Punjab was fast becoming the irrigation province *par excellence*: 'canals . . . may not protect against famine', Sir Thomas Higham, chief irrigation engineer for Punjab had told the Irrigation Commission, 'but they may give an enormous return on your money'. From 1901 irrigation investment was concentrated on Punjab's huge irrigable margin, and on those schemes elsewhere which might be expected to produce results comparable to Punjab's: the Sukkur barrage in Sind, and in UP the Sarda Canal.

## Principal Irrigation Works: Environmental Costs

The costs imposed by physical conditions of climate and terrain were not only financial but also environmental: but the environmental costs of waterlogging, salinity and malaria, while documented in detail, were never satisfactorily entered in the irrigation accounts. An outline of the essential features of the semi-arid environment of the subcontinent makes clear why such costs were inevitably incurred.

### *I. Geomorphology*

The alluvium of the Ganges–Jumna and upper Indus Doab has been formed by the gradual shift of the upper reaches of the rivers from east to west. Wilhelmy has demonstrated the principle in a remarkable study of the Indus[4] in which he deduced the phases of river-shift from nineteenth and twentieth century observations, and from the archaeological ruins of towns located on a succession of tributaries; these are plotted on a historical time-scale, from *c.* 2000 BC to 1940 AD. From these patterns, Wilhelmy derived a 'law of westward stream migration' which governs the geomorphological events leading to the formation of doabs, the mechanics determined by silting, the rate and extent of which is in turn determined by climate and geology. The help of archaeologists

[4] H. Wilhelmy, 'Das Urstromtal am Ostrand der Indusebene und das Sarasvati-Problem', *Zeitschrift f. Geomorphologie*, N.F., Suppl.-Bd 8, 1969, pp. 76–93; cf. G.S. Roonwal, 'The Wandering Rivers of the Punjab, India' *Palaeogeography, Palaeoclimatology, Palaeoecology*, 4, 1968, pp. 155–9.

should be solicited in establishing the patterns characteristic of the Ganges–Jumna Doab.

This westward migration leaves behind obsolescent and ultimately obsolete channels, 'dead' rivers, or riverains, in low-lying tracts which form series of shallow basins, great and small. These *jhils*, as they are known in Hindustani, are most conspicuous in the central and lower reaches of the doabs, where the gradient is barely one foot per mile, and the surface drainage therefore sluggish and, in the case of jhils, non-existent.

### *II. Rainfall*

Rainfall is characterized by extreme seasonal variation, the curve of annual precipitation being markedly skewed, with maximum rainfall in the third quarter. For these months, precipitation frequently exceeds runoff; the risk of prolonged pooling is increased by restricted surface drainage, with waterlogging where drainage is impeded, especially in and around jhils. Excessive monsoon rainfall, irregularly distributed through the third quarter, as recorded roughly one year in every five, increases the risk.

### *III. Temperature*

Extreme seasonal variation characterizes the annual temperature curve, with maximum values recorded for the second and early third quarters, thus overlapping with the season of maximal precipitation.

### *IV. Soil Profile*

Semi-arid alluvium contains salts, dispersed through the profile by the annual rainfall. Pooling, where surface drainage is inadequate, increases subsoil moisture. Where vertical drainage is also restricted, as in long-standing jhils, by the formation of indurated layers by the accumulation of insoluble salts—carbonates (*kankar* in Hindustani)—the water-table rises, subsoil moisture reaches saturation, and salts which cannot be washed down accumulate in greater concentrations in solution in the subsoil. In the dry months following the rains, soil moisture is drawn up to the surface by capillary action with its content of salts. With the high temperatures of the later first and the second quarters, the rate of evaporation increases to maximum, and the soluble salts—chlorides, (*reh* in Hindustani)—crystallize on the surface. Tracts of impeded drainage thus mark the landscape like giant evaporating dishes, the insoluble kankar at their base and an efflorescence of white, powdery reh up the sides.

The construction of high-level canals as well as all-weather roads and railway, carried necessarily on embankments, risked obstruction to surface drainage even where, in the upper reaches of the Doab, it was adequate for the annual monsoon precipitation. The risk of pooling in the event of excessive rains therefore intensified in these areas. In the vast low-lying reaches of the central and lower Doab, embankments aggravated the effects of the natural impediments to drainage—surface and vertical. Cautley described and measured great acreages of saline-alkali marginal land in the districts of Mainpuri and Etawah, UP, in his survey for the lower Ganges Canal.[5] Severe waterlogging and salinity was persistently reported in these areas from the 1860s. In 1876, at the first official enquiry into waterlogging and salinity, Sir Edward Buck described cultivation as no more than 'a few patches of crops in the salt-covered desert around them'.[6]

The description of districts of the Doab, (still the heartland of agriculture in the north) as desert is arresting: still more so when one considers the density of its population, overwhelmingly agricultural, numbering in the late-nineteenth century upwards of 500–600 per square mile. In this cultivated desert it was not only the soil, the groundwater beneath the soil and the crops which grew on it which suffered from waterlogging and its correlate, salinity. The people who lived on the land suffered similarly, from the diseases of waterlogging and fevers, principally malaria.

[5] P.T. Cautley, *Report on the Ganges Canal Works from their Commencement until the Opening of the Canal–1854*, vol. 1, (London, 1866), pp. 265–7.

[6] E. Whitcombe, *Agrarian Conditions in Northern India*, 1, (Berkeley, 1972), Appendix 5.

Malaria may well have been known in the subcontinent since ancient times. The first modern observations in the nineteenth century noted that 'malarious fevers' were traditionally associated, in the semi-arid zone, with pooling of fresh water from the annual monsoon. Nineteenth-century medical opinion correctly identified climatic determinants: high temperatures in association with the rains. The conventional but mistaken conclusion that the cause of malaria must be 'noxious exhalations' from the overheated soil saturated by rain was disproved by the discovery of the biological agents: first the parasite, plasmodium spp., by Alphonse Laveran in Algeria in 1888, then the vector, the female anopheline mosquito, as postulated by Patrick Manson in 1896, and confirmed experimentally by Ronald Ross in 1899. Ross demonstrated the agent and the mode of transmission. Colleagues in the Malaria Survey of India provided the correlation with specific environmental factors, notably S.R. Christophers and C.A. Gill in Punjab: the critical climatic factor in transmission was not rainfall as such in association with maximal annual temperatures, nor pooling, nor soil-saturation, but atmospheric humidity. By 1920 Gill had established that a level of approximately 63 per cent humidity represented a threshold, below which the vector was unlikely to survive long enough, still less to proliferate on a sufficient scale, for the infection to be transmitted.[7] The climatic characteristics of the third quarter, annually, in the semi-arid zone, the persistence of high temperatures in conjunction with maximum precipitation, drove atmospheric humidity in 'normal' years to well above this threshold, prolonging the longevity of anophelines and thereby intensifying their breeding capacity.

Tropical malaria, as described in the medical and scientific literature of British India, had two characteristic, 'endemic' forms. Benign tertian occurred in two seasonal waves. The first was low,

[7] S.R. Christophers, 'Malaria in the Punjab', *Scientific Memoirs by the Officers of the Medical and Sanitary Departments of the Government of India*, NS, 46, 1911; C.A. Gill, *The Seasonal Periodicity of Malaria and the Mechanism of the Epidemic Wave*, (London, 1938).

in the second quarter, reaching maximum infectivity in May, and clinically mild, with no appreciable mortality. The second wave, which began abruptly in August and reached maximum infectivity towards the end of September into October, was a regular cause of significant morbidity and mortality. The second form, malignant tertian, consisted of a single seasonal wave, identical in form to the 'benign autumnal' but of greater virulence. It was endemic malaria of 'autumnal' incidence which was the 'truly "Imperial" disease, the chronic relapsing malaria which saps life and energy, alters mentality and leads to invalidism and poverty'. In 1936 J.A. Sinton, Director of the Malaria Survey of India, estimated the annual prevalence of endemic malaria at no less than 100,000,000 with an annual mortality of 2,000,000. Incidence was highest where atmospheric humidity was highest: in submontane tracts, and in waterlogged areas of the plains. This 'stable' pattern in the incidence of malaria could be destabilized by excessive rainfall, a major determinant of the incidence of epidemic malaria. Here, too, incidence was inevitably highest in tracts waterlogged naturally, or as a consequence of irrigation. Sinton estimated that an outbreak of epidemic malaria added between 250 and 500,000 to the annual mortality.[8]

Precisely where, when and how the introduction of large-scale perennial irrigation, by compounding natural disadvantages of drainage, increased the risk of malaria, endemic and epidemic, may be demonstrated from the history of regional canal systems.

## Western Jumna Canal

By 1846, twenty-five years after its opening, the canal was still showing 'excellent financial results'. But there were at the same time persistent reports of 'unhealthiness' apparently associated with the irrigation works at Karnal, not least at the barracks, and at various localities in and to the south of that district. A commit-

[8] J.A. Sinton, 'What Malaria Costs India, Nationally, Socially and Economically', *Records of the Malaria Survey of India*, 5:3, 1935, pp. 226, 263–4.

tee, consisting of Major Baker, Surgeon Dempster and Lieutenant Yule was appointed to assess conditions on the Western Jumna Canal and estimate the risk of the 'unhealthiness' occurring in the command of the Ganges Canal, now under construction. The modern epidemiology of malaria begins with this committee. The officers travelled 1400 miles through the canal tract, visiting more than 300 'inhabited localities'. Surgeon Dempster physically examined more than 12,000 individuals. He devised the spleen-rate as the index of malarial infection, which remained in clinical use until the introduction of the parasitaemia index in the late 1940s. The committee concluded that the epidemic of 'fever' which had occurred during and after the excessive rains of 1843 had been generally more prevalent and severe in canal-irrigated districts, especially in villages within a half-mile of the canal, comparable to the waterlogged tracts of the Najafghar jhil near Delhi and the Jumna *khadir:* that spleen-rates, indicating persistent infection, were highest in these areas: that similar conditions were found in the central, low-lying, division of the Eastern Jumna Canal.[9]

Action was taken. In the 1850s a number of works were sanctioned to relieve the 'pestiferous swamps'. Some of the more tortuous stretches of the Western Jumna Canal were realigned: the slope of the canal bed was regulated in the central division of the Eastern Jumna Canal: surface drainage cuts were provided for the Najafghar jhil. But the swamps persisted, and so did the wretchedness. In 1863, Yule revisited the Karnal and Delhi divisions of the Western Jumna Canal with the Superintendent, Baird Smith, noting the swamps caused by the percolation of canal water, and the salinity. More preventive measures were recommended. 'Line the canal', said Baird Smith. The expense was beyond government, which sanctioned a more modest scheme for further realignment. But when, five years later, Taylor resurveyed the 'fever-tract' of the Western Jumna Canal, he found the prevalence as high as in 1846. The distribution of benefits and costs,

[9] W.E. Baker, T.E. Dempster, H. Yule, *Report,* 1846, reprinted in *Records of the Malaria Survey of India,* 2, 1930, pp. 1–68.

physical as well as financial, continued unchanged. In 1883 it was said of the Western Jumna Canal that 'nowhere has irrigation been financially more successful; but nowhere are the evils more or less associated with a faulty system so apparent, and certainly nowhere are the remedial conditions more complex'. The melancholy catalogue was reiterated: drainage lines and swamps intersected by the canals, oversaturation of the soil from seepage and uncontrolled irrigation, 'undue' rise of groundwater levels, saline efflorescence, 'malariousness'.[10] The same remedies were proposed: realignment, surface drainage cuts, which, since water sat in them immobilized by the slightness of the gradient, merely aggravated the swamps. Lining was again mooted, and even the restriction of irrigation: neither was seriously contemplated, the former for reasons of cost, the latter for its impracticality and compromising of revenue. By 1891 the Eastern Jumna Canal, 870 miles long, now had 327 miles of drainage cuts in the central division: but the groundwater level there was still 'dangerously high' and fever as prevalent as ever. The government now admitted that 'it was doubtful if the construction of surface drains will ever materially affect the spring level'.[11] From 1890–9 vital statistics were collected annually for villages of the four southern divisions of the Western Jumna Canal, where 'fever mortality' was registered as highest in Punjab, the province with the highest 'fever mortality' in British India.[12] In 1900 the series was discontinued.

### Ganges Canal

Construction had proceeded with the example of the Jumna Canals in view. Cautley had been confident that problems of terrain could be overcome by skilfull engineering. His ingenious

[10] E.E. Oliver, 'Report on the Reh, Swamp and Drainage of the Western Jumna Canal Districts', *Professional Papers on Indian Engineering*, 3rd series, 1, 1883, pp. 63–87.

[11] *India, Public Works Department, Irrigation, Proceedings*, July 1897.

[12] Punjab, Sanitary Commissioner, *Reports*, 1890–9, Appendices H, I.

construction of siphons and aqueducts to carry the canal under and over the torrents from the Siwaliks solved the problems of the upper reaches. Here the Ganges Canal enhanced the natural advantages of the Meerut division. But south-east from Aligarh, the chronicle of poor drainage, waterlogging, salinity and 'fever' so familiar from the Jumna systems, reappeared. By 1866, twelve years after opening, sixty-six drainage cuts had been made.[13] But whenever rains were 'more than moderate'—on average, two in every five years—waterlogging recurred, and with it malarious fever. Annually, from 1867 to 1870, the Sanitary Commissioner reported an 'unusual prevalence' of fever: the area affected, the period of prevalence, and the intensity of attack all very greatly increased since the introduction of canal-irrigation, 'this prevalence and intensity being fairly measurable by the increased moisture of the soil, and consequently the atmosphere . . . by the permanent rise in the spring level . . . which must be due to canal-irrigation'. The trend persisted. Mortality for UP in a 'good' year, in which the principal cause, the 'fever-rate', was low, ranged from 15 to 22 per mille. In years of excessive rainfall, 1885 for example, mortality shot up to 38.9 per mille: the fever-rate was 35.5 per mille, the highest incidence recorded in 'tracts with the heaviest rainfall and under the immediate influence of canals'.

The Irrigation Department pointed in confidence to the 100 miles of drainage cuts in the canal command area. The Sanitary Commissioner pointed out that these were barely sufficient to carry off 'ordinary' rainfall and in years of extraordinary rainfall the fever rate in the irrigated districts continued, inevitably, to top the province. 1894 saw an epidemic of malaria, with mortality in hundreds of thousands. More drainage cuts were dug along the Ganges canal: but the annual fever rates showed no change and in 1908, another epidemic struck the province and the mortality rate was highest in the submontane and the western-central canal-irrigated districts. The limitations of surface drainage in such

[13] *India, Public Works Department, Irrigation, Proceedings*, April 1867, *Appendix, Irrigation: Ganges Canal.*

conditions were now obvious to the canal department. Official attention turned to malaria prevention, the supply of quinine and the spraying of ponds with kerosene oil, in so far as the budget of the Sanitary Commissioner permitted it, a few hundred rupees per district.[14]

## Bari Doab Canal

The UP experience was repeated in Punjab, as physical conditions prescribed. In Amritsar district, by 1868, a mere nine years after the opening of the Bari Doab Canal, waterlogging was persistently reported. By 1901 the Mian Mir subdivision had become a byword for the ill-effects of irrigation. The malaria epidemic of 1908 ravaged Punjab, again especially the canal-irrigated tracts, notoriously Amritsar district. In 1917 the great colonization scheme of the Triple Canal Project—Chenab, Jhelum and Lower Bari Doab Canals—was opened.[15] By 1922 an increasing incidence of endemic malaria was reported in the colonies, 'a serious menace [which] if it does not altogether nullify the good [such] schemes bring, at least detracts largely from them'. The clinical signs long familiar in waterlogged tracts of the older canals were observed in the colonies: chronic malarial cachexia, retarded recovery and repeated relapses, the adult population poverty-stricken and anaemic, few children on account of high infant mortality and low birth rate.[16]

The Punjab Irrigation Institute was established at Lahore in the first decade of the twentieth century with a research division, the chief function of which was the assessment and rectification

[14] NWP and Oudh, Sanitary Commissioner, *Reports*, 1867–70; 1885; 1894; J.C. White, 'Report on the Outbreak of Malarial Fever in UP . . . 1908', UP, Sanitary Commissioner, *Report*, 1909.

[15] C.A. Gill, 'The Relationship of Canal Irrigation and Malaria', *Records of the Malaria Survey of India*, 1:3, 1929–30, pp. 417–22; S.R. Christophers, 'Malaria in the Punjab', sup., n. 7.

[16] A. Taylor, E. McKenzie, M.L. Mehta, 'Some Irrigation Problems in the Punjab', *Records of the Malaria Survey of India*, 11, 1941, pp. 137–69.

of waterlogging and salinity.[17] The first significant successes were achieved by exploiting vertical drainage where practicable: in a handful of projects, including parts of the waterlogged tract of Mian Mir, the water-table was driven down to safe limits by tubewells, and a few thousand acres were reclaimed.

The achievements of reclamation, limited also by natural conditions and financial constraints, by the viability, technical and economic, of tubewells, did not change the overall picture presented by canal irrigation in the Punjab at the close of the British period. In 1944 Sir William Stampe could truthfully describe irrigated Punjab as the granary of India. The latest canals, of the Ravi-Jhelum tract, operated at an aggregate discharge of 24,000 cusecs, commanding between three and four million acres. The annual return on the capital investment ran at 20 per cent. But in the twenty years since the canals first opened, the spring-level was reported to be steadily rising in many thousands of square miles, to within seven feet or so of the surface: an estimated 50,000 acres were going out of cultivation annually, and on several hundred thousand acres more, yields were down by some 75 per cent.[18]

The adverse effects were to some extent offset and disguised by a net annual increase in canal-irrigated area, by a rise in prices sufficient to compensate for reduction in yield, and by a reduction in the land-revenue demand. Nonetheless, waterlogging and salinity now accounted for at least 1,000,000 acres of former cultivated land made barren by perennial irrigation.

## Sukkur (Lloyd) Barrage

The physiography of the lower Indus and its deltas in Sind has been determined by the same forces of semi-arid geomorphology operative in the north. Wilhelmy has also reconstructed the time-

[17] B.H. Wilsdon, R. Parthasarathy, 'A Statistical Examination of the Sensitivity of a Watertable to Rainfall and Irrigation', *Memoirs of the Punjab Irrigation Research Laboratory*, 1:1, 1927, pp. 1–51; 1:2, 1928, pp. 1–24.

[18] Sir W.E. Stampe, *Planning for Plenty* (Delhi, 1944).

sequence of westward river shift for the Indus delta.[19] Climatic parameters are similar to Punjab–West UP, but with more extreme seasonal variation, lower maximum precipitation and higher maximum temperatures. A perennial irrigation system taking off from a barrage across the lower Indus at Sukkur had been put forward by the Government of Bombay in the 1860s, but was rejected on grounds of projected costs outweighing predictable benefits. The provincial government submitted a revised scheme in 1912. After much debate the India Office refused its sanction: it saw no need for a very expensive remedial scheme of perennial irrigation: the project would not prove productive (remunerative). Sir George Lloyd considered the project so desirable, on his own assessment of its protective and productive capacity, that he flouted London's decision, pushed the scheme through the Legislative Council in Bombay, and authorized construction to begin in 1923.[20]

In 1930 five years before the opening of the barrage and the first canals, the Irrigation Department set up a research division on the model of Punjab's, to investigate groundwater conditions in the potential command area. G. Covell and J.D. Baily meanwhile surveyed every village, from 1925 to 1935, for the Malaria Survey of India.[21] From these investigations it emerged that the potential command area of the Sukkur barrage was characterized by great variation in annual rainfall, from less than 1 inch to 25, even 50 inches in different districts in different years. The incidence of malaria varied similarly. hyperendemic in the heavily-irrigated rice-growing tracts and riverains: the Sind *dhouro*, for example, abandoned in the westward shift of the delta streams, was 'highly malarious'. Records showed that there had been

[19] H. Wilhelmy, 'Indusdelta und Rann of Kutch', *Erdkunde*, 22:3, 1968, 176–91; 'Verschollence Stadte im Indusdelta', *Geographische Zeitschrift*, 56, 1968, pp. 256–94.

[20] *India, Public Works Department, Irrigation, Proceedings*, July 1914, 1–9; July 1916, 21–6; June 1921, 1–2; C.L. Setalvad, *Recollections and Reflections*, (Bombay, 1946), pp. 333–7.

[21] G. Covell, 'Malaria and Irrigation in India', *Journal of the Malaria Institute of India*, 6, 1946, p. 403; G. Covell, and J.D. Baily, 'Malaria in Sind, xv', *Records of the Malaria Survey of India*, 6:3, 1936, pp. 327–409.

regional epidemics at intervals, associated primarily with 'unseasonably heavy rainfall'.

Covell predicted a rise in the rate of endemic malaria would follow the opening of the Sukkur scheme. His prediction was confirmed. Seepage pushed up the spring level adjacent to the main lines and distributaries, and persisted during the winter months: swamps and ponds, once dry through the winter, became perennial marshes. Old inundation canals, intersected by the new canal system, were converted into a new set of riverains. Irrigation intensified in the rice tracts on the right bank of the Indus and, with seepage, the subsoil water rose within a few years from a depth of three to twelve feet to the surface: the spring level also rose in the former dry-crop areas brought under the new system. The waterlogging of hundreds of thousands of acres was compounded by two years of unusually heavy rainfall following the opening of the scheme. The result was increased atmospheric humidity in the second and third quarters, the crucial climatic factor promoting increased transmission of malaria. In Sukkur district, in 1935, Covell and Baily recorded spleen-rates of 80–90 per cent as against 15 per cent in 1927–8: hyperendemicity persisted in Larkana and Dadu and was now a uniform finding throughout the Sind dhouro and rice-growing tracts.

## Sarda Canal

Sarda was the last and the largest of the great British Indian canal systems to be constructed. Like the Sukkur barrage, the Sarda canal had its origins in a project submitted decades before, in 1871. It had met with violent opposition from the talukdars of Oudh, on grounds set out in their petition of 1872:

(1) the cultivators' need for irrigation was already met by wells since groundwater was accessible;

(2) there was no evidence that drought, or famine and scarcity from drought, had ever been a problem in Oudh;

(3) the Sarda canal would cause deterioration in the condition of the

soil, as the Jumna and Ganges canals had done, through water-logging and salinity, 'and disease would follow in its train';

(4) the canal would add to the fiscal burden, in water-rent and increment to land-revenue;

(5) it would not pay

In 1872, fifteen years after the Mutiny, the opinions of the talukdars demanded attention. The project, its remunerativeness far from assured, was shelved.[22] But the Irrigation Commission of 1901–3 retrieved it, and smiled on it. A revised project was sanctioned in 1924. In 1928 the first section of the Sarda Canal was opened to the sound of imperial trumpets. The huge tracts of saline-alkali waste- and semi-wasteland which today surround the central and lower reaches of the canal have regretably vindicated the talukdars in their opposition. Sarda's malaria history has yet to be written.

## Conclusion

The great lesson of British India's irrigation history is that it succeeded, financially and physically, where the natural order permitted. It failed where nature so dictated—where the technical and economic resources of government were insufficient to solve the problems posed by the environment and the interaction of perennial irrigation with it. Canals did not control the vagaries of nature, but compounded them. The lesson can be learnt better in the subcontinent than anywhere else in the world. The gigantic canal system, still the mainstay of agricultural development, was a gigantic experiment in the correction of nature, philanthropic in part but heavily underwritten by the commercial principle. The prodigious detail of its history, interpreted in the light of modern science, provides us with the means to reconstruct the patterns of formation and deformation in climate, rivers, soil, groundwater and public health, over historical (not geological) time. This is

22 *NWP, Public Works Department, Irrigation, Proceedings*, December 1872, 5–9.

invaluable as an exercise in the historical analysis of the great agrarian problems of the subcontinent, and for the prediction of future risk.

Chapter Nine

# Inland Waters and Freshwater Fisheries: Issues of Control, Access and Conservation in Colonial India*

PETER REEVES

In the late-eighteenth and through the nineteenth century, the British created a new regime for control over, access to, and exploitation of, inland waters in India. This new regime was the result of various activities: decisions about riparian rights implicit in the development of British systems for the control and administration of land and the settlement of land revenues; the building of irrigation works to support agriculture and other engineering works; and a range of new uses to which rivers were put in relation to growing urban and industrial areas.

By its very nature, this new regime affected colonial India's freshwater fisheries. This essay looks at the ways in which these changes produced, in turn, a need for new regulatory procedures which had still further effects on those fisheries and the people who depended on them. It attempts, firstly, to outline the nature of pre-colonial fisheries in India. It then examines the way in which the grant of riparian rights to zamindars in Bengal affected the control of fisheries and, hence, access to them; the all-India debate in the late-nineteenth century about the need to legislate to control

* Research for this paper was supported by an Australian Research Council Small Grant awarded through Curtin University of Technology for 1991 and 1992.

fishing methods which illuminates the ambiguities in the colonial position on control and conservation of fisheries; and popular demands for free access to fisheries in Bengal in the early twentieth century.

## Fisheries in Pre-Colonial India

Fishing was certainly an occupation of great antiquity in India but an adequate description of its practices, and the controls upon it in pre-colonial times, is not readily available. In part this is because there often seems to be in the literature dealing with fishing in earlier times a concern to identify it as an occupation of lesser people; and in part it is because fisheries are never seen as being of the same importance as agriculture on the one hand, or artisanal manufactures on the other. So at this time it is possible only to give a fragmentary view of the pre-colonial situation.

Fishing is referred to in the earliest Indian texts, although it has been argued that it was the occupation of the pre-Aryan inhabitants of India, and not an occupation which the Aryans ever followed. Tarak Chandra Das wrote, in 1931, 'Fish is mentioned only once in the *Rigveda* (X.68,8) where a whole Sukta is devoted to it. But it does not indicate fish as an article of food among the Rigvedic Aryas. It refers to the method of catching them with nets and that also by peoples probably belonging to a different racial stock.'[1] From the Vajasaneyi Samhita and the Taittiriya Brahmana he points to the list of names of those who lived by fishing—'the Kaivarta or Kervarta, Puanjistha, Dasa, Mainala, . . . and perhaps the Bainda and the Anda, who seem to have been some sort of fishermen'.[2] He then goes on to cite Macdonell and Keith's *Vedic Index* concerning the descriptions given by Sayana of the different fishing methods used by these groups:

While commenting on the Taittiriya Brahmana, Sayana has attempted

[1] Tarak Chandra Das, 'The cultural significance of fish in Bengal, V', *Man in India*, XI (1931), p. 294.

[2] Ibid., p. 295.

to explain the different modes of catching fish, prevalent in those days, from the various terms indicating 'fisherman' but the authors of the '*Vedic Index*' do not regard these explanations as of much authority. Thus, 'Sayana says that Dhaivara is one who takes fish by netting a tank on either side, Dasa and Sauskala do so by means of a fish-hook (badisa), Baind, Kaivarta and Mainala by means of a net (jala), Margara catches fish in the water with his hands, Anda by putting pegs at a ford (apparently by building a sort of dam), Parnaka by putting a poisoned leaf on the water.'[3]

No reason is given for Macdonell and Keith spurning this list, which certainly seems to include many of the methods that are used by Indian fishers. If spearing, and shooting with an arrow, were added—and Sunder Lal Hora finds these described, along with angling, in the *Ramayana*—it suggests that the classical texts provide evidence of a well-developed fishing 'sector' from an early period onwards.[4]

There were, however, as Sunder Lal Hora indicates in another article, Hindu concerns about fish—or certain classes of fish—as food:

It can be safely concluded that during the period 600 BC to 200 AD, fish was generally considered a valuable article of food among the Hindus, though certain species or kinds of fish, for one reason or another, were forbidden to be eaten. Among those regarded [as] suitable for eating, there was a regular gradation in quality or value . . . The *Smritis* contain contradictory statements about the use of fish as food which shows the working of the social, religious and political influences by which taking of any kind of animal flesh became a taboo afterwards.[5]

[3] Ibid., p. 295.

[4] Sunder Lal Hora, 'Fish in the Ramayana', *Journal of the Asiatic Society of Bengal. Letters*, XVIII, 2 (1952), pp. 66–7, 68–9.

[5] Sunder Lal Hora, 'Knowledge of the Ancient Hindus concerning fish', *Journal of the Asiatic Society of Bengal. Letters*, XIX, 2 (1953), p. 75. Das, in the fourth of his articles on 'The cultural significance of fish in Bengal' makes a slightly different point: 'From the Rig Vedic time up to the Grihya Sutra period we do meet with several references to fishing and fishermen but it is never mentioned as an article of food. But as soon as we reach the Dharmasutra period

If we can, in this way, point to the existence of fisheries and fishing peoples over a long period in India, we can also point to evidence of the recognition of rights to fisheries and of fishing as an occupation by local political powers up to the colonial period. Pre-colonial sales of *mirasi* rights in south India specifically mention the waters that are transferred to the purchaser.[6] Certainly, the early Madras administrators freely interpreted the reference to 'waters' as referring to 'fisheries'. F.W. Ellis lists 'fisheries' as one of the 'eight incidents of ownership contained in the Sanscrit text' on which he relied for his answer to the question 'Is Merassy right ever sold?'.[7] And Sir Thomas Munro refers to the same list in his discussion of Ellis' views in his Minute 'On the state of the country and the condition of the people' in 1824.[8]

Fishermen, along with other non-agriculturists, appear everywhere to have been subject to the 'tax on trades and professions' known as *muhtarifa* (usually rendered into English as *mohturfa* or a variant along those lines) which was an item in the *sayar* income of land controllers.[9] The note in H.H. Wilson's *Glossary* provides an overview:

---

we find elaborate rules about fish-eating. Almost all the writers on Dharmasutras and Smritis first prohibit fish-eating in general terms and then introduce certain exceptions to this rule and thereby allow consumption of certain kinds of fish.': *Man in India*, XI (1931), p. 114.

6 A. Sarada Raju, *Economic Conditions in the Madras Presidency, 1800–1850* (Madras, 1941), p. 32, and the specimen deed of sale given in full in App. II, p. 298. See also Francis W. Ellis, *Papers . . . Relative to Mirasi Right* (1818), p. 47. Kathleen Gough's description from Tanjore in the early 1950s perhaps illustrates what would have been the case then: 'Adi-Dravidas', she recorded, fished in the irrigation channels for 'minnows and small crabs . . . The larger fish in the village bathing pools belonged to resident village landlords and were sold by them once a year to local or migrant fishermen.': *Rural Society in Southeast India* (Cambridge, 1981), p. 13.

7 Ellis, *Mirasi Right*, pp. lxxxiii–lxxxiv, and p. 46 for the question.

8 Sir Thomas Munro, *Selections from his Minutes and Other Official Writings*, Sir A.J. Arbuthnot (ed.) (Madras, 2nd ed., 1886), p. 234.

9 F. Steingass, *A Comprehensive Persian-English Dictionary* (London, 1892), p. 1183, 'muhtarifa'; H. Yule and A.C. Burnell, *Hobson-Jobson*, new ed. by

A tax or taxes levied on trades and professions, on the artificers of a village or their implements, as upon the weaver's loom, upon tradesmen and their shops and stalls, and sometimes upon houses: in some places under the Madras Presidency, it is properly a poll-tax upon artificers, the taxes upon shops being termed *Pandari* and those on the profits of trade *Visabadi*; but the term is used in a general way to designate the several personal taxes above mentioned: the designation is in a great measure peculiar to the provinces of the presidencies of Madras and Bombay, the taxes of a similar nature formerly levied in Bengal being included in the general denomination of *sair*.

Baden Powell makes the point that in Bengal it was understood as 'a house tax, or kind of ground rent levied by the landlord, or a landlord community, on the non-agricultural residents in the village' and was known as 'parjot' '(or in Persian "muhtarfa")'.[10] Munro thought of it as a 'tax upon income'; although he then adds, 'In the case of labourers and other poorer orders of the inhabitants, where it does not exceed one or two rupees, it may be called a house rent . . .'.[11]

Ravinder Kumar, in his study of Maharashtra in the nineteenth century, gives an important role to muhtarifa in the social consciousness of the Maharashtrian community. 'The popularity of social values which favoured equality at the cost of progress', he argues, 'is best reflected in the *mohturfa* tax, which was levied on the artisan and commercial castes.' This was because mohturfa was levied not on individuals but on caste groups; the head of the caste was told of the demand on his group and the group then distributed this demand among the caste. This, he argues, could have led to the demand being imposed by the stronger members on the weaker; 'but in fact this never happened and the mohturfa

W. Crooke (London, 1903, rep. 1969), p. 591, 'moturpha'; H.H. Wilson, *A Glossary of Judicial and Revenue Terms*, enlarged ed. by A.C. Ganguli and N.D. Basu (Calcutta, 1940), p. 556, 'muhtarafa'.

[10] B.H. Baden Powell, *The Land Systems of British India*, 3 vols (Oxford, 1892), vol. I, p. 516.

[11] Munro, 'The importance of a tax on incomes in the form of a house tax', 15 August 1807, *Selections*, p. 103.

was distributed among the members of the caste according to their ability to contribute to the collective obligation'.[12] Whether this held equally true for muhtarifa throughout India and for all of the trades and occupations covered by it remains to be seen.[13]

There is, however, no doubt that muhtarifa was exacted from fishermen. S.M. Edwardes, in discussing Maratha taxation, makes the point that the Marathas charged muhtarifa on boats, which may be a synonym for fishermen, as well as 'palanquins, shops, oil mills and potters' wheels'.[14] A. Sarada Raju points out that in the Madras Presidency, it was charged across the entire spectrum of 'trades and professions'; 'Even the meanest and poorest—fishermen, potters, dhobis, etc.—were not exempt'.[15] These, together with Baden Powell's point about the Bengal levying of 'parjot' (as well as the existence within the sayar income of Bengali zamindars of income for 'the use of the produce of water'—called *jalkar*—which we will discuss in the next section) indicates that throughout pre-colonial India fishermen were subject to taxes on their occupation through a variety of assessments.

This can be illustrated briefly by reference to Bombay material both from the period prior to the assumption of colonial control of the 'Continental' territories and from shortly afterwards. The existence of fishing activity itself in both the Bombay territories of the East India Company and the Maratha territories on the mainland shortly before annexation is highlighted in the following passages from the Bombay Revenue Consultations for 1810–11:

[1810] Letter from Judge-Magistrate and Acting Collector [of Salsette]

[12] Ravinder Kumar, *Western India in the Nineteenth Century* (London, 1968), pp. 36–7.

[13] For some preliminary work on this area see my paper 'The Koli and the British at Bombay: the structure of their relationship until the mid-nineteenth century', paper read at the 9th Biennial Conference of the Asian Studies Association of Australia, Armidale, 6–9 July 1992.

[14] S.M. Edwardes, 'Maratha Administration', ch. xxiii in H.H. Dodwell (ed.), *The Cambridge History of India*, vol. V, *British India 1497–1858* (Delhi, reprint, 1963), p. 397.

[15] Sarada Raju, *Economic Conditions*, p. 5.

reporting on a petition from Sundry Coolies [Kolis, the fishing caste of the area] of Chindney desiring that the Mahrattas might be prevented from molesting them while fishing in the Salsette River. To instruct the Engineer Officer at Tannah [Thana] to make a chart of the river and point out therein the limits of the [fishing] stakes. The Judge-Magistrate and Collector of Salsette to report whether the Chindney Coolies have made any encroachments beyond their limits.[16]

[1811] From Salsette Judge-Magistrate, reporting the result of his enquiry into the rights of the Salsette Coolies to fish near the Mahratta shore which is complained of by the Subedar of Bellapoor and Transmitting a chart of the river . . . Secretary of Coolie Correspondence Office to intimate to the Soubhedar [*sic*] the impropriety of his preventing the Salsette Coolies from fishing near the Salsette Coast. To Subedar of Belapoor [*sic*] relative to the obstruction while fishing which the Chindney Coolies have met with from the Mahrattas [*sic*]. Translation of a letter from the Subedar of Bellapore [*sic*] asserting the right of the Coolies on the continent to prevent those of Chindney from fishing near their coast. From the Resident [15 April 1811] reporting he had applied to the Poona Government for an order on the Subedar of Bellapore prohibiting him from molesting the Tannah Coolies. Advising that the right of the Chindney Coolies to fish in the Tannah river is of too long standing to be termed an innovation. From the Resident [11 May 1811] transmitting answer to Subedar not to molest the Fishing Coolies belonging to the Company's Government. Letter to be sent to the Subedar by the Judge-Magistrate Salsette.[17]

Later, in the 1830s, in the process of simplifying the very diverse situation with regard to taxes on fishermen that they found within the continental territories which they gained after 1817, the Company's servants had to review the situation in various parts of the greatly expanded Presidency. Arthur Elphinston's recommendations provide a neat summary for Ratnagiri. He recommended

[16] British Library, Oriental and India Office Collections [OIOC], Z/P/3444, Bombay Revenue Consultations, Index for 1810, 1719–21. The stakes referred to are the stakes driven into the bed of the sea or river to which the nets are attached.

[17] OIOC, Z/P/3445, Bombay Rev. Cons., Index for 1811, 100, 103, 753–5.

that all fishermen between the ages of 16 and 60 who lived within 2 coss of the sea coast should be subject to a poll of no more than Rs 2 per head; that fishermen beyond 2 coss should pay a poll tax of Re 1 per head; 'that the Bhoees and other fishermen (many of them cultivators of the soil, who *never* go to fish at sea, but confine themselves to fishing up the creeks and rivers) should, between the above ages, be subject to a poll tax of half a Rupee per head'.[18]

## Change in the Nature of Jalkar: 'Private Fisheries' in Bengal

In the colonial situation there were changes to the way in which control over access to water was treated and to the position of customary dues within the colonial financial structure. We can see this illustrated in the case of colonial Bengal where British decisions on the rights to muhtarifa and jalkar produced a very new situation with regard to freshwater fisheries in that Presidency.

As part of the arrangements under the Permanent Settlement of 1793 in Bengal, the government—by Regulation XXVII of 1793[19]—gave rights over the fisheries bounded by their 'estate' (*mahal*) to the zamindars as part of their *sayar* income. Baden Powell explained the procedure adopted:

> As to the sayer [*sic*] dues, those which were in the nature of separate taxes—excise and the like—the Government took into its own hands, severing them entirely from the land revenue account. Others, which were oppressive, as transit dues, taxes on pilgrims and the like, it gradually abolished. Such dues of this class as represented payment for the use of produce of land or water, the Government handed over to the landowners to augment their legitimate profits.[20]

[18] OIOC, P/373/13, Bombay Rev. Cons., 19 March 1840, 1755, A. Elphinston, Collector Rutnageerie to J. Vibart, Revenue Commissioner, Poona, 23 November 1839, para 4.

[19] Bengal, *An Abstract of the Regulations Enacted for the Assessment and Realization of the Land Revenues in Bengal, Bihar and Orissa for the Years 1793 to 1824, inclusive* (4 vols, Calcutta, 1826), vol. III, p. xx.

[20] Baden-Powell, *Land Systems*, vol. I, p. 421; see also pp. 422, 516.

Among the dues 'abolished' in these moves was muhtarifa,[21] so that fishermen were in a different situation from the outset of the Permanent Settlement. What was more, jalkar was given a quite new meaning and power: 'Such dues . . . as represented payment for the use of produce of . . . water' was, of course, jalkar. It is instructive, however, to see that nineteenth-century glossaries came to define jalkar as 'profits or rents derived from a fishery' rather than merely as 'produce of water'.[22] This can be seen in Colebrook and Lambert's comment on jalkar as early as 1804: 'The rent of piscaries is obtained by occasionally drawing the fishery on the landholder's account, after which any person may fish as a gleaner; or fishermen are licensed for fixed sums, or for a proportion of the produce, regulated by rates or by express agreements. In general piscaries, as well as pastures and grasslands, are let in farm.'[23]

More detailed accounts were contained in Buchanan-Hamilton's reports which he compiled between 1807 and 1813 when he was engaged to make 'a minute investigation into the history past and present, as well as the natural resources in all its branches, of the various Districts then under the Government of Bengal',[24]

[21] Dharma Kumar, 'Agrarian relations: South India', in D. Kumar (ed.), *The Cambridge Economic History of India*, vol. II, *c. 1757–c. 1970* (Cambridge, 1982), p. 369.

[22] Government of India, Department of Revenue, Agriculture and Commerce, *A Glossary of Vernacular Judicial and Revenue Terms or Other Useful Words Occurring in Official Documents Relating to the Administration of British India* (Calcutta, 1874); it does add, for Bengal: 'Tanks, wells, and rivers in a village: Water rights, meaning fishing rights'. This *Glossary* gives similar definitions for the North-Western Provinces, Central Provinces and Punjab. See also Wilson, *Glossary of Judicial and Revenue Terms*, p. 354: 'Profits or rents derived from the water, lakes, ponds, or the like, upon a tract of country or an estate, with the right of fishing, and of cultivating the bed if dry; also used laxly for a fishery or right of fishing'.

[23] F.H.T. Colebrook and A. Lambert, *Remarks on the Husbandry and Internal Commerce of Bengal* (Calcutta, 1804), p. 69.

[24] W.W. Hunter, *A Statistical Account of Bengal*, vol. XX, *Fisheries and Botany of Bengal* by Surgeon-Majors Day, Buchanan-Hamilton, King, and Mr Kurz (London, 1877; rep. Delhi, 1976); Francis Day, 'Introductory note' to 'The

although these appear to have remained unused until Francis Day used them as the basis for his 'The Fish and Fisheries of Bengal' in volume XX of Hunter's *Statistical Account of Bengal* in 1877. Writing of Dinajpur, Buchanan-Hamilton outlined the system in general. 'Wherever the fishery' employed 'regular fishermen', he wrote, 'the landlord exacts a revenue'. However, he went on,

> In this District the property in the fisheries (Jalkar) has in many places been separated from that of the adjacent land, which seems to me to be a great loss, as it is the proprietor of the neighbouring land alone that can take care either of the fish or fishermen . . . Even the fish in ponds do not always belong to the proprietor of the banks, who, of course, will never care to stock them, and who is the only person that can prevent poaching, so that probably not one-fourth of the fish is produced for use that might be by proper care. The same may be said of Bils or watercourses.
>
> The duties that are levied on the fishermen are in general moderate enough, and do not amount to a considerable sum. The largest proprietor of whom I heard (Balaram Joti) receives only 2000 rupees a year, and I believe that part of this arises from some duties he levies on ferries. The proprietors generally let their fisheries from year to year, and the farmers (Ijaradars) sometimes employ fishermen to catch the fish, either for wages or for a share; and sometimes levy so much money for each man or boat employed. Thus a watercourse (Bil) in the Maldah District pays to the proprietor 130 rupees a year. The farmer employs fourteen men to fish with the Byana [a screen used to surround the fish so that the fishermen could take them by hand], and these give him one-half of the fish. They fish for nine months of the year, and each can make about four rupees a month, out of which, however, they have to deduct all expenses; but these are inconsiderable, as they require no boat, and make the whole apparatus. The farmer therefore receives about 500 rupees, out of which is only to be deducted the rent, and the charge of watching to prevent imposition. Small traders come and purchase the fish, which they retail at different markets.
>
> These fishermen, when they fish with the trap (Onta), pay two rupees a head for the season of three months. Their profit is then still greater,

---

and fisheries of Bengal', p. 1.

and they have a remarkably good market in the manufacturing towns. Those who fish on the Mahananda pay twelve anas [sic] a head yearly for the dry season, and the same sum, with four rupees for each boat that is wrought by five men, if they are employed in the Ilish [Hilsa] fishery. In this case, the more wealthy men furnish the boats and nets, and take one half of the fish, while each man pays his share of the duty. The profits of those who fish with nets and boats, is more considerable than those who use the screen and the traps.[25]

The rental nature of jalkar to the zamindars was so important by the time he was writing, in fact, that Buchanan-Hamilton expressed frustration on occasions at the difficulty of getting accurate information. 'There seems to be an uncommon alarm on the subject of the fisheries', he reported from Bhagalpur, 'so that I could procure no satisfactory account either of the number of the men employed, of the nature of the tenures, of the means used, or even of the kinds caught . . . The aversion shown by the owners and managers of the fisheries proceeds, I suspect, either from deficiencies of title or consciousness of fraud'.[26] Notwithstanding these difficulties, he detailed many of these same features in descriptions of fisheries in Purniah (Purnea), Bhagalpur, Patna and Shahabad districts. In all of these cases, moreover, he took pains to spell out, as he did in the case of Dinajpur, the change that was taking place. 'The property in the fisheries, Jalkar, has in many places been separated from that of the adjacent land', he reported; that is, jalkar was increasingly being separated from zamindari. It was thus becoming a *financial* right, the real profits (from production) of which went to a lessee and not a zamindar, and as a result, access was granted only to those who paid for the privilege.[27]

There was an important additional element on which Buchanan-Hamilton reported in these later sections: this was the existence of 'great' or 'exclusive' fisheries in particular hands on important stretches of the major rivers. There was an implication in his

25 *Statistical Account*, pp. 25–7.

26 Ibid., p. 69.

27 Ibid., pp. 55, 69–71, 84, 93.

descriptions that these were different in nature to jalkar within zamindari but, he suggested in a number of places, these 'great fisheries' were also often falling into a similar leased mode of operation. The 'greatest fishing' in the Ganges in Purniah district, he noted, 'belongs to a lady, who resides at Rajmahal in Bhagalpur and many fishermen in this District are in her employ' although in his report on Bhagalpur he notes that this Rajmahal fishery had now been purchased—at an auction for arrears—by the Government and 'farmed' to a Muslim for Rs 1,001 per annum.[28]

The other 'great fishery' Buchanan-Hamilton reports from Bhagalpur was that of 'Dihi-Mirzapur' which 'includes what is called the Gangapanth, or the fishery on the Ganges and all its creeks and branches'. Some five hundred families, he reported, paid 'from a-half to three rupees a-year' for rights to work this fishery.

> These people have the exclusive privilege of using the fishery of the Gangapanth, wherever the stream runs, but this is chiefly used in the rainy season, and in the dry, the fish are mostly caught in the branches and creeks (Kol or Damas), that are stagnant, and the privileged fishermen, if they fish there, must give one half of all they take to the renter of the fishery, and he may employ as many other people as he pleases. The 500 privileged families have 400 boats, and cannot well contain less than 1000 able-bodied men. The rent, according to some, is Rs 900; according to others, Rs 1100, and for the expense of collection (Saranjami) the renter is allowed a deduction of Rs 125.[29]

'Similar customs', he continued, existed in other fisheries. However, he had to conclude, 'as these fisheries are here also in general farmed, there is no knowing their real value, even if we had access to see the books of the estate, for the renter either pays a present (Salami) for his lease, or receives it at a trifle as a reward for his services'.[30]

On the basis of Buchanan-Hamilton's material, then, it is

28 Ibid., pp. 55, 70.
29 Ibid., p. 71.
30 Ibid., p. 71.

possible to conclude that in the first twenty years of the Permanent Settlement, jalkar rights were recognized as part of zamindari; but they were also recognized as being, in general, leased out by the zamindar. Moreover, other river fisheries were leased in the same way.

Did later modifications to the Permanent Settlement arrangements make any further difference to the position of jalkar? Starting about twenty-five years after the decisions of 1793, Bengal governments sought to gain a share of the growing revenues of Bengal—i.e. to circumvent the restrictions placed on their finances by the Permanent Settlement—by looking to 'resume' lands 'concealed' by the zamindars in the earlier settlement operations or new lands created by alluvial action (which would necessarily raise questions of water rights and fisheries) on which it hoped to be able to enact a 'sub-ryotwari settlement'.[31] Regulation II of 1819 and Regulation III of 1828 made provision for these resumptions and the assessment of land revenues on land so acquired.[32] Some fisheries do appear to have been acquired by government in these resumptions of alluvial lands which secured rights in the waters bounded by those lands.[33] Overall, however, these resumption procedures do not appear to have modified zamindari ownership

[31] C. Palit, *Tensions in Bengal Rural Society: Landlords, Planters and Colonial Rule, 1830–1860* (Calcutta, 1975), p. 28.

[32] F.G. Wigley (ed.), *The Bengal Code, In Four Volumes* (Calcutta, 4th ed., 1913), vol. I, pp. 171–84. (Hereafter *Bengal Code*).

[33] Mahbub Ullah describes the contemporary Bangladesh situation entirely in terms of these 'resumed mahals'; see his 'Fishing rights, production relations, and profitability: a case study of Jamuna fishermen in Bangladesh' in T. Panayotou (ed.), *Small-Scale Fisheries in Asia: Socioeconomic Analysis and Policy* (Ottawa, 1985), p. 212. It is worth noting, however, that Mahbub Ullah refers to the resumptions being on the basis of the principles in Government Order 341 of 12 September 1859 which, I think, indicates that the resumptions to which he refers came from the actions foreshadowed in the correspondence between the Lieutenant-Governor and the Board in 1859 outlined below. The early twentieth-century official report by Kiran Chandra De, ICS, reported that fisheries 'acquired by Government' were settled temporarily: *Report on the Fisheries of Eastern Bengal and Assam* (Shillong, 1910), p. 10, para 43.

of the majority of the Bengal fisheries, or the pattern of leases that had developed in these fisheries.

This is borne out in correspondence between the Revenue Department and the Board of Revenue in Bengal in 1859. The Board of Revenue, in answering in the affirmative a request from the Lieutenant-Governor for support for the government to levy 'a Tax on the Fisheries of navigable rivers, such as the Hooghly and Ganges', was quite clear as to the position regarding the river fisheries. The Board maintained that while there were 'some particular instances' of fishery rights on large navigable rivers being given, these were 'exceptions':

> the general rule is the non-existence of any declared or acknowledged rights on the part of Zemindars to levy a cess from the Julkur of such Rivers . . . The Zemindars and others have in some way or other usurped the rents of many of the fisheries in the large navigable Rivers which run by the borders or through their Estates, but the Board do not consider that they can show any good title, and they see no reason why the State should not avail itself of these resources. Doubtless the Zemindars will plead prescriptive rights which in many instances they will try to support by documentary and other evidence; but very few of the large navigable Rivers are likely to have come within the pale of the Decennial Settlement. This, however, is a point which can be ascertained only by regular investigation under Regulation II of 1819. Though the plea of prescription, even if made good, may confer the right of engaging for the Revenue from Julkur Mehals, it cannot give the Zemindars the right to hold them rent-free as they have hitherto generally done.

There were, the Board further reported, 'very valuable fisheries' in the Sundarbans, but the 'Grantees' of these fisheries 'have no rights of fishing beyond the limits of their grants'.[34]

With respect to fisheries in other inland waters there was no doubt in the Board's mind as to the position of the zamindars. 'As a general rule', the Board maintained, 'the fishery rights in Beels and Jheels are vested in the Zemindars, except in regard to

[34] OIOC, P/66/23, Bengal Revenue Proceedings, A 15 September 1859, 18: E.T. Trevor, Sec. Board of Revenue, Lower Provinces to Sec., Govt of Bengal, 344, 2 August 1859, paras 2–5.

very extensive low land not situated within single Estates, but surrounded by several Estates, such as the Beels in Backergunge, Pubna and Rajshahye, the Government title to which can only be established by suit under Regulation II of 1819'.[35] This view, moreover, was endorsed by the Lieutenant-Governor. He asked the Board, with regard to the navigable rivers, 'to carry out the measure by dividing the Fisheries into convenient sections or blocks and inviting farming tenders for them'.[36] But he underlined the fact that jalkar rights in zamindari estates were to be scrupulously guaranteed; 'The Board will . . . be careful to see that the arrangements to be made do not affect any questions as to the rights of Jhulkur in any other waters'.[37]

The position of jalkar as assets at the disposal of the zamindars, remained clear enough, therefore, at the point at which the British Crown assumed the government of India. The new regime, moreover, clearly intended that such a position should be maintained. In 1883, C.D. Field, in his authoritative text on landlord-tenant relations in Bengal, spoke of *jalkar* rights in the same terms as the Board and the Lieutenant-Governor in 1859:

> Fisheries are private property, and are strictly preserved, the slightest invasion of a *julkar* [*sic*] or right of fishery, being invariably followed by a civil or criminal suit. . . . The *Julkar* or right of fishery in all large natural waters is regarded as a valuable property, and is usually let by the zemindar at an annual rent, which is sometimes considerable.[38]

By the time Field was writing, however, important contradictions between the property rights created in fisheries and the legal concepts of British-Indian law with regard to rights to water and property rights in fish were beginning to appear. Through the

[35] Ibid.

[36] OIOC, P/66/23, Bengal Revenue Proceedings, A 15 September 1859, 19: E.H. Lushington, Offg. Sec., Govt of Bengal to Sec., Board of Revenue Lower Provinces, 341, 12 September 1859, para 2.

[37] Ibid., para 3.

[38] C.D. Field, *Landholding in the Relations of Landlord and Tenant in Various Countries* (Calcutta, 1883), pp. 54n, 707n.

1870s and 1880s, therefore, the effectiveness of the litigation which Field noted as 'invariably' following transgressions of jalkar rights, had run into difficulties which were highlighted by the widely-discussed 'Meherpore Case' in 1888. Given an opportunity by the Government of India to discuss the desirability of fishery legislation in India, the Government of Bengal decided to act[39] to protect jalkar rights because it was concerned that the zamindars were alarmed at what they conceived to be the undermining by the courts of their rights and, hence, their financial position.[40]

The problem came to the government in a memorial from the zamindars' British Indian Association. It arose from the popular conception that fish in the waters over which *amindars* exercised their jalkar rights *belonged* to the zamindars, so that anyone taking those fish without permission was guilty of theft. This, it was now clear, was not in accordance with the Common Law view of property in fish which the Bengal courts followed in cases dealing with unauthorized fishing in jalkar waters.

The Chief Secretary of the Bengal Government, raised this as the key fisheries issue in the Presidency when he wrote to the Government of India. He based his presentation on a memorandum prepared in the Judicial Department of the Bengal Government, 'Notes on the Criminal Law in India affecting Julkurs'. Jalkar incomes, he asserted, were part of the complete assets of zamindari which meant, therefore, that they were connected with the land revenue of the Presidency and hence with government

[39] OIOC, P/3449, India (Revenue and Agriculture Proceedings—Fisheries), A January 1889, 1–9, 'Mr Thomas' Draft Fisheries Bill'. The Bengal material is no. 6: J. Ware Edgar, Ch. Sec., Bengal to Sec., Rev. and Agric., Govt of India, 8 September 1888, 4016J. The Meherpore Case of 6 June 1887 is outlined in Beeby's 'Note on the Criminal Law in India Affecting Julkars' which is an enclosure to Edgar's letter; the case was reported in I.L.R. 15 Cal 390.

[40] Ch. Sec., Bengal to Govt of India, 8 September 1888, para 1; this indicates that Edgar is forwarding a memorial from the British Indian Association of Calcutta—the zamindars' association—'on the subject of the existing state of the law relating to private fisheries' signed, he indicated, 'by many influential people'.

finances. In this way, he implied, the issue could not be construed as one of narrow sectional interest. 'Ever since we came into possession of the country, the exclusive rights of fishing in internal waters, technically known as julkar, has been the subject of revenue assessment which, in the permanent settlement of Bengal, is generally lumped together with other assets from the land, and not separately entered in the revenue roll'.[41] It was true, he admitted, that there were no records kept which made it possible to give 'even an approximate figure of the revenue derived by Government from the assessment of fisheries'; but, he indicated, the Board of Revenue believed that 'the zemindari rental' from jalkar was very much more than ('must largely exceed') three lakhs of rupees.[42]

Against this background the Chief Secretary outlined the problem faced by the zamindars and—significantly, because he makes such a point of mentioning them—the lessees of *jalkar* rights. The problem derived from the legal definition of property in fish. The law, on which the Bengal courts depended, took the following view of this matter: 'The fact of fish being in a public river does not make the fish the property of the person who has the fishing right in such river, and nobody can be said to be in possession of them, as they are *ferae naturae*. The right of fishing is not property of such a nature that a man who infringes it can be said to commit criminal trespass.'[43]

Even fish in an enclosed tank which overflowed in times of flood were held to be *ferae naturae*; 'Wild fish in a bhil are not the property of any person till caught, nor are fish in a creek or in an open tank made for purposes of irrigation'. The one situation in which taking fish was theft was when they were in 'an enclosed tank . . . restrained of their natural liberty' and 'liable to be taken at any time by the owner of the tank'.

'The courts', he went on, 'had held this view consistently',

but it must be acknowledged that the public generally, including most

[41] Ibid., para 2.

[42] Ibid., para 2.

[43] Ibid., paras 3–5. This is also the source of the following two paragraphs.

of the Officers of the Government, and many of the Subordinate Courts, have always believed the law to be different, and that it was a criminal offence punishable as theft to catch fish in private waters without the consent of the owner, or in those held in julkar lease without the consent of the lessees. There can be little doubt, therefore, that the value of julkar property will be seriously impaired, if not altogether destroyed, when the real state of the law becomes generally known, and when the mass of the people realise that violation of julkar rights is not a criminal offence; for the people likely to commit such violations belong to the poorest classes, and it would be a mere waste of money to send them to the Civil Court. The result is that proprietors and lessees of julkars have practically no remedy when their rights are attacked.

The zemindars are clearly entitled on equitable grounds to ask that Government should provide adequate protection for property, from which it derives a considerable revenue, and the special character of which has been recognised throughout the entire period of our rule in India. The argument from expediency is equally strong. There can be no doubt that, when the state of the law gets generally known, there will be constant attempts made everywhere to fish in private fisheries without the consent of the owners. The landholding classes, if they find that the law does not afford them adequate protection in such cases, will take other means to protect rights to which they attach great value, and there will certainly be many cases in which violence will be used on one or both sides if the law is left as at present.

In addition, he argued, there were conservation arguments to be addressed: 'unless these rights are protected, there will be a serious diminution in the fish supply owing to the wanton destruction and waste of fish which will result . . . the promiscuous killing of fish by a crowd of persons is much to be deprecated', for while the benefit of the poorer classes could only be temporary, it would certainly be purchased at the cost of a diminution of the fish supply in the future.

Similar problems in English fisheries, he continued, had recently been addressed by special legislation.

The Lieutenant Governor understands the law in England to be that every person poaching in an enclosed fishery can be summoned for an offence, and is liable to a fine of 5 pounds over and above the value of the fish taken. A fish poacher caught *flagranti delicto* may be apprehended by anybody unless he escapes to the highway or the lands of another before arrest. In other cases he must be summoned. So, too, an *angler* fishing in the daytime cannot be arrested, but must be summoned. Under the Larceny Act (24 & 25 Vict. cap 96, sec 25) the proprietor of the fishery may demand from the poacher, and, if refused, seize his nets, implements and tackle.

These English moves, the Chief Secretary noted, led the Lieutenant-Governor to recommend that similar legislation was needed for Bengal.

Sir Steuart Bayley does not think the remedies provided need go much, if at all, beyond those provided in the English laws, except that the injured party should have the aid of the police in bringing the offender to justice. The fisheries to be protected should be all those existing within the boundaries of lands which are private property, and all those for which revenue is paid directly to the State.

The Government of India—which, as we will see in the next section, procrastinated for another eight years before it found itself able to legislate for the protection of Indian fisheries—agreed, without hesitation, to this request for criminal legislation.[44] The result was Bengal Act II of 1889—The Private Fisheries Protection Act, 1889—which received assent on 26 June 1889.[45] This provided, in clause 3:

Any person who (a) fishes in any private waters, not having a right to fish therein, (b) erects, places, maintains or uses any fixed engine in private waters, or puts, or knowingly permits to be put, therein any matter for the purpose of catching or destroying fish without the permission of the person to whom the right of the fishing belongs; shall be guilty of an offence and shall be punished for a first offence with a fine not exceeding fifty rupees; and for a subsequent offence with imprisonment

[44] OIOC, P/3449 India, Revenue and Agriculture Proceedings—Fisheries, A January 1889, no. 6: S.W. Edgerly, Offg. Sec., Govt of India to Chief Sec., Bengal, 9 November 1888, 1715.

[45] *Bengal Code*, vol. II, pp. 993–4.

which may be simple or rigorous for a term not exceeding six months, or with a fine not exceeding two hundred rupees, or both.

Under clause 5, even to enter on to 'land in possession of another or upon private waters' with the 'intent' of committing any of the offences in clause 3 warranted a fine of Rs 50.

This legislation to resolve the perceived problems in 'private fisheries' in Bengal emerged from a wider consideration of problems that were seen to have arisen within artisanal fisheries in colonial India by the later nineteenth century; and it is to that debate and its outcome that we now turn.

## Control and Conservation: 'The Fisherman's Problem' in Colonial India

Arthur McEvoy defines 'the fisherman's problem' in his masterly study of the California fisheries between 1850 and 1980:

> A self-preserving fishing industry would respect the biological limits of its resource's productivity, limiting its seasonal take to some safe minimum so as to guarantee future harvests. Fishing industries, however, do not generally manage their affairs in such a rational way. This is primarily because fishery stocks are 'common property' resources; that is, although many different individuals or firms may compete with each other for fish, no one of them owns the resource so as to keep others away from it. As a result, everyone has an incentive to keep fishing so long as there is any money to be made in the effort, whereas no one has an individual incentive to refrain from fishing so as to conserve the stock. Every harvester knows that if he or she leaves a fish in the water someone else will get it, and the profit, instead. This is what economists call 'the fisherman's problem': In a competitive economy, no market mechanism ordinarily exists to reward individual forbearance in the use of shared resources.[46]

It was just such a situation that Major Surgeon Francis Day described in his *Report on the Freshwater Fish and Fisheries of India*

[46] Arthur F. McEvoy, *The Fisherman's Problem: Ecology and Law in the California Fisheries, 1850–1980* (Cambridge, 1986), pp. 10–11.

*and Burma* to the Government of India in 1873. He recorded his dismay at the 'wasteful destruction' he had observed.[47] The reason for that alarming situation, he insisted, was the lack of effective regulation 'of how those fisheries should have been worked' since the British assumption of the administration.[48] That lack of regulation had allowed unbridled competition: 'It becomes simply a scramble on the principle—"Should I not catch them, somebody else will"'.[49] He maintained that fishers, as well as those fishing to feed themselves, acted in this way:

> At present everyone encroaches on the fishermen's calling, who seeing others slaughtering breeding fish and fry, do the same: as remarked to me in Burra,—why should we save them if others kill them? or in the Panjab, where they complained that their nets with 1 1/4 inch meshes could not take fry, whereas such were permitted to be sold in the bazaar by people not fishermen.[50]

Day's concerns were clearly spelt out: the supply of freshwater fish was decreasing everywhere and the 'recruitment' of future stock was jeopardized by the 'wasteful destruction' of breeding fish and the young fish fry.[51] He gave, as examples, developments from Madras and from Burma:

> . . . in Madras, the moturfa tax [which, he had earlier defined as 'clearly a licence to net, either in the form of a capitation tax on the fisherman, or one on his implements of chase] was abolished . . . and . . . many leased fisheries were given up to the general public. This intended boon has eventuated in their almost depopulation, now termed a 'free industry' and with which it is proposed 'no interference' should be permitted, although their almost ruined state must be evident in many localities where such licence has been allowed. The absolute giving-up of freshwater

[47] F. Day, *Report on the Freshwater Fish and Fisheries of India and Burma* (Calcutta, 1873), p. 48.

[48] Ibid., p. 47.

[49] Ibid., p. 55.

[50] Ibid., p. 50. See also his 'Introductory Note' to 'The fish and fisheries of Bengal' in *Statistical Account*, p. 18, for a similar view.

[51] Day, *Report*, pp. 41–4.

fisheries to the people without any restrictions, experience in every part of the globe, shows, always eventuates in their utter annihilation. These 'free industries' would be more aptly termed 'free poaching' or 'wasteful destruction' and as such, I consider, strongly to be condemned, and for the following reasons: That numerous individuals now fritter away their time on these fisheries instead of working at their legitimate occupations, and whilst doing so, are permitted to poach the breeding fish and fry as freely as they please—a license which they are not slow in availing themselves of. I assert that this is one of the chief causes of the present decrease of animal food . . . and that it is not only unfair to the fisheries, but also to the legitimate fishermen, whose occupation in many places is now a thing of the past . . .

. . . Burma [an area where leasing of fisheries had been traditional practice] will be especially interesting as the country which has most recently come under British rule. . . . At the present time, creeks not claimed by the fishing lessees ['Een Thoogyee'] fall to the share of the villagers, who forthwith choke them up in all directions with small dams. It appears, under the Burmese Government, dams were not allowed in any of the main streams. In the year 1861, the fishery laws in Burma were passed, and from this date, I believe, injuries to fisheries may be chiefly dated. From this period, I was informed, the practice of employing fixed engines in irrigated fields and water courses, untaxed, commenced; weirs have largely augmented, any one being allowed to take fish any way he pleases, without payment for home consumption, whilst no regulations were instituted for the protection of the fisheries from wasteful destruction. Irrespective of this, certain localities were set aside as free fisheries. The result is, that the fish are reported to be decreasing; for, if it is for one moment considered as to what such a course inevitably eventuates in, surely it must be admitted that unlimited license will cause unlimited waste. If persons may help themselves as they please, they will take those captured with the least trouble, and thus breeding-fish and fry are destroyed where they should be preserved. The people cannot be blamed for this: fishermen will do it, whether in Europe or in India, if so permitted . . . [52]

Day was not alone, moreover, in seeing the problem in these terms. The Collector of South Canara, Henry Sullivan Thomas,

[52] Ibid., pp. 47–9.

who like his friend Francis Day was a keen ichthyologist, had already investigated and reported a number of the problems which Day saw in the fisheries of his district in 1870.[53] Moreover, it was indicative that when Day began the investigations (as Inspector-General of Fisheries) which led to his Report, a number of district officers spoke to him in these terms; it was as though the occasion of his investigation released a pent-up concern about fisheries and fishers that had not been allowed to express itself.[54]

Day was convinced that this was not the necessary condition of the Indian fisheries. He held that it was wrong to imagine that Indian fisheries were being conducted as they always had been: 'I believe that great and destructive innovations have been or are being permitted, and that the British, with the most philanthropic intentions, have given to the people license in fishing that has been greatly abused, and is now destroying the fisheries'.[55] And he was convinced that regulation had to be introduced: 'future generations will have even more reason to complain than those of the present time, if we do not revert to native precedent'.[56]

How was it best to do that? Day recommended that 'native precedent' should be 'modified by British law, not as proposed in India but as existing in England'.[57] But this introduced new (and, for some, unwelcome) features. English law itself had been quite recently introduced or amended by the Salmon Acts of 1861 and 1865 and had, by this time, a range of restrictions and supervisory practices.[58] Day would have had these features in mind when he wrote: 'If it is still decided that these fisheries shall be continued

[53] H.S. Thomas, *Report on Pisciculture in South Canara* (London, 1870); pp. 3–8 (poisoning), 13–17, 24 (fry), 28–30 (fixed engines), 31–5 (meshes).

[54] See Day, *Report*, pp. 2–3.

[55] Ibid., p. 44.

[56] Ibid., p. 46.

[57] Ibid., p. 46.

[58] Thomas Baker, *The Laws Relating to Salmon Fisheries in Great Britain* (2nd edn., London, 1868), pp. 1–9; cf Day, *Report*, p. 108. Day also cites James Paterson, *Treatise on the Fishery Laws of the United Kingdom, Including the Laws of Angling* (1863); see *Report*, pp. 101, 107–8.

open to all, and their comparative utter annihilation is not wished for, restrictions as to the use of fixed engines, poisoning of waters, and perhaps the size of the meshes of nets employed, etc., will have to be laid down by authority, and to see them properly carried out, watchers or water-bailiffs would be necessary'.[59] Such restrictions and supervision raised the question of expense and hence of licences and taxes and it was these questions which ensured, despite the continued pressure over the years of a pro-fishery/pro-regulation lobby, that there was no legislation for India as a whole for a further twenty-five years.

Certainly, there were very negative attitudes within the administration about the importance of fisheries, the value of the fisher-people and their skills, and the degree of responsibility that the administration should have towards both fisheries and fishers. For each of the Days and Thomases with their expressions of concern there were several officers who thought that the fisheries were of no importance and that there was nothing that needed to be done. Day's own appointment as Inspector-General had been derided by officers in one province by dubbing him 'Inspector-General of Sticklebacks' in the ICS 'club' newspaper, *The Pioneer*,[60] and there was a good deal of ill-feeling and reluctance to assist his enquiries among district officers.

Matters went much further, however, than personal likes and dislikes. A major reason for dismissing fisheries as unimportant was clearly a view among officials that they were not sufficiently remunerative to warrant attention; land revenue was the chief source of colonial finance in the nineteenth century and subjects which could not produce revenue on that scale were not worth the trouble. One Sind official put it very succinctly: 'If the fishing

59 Day, *Report*, p. 48; note that he has a long discussion of his proposals for legislation on pp. 85–118.

60 *The Pioneer*, December 1871: pasted in cutting book in the 'Day Library of Natural History', Cheltenham Public Library, vol. 'Q658; see also P.J.P. Whitehead and P.K. Talwar, *Francis Day (1829–1889) and his Collection of Indian Fishes (Bulletin of the British Museum of Natural History), Historical Series*, 5, 1 (1976), p. 47.

ceased, the people now employed therein would have to take to agriculture, and, as there is abundance of land with scarcity of population, this would be an advantage rather than otherwise'.[61]

Most important as a block to legislation for control was the persistent argument that to take any action meant, firstly, additional expense and, secondly, the danger of creating agencies which would find new ways to intrude into the people's lives and to oppress them. Day recognized that this argument was present and commented directly on it:

It appears almost ludicrous, were it not lamentable, to observe many well-informed officials, who, in the following reports, have given their opinions, *very strongly*, that it will be hard on the people if Government issue any regulations to protect their own fisheries from a threatened destruction, and that the license now permitted and so grossly abused should be allowed to be continued in every species of poaching manner and without limitation.[62]

Such views, however, were very prevalent and they seem to have been able to undermine all suggestions for legislation and greater regulation in the 1880s.

A note prepared in the Revenue and Agriculture Department of the Government of India, as background to a conference called in 1888 to consider legislation to protect freshwater fish and fisheries, gave an insight into the attitude of the Government of India on earlier suggestions from the provinces since the time of Day's report. Except for Burma, where the government had been anxious to get as much as possible by auctioning leases and where an Act was passed in 1875, no province had a Fisheries Act.[63] When in 1879–80 the Punjab Government raised the possibility

[61] OIOC, P/695, India, Agriculture, Revenue & Commerce Proceedings—Fisheries, A October 1874, 1, Merewether, Sind to Governor in Council, Bombay, 12 December 1873, para 11, attachment to Bombay to Govt of India, 15 June 1874.

[62] Day, *Report*, p. 48.

[63] OIOC, P/3219, India, Revenue and Agriculture—Fisheries, A June 1888, prog. 5A, Revenue and Agriculture Department, 'Proposals for protection of freshwater fish and fisheries in India', February 1888, para 15.

of legislation to give the provincial government 'power to frame rules for the protection of spawn and young fish against . . . indiscriminate destruction' the Government of India held that, as it was the only province pressing for legislation at the time, there was not a sufficient case.[64] In 1881 when the Bombay Government wanted 'to provide for the preservation of Game and *Fish'* [sic], the Government of India 'withheld its assent, as it doubted the advantage of introducing restrictions which may be irksome to, and misunderstood by, the people. The public interests involved in the preservation of birds and fish were not, in the opinion of the Government of India, sufficiently strong to warrant interference with the habits of the rural population.'[65]

Similarly, a draft fisheries bill prepared by H.S. Thomas for Madras in 1883 was returned for circulation and 'for the opinion of the Board of Revenue and the Collectors of Districts'. Five years later the Government of India could report that 'Nothing further has been heard on the subject, however, from Madras. The Bill . . . involved a considerable amount of interference with private rights, and would require large and expensive establishments to be worked effectively.'[66]

The question of 'intrusion' was seen, therefore, as a question about licensing and taxing powers. If there was to be a regulatory regime that required inspections and continuous supervision (Day's 'water bailiffs') then the question of licence fees and other forms of taxation became relevant because colonial finances could not afford the additional establishment at their existing level. The introduction of such new licences and taxes, however, raised issues which the colonial government did not wish to raise at that time. So there was a strong disincentive to accept the essentially conservationist arguments for control; better, it seemed to argue either

[64] Ibid., paras 10–14.

[65] Ibid., para 7. Note that this reveals a split between the Commissioner of the Northern Division, G.F. Sheppard, who was in favour of legislation, and the Conservator of Forests, Northern Circle, A.T. Shuttleworth, who claimed that protection could be effected with reserves and without special legislation.

[66] Ibid., para 9.

that the fisheries were of no account or, if they were, to argue that the most effective controls were exercised by proprietors or lessees who stood to gain financially from them and so could be relied upon to conserve them. In the late 1880s, therefore, in a new round of discussion of legislation, the only form of legislation that received an effective hearing was for legislation to protect rights in private fisheries.

In 1887–8 there were signs that the provinces intended to move again to attempt to legislate. Both Madras and Bombay indicated in March 1888 that legislation was under consideration.[67] Madras notified the Government of India that Mr Thomas was to be placed on special duty to draft a 'simpler' Bill than he had prepared in 1883. The fact that H.S. Thomas had become First Member of the Board of Revenue in Madras by 1888 may well help to account for the decision to move again on fisheries legislation, for the proceedings of the earlier Board of Revenue made it clear that local officers then were completely opposed to any idea that licence fees would become a part of fisheries administration. In March 1888, Bombay sent correspondence from H.N.B. Erskine, the Commissioner in Sind, indicating that he believed that there should be legislation to protect the rights of lessees of Government fisheries against poaching. Correspondence with the Commissioners of other Divisions, however, revealed the deep divisions that existed on the subject. Mr Sinclair, in Kolaba, deprecated 'any recourse to legislation on the fisheries of the Regulation Provinces' because 'I do not think that we possess the machinery for enforcing any fishery laws'. The Commissioner of the Central Division, E.P. Robertson, on the other hand, ended on a vehement note—in which he suggested that his own Collectors did not properly understand the matter, since they were lukewarm on the matter of legislation—by declaring that the fact that his Division did not have a large income from fisheries was not 'any reason why the subject of fisheries should be any longer neglected in this Presidency'. In April 1888, the

[67] Ibid., progs 8 & 9.

Chief Commissioner of Assam indicated that he believed that there was a need to legislate to protect lessees of government fisheries against poaching.[68]

In the light of these developments, the Government of India convened a conference on freshwater fisheries on 31 March and 3 April 1888. It agreed, after airing considerable disagreements and reluctance on the part of some provinces to move too quickly or too widely, that Mr Thomas should draft an Indian Fisheries Bill which would be applicable in all provinces and which would certainly (a) prevent the use of dynamite or poisons in fishing; (b) regulate fixed engines; and (c) protect stock-pools. There was no unanimity, however, on the regulation of mesh size; the catching of fish by damming streams and baling out the water; and the declaration by government of a right to fish in particular waters.[69]

The draft Bill was ready by mid-1888;[70] it was circulated for provincial comment in January 1889. The Government of India's attitude was hardly such as to promote the draft. Its caveat that it did not 'endorse' the principles in the draft Bill was perhaps only to be expected, but its further point rather suggested that it anticipated that the provinces would want something different: 'whatever opinion may be formed as to the applicability of Mr Thomas's proposals, or any part of them to the province . . . the subject is one on which the Government of India will . . . be glad to receive definite suggestions independently of those which are put forward in the Draft Bill'.[71] It is indicative of the situation that the only legislation that emerged from the responses to this draft Bill was the Bengal Private Fisheries Protection Act, II of 1889, which was detailed in the preceding section.

All-India legislation—the Indian Fisheries Act, IV of 1897—followed eight years later. It outlawed the use of dynamite and poisons but it left with the provincial governments the tasks of

68 Ibid., no. 11.

69 Ibid., prog. 12.

70 OIOC, P/3449, India, Revenue and Agriculture—Fisheries, A January 1889, progs 1–2.

71 Ibid., prog. 8.

making rules applicable to the province or applicable to particular waters and of making rules to regulate fixed engines, weirs and the dimensions of nets; in other words, provincial governments had to make the choice themselves of how to impose (and pay for) such regulations. There was provision for fines for breaches of the rules and for the forfeiture of fixed engines and fish taken illegally.[72] By 1904 Bengal, Punjab, United Provinces, Coorg and the North-West Frontier Province had made rules under the Act; Bombay, Madras, Assam, Central Provinces and Ajmer-Mewara had not.[73] It would be fair to conclude that there was still considerable ambiguity in colonial attitudes to the question of regulating—and conserving—inland fisheries.

## The Question of Free Fisheries: The Bengal Case

The effect of settlement procedures and legislation in Bengal was to ensure that all fisheries were under the control of *zamindars*, those who leased jalkar from the zamindars, or were in Government hands and leased out. Reporting officially in 1910 on the fisheries of Eastern Bengal and Assam, Kiran Chandra De made the point that fisheries were either in the possession of zamindars or 'intermediate tenure holders' and were permanently settled, or they were in the possession of the Government and 'temporarily settled'. As a result, he argued, 'There are no free fisheries, in which the public have right to fish without license [*sic*], except the sea'.[74] (It should be noted that Bengal Act II of 1889 did in fact allow

[72] OIOC, V/8/62, *India Acts 1897–98*; the Act received assent on 4 February 1897.

[73] OIOC, P/6833, India, Revenue and Agriculture—Fisheries, B May 1904, 1–14.

[74] K.C. De, *Report*, p. 10, para 43. See also T. Southwell, *Notes on the Fisheries of Bengal, Bihar and Orissa* in Department of Fisheries, Bengal, Bihar and Orissa, Bulletin no. 4; *Some Remarks on Fishery Questions in Bengal* by T. Southwell (Calcutta, 1914), p. 7: 'it is to be noted that the fishery rights in some cases belong to the zamindars and in other cases to the Government. In nearly every

'angling with a rod and line or with a line only in . . . a navigable river' which, it might be said, was better than nothing.)[75]

De followed his point about the lack of public access to fisheries with a more revealing observation. 'Poaching', he claimed, was virtually unknown in Eastern Bengal: 'But in every district of Eastern Bengal there is a custom of openly defying the lessees and owners of *bhils, hoars*, or smaller *khals*, by fishing with *polos* and other hand traps'.[76] In his view the people who suffered most from these incursions were the fishermen: 'The fishermen are generally meek and timid people, and thus are often bullied by the sturdier cultivators and others' into putting up with these 'depredations' and into making presents of fish from their catch or selling at 'absurdly low prices'.[77] There may be some substance in this suggestion, but it would seem to be clear from other evidence that these defiant attacks on private fisheries had a still more serious meaning.

Two recent studies point the way to this interpretation. Ranajit Guha underlines the potency—as an instrument of peasant mobilization against the zamindars—of 'rebel' threats to bring the *polo* (trap) 'to fish in the beel, close by your village' in Pabna district as early as 1873: 'The polo in its turn', he writes, 'was regarded as a badge of insurgency. It gave to the movement and its participants their respective folk names—"Polo Bidroha" and "Polowallahs"'.[78] He also points to Santal use of collective fishing of this kind as a means of mobilizing for protest.[79]

Sumit Sarkar extends this discussion into the 1920s. He comments on a number of instances in 1922 and 1923:

---

case these fishing rights are leased out, so that public fishing in the rivers is generally not allowed.' Southwell was Deputy Director of Fisheries for Bengal, Bihar and Orissa.

75 *Bengal Code*, vol. II, p. 994, proviso to clause 3.

76 De, *Report*, p. 11, para 46.

77 Ibid.

78 Ranajit Guha, *Elementary Aspects of Peasant Insurgency in Colonial India* (Delhi, 1983), pp. 127–8, also p. 229.

79 Ibid., pp. 134–5, 237.

> Haat- and fish-pond looting by Santals in north-west Midnapur and Bankura in 1922 and 1923 however was clearly part of a broader upsurge and had more to do as we shall see with rumours of a crisis in authority than economic distress alone . . . In April 1923 for instance there was a wave of looting of fish-ponds and violation of forest rights over an area of 200 square miles extending from Jambori and Gopiballabhpur (Jhargram subdivision, Midnapur) westward to Ghatsila (in Singhbhum district of Bihar) and northwards through Silda and Binpur to Raipur police station in Bankura district . . . Crowds of up to 5,000 consisting of Santals as well as low caste Bengali peasants looted fish-ponds in daylight, asserting what they felt was a natural right.[80]

Sumit Sarkar's evidence, moreover, points to the deeper meaning of these 'attacks':

> The Santal, an official reported, 'will tell you how in his father's time all jungles were free, all *bandhs* (ponds) open to the public . . . Sometimes he is right.' . . . Santals in 1923 'believed that they were simply carrying on an old tradition', bringing back a 'golden age' when 'all jungles were free' . . . Gurusaday Dutt, the DM of Bankura, reported in 1923 that Santals freely admitted looting of fish ponds to be illegal, but 'they considered tank-raiding might act as an inducement to zamindars to concede their old customary rights over jungles'.
>
> In the Midnapur Santal rising of April 1923 the dispossessed Raja, Pratap Dal, was rumoured to have given permission to take wood and fish freely, and so there was a 'genuine belief by 90 per cent of the crowd that they were doing nothing illegal'.[81]

On this evidence, then, it is possible to suggest that 'pond-looting' was an assertion of a 'traditional' claim to access; a claim to access, that is, which pre-dates the refashioning of jalkar under the colonial land revenue system. In that earlier situation, the peasants—whether fishers, labourers or agriculturists—could fish and, in return, pay (or have exacted from them) 'dues' for the

[80] Sumit Sarkar, 'The conditions and nature of subaltern militancy: Bengal from Swadeshi to Non-Co-operation, *c.* 1905–22' in Ranajit Guha (ed.), *Subaltern Studies III* (Delhi, 1984), p. 303.

[81] Ibid., pp. 303, 306–8.

zamindar. In the new situation, peasants could only fish if they bought the right to do so from the lessee or were employed by the lessee. The nature of controls over water and fisheries—and, with this control, the nature of rights of access to, and utilization of, the fisheries—had been fundamentally altered by the Permanent Settlement and the legislation and regulations which flowed from it; but the memory of that freer period remained. (Perhaps it was particularly strong in connection with what, in Bengal, is called not simply 'freshwater' but, '*sweetwater*', fish!)

## Conclusion

Colonial rule made far-reaching changes in freshwater fisheries in India, changes which shifted control from landholders and fishers to lessees (who were most likely to be, because of the resources involved, local capitalists); denied to fishers levels of access they had previously had to fisheries; and seriously compromised—for essentially political reasons—the real conservation needs of the fisheries. As yet we do not have the data to measure accurately the effects of these changes on the fisheries or the fishers, apart from reports by officials with 'fisheries interests' such as Francis Day and H.S. Thomas, in the nineteenth century, and T. Southwell in the twentieth; but there is sufficient evidence in the material reviewed above to indicate that the problems were very real.

What is also clear is that the main vehicle for the colonial impact was the regime of 'legislation'—beginning with the Bengal Regulations which enshrined the bases of the Permanent Settlement, the later Regulations for the 'Resumed Mahals', through the later nineteenth-century Acts of the Indian legislature which governed the Burma and Bengal Private fisheries, and, finally, to the Indian Fisheries Act of 1897 (even though this applied to less than half of the territory of British India). What this means is that the colonial state was deeply and directly implicated in the condition of the Indian fisheries—and of Indian fishers—by the late colonial period. There were direct and conscious policy decisions taken by colonial officials behind each of the situations which affected India's fisheries—although not always in the eventual form which those situations assumed—decisions to give away traditional controls as well as not to take up, when the situation warranted it, new forms of control.[82]

[82] Some sense of this, perhaps, is conveyed in Southwell's very negative tone in his *Notes on the Fisheries of Bengal, Bihar and Orissa*. In the paper, published in 1914, the Deputy Director of Fisheries in the Bengal Presidency, maintained (p. 7) that 'Fishing operations in Bengal are generally carried out casually and in the old time way, viz., intensive fishing over small areas, a method which is most destructive and which is detrimental to the best interests of the fishermen themselves.' But he insisted that it was not his place to bring about change. 'The particular conditions in Bengal which render the development of the inland fisheries a matter of some difficulty does [sic] not however preclude the possibility, or desirability, of improving the present position, but from what statistical data is available it would seem almost certain that these freshwater fisheries are quite incapable of supplying the demand for fish, even if the output could be increased four-fold, and as the development of these fisheries is a question which almost wholly concerns Indian lessees, and zamindars owning the fishing rights, I do not propose discussing the question further here.' (Ibid., p. 7).

Chapter Ten

# The Conquest of Smoke: Legislation and Pollution in Colonial Calcutta[1]

M.R. ANDERSON

In India's recent history urban air pollution has occurred in so many cities, and with such intensity, that both popular discontent and government intervention have become routine features of public life. As the law relating to air pollution has grown,[2] the questions of social context and technical implementation have acquired greater urgency. Nowhere has this been more true than in Calcutta, one of the most polluted cities on earth.[3] And yet, for all the scholarly and popular attention devoted to Calcutta's smoke in the late twentieth century, the historical dimension of the problem has gone almost entirely unexplored.[4]

[1] I am indebted to Catherine Bowler and Peter Brimblecombe for advice on smoke abatement, and to David Arnold and Elleke Boehmer for their helpful comments on an earlier draft of this essay.

[2] A. Rosencranz, S. Divan and M.L. Noble, *Environmental Law and Policy in India* (Bombay, 1991), chap. 6.

[3] National Environmental Engineering Research Institute, *Air Quality in Ten Cities, India,* 1982–1985 (Nagpur, 1988); Cf. UNEP and WHO, *Urban Air Pollution in Mega-Cities of the World* (Oxford, 1992).

[4] W.A. Bladen and P.P. Karan, 'Environmental pollution and its perception in the Calcutta-Hooghlyside area' in A.G. Noble and A.K. Dutt (eds.), *Indian Urbanization and Planning: Vehicles of Modernization* (Delhi, 1977); P.P. Karan, 'Changes in the environmental perception of pollution in the Calcutta-Hooghlyside industrial strip of India', *International Journal of Environmental Studies,*

There is nothing new in this. Successive generations of Calcuttans have taken the view that the city's acrid odours and obscured horizons are a recent problem, set against a relatively smokeless past.

However, a much longer history of air pollution is apparent from earlier accounts. By the eighteenth century, smoke was cited, along with heat, dust, humidity, and noisome smells, as one of the attendant hardships and health hazards for Europeans in Calcutta.[5] The city was renowned for its insalubrious air. Calcutta was proudly labelled the 'City of Palaces' and the 'Second City of the Empire', but its architecture was obscured by thick winter mists while its cosmopolitan inhabitants were forced to breath a grey-brown muck. Colonial governments attended to the problem with a concern and level of expenditure which betrayed real anxiety. Calcutta became one of the first cities in the world to adopt smoke nuisance legislation in 1863[6]—only ten years after London, and well before many European and North American cities.[7] A special committee was formed to investigate the problem in 1879,[8]

---

15, 1980, pp. 185–9; P.P. Karan, 'Public awareness of environmental problems in Calcutta Metropolitan area', *National Geographical Journal of India*, 26, 1980, pp. 29–34; M.L. Upadhyaya, 'The extent of application of the Bengal Smoke Nuisances Act' in S.L. Agarwal (ed.), *Legal Control of Environmental Pollution* (Delhi, 1980).

[5] P. Thankappan Nair (ed.), *Calcutta in the 18th Century: Impressions of Travellers* (Calcutta, 1984), esp. pp. 4, 111, 133–4, 147, 181, 221.

[6] The *Calcutta and Howrah Smoke-Nuisances Act* (Bengal Act II of 1863).

[7] For comparative historical studies, see: E. Ashby and M. Anderson, *The Politics of Clean Air* (Oxford, 1981) for England generally; P. Brimblecombe, *The Big Smoke* (London, 1987) for London; D.E. Grinder, 'The battle for clean air: the smoke problem in post-civil war America' in M.V. Melosi (ed.), *Pollution and Reform in American Cities* (Austin, 1980) on the USA; and essays in P. Brimblecombe and C. Pfister (eds.), *The Silent Countdown: Essays in European Environmental History* (Berlin, 1990) for Leiden, York, and the Ruhr basin.

[8] *Report of the Special Committee Appointed by the Government of Bengal to Consider the Subject of the Smoke Nuisance and Suggest Measures for Its Abatement*, March 1880. In India Office Library and Records (hereafter IOLR), Bengal Judicial Proceedings (hereafter *BenJP*), 1880, pp. 335–6.

and in 1902 the Smoke Inspector for Leeds, Frederick Grover, was employed at great expense to survey Calcutta's smoke and make recommendations for its abatement.[9] Grover's report gave rise to the *Bengal Smoke Nuisances Act* of 1905, and the subsequent establishment of the Bengal Smoke Nuisances Commission, which carried out a systematic but selective smoke abatement programme throughout the colonial period.[10]

The political urgency of Calcutta's smoke problem was closely bound up with the history and function of the city within the empire of British India. The seat of government until 1911 and the commercial capital of the subcontinent until the First World War, Calcutta housed a high proportion of the European military, administrative and mercantile groups which made up the ruling classes. But for all its imperial power, Calcutta was a city nestled in swamps, with longstanding problems of overcrowding, disease, and extreme poverty.[11] Its rapid population increase, with over one million inhabitants by 1911 and over two million by 1941, intensified problems further. In these conditions, the ethos of urban improvement was strong. The dominant European ideology contended that Calcutta was liveable only because the inherent dangers of an Asiatic city had been subordinated to the discipline of scientific control.[12]

But smoke raised a different problem. It highlighted that Calcutta combined two radically different sets of ecological problems—one, the crowded streets and poor sanitation which Europeans associated with colonial Asia, and the other, the social disruption and heavy pollution more familiar from European industrialization. The combination unsettled common stereotypes,

[9] F. Grover, *Report on the Smoke Nuisance in Calcutta* (Simla, 1903).

[10] *Report of the Bengal Smoke-Nuisance Commission* (hereafter *RBenSNC*), Annual Series, Calcutta, commencing in 1907.

[11] D. Arnold, 'The Indian Ocean as a disease zone 1500–1950', *South Asia*, 14, 2 (1991); A. Bagchi, 'Wealth and work in Calcutta 1860–1921' in S. Chaudhuri (ed.), *Calcutta: The Living City*, vol. 1 (Delhi, 1990).

[12] This view is neatly summarized in 'Calcutta', *Encyclopaedia Britannica*, ninth ed. (Edinburgh, 1888).

causing Lord Curzon to despair that smoke 'makes one forget that this is an Asiatic capital'.[13] Though industrial smoke was not a prominent political issue among either imperialists or nationalists, it was an important focus for social conflict since it posed difficult questions, not only about the nature of urban society and the prospects for industrialization in India, but also the role and responsibilities of the state in the context of environmental degradation. Many of the features which are now axiomatic in environmental regulation—systematic monitoring, reliance on technical experts, technological remedies, and close collusion between industry and bureaucracy—were consolidated under the aegis of the Smoke Nuisance Acts. So, too, it was under the Acts that new techniques for policing industrial labour and disciplining the social practices of subordinate classes were introduced and consolidated. Through these developments the state acquired the capacity to construe and manipulate the quotidian experience of air pollution in an industrial city.

## The Incidence and Character of Smoke

Calcutta was uniquely situated to suffer from air pollution. A centre for heavy industry located close to the Bengal coal fields, the city was host to many types of emissions. Moreover, its topographical and meteorological characteristics tended to prevent the dissipation of smoke into the surrounding atmospheric sink. The combined effect of heavy emissions and poor atmospheric clearing bore directly upon the physical comfort of inhabitants, and many complaints were lodged. Official correspondence before 1900 reveals major smoke inundations had become a routine feature of Calcutta life by the late 1870s. Before considering the social responses to this problem, it is necessary to consider the general incidence of smoke in Calcutta's urban environment.

The perception and incidence of smoke are difficult to treat as separate issues. In general, the darker and stronger-smelling

[13] T. Raleigh (ed.), *Lord Curzon in India* (London, 1906), p. 269.

varieties of smoke elicited more comment, even though they were not necessarily the most prevalent or the most deleterious in their effects. Some fuels emitted relatively little perceptible smoke and yet produced compounds harmful to plant and animal life.[14] Smoke, like any other physical phenomenon, is perceived in ways largely determined by conditioning and cultural associations. The extensive burning of dung and other light biomass fuels such as straw and crop residues was a distinctly Indian practice, and served to mark out differences between South Asian and European technologies. François Bernier, travelling with Aurangzeb in 1665, complained that the evening meal was typically cooked over a fire of 'cow and camel dung and green wood' which produced a smoke that was 'highly offensive, and involves the atmosphere in total darkness'.[15] Bernier was not alone in finding Indian smoke repugnant. Since dung and light biomass remained popular domestic fuels in Calcutta throughout the nineteenth and early twentieth centuries, there was ample opportunity for complaint from European quarters. On the other hand, Europeans tended to tolerate and even romanticize woodsmoke from domestic fireplaces. Bengalis were inclined to ignore dungsmoke, but like Europeans, they frequently complained of industrial coal emissions.

Calcutta had well-established markets for wood, charcoal, and dung before the nineteenth century, and there was a lively trade from rural areas to feed urban demand.[16] Dung was carefully collected, often mixed with straw or rice-husks, and then shaped

[14] Cf. Peter Brimblecombe, *Air Composition and Chemistry* (London, 1986); Kirk R. Smith, *Biofuels, Air Pollution, and Health: A Global Review* (New York, 1987).

[15] When Archibald Constable translated the text in 1891, he commented on the familiarity of this common experience in northern India. See François Bernier, *Travels in the Mogul Empire, 1656–1668*, 2nd ed. (V.A. Smith, ed.) (London, 1914), p. 368.

[16] See, for instance, Nair, *Calcutta in the 18th Century*, p. 217. The high price of wood relative to dung was noted in Jahingir's day, and remained a constant feature of the fuel market in later centuries. See Francisco Pelsaert, *Remonstrantie*, published as *Jahingir's India* (Cambridge, 1925), p. 48.

into cakes for burning.[17] Dung-drying was extensive within Calcutta itself: in 1848 the Municipal Commissioners recommended that the drying of dung for fuel be prohibited as a nuisance, though the proposal was not translated into law.[18] Wood seems to have been preferred as a source of fuel where available, but it is possible that deforestation and increased urban demand brought about a greater reliance on dung, straw, and other low-grade biomass fuels. In some contexts, dung was clearly preferred over wood. Dung was not only touted as one of the five sacred products of the cow, it also offered the advantage of a longer cooking duration over a safe flame. Nevertheless, dung was the principal fuel only for the poor; those who could afford to do so purchased wood—and later coal, coke, and gas—for domestic purposes.[19]

Despite the prevalence of biomass smoke throughout the colonial period, it was the dense black smoke from coal which attracted the most attention. The use of coal as a high-grade fuel was not entirely new, but it was only with the introduction of the steam engine that coal was used on a much larger scale. Steam engines were introduced for river navigation and modest industrial efforts by 1830.[20] Coal did not immediately supplant wood as the

[17] Colebrook's early condemnation of the 'abuse of dung employed for fuel, instead of being used as manure' was echoed throughout the colonial period. T.H. Colebrook, *Remarks on the Husbandry and Internal Commerce of Bengal* (London, 1806), p. 43. The argument was further endorsed by Francis Buchanan. See F. Buchanan, *An Account of the District of Purnea in 1809–10* (V.H. Jackson, ed.) (Patna, 1928), pp. 152–5.

[18] *First Half Yearly Report of the Commissioner for the Improvement of Calcutta* [hereafter *Municipal Commission Report*] (Calcutta, 1848), p. 41.

[19] Fuel preferences also depended on the practical and ritual uses of smoke—especially for purification, curing disease, and repelling mosquitoes. Though the place of smoke in popular consciousness is beyond the scope of this paper, a careful survey of domestic burning practices conducted in Calcutta in 1958 suggested that smokiness was a much less important criterion in fuel selection than either convenience or cost. National Council of Applied Economic Research, *Domestic Fuels in India* (Bombay, 1959), p. 109.

[20] M.T. Bernstein, *Steamboats on the Ganges* (Agra, 1960); J. Tann and J. Aitken, 'The diffusion of the stationary steam engine from Britain to India,

primary fuel for raising steam, since unreliable supplies and high prices impeded coal consumption. But in February 1855 India's first proper railway was opened between Calcutta and the Raniganj coal fields, permitting a massive increase in the supply and distribution of indigenous coal. In the decades which followed, Calcutta was transformed into the centre of the Hooghly industrial corridor—an Asian equivalent of the Ruhr valley—with high levels of production and correspondingly high levels of air pollution. With its government mint, municipal water pumps, river vessels, ocean-going ships, railway locomotives, engineering workshops, and the growing number of jute mills and other industrial undertakings, Calcutta hosted nearly every type of steam engine then operating in South Asia.

Early on the British complained of the quality of Indian coal. In his 1867 survey of India's coal resources, Thomas Oldham concluded that Indian coals were high in ash content and normally provided only ½ to ⅓ the heat of average English coal.[21] In Grover's more detailed study of 1903, he found that Indian coals could contain from 14.8 per cent to 47 per cent ash by weight, depending upon the variety and source.[22] Apart from a higher ash content and lower calorific value, Indian coals produced more smoke than English coals, though a small number of clean-burning coals were available. Generally, cheaper types of coal smoked more and produced less heat than more expensive varieties. Since most coals in India were found to produce a soft, poor-quality coke, the possibilities for developing a supply of smokeless fuels were strictly limited.

In addition to biomass and coal, a third category of fuels included oil and gas. The use of vegetable oils for lighting and cooking was widespread in the eighteenth century and continued into the colonial period.[23] Coconut oil was used initially for Calcutta's street

---

1790–1830'. *Indian Economic and Social History Review*, 29, 1992.

[21] T. Oldham, *The Coal Resources and Production of India* (Calcutta, 1867), p. 22.

[22] Grover, *Report*, p. 41.

[23] In his survey of fuels in Purnea, Buchanan found widespread use of castor,

lighting, but was gradually replaced by kerosene and then gas.[24] In 1857, the Oriental Gas Company, which extracted volatile gases from coal, contracted with the Calcutta Corporation to provide street lighting. Gas remained expensive, and did not see wide use beyond street lamps, though wealthier households were able to afford gas heating and cooking appliances after 1910.[25] Petroleum distillates appeared in the 1880s to fuel oil-fired furnaces for raising steam, but did not receive widespread use until the upper Burma oil fields were developed after 1896. Petroleum use increased dramatically after the First World War, when internal combustion engines came to be used more widely in ships and factories.

The pattern of fuel consumption suggests that Calcutta's air pollution can be divided into three broad historical periods. In the first period, prior to 1855, domestic burning of wood, charcoal, dung, and illuminating vegetable oils was the major source of smoke, though coal-burning became a more common feature after 1820. The second period, spanning the middle decades of the nineteenth century, witnessed a large increase in coal smoke on top of a substratum of biomass emissions. After 1855, the use of coal increased dramatically, and by 1880 the incidence of coal smoke, both in boilers and for domestic use, had fundamentally altered Calcutta's ambient air quality.[26] The problem was particularly acute near the textile mills located close to the river.[27] In 1903, Grover identified six principal sources of smoke in the Calcutta area: (i) domestic fire-places in 'native' huts, (ii) steam launches and ocean-going steamers, (iii) lime and brick kilns, (iv) the manufacture of coke on the banks of the Hooghly, (v) furnaces used for heating plates and metal ingots, and (vi) mill and factory

safflower, sesame, linseed, and mustard seed oils. Buchanan, *An Account*, p. 606.

[24] M. Massey, *Recollections of Calcutta for Over Half a Century* (Calcutta, 1918), p. 64.

[25] See figures provided in *RBenSNC* after 1908.

[26] IOLR, *BenJP*, March 1880.

[27] *In re John Beat, Manager of Howrah Jute Mills*, Howrah Magistrate, 14 August 1898, in IOLR, *BenJP*, July 1902.

boilers used for the purpose of raising steam.[28] Though he attributed the greatest proportion of smoke in Calcutta to the land boilers contained within the jute and cotton mills, it is likely that domestic smoke arising from both coal and biomass still accounted for a very large proportion of the city's haze. The industrial use of coal increased at a rapid rate until well into the twentieth century. The number of registered steam boilers in Calcutta reached 2039 in 1912, and 2582 in 1923. Boiler registrations increased only slightly before peaking in 1926, and then began a slow decline which continued throughout the Depression years.[29] The increasing popularity of oil for raising steam reduced demand for industrial coal, though this was probably outweighed by large increases in the use of soft coke for domestic purposes in the inter-war period.[30]

The third phase was marked by the increasing use of petroleum fuels for internal combustion engines, particularly in industry, but also in ships and automobiles. Though the internal combustion engine was the industrial power plant of preference by 1921,[31] Calcutta industries were generally slow to switch from steam to petroleum power, perhaps due to undercapitalization. The change was only effected on a very large scale with the rapid industrialization of the 1940s. Petroleum distillates brought new types of pollutants even as the smoke of coal and biomass continued.

Calcutta's air pollution was exacerbated by its geographical

[28] Grover, *Report*, p. 2. Grover estimated the total consumption of coal in Calcutta at 320 tonnes per day (p. 3), or nearly 116,800 tonnes per year. But by 1917 the Calcutta Coal Controller estimated that domestic consumption alone amounted to 200,000 tonnes per year. See *Census of Coal Consumption in India During 1917* (Calcutta, 1910), p. 39.

[29] *Report of the Commission for the Inspection of Steam-Boilers and Prime Movers*, Annual Series, 1903/4–1940.

[30] Speech of Mr Alec Aikman, Chair of the Bengal Coal Company, 23 December 1935. Microfilm 8 (3), Indian Institute Library, Oxford.

[31] A.T. Weston, *Factory Construction and Installation in Bengal* (Bulletin of Industries and Labour, No. 14) (Calcutta, 1921), pp. 20–5.

setting and prevailing meteorological conditions. Unlike Bombay or Madras, Calcutta could not count on consistent sea winds to dilute smoke. Particularly in the months from November to March, weeks could go by without a significant breeze. The effect of the still air was compounded by a lack of rain during these months.[32] To make matters worse, local meteorological conditions made Calcutta vulnerable to frequent temperature inversions which prevented vertical ventilation and trapped smoke in the lower atmosphere.[33] And like London, Calcutta suffered from recurrent fogs, which became more intense and of longer duration as smoke emissions increased. The fogs, which were common in this part of Bengal,[34] arose in part from the marshes which surrounded the city. Yet the programmes of draining and 'improving' the wetlands during the nineteenth century did little to abate the fog.[35] A partial series of fog data for the period 1879 to 1894 reveals that though fog was almost non-existent in the months of May to September, it was a standard feature in the period from October to March, when the proportion of days with fog ranged between 13 per cent and 48 per cent.[36] Fog often settled in for long periods. The month of January 1884, for instance, saw twenty-nine days of fog. Smoke aggravated the phenomenon, mixing with fog to create thick sulphurous smogs.[37] And like the

[32] See the Alipore Observatory records in *Meteorological Observations Recorded at Six Stations in India*, Annual Series, 1879–1894. The observation methodology and system of notation are described in Henry F. Blanford, *The Indian Meteorologist's Vade-Mecum* (Calcutta, 1877), pp. 58–60; see also *Meteorological Observations at St. Xavier's College, Calcutta, 1868–1917* (Calcutta, 1918).

[33] S.C. Basu, 'Fog forecasting over Calcutta and neighbourhood', *Indian Journal of Meteorology and Geophysics*, 3:4 (October 1952), p. 281.

[34] Colebrook, *Remarks*, p. 7.

[35] See Christine Furedy, 'From waste land to waste-not land: the role of the Salt Lakes, East Calcutta, in waste treatment and recycling, 1854–1930' in P. Sinha (ed.), *The Urban Experience: Calcutta* (Calcutta, 1987).

[36] Derived from the Alipore observations in *Meteorological Observations Recorded at Six Stations in India*.

[37] IOLR, *BenJP*, March 1880, p. 335; see also Amal Basu, 'Frequency of

great industrial centres of Belgium and Pennsylvania, Calcutta experienced smogs intense enough to disrupt the conduct of everyday business and cause real hardship for residents with respiratory problems. By 1927, when the health effects of smoke came to preoccupy official concern, it was estimated that the death rate from respiratory disease tripled during especially smoky periods.[38]

Despite the severity of Calcutta's industrial smoke, it is clear that not everyone regarded smoke as a nuisance. For some, 'volumes of thick black smoke pouring from factory chimneys' were signs of 'hustle and prosperity'.[39] Supporters of industry equated smoke with prosperity and the bracing technological achievements of the Victorian age. However, the experience of winter smogs in Calcutta prompted many others to complain. Early official writings focus on the 'nuisance' of smoke—its impact on the physical comfort of Calcutta's residents, especially Europeans. There was more at stake than just smoke. Most protests against factory smoke were accompanied by charges of untidiness, noise, vibration, irregular hours, and the general disruption of neighbourhood life. Memories of an older Calcutta—a centre of stately poise, concerned with administration and shipping rather than industry and engineering—were invoked against rapid industrialization.[40] Behind smoke nuisance lurked a deeper concern about the appropriateness of industrialization to Indian conditions, as well as a nostalgia for 'traditional' India that seemed to be passing away before the eyes of observers.

## The New Nuisance

Though Calcutta's winter haze was patently a product of human activity, administrators of the East India Company were initially

---

fog at Alipore, Dum Dum, and Barrackpore', *Indian Journal of Meteorology and Geophysics*, 5:4 (October 1954), p. 352.

[38] *RBenSNC*, 1927, p. 4.

[39] *RBenSNC*, 1918–19, p. 1.

[40] See, for instance, Sir Henry Craik, *Impressions of India* (London, 1908), pp. 212–14.

inclined to treat it as a pernicious but permanent feature of the Bengal landscape. Apart from anecdotal complaints, neither Company officials nor their associates devoted serious attention to Calcutta's smoke before 1855. There was, however, extensive concern for good ventilation, both in individual houses and in the town more generally. A strong current of European medical thought stressed the health dangers associated with miasmas—pathogenic emanations from putrescent organic matter—said to arise from swamps, sewers, and other unwholesome locales. Situated amidst marshes and waterways, Calcutta was famous for its unhealthy air, which was also attributed to the slovenly habits of natives.[41] The principal concern of early nineteenth-century administrators was to 'ameliorate the climate' so as to render the seat of government 'a place where Englishmen, having the usual constitutions of their race, can live in full possession of their faculties, and their vigour'.[42] Extensive thought was put into draining stagnant waters and opening up streets in order to provide the city with good ventilation. Following an influential report by the Fever Hospital Committee in 1839, the Municipal Commission was constituted in 1848 with a view to coordinating sanitary, commercial, and political improvements in the urban environment. The Commission articulated anxieties about the ventilation problems in the 'native' district of northern Calcutta, which was becoming 'thickly populated' with a 'class of people indifferent to cleanliness', posing a 'danger to health, life, and property'.[43] While many bustees in the native town were cleared out to provide better ventilation into the city, the Commission continued its work of watering the streets in the European town to minimize the 'great discomfort produced by dust'.[44]

[41] F.P. Strong, *Extracts from the Topography and Vital Statistics of Calcutta* (Calcutta, 1837).

[42] Marquis of Wellesley, Minute of 16 June 1803, quoted in *Abridgment of the Report of the Committee Appointed for the Establishment of a Fever Hospital* (Calcutta, 1840), pp. 62, 64.

[43] *Municipal Commission Report*, 1860, p. 42.

[44] *Municipal Commission Report*, 1861, p. 12.

HIGHEST Award and First-class Certificate,
Calcutta International Exhibition, 1883-4

The Pioneer Paper Mills of India.

**The Bally Paper Mills Co., Ld.,**
Calcutta.

Paper Makers and Manufacturing Stationers: Contractors to the Government of India.

Mills: BALLY. | Stationery Dept.: 13, STRAND ROAD.

*Managing Agents:*

**Geo. Henderson & Co.,**
*100, Clive Street, CALCUTTA.*

Illustration 1. The Bally Paper Mills (an advertisement)

Illustration 2. The Bally Paper Mills

Thus, prior to 1855, the extensive attentions devoted to ventilation were concerned principally with miasmas rather than smoke. In this context, the 1863 Calcutta and Howrah Smoke Nuisance Act presents itself as an innovation largely without precedent or purpose. What gave rise to the new state interventionism in the matter of industrial smoke? Several factors were important. One explanation lies in the relation between Calcutta—the 'British Metropolis in the East'[45]—and the industrial towns of England, particularly metropolitan London which had mounted a campaign against smoke in the 1850s. By this time Calcutta was seen as an emblem of a more confident British Empire, and its policies had to endure comparison with other world-class cities. Early pressures to evolve a policy on smoke abatement arose principally among the European administrative and mercantile groups who not only made their lives in Calcutta, but were aware of the commercial and political importance of the urban environment. Also, the Act must be understood in the context of the early 1860s which witnessed a great expansion in criminal legislation. The new Penal Code and the various Police Acts signalled a maturation in the colonial state, now increasingly prepared to intervene in the conduct of everyday life.[46]

But the main explanation must lie in this: that starting in 1855 with the ready availability of Raniganj coal, the city witnessed a sudden change in the character of its atmosphere. It was not so much that aggregate levels of haze had increased, but rather that the dense black smoke of industrial chimneys focused attention on air quality in a new way. In these new circumstances, the temptation to regard smoke as a fixed feature of the landscape diminished. The new sources of smoke were clearly identifiable and obviously a product of human action. In a city where domestic chimneys were uncommon, the smokestacks of steamships and

[45] *Municipal Commission Report*, 1859, p. 2.

[46] M.R. Anderson, 'Public Nuisance and Private Purpose: Policed Environments in British India, 1860–1947', SOAS Law Department Working Paper No. 1 (1992).

factories prominently displayed their dense coal smoke against the backdrop of sky. In addition to steamships, the principal culprits were the new jute mills located near the river which were transforming the character of Calcutta life with their noisy machinery and expanding labour force. The concentration of factories along the river, closely adjacent to the administrative nerve centre of India as well as the businesses and residences of the influential public, raised fears of conflagration and other industrial hazards. European industry was interfering with European (and increasingly Bengali) comfort and pride. In response to these concerns, the Municipal Commission recommended in 1860 that certain jute works be moved outside of the city entirely.[47]

As things turned out, the jute mills were allowed to stay, but their emissions were made subject to new regulation. In January 1863, the Bengal Council promulgated the Calcutta and Howrah Smoke-Nuisances Act, modelled on the London legislation which Palmerston had forced through Parliament ten years before.[48] The Act required that any furnace employed for the operation of a steam engine or used for any other purposes of trade or manufacture should be constructed 'so as to consume or burn its own smoke'. In keeping with the English legislation, the Act did not require a furnace to consume or burn *every* particle of smoke, but rather that the furnace employ 'the best practicable means for preventing or counteracting such smoke' and that the fire be carefully attended so as to burn, 'as far as possible, all the smoke' arising from the furnace.[49] The Act was principally aimed at land-based steam engines, and did not apply to domestic fires, locomotives, or steam vessels other than ferries.

[47] *Municipal Commission Report*, 1860, p. 44.

[48] Bengal Council Act II of 1863, based on the *Smoke Nuisance Abatement (Metropolis) Act* of 1853 (16 & 17 Vict cap 128). Though a similar Act was introduced in Bombay slightly earlier (Bombay Act VIII of 1862), Bombay's meteorological conditions made the matter much less pressing.

[49] Magistrates were empowered to order furnace inspections. Violations of the Act were cognizable upon Magistrate's orders, and a first violation carried a maximum fine of 50 Rupees, doubling for every violation thereafter.

The Act produced few prosecutions—no more than six in any given year, and most years saw only one or two convictions.[50] This much is perhaps not surprising. In London, the 1853 Act became effective only because Palmerston's tenacious supervision overcame the reluctance of police and magistrates to make it stick.[51] The Calcutta Act was not enforced with the same enthusiasm. Though the Act was initially publicized, little effort was put into enforcement, and the Act 'was allowed to remain almost a dead letter' until 1879.[52] Prior to that time, the very few actions taken against smoke nuisance were brought by residents who could mobilize either political influence or sufficient resources to retain legal counsel. In one celebrated case of 1872, Rajmohun Bose, who owned a house adjacent the Howrah workshops of the East India Railway Company, brought a civil action before the High Court objecting to the smoke and smuts which entered his house, arising from the workshop's forges and furnaces.[53] The Court found in favour of Bose, and ordered that the Railway abate the nuisance within a period of three months. The costly and slow process of litigation proved worthwhile only where a major source of smoke caused immediate and obvious damage. For more distant and generalized smoke, there was no remedy other than complaint.

Public protest against smoke escalated in the winter of 1878–9, and following the personal intervention of Sir Ashley Eden—a longtime Calcutta resident newly appointed as Lieutenant-Governor of Bengal—the government convened a special committee to consider the smoke problem.[54] The committee concluded that

[50] *Report on the Administration of Criminal Justice in the Lower Provinces of Bengal*, Annual Series, 1879–1905.

[51] With strong central guidance, Palmerston had been able to secure 124 convictions in one eight-month period. Ashby and Anderson, *Politics of Clean Air*, p. 18.

[52] IOLR, *BenJP*, March 1880, Secretary, Government of Bengal to Calcutta Commissioner of Police, 16 March 1880.

[53] *Rajmohun Bose v East India Railway Company*, 10 Bengal Law Reporter 241 (1872), p. 242.

[54] IOLR, *BenJP*, 1879.

smoke from land-boilers had increased only slightly, and that the most problematic emissions arose from steam vessels which fell outside the purview of the 1863 Act.[55] On the committee's recommendation, the Bengal government took steps to enforce the Smoke Nuisance Act more rigorously, and from 1880, the systematic inspection of smoke emissions was entrusted to the Boiler Commission Inspector, whose primary duties related to the structural integrity and safety of boiler equipment.[56] Government concern peaked following serious bouts of smog, and major campaigns against smoke were mounted in 1880–1, 1883, 1891–2, and 1898–1902.[57] In each of these episodes, the Lieutenant-Governor of Bengal responded to numerous complaints with personal intervention in the business of smoke abatement. Though the record of complaints is sketchy, they were lodged by both Indian and European residents of Calcutta, usually against a particular chimney or set of chimneys rather than against the smoky city as a whole.

In 1892 G.E. Marklew, a jute warehouse inspector, was appointed to act as a special smoke inspector on a part-time basis. He was reappointed in 1898 on a temporary basis which was made permanent in 1901. Using coloured diagrams of four shades to approximate the colour of smoke, he recorded observations of the density and duration of chimney emissions, issued warnings to managers, and initiated prosecutions. Since the authorities preferred to maintain a system of consultation and advice, managers could expect multiple warnings before prosecution.[58] A number of plant operators minimized smoke emissions through a mixture of new boilers and careful firing, thus avoiding prosecutions entirely. Even within a fundamentally pro-industrial mode of thought it was possible to condemn 'excessive' emissions of

55 IOLR, *BenJP*, March 1880, pp. 335–6.

56 IOLR, *BenJP*, March 1880, Secretary, Government of Bengal to Calcutta Commissioner of Police, 16 March 1880.

57 IOLR, *BenJP*, 1880–1905.

58 Between 1898 and 1901, the Sibpur Jute Mill was warned on twelve occasions, but prosecuted only once.

smoke. Adjacent chimneys invited comparison, and considerable discrepancies in the volume and density of smoke labelled particular mills 'dirty'. Acceptable levels of smoke were determined more by comparison than by absolute emissions: managers were exhorted to adopt the practices of the Alipore Jute Mill, which kept emissions comparatively low.[59] Other chimneys were found to 'smoke intolerably without cessation the whole day'.[60] The Ganges Jute Mill failed to reduce emissions, and was repeatedly warned and prosecuted for smoke nuisance, with multiple convictions between 1879 and 1902.[61] In general, Indian managers were readily prosecuted after a small number of warnings while European managers could except greater forbearance. Even with Indian mills, prosecutions were handled casually, so the provision of the Act which required the fine to double on each subsequent conviction was often ignored. Some of the most important polluters, including the mint and water-pumping stations, were government operated, and thereby exempt from prosecution.

Even where prosecutions were mounted, securing a conviction could be difficult. Legally, the key enforcement problem was how to define whether any given furnace was burning its own smoke 'as far as practicable' as required under the Act. Early convictions were secured with ease, but the mills began to mount a more vigorous defence in 1892,[62] and by 1898 the magistracy was siding firmly with mill owners. The turning point came in *Emperor vs Burn.*[63] Burn & Co. admitted that the chimney of their jute mill emitted black smoke for eight to nineteen minutes in each hour, but that they had taken reasonable steps to abate the smoke in using

[59] IOLR, *BenJP*, February 1879, P. Donaldson, Memorandum on the prevention of smoke in steam generators burning Indian coal, 3 February 1879.

[60] IOLR, *BenJP*, 1879, Magistrate of Howrah to Commissioner of the Burdwan District, 19 February 1879.

[61] IOLR, *BenJP*, March 1880, March 1892, May 1902.

[62] The evidence of the inspectors and permissible levels of smoke were both called into question in *Boiler Commission v Central Jute Mills*, Howrah District Magistrate, 21 May 1892 (IOLR, *BenJP*, July 1902).

[63] Calcutta Magistrate, 22 May 1898, in IOLR, *BenJP*, July 1902.

good quality coal and adopting firing methods recommended by the Boiler Commission. The magistrate held that mere presence of smoke was insufficient to secure a conviction, and that the prosecution would have to demonstrate that either the plant design or the firing practices fell below accepted standards. A similar result was obtained in *Emperor vs Eustace, of Calcutta Electric Supply* in 1902.[64] The cases established a precedent whereby a successful prosecution would require either evidence of negligence or expert testimony as to the inadequate technical parameters of the furnace. Henceforth the burden of proof was so high as to make successful prosecution 'almost impossible'.[65] Moreover, any excessive smoke resulting from the use of poor quality coal or heavy firing could not give rise to a conviction. Instead an inadequacy had to be found in the design and construction of the furnace. In effect, conviction required 'the very highest expert knowledge' in a context without trained combustion experts.[66] Without the imminent threat of criminal conviction, managers could easily afford to ignore the cajoling smoke inspector.

### The Politics of Professional Policing

From the outset, the predominantly European manufacturing community in Calcutta opposed smoke abatement on the grounds of higher costs and technical barriers. Against this, a broad mix of the European and Bengali populace—particularly professionals, administrators, and mercantile groups—had a keen interest in the aesthetic quality of the cityscape.[67] Inevitably, the anti-smoke lobby had greater influence with government, so when Curzon assumed office he was battered with complaints about smoke, and

[64] Calcutta Magistrate, May 1902, in IOLR, *BenJP*, July 1902.

[65] Grover, *Report*, p. 21.

[66] Grover, *Report*, p. 23.

[67] It is unclear to what extent Calcutta's residents were aware of parallel developments in England where the National Fog and Smoke Committee and its successors lobbied for government action throughout the 1880s and 1890s. Ashby and Anderson, *Politics of Clean Air*, chp. 5.

soon took a direct interest in the question. There was a political motive here too: following the debacle of the 1899 Calcutta Corporation Act,[68] smoke abatement was one of the few issues which could unite the *bhadralok* and influential Europeans in the period immediately prior to Swadeshi politics. Curzon appreciated the political significance of urban environments, and placed them on his highly authoritarian agenda. Seizing on the smoke issue with his celebrated decisiveness, Curzon upbraided Marklew for incompetence, and sent to London for expert advice in July 1902.[69] Lord Hamilton, the Secretary of State for India, replied with a short memorandum on smoke abatement, cautioning that a qualified smoke inspector would be expensive.[70] But Curzon insisted, and in February 1903 Grover was employed for four months at the sum of £800 plus expenses.[71] In the same month, Curzon lectured the Bengal Chamber of Commerce on the urgency of reducing Calcutta's smoke, which 'besmirches the mid-day sky with its vulgar tar brush and turns our sunsets into a murky gloom'. He further warned that this 'insidious and growing danger' would surely destroy one half of the city's amenities unless checked by new legal measures.[72]

When Grover arrived, Calcutta represented something of a smoke-inspector's paradise: with strong government support, he was able to design a state of the art system for abating smoke. The new Smoke Nuisance Bill, which largely adopted his recommendations,[73] provided the machinery for more intensive monitoring

68 Chris Furedy, 'Lord Curzon and the reform of the Calcutta Corporation, 1899: A case study in imperial decision-making', *South Asia*, 1, 1 (March 1978).

69 IOLR, *BenJP*, July 1902, Governor-General in Council to Lord George Francis Hamilton, 10 July 1902.

70 Dr Theodore Thomson, Minute on Smoke Nuisance in Calcutta, August 1902, in IOLR, *BenJP*, October 1903.

71 IOLR, *BenJP*, October 1903.

72 Raleigh, *Lord Curzon*, p. 269.

73 A number of Grover's proposals were watered down in the Bengal Legislative Council: The fines were reduced, existing kilns were excluded from license requirements, and a partial exclusion was introduced for ocean-going steamers. *Calcutta Gazette*, part IV, 1905, p. 11.

and regulation through four key features. First, a new Commission, composed of equal numbers of bureaucrats and industry representatives, was to be set up to supervise the work of a permanent inspectorate. For Grover, himself a product of the growing professionalization of air pollution control in England,[74] a technically-competent and professionally-committed Chief Inspector was essential to the scheme's success. This was the culmination of a trend, already present in the smoke abatement efforts of the 1880s, to invest bureaucratic power in technical experts rather than amateur colonial administrators. Second, new powers were to be provided to prohibit the urban operation of certain industries, including brick and lime kilns, smelting and calcing works, iron works, and coke manufacture. Third, conviction was made to depend on observed smoke emissions rather than questions of technology and firing practices. Fourth, rather than permitting the magistracy to determine levels of permissible smoke on a case by case basis, a systematic set of standards was adopted for measuring the density and duration of smoke so that a consistent threshold could be deployed in enforcement. Henceforth, smoke would be monitored, measured, and recorded on a daily basis.

Once the smoke legislation was mooted, the British India Association successfully pressed to extend emission standards to steam rollers, urban railways, and miscellaneous workshops.[75] The strong support for smoke abatement among the *bhadralok* was reflected in the speech of Nalin Behari Sircar before the Legislative Council in January 1905:

> The innumerable chimneys that have sprung up . . . are a constant source of considerable trouble, inconvenience, and mischief to the residents in their neighbourhood. In Calcutta, Wards 3 and 4 and possibly

[74] See R.M. MacLeod, 'The Alkali Acts administration 1863–84: The emergence of the civil scientist', *Victorian Studies*, 9, 1965, pp. 86–112; P. Brimblecombe and C. Bowler, 'Air Pollution in York 1850–1900' in Brimblecombe and Pfister (eds.), *The Silent Countdown*.

[75] Proceedings of the Bengal Legislative Council, 11 January 1905.

also Ward 2 are the worst sufferers in this respect, and I can bear my personal testimony to the great annoyance to which the unfortunate residents of this locality are constantly subjected.[76]

The Bengali middle classes had been protesting against smoke for decades, but Curzon's intensely autocratic approach gave pause for caution. The *Bangavasi* welcomed the prospect of reduced smoke, but warned that the Act should not be a device for 'some sort of oppression'.[77] Inevitably, both European and Indian manufacturing interests opposed the measure, but great efforts were made to secure their co-operation. Even before Grover set foot on Indian shores, representatives of the Calcutta Port, the Jute Mills Association, and the European managing agency houses of Bird & Co. and Jessop & Co. were summoned for a meeting with H.H. Risley, Secretary to the Government of Bengal, who made the case for close cooperation in scientific smoke management.[78] The promise of technical expertise rather than government meddling was held out as an incentive for managers. So too, private enterprise could take comfort in the knowledge that unlike the 1863 legislation, the new Act would apply equally to government and private smoke. The Bengal Chamber of Commerce was consulted during the drafting stages, and was able to secure important concessions, most notably a massive reduction in the first conviction fine from Rs 1000 to Rs 50.[79]

Both the Bengal Chamber of Commerce and the Bengal National Chamber of Commerce found representation on the Smoke Nuisance Commission, though the local government always retained majority control through the chair. The Commission began its work in 1906, with W. Nicholson, a Sheffield Smoke Inspector, employed to train a local engineer, John Robson, who

76 Ibid.

77 *Bangavasi*, 16 January 1905, in *Reports From Native Papers, Bengal* (Calcutta, 1905).

78 IOLR, *BenJP*, March 1903, Conference at the Home Office to Consider the Smoke Nuisance in Calcutta, 23 February 1903.

79 *Proceedings of the Bengal Legislative Council*, 8 March 1905.

subsequently served as smoke inspector until 1932. Robson adhered to a strong ideology of professionalism; in his twenty-five year tenure he repeatedly stressed the importance of scientific inquiry and innovative engineering. Perhaps more importantly, he was committed to smoke abatement as a vocation, and clearly took delight in the prospect of bringing real improvement to Calcutta's atmosphere. Robson's enthusiasm placed his actions on a world stage. He regularly referred to smoke abatement developments abroad, and compared Calcutta with Manchester, New York, and Glasgow. Smoke inspectors were accorded considerable status, and after 1922 were entitled to benefits normally reserved for more senior servants under the Civil Service Regulations.[80] Robson and his two assistants served a didactic as well as a police function. The inspectorate, which was consistently understaffed during much of the inter-war period, was not only responsible for monitoring smoke emissions and recommending prosecutions, but also receiving complaints, approving building designs, training stokers, and in certain cases, designing smoke-abating devices.

The key feature of the new system—both conceptually and practically—was the way it linked prosecution to quantified levels of smoke. Rather than relying upon subjective perceptions of nuisance, the impact of smoke was made subject to a putatively objective, and hence 'scientific' measure. For this purpose a series of grey scales based on those developed in France by Ringelmann was adopted (see Fig. 1). When held at a distance, the density of the Ringelmann chart could be compared by eye with the density of emissions from particular chimneys. Thus changing densities were observed over time, and the result could be statistically manipulated to arrive at an overall measurement of smoke.[81] Since inspectors were unable to observe all chimneys simultaneously, they concentrated on the chimneys thought to be emitting the worst smoke. Of course not all smoke fit neatly on the grey

[80] IOLR: L/E/7/1106.

[81] In order to express the resulting observation as a single figure, a conversion system was devised so that 1 minute of scale 6 smoke was deemed equivalent to 1.81 minutes of scale 5 smoke or 2.7 minutes of scale 4 smoke.

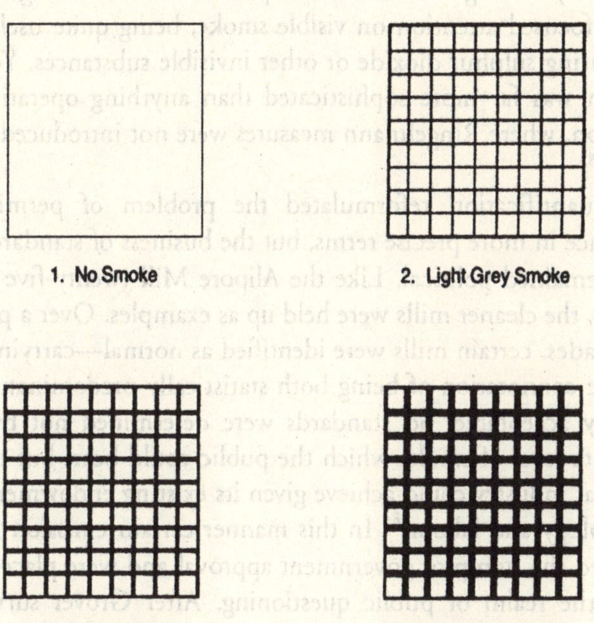


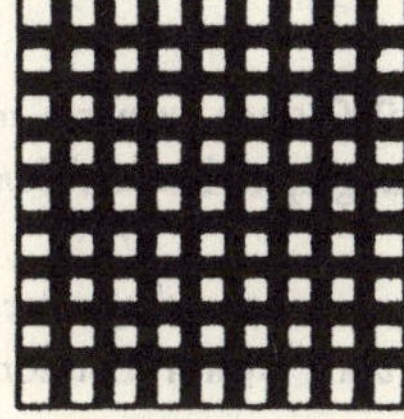

5. Black Smoke

6. Dense Black Smoke

Fig. 1. Bengal Smoke Gauge.

scales—biomass smoke was predominantly white or yellow in colour[82]—but the chart did provide an index of coal burning efficiency. Later generations would point out that the Ringelmann chart focused attention on visible smoke, being quite useless in measuring sulphur dioxide or other invisible substances. Yet the system was far more sophisticated than anything operating in London, where Ringelmann measures were not introduced until 1956.[83]

Quantification reformulated the problem of permissible nuisance in more precise terms, but the business of standard-setting remained political. Like the Alipore Mill twenty-five years earlier, the cleaner mills were held up as examples. Over a period of decades, certain mills were identified as normal—carrying the double connotation of being both statistically predominant and socially acceptable. So standards were determined not by the absolute level of smoke which the public could bear, but rather by what industry could achieve given its existing endowments of technology and labour.[84] In this manner certain emission levels received the stamp of government approval and were placed beyond the realm of public questioning. After Grover surveyed Calcutta emissions, he opined that the mix of Bengal coal and coolie labour made abatement more difficult in Calcutta, and suggested a maximum of ten minutes of black smoke in the hour —more lax than standards in some English provincial towns.[85]

[82] In 1914, the Commission estimated that 8,000 trade furnaces in and around Calcutta emitted smoke of colours other than grey or black. *RBenSNC*, 1913–14, p. 2.

[83] Indeed, one of the objections to Curzon's reforms was that they were more stringent than the existing London legislation, the Public Health (London) Act of 1891 [54 & 55 Vic ch 76].

[84] The Boiler Commission had used an informal measure after 1891, initiating prosecution when a chimney exceeded twelve minutes of 'black smoke' in one hour. In May 1902 the Commission proposed to reduce the level to six minutes.

[85] Comparable English levels were six minutes in Bolton, twelve minutes in Oldham, and one to three minutes in Leeds. Grover, *Report*, p. 145.

He recommended the 'lenient scale to prevent any ill-feeling with the commencement of the Act' but proposed that the limit be gradually reduced as the working of furnaces improved.[86] In early 1910, Howrah laboured for days under a thick evening smoke trapped by a temperature inversion. The Commission was powerless to act since no individual chimney was found to be violating the Ringelmann standard.[87] Two years later, the 'unnecessarily liberal' emission limits were made significantly more stringent.[88]

In its first few years of operation, the Commission was able to secure a dramatic decline in the observed level of dense black smoke (see Table 1). Early improvements resulted from intensive lobbying and consultation with managers, especially those of the Bengali-owned oil and flour mills in north Calcutta. Robson lobbied for good stoking and better furnace design. After good stoking, probably the single most important factor in reducing smoke emissions from coal-burning furnaces was the construction of well-designed chimneys. A tall chimney raised smoke above inhabited space, but more importantly, it improved burning efficiency by increasing draught. The city experienced a small-scale architectural revolution between 1906 and 1912 as the Commission ordered 207 chimneys to be heightened, and many more were raised voluntarily. After 1915 owners were required to submit for the Commission's approval architectural drawings for all new furnaces, flues, and chimneys.[89] Where it was impossible to raise chimneys, the inspectors endeavoured to have gas, electric, or other smokeless furnaces installed.

Like the Alkali Inspectors in England, the Bengal Smoke Inspectors sought a close working relationship with factory owners and managers. Once the statutory rules were officially approved, prosecutions became possible and there followed a brief period in

86 Grover, *Report*, pp. 145–6.

87 *RBenSNC*, 1909–10, p. 4.

88 The new rules prohibited Scale 6 smoke entirely, while the limit of scales 4 and 5, mathematically expressed in terms of scale 6, was reduced to 2.21 minutes per hour for a single furnace. *RBenSNC*, 1912–13, p. 1.

89 *Bengal Smoke-Nuisances (Amendment) Act*, 1915.

Table 1
Smoke Observations in Calcutta and Howrah, 1898–1944

| *Year* | *Average min/hr* | *Year* | *Average min/hr* | *Year* | *Average min/hr* |
|---|---|---|---|---|---|
| 1898/9 | 17.00 | 1917 | 1.31 | 1932 | 0.08 |
| 1899/0 | 10.88 | 1918 | 1.29 | 1933 | 0.08 |
| 1900/1 | 7.44 | 1919 | 1.27 | 1934 | 0.07 |
| 1901/2 | 8.16 | 1920 | 1.22 | 1935 | 0.07 |
| 1906 | 13.10 | 1921 | 1.60 | 1936 | 0.08 |
| 1907 | 3.51 | 1922 | 1.68 | 1937 | 0.08 |
| 1908 | 2.50 | 1923 | 1.49 | 1938 | 0.09 |
| 1909 | 2.04 | 1924 | 1.39 | 1939 | 0.10 |
| 1910 | 1.94 | 1925 | 1.19 | 1940 | 0.09 |
| 1911 | 1.85 | 1926 | 0.98 | 1941 | 0.08 |
| 1912 | 1.84 | 1927 | 0.68 | 1942 | 0.11 |
| 1913 | 1.82 | 1928 | 0.48 | 1943 | 0.12 |
| 1914 | 1.74 | 1929 | 0.30 | 1944 | 0.12 |
| 1915 | 1.66 | 1930 | 0.18 | | |
| 1916 | 1.40 | 1931 | 0.08 | | |

The averages for 1898–1902 based on observations of minutes of 'black smoke' emitted from 18 chimneys.

Source: *Bengal Judicial Proceedings*, July 1902, p. 1381. After 1906, averages are based on Ringelmann chart observations, expressed in terms of Scale 6. Source: *Reports of the Bengal Smoke Nuisance Commission*, 1907–44.

which the Commission displayed its willingness to take mill-owners to court. However, with substantial industry representation on the Commission, the confrontations could not last, and after 1912, a new approach was adopted. Aiming to reduce prosecutions, the Commission incorporated the owners, managers, and superintendents of large undertakings into the system of enforcement. Upon sighting excessive levels of smoke, the Inspector issued a notice to the factory manager, who would then take action departmentally, levying a fine on allegedly negligent or inefficient stokers. It is difficult to overstate the import of this change. In effect, the responsibility for smoke was neatly shifted from employers to workers. As managers began to dispense punishments and warnings to their workers, they were incorporated into the state's authority system with police-like powers. Meanwhile, stokers, who were required to work with the existing technology, became subject to docked pay, punishments, and unpredictable sackings.[90] In using the power relations of the workplace to its advantage, the Commission was able to mollify owners, avoid courtroom confrontations, and introduce a highly coercive system to ensure careful stoking. This approach was employed primarily within factories, but also in cases of ships, launches, locomotives, and road-rollers. The level of industrial smoke fell dramatically as the number of departmental notices increased. The Commission was so pleased with the result that departmental notices replaced prosecutions entirely for the years between 1925 and 1932. When R. Grant replaced Robson as Chief Smoke Inspector in 1932, he initiated a handful of prosecutions, but continued to rely most heavily on the departmental notice system. Government and capital had reached a lasting compromise—crucial to the scheme's overall success—which shifted the moral and physical burdens of smoke abatement onto labour.

In contrast to the close collusion between inspectors and mill-owners, other types of polluters were subjected to more coercive policing. An important source of smoke was the small-scale manufacture of coke from raw coal, frequently carried out by mobile entrepreneurs operating on 'waste' land, usually at night when the smoke was not easily observed.[91] Often drawing on scavenged or stolen coal, petty coke-producers filled a key niche in the Calcutta fuel market, providing inferior quality coke at prices within reach of potters, blacksmiths, and domestic consumers. In July 1909 the Commission introduced rules to prohibit the making of coke

[90] There was a precedent for this approach. In 1879 the magistrate of Howrah undertook to prosecute and fine the 'coolie' stokers feeding the furnaces rather than mill owners. IOLR, *BenJP*, 1879, Magistrate of Howrah to Commissioner of the Burdwan District, 26 February 1879.

[91] *RBenSNC*, 1918–19, p. 2.

without ovens or special appliances within Calcutta and its suburbs, successfully prosecuting twenty-six offenders.[92]

Systematic enforcement proved difficult since 'the irresponsible class of petty shop-keepers' who engaged in the activity were able to move on before being detected.[93] After 1915, criminal liability was extended to the owner of the land on which the coke was produced.[94] With the rise in coke prices following 1919, there was a massive upturn in small-scale coke production in 1920, processing as much as 70 tonnes of raw coal per day.[95] In 1921 the Commission requested intensified police efforts to arrest coke manufacturers, and proceedings were initiated in fifty-three cases.[96]

Over the years the Commission received complaints regarding blacksmiths, bakeries, potteries, cooking shops, brickfields, lime-kilns, construction works, and iron foundries, though by the 1930s most complaints were directed at domestic smoke which was beyond its jurisdiction. Locomotives and steamships caused frequent complaint, in part because they vented emissions at a low altitude near residential communities, and in part because their smaller boilers made design innovations extremely difficult. The inspectorate emphasized good firing for each, and relied heavily on the departmental notice system to put pressure on stokers. After 1918, a number of ships converted from coal to oil-burning boilers. The initial experiments were disastrous. In January and February of 1920, Calcutta was deluged with the accumulated thick, oily smoke of ocean-going vessels. The dense rain of oily smuts produced a public outcry in the press which only subsided after the Commission supervised adjustments to the burners.

Despite such minor disasters, there is no reason to doubt that the inspectorate efforts dramatically reduced the volume and density of coal smoke from Calcutta's chimneys. Robson's figures indicate that by 1916 the most noxious chimneys were emitting,

92 *RBenSNC*, 1909–10, p. 3.

93 *RBenSNC*, 1920, p. 4.

94 *Bengal Smoke Nuisances (Amendment) Act*, 1915.

95 *RBenSNC*, December 1920, p. 3.

96 *RBenSNC*, 1921, p. 3.

on average, only 11 per cent of the black smoke which they had discharged ten years previously.[97] By 1922, the Commission could boast that despite a doubling in the number of mills since 1907, Calcutta's air was cleaner than that in the industrial and shipping centres of Europe.

In 1926, a Central Smoke Observatory was established atop one of the highest buildings in Calcutta. Suddenly it became possible to survey the entire 80 square miles under the Inspectorate's control. Nearly every factory chimney could be seen from the observatory at once, and the number of departmental notices jumped from 2759 in 1925 to 4170 in 1926, and 7433 in 1927. The Observatory was fitted with a telephone to facilitate immediate conversation with the offending party. The effect was dramatic. Henceforth, the whole of the city became subject to surveillance during daylight hours, and stokers were made aware that their furnaces were under constant scrutiny. 'Engineers and firemen' admonished the Commission, 'will not reduce smoke unless they know they are constantly watched, that every offence is detected and quickly followed up'.[98] Probably no other industrial city in the world, before or since, has operated a pollution notification system so ambitiously conceived, so comprehensive in range, or so penetrating in its disciplinary effects.

## Labour and Technology

Smoke from steam boilers could be abated either through investment in superior technology, or through highly-skilled stoking practices, or both. Over the years, Calcutta firms experimented with both labour-intensive and capital-intensive forms of abatement; their choices reveal much about attitudes to technology and labour in colonial circumstances. The basic elements of smoke abatement had been fully described in England by the middle of

[97] That this was reduced to 7.4 per cent by 1926, and 0.6 per cent in 1936 is testimony to the inspectorate's very real influence.

[98] *RBenSNC*, 1927, p. 5.

the nineteenth century, and were first discussed in India no later than 1877 when the Calcutta Port Commissioners held an inquiry into the subject.[99] Prior to Grover's report, the Bengal government received technical advice from England in 1891, 1895, 1901, and 1902;[100] each instance reiterated essentially the same advice, which was also available from the *Encyclopaedia Britannica.*[101] Adequate boiler power, careful stoking, tall chimneys and good quality coal were widely recommended. It was usually lamented that in Indian conditions, efforts to reduce pollution would never match the perfection of smoke abatement which existed in England—the inferiority of coal, technology, and skilled labour was simply presumed.

Among mill-owners, the most frequent scapegoat for smoke was the indolent Indian stoker. The task of the stoker was onerous: in order to burn coal with a minimum of smoke, the correct proportions of air and fuel had to be maintained at a high temperature. Excess air would reduce the temperature of the smoke below ignition point, while too little air would supply inadequate amounts of oxygen to combust volatile materials and unburnt carbon. Executed properly, the task of stoking involved a high degree of skill and mental concentration. The coal needed to be added regularly in small quantities, and spread evenly over the burning bed—an especially demanding exercise in India where the coal was not sorted by size. The stoker's job was even more difficult where the Managing Agent of the mill also operated a colliery, since the best coal was reserved for sale on the open market

[99] IOLR, *BenJP*, 1880, Vice-Chairman, Port Commissioners to Secretary, Government of Bengal, 24 April 1880.

[100] See, respectively: note on smoke abatement by R. Bushby, 8 December 1891 (*BenJP*, January 1892); paper by Mr Curruthers Thomson, Engineer to the Smoke Abatement Association, 1895 (*BenJP*, January 1902), letter from Mssrs Hargreaves & Co of Soho Iron Works, 1901 (*BenJP*, July 1902), minute on smoke nuisance in Calcutta by Dr Theodore Thomson, 1902 (*BenJP*, July 1902).

[101] 'Smoke Abatement', *Encyclopaedia Britannica*, ninth ed., vol. 22 (Edinburgh, 1888).

while the poorest fuel was diverted to the mills. Under a general regime of low investment, boiler equipment was not only inefficient, it was often cracked, corroded, and highly dangerous.[102] Since boilers were inadequately insulated, stokers worked in conditions of intolerably high temperatures which militated against careful tending of air-fuel mixtures. In these circumstances, the best strategy available to stokers, both for comfort and safety, was to shovel in a large amount of coal as quickly as possible, and then retreat to a cooler place away from the furnace. Not surprisingly, this seems to be what many stokers did.

The twin factors of race and class made stokers easy objects of abuse. Grover reflected the views of European managers when he concluded that 'the low standard of intelligence of the native fireman' constituted the largest obstacle to smoke abatement in Calcutta.[103] He observed that the typical fireman displayed a 'stolid indifference' and 'passive resistance' to the demands of smoke abatement. Racist prejudices aside, stokers did take action to defy their ridiculous working conditions. Most stokers were classified as 'coolie' labour, employed at the lowest possible wages.[104] Training was minimal since the majority of mill-owners placed a low priority on technical education of workers.[105] The working conditions exacerbated a high rate of turn-over, attributable in part to the seasonal character of employment, with many stokers involved in agricultural pursuits. Though some stokers adopted the ways of a more settled work-force and became highly skilled,[106] the majority remained transient and did not have the opportunity to develop smoke abatement expertise.

102 *Report of the Commission for the Inspection of Steam-Boilers and Prime Movers*, Annual Series, 1903/4–1940.

103 Grover, *Report*, p. 44.

104 IOLR: L/E/7/1381/(File 886), Memorandum on Hours and Wages in Jute Mills, 1926; and S.R. Deshpande, *An Enquiry into Conditions of Labour in the Jute Mill Industry of India* (Simla, 1946).

105 D. Chakrabarty, *Rethinking Working-Class History: Bengal 1890–1940* (Princeton, 1989), pp. 88–92.

106 *RBenSNC*, 1926, p. 3.

In March 1914 the Commission established a training programme for stokers, with the promise of a certificate for those who completed the course. Few labourers appeared for the scheme, and the Commission reduced the training fees in an unsuccessful attempt to attract more interest.[107] With European employers reluctant to sponsor their workers, the scheme was shut down in frustration after nine years. Between 1914 and 1923 only 133 stokers were trained in this way, and of these, the majority came from boiler-rooms operated by Indians. In practice, smoke abatement skills were imparted by Robson and his assistants during the thousands of on-site furnace inspections they made every year. The reluctance of European employers to sponsor their workers for training perplexed the Commission, but it was in keeping with a larger pattern among European managers who tenaciously refused to invest in employee education. In contrast, Indian-operated businesses were more forthcoming with smoke abatement. In 1908, nearly one hundred oil and flour mills under Bengali management in northern Calcutta employed a special engineer to abate smoke from their furnaces. The engineer's pay was linked to a bonus contingent on the absence of prosecutions under the Smoke Nuisance Act. The scheme was a success, but European managers refused to take up similar initiatives.

If European capital reviled workers, it was perpetually drawn to the notion of an easy technical fix for smoke nuisance. The market for abatement devices was well-established by the early 1870s, and many firms imported the latest patent furnaces, fuel beds, and fashionable gadgets from London. Some measures—particularly those which increased furnace size or facilitated good draughts—were successful if tended with vigilance.[108] Others were

107 *RBenSNC*, 1916–17, p. 2.

108 Without skilled operators, most smoke-abating furnaces suffered from clogged apertures or improper fuel loading. Though these problems were identified as early as 1882, few changes were introduced in labour processes. IOLR, *BenJP*, February 1883, President, Boiler Commission to Secretary, Government of Bengal, 28 July 1882.

improperly installed or operated, or were ill-suited to Indian coal, or were simply fraudulent devices ineffective in actually changing the character of combustion.[109] Dozens of different devices were tried. Calcutta offered particularly rich pickings for charlatan entrepreneurs: one mill insisted that its clean chimneys could be attributed to a sprinkling of newly-invented powder on the coal; however, Grover noted that the agents for the mill were also the agents for the powder.[110]

As early as 1879 the magistrate of Howrah suggested that managers would do better to concentrate on good stoking rather than spending exorbitant sums on patent smoke abating machinery.[111] However, mill managers were hesitant to rely on stoking, since the predominant view held, in 1891, that 'the quality of workmen available here is hardly capable of firing a boiler so as to reduce the volume of smoke'.[112] Throughout the 1890s mill-owners were counselled to seek the latest improved appliances to deal with the problem, but with small success. By 1903 the failure of technical solutions had frequently 'given rise to the opinion [among mill-owners] that nothing further can be done' while the benefits of good stoking were ignored since 'too much reliance has been placed on automatic devices'.[113] Grover suggested that technical solutions would only be feasible once Calcutta had developed a pool of labour power capable of managing the complicated machinery. What the European managers failed to appreciate was that improved technology was largely useless without more highly-skilled labour. Their fascination and trust in machines, when combined with a refusal to support a more skilled workforce, consigned many early abatement efforts to failure.

109 IOLR, *BenJP*, March 1900, Secretary, Government of Bengal to Secretary, Government of India, 12 January 1900.

110 Grover, *Report*, p. 11.

111 IOLR, *BenJP*, 1879, Magistrate of Howrah to Commissioner of Burdwan, 26 February 1879.

112 IOLR, *BenJP*, January 1892, Magistrate of Howrah to Commissioner of Burdwan, 4 September 1891.

113 Grover, *Report*, p. 18.

Robson and his assistants were able to impress upon managers the importance of good stoking, but after the collapse of the stoker training scheme, inspectors seem to have devoted greater efforts to encouraging capital-intensive methods of smoke abatement. In the mid-1920s a number of jute mills began to adopt more sophisticated technology including grit-removers, smoke washers, and devices to pre-heat and super-heat air for combustion.

Of course there were many instances where innovations in engineering brought about spectacular improvements. For instance, in 1920 a number of rice mills turned away from the inflation-bloated price of coal, and began to burn rice husks, which generated a light but copious smoke laden with soot and ash. Since the mills operated in the predominantly European Tollygunge area, residents were quick to complain that 'the air is filled up with black soot which falls like drizzling rain from morning till night, and it has become impossible to live'.[114] Though the soot did not transgress the Ringelmann chart standards, Robson successfully designed a series of devices to reduce the emissions, effectively settling the problem with a purely mechanical solution. But even with such technological improvements, skilled operation remained an essential ingredient of efficient combustion. The 'human element' remained 'the last barrier to the realization of a smokeless city'.[115]

### Smoke and Social 'Improvement'

Though the basic techniques of smoke abatement remained reasonably constant, its social audience and cultural significance changed dramatically over the spread of the colonial period. What began as a palliative to influential Europeans successively became a matter of middle-class Indian concern, a check on unplanned industrial growth, and finally a component in the state's public health policy. This last feature assumed greater prominence in the

[114] *RBenSNC*, 1921, p. 3.

[115] *RBenSNC*, 1927, p. 10.

period following the First World War, especially as the Smoke Nuisance Commission assumed a more didactic tone and turned its attentions to the well-being of the subordinate classes.

The link between smoke and health had been in the background during the early nineteenth century when the emphasis fell mainly on the nuisance and discomfort smoke introduced to urban life. In the extended writings on sanitation, drainage, and improved ventilation, virtually no attention was devoted to smoke *per se.* The problem appears to have been viewed independently of miasmas and pathogenic landscapes. But the miasma theory maintained its hold over European imaginations until well into the 1890s,[116] and its emphasis on ventilation continued to inform later medical debates on smoke.

In 1920 the Commission endorsed the theory that smoke 'renders the system susceptible to distemper of diverse kinds', and opined that the rise in tuberculosis was 'greatly, if not wholly due to this cause'.[117] This marked a considerable shift from Lankester's comprehensive report on tuberculosis, published only five years previously, which made no mention of smoke.[118] The Commission developed the theme further throughout the 1920s. Noting that one-fifth of the total death-rate in Calcutta could be attributed to diseases of the breathing organs, it stressed that 'smoke nuisance lowers the public health and renders it susceptible to other diseases'.[119] In response to increasing concern for the effects of smoke on public health, the Director of Public Health for Bengal was appointed to the Smoke Nuisance Commission in 1927. That year a statistical analysis showed that the weekly death rate rose from 80 to 240 during especially smoky periods.[120] Though a link with respiratory disorders was identified as the primary causal factor, the Commission also opined that smoke had a more general

116 See, for example, 'The City of Calcutta and its municipal constitution', *Calcutta Review*, 70, 1880.

117 *RBenSNC*, December 1920, p. 4.

118 A. Lankester, *Report on Tuberculosis in India* (Simla, 1915).

119 *RBenSNC*, 1926, p. 2.

120 *RBenSNC*, 1927, p. 4.

effect in lowering the public vitality since it cut off 'the sun's health-giving ultraviolet rays'.[121]

Toward the end of the 1920s, as the incidence of black coal smoke from industry declined, the principal health issues arose in relation to domestic smoke. The effects of domestic smoke were highlighted after a much higher death rate was noted in residential areas than in industrial areas.[122] Even though domestic smoke lay beyond the Commission's legal remit, the epidemiological evidence was a convenient scientific justification to pursue what had already been a longstanding irritation. In its first report, the Commission noted that much of the smoke nuisance derived from domestic fires, which were not covered by the Act.[123] The problem was 'aggravated by the fact that such smoke is discharged at almost ground level, as compared with the discharges from chimneys in European cities'.[124] The most severe smoke occurred in the evening and early morning, when cooking activity peaked and the air was still. At its worst, the stagnant low smoke could be so dense that 'the street lights cannot be seen a few yards distant'.[125] This 'low-lying smoke' was regarded as 'the most deadly' form of smoke after 1920.[126] Observations indicated that the smoke from domestic fires was worst where raw coal was used as the chief source of fuel.[127] In 1914 the Commission recommended to the government that the burning of raw coal in domestic fireplaces be prohibited, but the proposal was politically untenable.[128] The inspectorate encouraged the replacement of coal domestic cookers with gas, and generally urged more extensive use of gas and electricity in all homes. But these options were available only to the tiny percentage of the population able to afford such extravagances. The problem

[121] *RBenSNC*, 1928, p. 2.
[122] *RBenSNC*, 1928, p. 7.
[123] *RBenSNC*, 1906–7, p. 3.
[124] *RBenSNC*, 1907–8, p. 3.
[125] *RBenSNC*, 1927, p. 9.
[126] *RBenSNC*, 1925, p. 3.
[127] *RBenSNC*, 1913–14, p. 2.
[128] *RBenSNC*, 1914–15, p. 2.

grew more acute as Calcutta's population increased in size and density. 'Collectively, in the suburbs, particularly in the cold weather evenings, localities are enveloped for several hours in a low-lying suffocating smoke pall, even on holidays when the mills are stopped'.[129]

The problem of domestic smoke did not yield easily to mere technical solutions. The conventional remedies for domestic smoke adopted in the metropole—taller chimneys, more efficient fire-places, and a switch to smokeless fuels—were unreal in the context of Calcutta's economic circumstances.[130] Some attempt was made to promote coke over coal, and to encourage more efficient burning of biofuels, but the Commission recognised that no relief would be obtained unless solid-fuel stoves could be replaced by appliances operated by gas or other smokeless fuels. However, such appliances were well beyond the means of most residents. Another tactic justified by health concerns was to reduce indoor air pollution. Europeans commented that most Indian dwellings, whether made of masonry or mud and straw did not normally include chimneys, the smoke being allowed to percolate through a porous ceiling construction.[131] The resulting accumulation of indoor smoke particularly affected women who were more likely to stay inside and work over smoky stoves. Efforts were made to introduce domestic chimneys and new cooking devices, which had also become markers of affluence and sophistication among the Bengali middle classes. After 1935 smoke inspectors began to make visits into residential areas, giving instruction in the smokeless firing of cooking stoves. Since the Commission had no legal power in the area of domestic smoke, it was forced to rely more heavily on persuasion than coercion. The strategy had little social effect, largely because the increased levels of heat and air required to make cooking fires smokeless also required more fuel. Nevertheless, the Commission

129 *RBenSNC*, 1923, p. 5.

130 *RBenSNC*, 1928, p. 7.

131 See, for example, W. Crooke, *Natives of Northern India* (London, 1907), p. 152.

continued a public campaign against smoke, aiming to temper criminal sanctions with public education. The Commission mounted displays showing the effects of smoke on mortality, food supplies, trees, and distant localities. And in a prescient anticipation of later developments, it commissioned a short film on smoke abatement to be shown in the Calcutta cinemas. The indifferent success of the campaign betrayed the limited range of its audience. Though the middle classes began to adopt gas appliances more readily, the Commission made little impact on aggregate levels of domestic smoke.

## Pollution, Legislation, and Hegemony

The conquest of smoke was a colonial enterprise. Since the colonial government catered more to urban administrative and mercantile elite than to manufacturing interests, it was able to regulate smoke enthusiastically within the constraints of available resources. A similar trajectory was not possible in Britain, where the industrial lobby frustrated smoke abatement efforts for many years.[132] An interventionist government located in a colonial setting was less constrained by laissez-faire doctrines than equivalent municipal governments in Britain.

Although the Smoke Nuisance Commission had a profound impact on the burning practices and level of industrial smoke during the late colonial period, there is a temptation to overemphasize its importance. The incidence and character of smoke in Calcutta had much to do with factors which were beyond the inspectorate's control. Changes in population, urban density, fuel prices, and socially-determined burning practices were as important as the introduction of new technologies. By 1950 the momentum of technological change had overtaken the Act. Coal-burning steam engines were becoming obsolete, and the Act was powerless against rising automobile pollution. And yet, while the smoke abatement efforts in Calcutta do need to be measured against their

132 Ashby and Anderson, *The Politics of Clean Air.*

primary purpose—the reduction of smoke—their other social consequences were perhaps equally important.

The ability to control smoke emissions was a critical test for the capacity of scientific reasoning to dominate the physical world. It also had important implications for the way in which Indians experienced industrialization. Environmental degradation was a ready charge against unpopular technological and economic change. In regulating smoke, the state acted to head off objections to industrialization before they mushroomed into serious social protest. The result was not to stop industrialization entirely, but merely to rein in its worst excesses. Perhaps too, this may be viewed as another instance of the colonial state's remarkable capacity to anticipate and intercept pressures for radical change.

Approaches to smoke abatement were closely bound up with attitudes to technology and the ideological bases of colonial rule.[133] In 1883, the Bengal government, then riding the crest of Victorian optimism, predicted that since engineering innovations would soon make the smoke problem obsolete, there was no point in producing new legislation until a successful apparatus for the consumption of smoke was discovered.[134] But by 1902 it was clear that Victorian technology had not provided a solution, and Calcutta was struggling under a blanket of smog which it could not throw off. In these circumstances, Curzon's administration was inclined to adopt a more urgent idiom, with overtones of apocalypse:

> [T]he continued prevalence of the nuisance which is even more aggravated now than it was two years ago, shows conclusively that those measures have not been sufficient. In the interest both of the comfort and health of the inhabitants of the city and fort and the future of Calcutta and its neighbourhood as a site of residence, it is essential that

[133] See, more generally, Michael Adas, *Machines as the Measure of Men: Science, Technology, and Ideologies of Western Dominance* (Ithaca, 1989).

[134] IOLR, *BenJP*, March 1883, Secretary, Government of Bengal to Commissioner, Burdwan, 30 March 1883.

the evil should be taken in hand at once, since every year's delay must increase the difficulties of grappling with it successfully.[135]

Curzon was keenly aware that Calcutta's melancholy murk had profound political implications that went beyond the immediate complaints of respectable citizens. At stake, even if only implicitly, was the core claim of imperialist ideology: that European technology and social organization improved the quality of human life. If the civilizing mission which depended on machines and industrial progress was discredited by the belching chimneys along the Hooghly, then the reassertion of European superiority required better engineering and more vigorous policing. In effect, the government was admitting the deleterious effects of industrialization even as it tried to abate and disguise them. Of course, European engineers never doubted the superiority of their technology, but the basis of their faith had to be publicly demonstrated. If the government could successfully control the longstanding problem of Calcutta smoke, a concrete example of the potential benefits of state power would be available. Smoke control helped to symbolize, in a practical way, the authority of the state, as well as demonstrate the potential benefits of state power.

The control of smoke provided a subtle way of asserting hegemony over social and productive life. Smoke was omnipresent and few could object to its diminution. As the administrative capacity to regulate smoke expanded, the frontiers of the state made an unobtrusive but significant advance. At the same time, the new profession of 'combustion engineering',[136] imparted a technical vocabulary for apprehending and manipulating the atmosphere. This professional cadre, operating under the banner of scientific expertise, was able to influence everything from policing to labour relations in the new Calcutta. Even though the allure of purely technological solutions led to frustration among managers and owners, the decision to treat smoke as a matter for technical

135 IOLR, *India Public Proceedings*, March 1902, Secretary, Government of India to Secretary, Government of Bengal, 3 March 1902.

136 *RBenSNC*, 1926, p. 2.

regulation rather than public debate was never questioned. Smoke abatement used the language of scientific administration to assert that given the correct mix of technological investment and administrative organization, the human environment could be made subject to political control. That smoke regulation in Calcutta relied upon heavy doses of coercion suggests that there might be more than a passing affinity between successful environmental intervention and authoritarian forms of governance.

## Chapter Eleven

# The Resurgence of Community Forest Management in the Jungle Mahals of West Bengal

MARK POFFENBERGER*

International concern over the rapid deterioration of the planet's forests has drawn attention to the dramatic changes in land cover in the tropics. Each year millions of hectares of natural forest lands continue to be cleared. Yet, in south-west Bengal and some other parts of South Asia, community groups have mobilized effectively to protect natural forests. With virtually no budget, relying on natural regeneration, over a million people have participated in the establishment of effective management for nearly one quarter million hectares of degraded *sal* (*Shorea robusta*) forests. This essay attempts to reconstruct the historical process through which this grassroots social movement emerged.

Too often, national resource management policy and development planning is based solely on an analysis of existing conditions and future need projections. Rarely is it based on a well grounded understanding of the history of environmental use patterns and the social, economic and political forces that shape them. I assume

* I would like to thank a number of persons who have commented on earlier drafts of this paper and provided valuable guidance in its development. Particular thanks are due to Ram Guha, Minoti Kaul, Cheryl Cort, David Arnold, and Prabir Guhathakurta. The author would also like to thank Jeff Campbell and the Ford Foundation for supporting the research.

that it is these factors that determine human behaviour *vis-à-vis* the environment and that effective resource policy and management systems must take these realities into consideration.

## The Pre-Colonial Context

It is apparent that prior to the colonial era, western Midnapore was covered by dense jungle tracts. While patches of forests, particularly along river plains had been cleared for agriculture, much of the area was wild and remote. For these reasons, the Jungle Mahals presented an ideal escape for tribal and other groups fleeing from oppression. Mukerji comments that during the late Mughal period large tracts of jungle inhabited by tribals (the Jharkhand) extended through the entire Chotanagpur area including Birbhum and western Burdwan (see Map 1). He notes further that 'although the Muslim Jagirdars were posted in Rajnagar in Birbhum, it seems a large number of tribal folk remained insular in the hilly regions'.[1] This essay examines the experiences emerging from an area known as the Jungle Mahals including the police stations (*thana*) of Garbetta, Binpur, Gopiballavpur, Salboni, Silda, and Jhargram in western Midnapore District (see Map 2). The region was primarily populated by Santal, Bhumij, and Mahato tribals, with some low-caste Hindus.[2]

In the pre-colonial period, while the Jungle Mahals were nominally under Mughal control, due to the inaccessibility of the area little attempt was made to extract revenues or exert political authority. The Santal and Bhumij tribal communities of forest inhabitants practised shifting (swidden) cultivation, as well as hunting and gathering forest products.[3] Wild fruits, roots, herbs

[1] S. Mukerji, 'A chapter on the tribal sources of Bengal history in the Muslim period', *Bulletin of the Cultural Research Institute*, 11, 1–2, 1975, pp. 20–4, as cited in Edward Duyker, *Tribal Guerrillas: The Santals of West Bengal and the Naxalite Movement* (Delhi, 1987), pp. 27–8.

[2] Swapan Dasgupta, 'Adivasi politics in Midnapur, *c.* 1760–1924', in Ranjit Guha (ed.), *Subaltern Studies IV* (Delhi, 1985), p. 102.

[3] Duyker, *Trial Guerrillas*, p. 28.

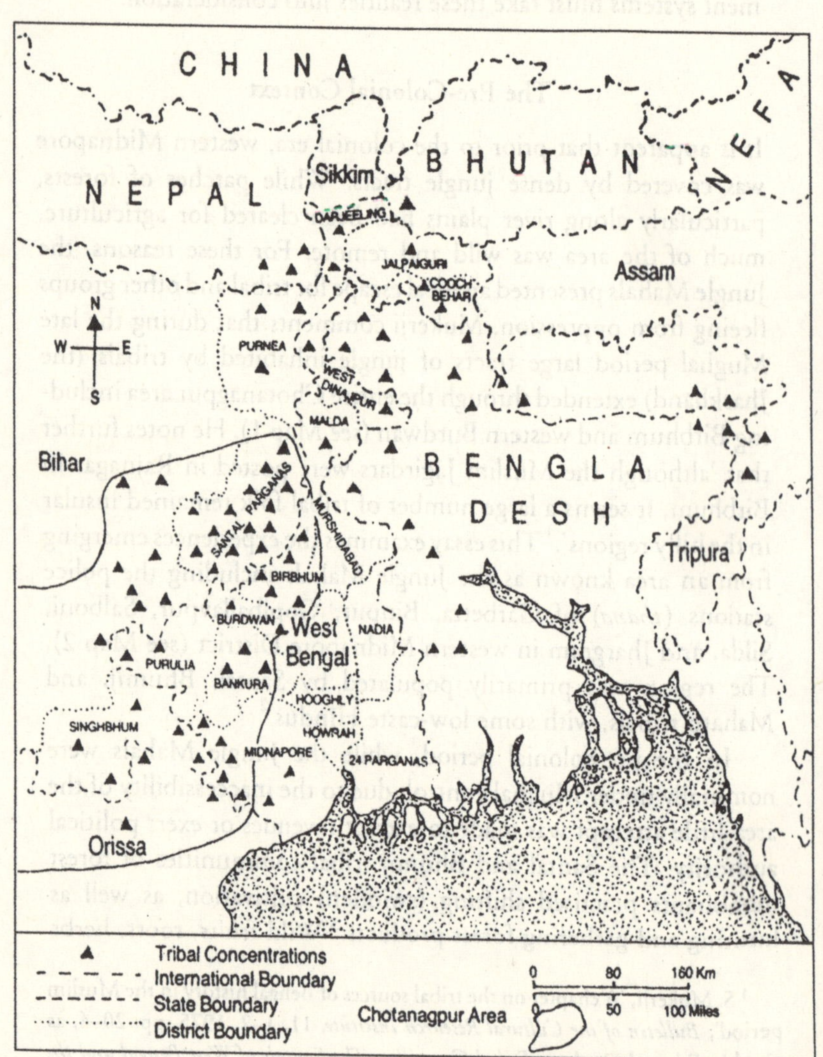


Map 1. Tribal Population Distribution in West Bengal.

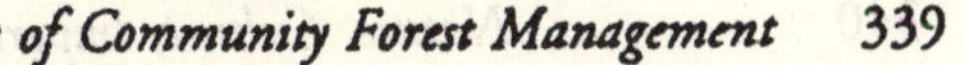

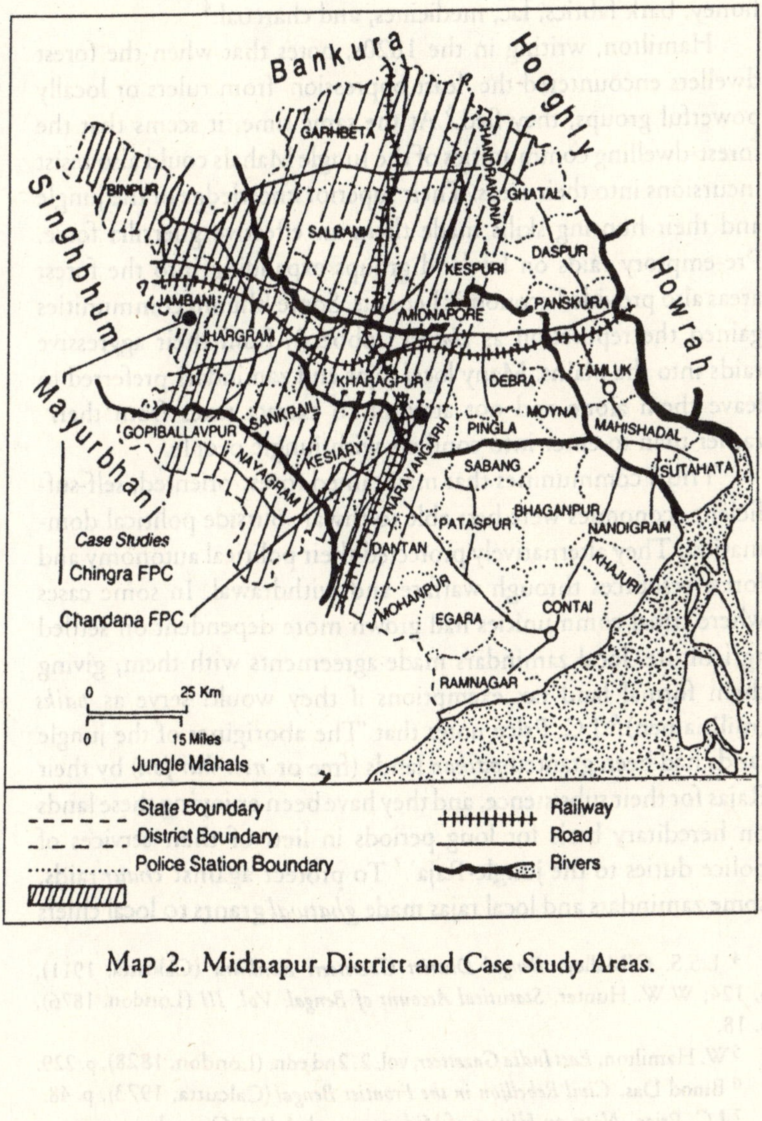

Map 2. Midnapur District and Case Study Areas.

and the nutritious flowers and fruit pulp of the Mahua tree provided much of the diet, making them less dependent on agriculture and highly mobile. Tribal villages were also actively engaged in trade in firewood, silk, resin, deer and buffalo horns, wax, honey, bark fabrics, lac, medicines, and charcoal.[4]

Hamilton, writing in the 1820s, notes that when the forest dwellers encountered the 'least oppression' from rulers or locally powerful groups, they fled.[5] At the same time, it seems that the forest-dwelling communities of the Jungle Mahals could also resist incursions into their areas. Their superior knowledge of the jungle and their hunting skills made them an effective guerrilla force. Pre-emptory raids on lowland groups expanding into the forest areas also provided economic benefits. Some Bhumij communities gained the reputation as *chaurs* (robbers), from their aggressive raids into the plains. Many local rajas and zamindars preferred to leave them alone and not attempt to extract taxes from then rather than to enter into conflicts with jungle people.

Tribal communities that maintained forest-oriented, self-sufficient economies were best able to thwart outside political domination. They alternatively protected their political autonomy and forest resources through warfare and withdrawal. In some cases where tribal communities had grown more dependent on settled agriculture, local zamindars made agreements with them, giving them formal land tax exemptions if they would serve as *paiks* (militiamen).[6] J.C. Price notes that 'The aborigines of the jungle lands had been granted *paikan* lands (free or *non-kar jots*) by their Rajas for their subsistence, and they have been enjoying these lands on hereditary basis for long periods in lieu of their services of police duties to the jungle-Raja'.[7] To protect against *chaur* raids, some zamindars and local rajas made *ghatwal* grants to local chiefs

[4] L.S.S. O'Malley, *Bengal District Gazetteer: Bankura* (Calcutta, 1911), p. 124; W.W. Hunter, *Statistical Account of Bengal: Vol. III* (London, 1876), p. 18.

[5] W. Hamilton, *East India Gazetteer*, vol. 2, 2nd edn. (London, 1828), p. 229.

[6] Binod Das, *Civil Rebellion in the Frontier Bengal* (Calcutta, 1973), p. 48.

[7] J.C. Price, *Notes on History of Midnapore*, vol. 1 (1876), p. 1.

if they would guard mountain passes. Baden-Powell noted that 'The chief (*ghatwal*) was allowed to take the revenue of a hill or frontier tract on the condition of maintaining a police or military force (*paiks*), to keep the peace and prevent raids of robbers on to the plain country below'.[8]

The polity of the Santal communities of south-west Bengal, and likely other tribal forest-dwelling groups, was either through community council or village chiefs. In the former case, the village was governed by a council of elders or panchayat whose membership is decided annually by community members. The traditional village council operates under a *pargana*, or council comprised of ten to twelve village panchayats, while final authority rests with the Lo Bir, or forest council, which may extend over an entire district and is the final court for dispute arbitration. The annual hunt organized by the Lo Bir provides the basis for inter-village political organizing, conflict resolution, military organizing and joint decision making—as well as a source of protein. Duyker reports that 'the social significance of the Lo Bir far outweighs its economic importance'.[9] More specifically, the Lo Bir appears to have provided a unifying mechanism among dispersed Santal communities, both over space and time. The council provided communication channels through which information regarding social and political issues could be exchanged and a organizational body through which some consensus on tribal policies might be reached. Due to the existence of this network of village and forest councils, it maybe that outside political operatives, like the Jharkhandis and the Naxalites, found it easier to work among the Santal in the later half of the twentieth century.

During the pre-colonial period, and up to the present, the belief systems of the forest communities were strongly grounded in the worship of nature. Religious festivals are tied to both the agricultural cycle and the flowering and fruiting of the forest trees. The Santal new year, for example, begins with the blossoming of

[8] B.H. Baden-Powell, *Land Systems of British India*, vol. 1 (Oxford, 1892), p. 393.

[9] Duyker, *Tribal Guerrillas*, p. 169.

the Sal tree in March. The links in tribal belief between the health of the forest, fertility, and prosperity are clear in the following lines from this Baha festival song.

> When the Sal trees are in leaf,
> On the mountain,
> How lovely they look,
> Wealth in the house . . .[10]

This subsistence-oriented, isolationist life of the tribal communities of the Jungle Mahals began to change with the emergence of British colonial power in Bengal in the late eighteenth century.

## Changing Forest Management During the Colonial Period

In 1760 the district of Midnapore was transferred to the East India Company by Mir Qasim, making it one of the first districts in India to be brought under British rule.[11] The area comprised vast tracts of forest, broken only by patches of farmland. Hamilton notes that 'these jungles were occupied by a poor miserable proscribed race of men called Santals . . . ', and the land was under the dominion of chieftains who had never been reduced to submission by the Moghuls and who 'never paid any regular rents for their lands'.[12]

During the late eighteenth century the British sent military expeditions into the Jungle Mahals in an attempt to extend their authority and extract land revenues. According to Richard Becher, an officer of the East India Company writing in 1769, 'When the English received the grant of the Dewani, their first consideration seems to have been the raising of as large sums from the country as could be collected to answer the pressing demands from home and to defray the large expenses here'.[13] The forest chieftains and

[10] W.G. Archer, *The Hill of Flutes, Love and Poetry in Tribal India: A Portrait of the Santals* (London, 1974), p. 237, cited in Duyker, *Tribal Guerrillas*, p. 169.

[11] Duyker, *Tribal Guerrillas*, p. 28.

[12] Ibid., p. 28.

[13] Cited in A.K. Sur, *History and Culture of Bengal* (1963), pp. 176–7

tribal communities resisted, ambushing British forces and harassing them whenever possible. According to one British source from the period.

As soon as the harvest is gathered in they carry their grain to the tops of the hills, or lodge it in other fastnesses that are impregnable; so that whenever they are pursued by a superior force they retire to these places, where they are quite secure, and bid defiance to any attack that can be made against them.[14]

Local zamindars also initially resisted the imposition of colonial authority, refusing to pay their taxes, organizing their paik militias to resist, and falling into arrears on their taxes. In 1798 widespread violent resistance disrupted revenue collection activities in the Midnapur area, forcing the Company to restore lands to hereditary chiefs that had been put up for sale for failure to pay taxes.[15]

Through superior force, however, the British did gradually succeed in extending their control in the area through the nineteenth century. As this process continued, the British empowered a new class of zamindars to control and tax local forest communities, encouraging them to open forest land for cultivation. Individual villages were established under Mandali tenure which could be incorporated into the revenue collection system. The Mandal, or village chief, brought tribal labourers with him to convert forest to agricultural land. The zamindar financed the migration of the tribal community (usually Santals), and their subsistence until the land became productive. Some of these zamindars were allocated huge tracts of land. For example, 'the Pargana Cundar was one of the largest Zamindaries of Midnapore . . . containing about 663 villages and over 130,000 bighas of land'.[16]

The tribal communities of the Jungle Mahals resisted the imposition of the taxation system through a series of armed revolts.

[14] Report from the Resident of Midnapore, 6 February 1773, cited in Gouripada Chatterjee, *Midnapore: The Forerunner of India's Freedom Struggle* (Delhi, 1986), p. 38.

[15] O'Malley, *Bankura*, p. 44.

[16] Chatterjee, p. 43.

The first, referred to as the Chuar Rebellions,[17] lasted from 1767 to 1800. Tribal guerrillas were so effective that 'even as late as 1800, after nearly forty years of British occupation, a collector reported that two thirds of Midnapore consisted of jungle, the greater part of which was inaccessible'.[18] Yet, gradually the East India Company succeeded in strengthening its control, despite subsequent revolts by forest people, such as the Naik Revolt (1806–16). By the early nineteenth century, while courts, jails, and district police were ineffective, collection of land revenue was becoming a routine matter. Under the Permanent Settlement Act by 1866, 1369 zamindari estates had been established in Midnapore, and given the absolute ownership of agricultural lands and forest tracts as long as they paid government revenues.[19] In order to meet their tax obligations, zamindars were anxious to bring in tribal and peasant cultivators to clear forest land and convert it to agricultural crops. Tribal communities often lost control of their paikan lands to zamindars and the Company, becoming tenant farmers. Due to the greater farming expertise of Hindu peasant cultivators, tribals were often displaced by zamindars in favour of the former, further exacerbating their social and environmental dislocation.

Tribal and low-caste families also suffered at the hands of moneylenders (*mahajans*). The *diku* (plains people) moneylenders who migrated into the Jungle Mahals began to displace the zamindars as sources of credit for small farmers. The mahajans were far more effective than the zamindars in converting outstanding loans into land mortgages and then foreclosing on them when the borrower failed to pay. Moneylenders often charged exorbitant interest rates of 50 per cent per year, forcing defaulters to migrate or become tenant farmers. Dasgupta cites McAlpin who reported at the time that many tribal and low-caste communities lost the

[17] The British adopted the Bengali term 'Chaur' meaning an outlandish or wild person, to refer to the tribal and low-caste people of the area.

[18] Chatterjee, *Midnapore*, pp. 17–18.

[19] Ibid., p. 72.

majority of their farm lands between 1892 and 1906. Of the 120 Santal villages who had owned land which McAlpin surveyed, '35 had sold their rights to pay off debts, 6 surrendered their rights, 19 had their rights forcibly taken away, and for 54 the process of loss was unknown'.[20] As Baden-Powell writes, 'The Mahajan entrenched himself in the rural economy which came to be dominated by him'.[21] With the elimination of tribal landowners, the Bengali mahajan landlords and the large zamindari companies came to control land resources, raising rents drastically and eliminating many of the forest use rights previously enjoyed by tribal and low-caste communities.

The process of forest clearing for agricultural land conversion had sweeping ecological implications, especially for river systems and soil conditions. Removal of the forest cover allowed torrential monsoon rains to wash away the shallow top soils, leaving an exposed laterite hard pan that made farming virtually impossible in many areas. Traditional forest based industries like tusar silk, indigo and *endi* declined dramatically, as did the population densities in Chandrakona, Ghatal and other regions of the Jungle Mahals as the forest was cleared.[22]

By the 1860s pressure on the forests of the Jungle Mahals grew further as the growing railway system demanded immense quantities of sal logs to provide sleepers for the rail bed. The construction and opening of the Ajay-Sainthia and Sainthia-Tinpahar railway lines in 1860 stimulated commercial felling, followed by the construction of the main line of the Bengal-Nagpur railway in 1898. Commercial demand for timber accelerated forest cutting, and raised the value of forest lands.[23] Timber merchants

20 M.C. McAlpin, *Report on the Condition of the Sonthals in the Districts of Birbhum, Bankura, Midnapore and North Balasore* (Calcutta, 1909), pp. 20–1, 31–3, 38–9, cited in Dasgupta, 'Adivasi Politics', p. 109.

21 Baden-Powell, *Land Systems*, I, p. 407.

22 *Midnapore District Census Report* (1951), p. LXV.

23 Kailash C. Malhotra and Debal Deb, 'History of deforestation and regeneration/plantation in Midnapore district of West Bengal, India', Paper prepared for the IUFRO International Conference on 'History of small scale

rushed in, even before the rail lines opened and began leasing or purchasing large tracts from the Midnapur Zamindari Company and other zamindars.[24] Leaseholders and zamindars began imposing strict controls on forest use by local communities as the value of the forest increased, restricting or eliminating traditional usufruct rights enjoyed under the mandali land tenure system. When tribals and low-caste groups appealed to the Settlement Department, their complaints were usually dismissed noting that the 'encroachments of the landlords were justified by "unavoidable economic circumstances" '. Dasgupta convincingly argues that 'it was with the active connivance and supervision of the imperial bureaucracy that the destruction of the traditional jungle rights was carried out'.[25] Tribal communities were charged fees to gather fuelwood or cut roofing poles. Zamindars sold lease rights for the collection of lac and cultivation of silk. They also carried out periodic searches of forest communities to detect illegally cut fuelwood or timber. If forest products were found, family members would be beaten and sometimes killed. Bradely-Birt notes for Chotanagpur that new zamindars also demanded tribals to pay taxes on mahua flowers and sometime cut down the trees and sold them for timber if they failed to pay.[26] As customary access to the forest was restricted, friction between tribal and low-caste communities and local zamindars grew.

In response to their growing marginalization, in early 1855 six to seven thousand Santal tribals from Birbhum, Bankura, Chotanagpur, and Hazaribagh began meeting to organize resistance. Under the messianic leadership of four Santal brothers, on 16 July 1855 some ten thousand tribal rebels 'stood their ground firmly and fought with bows and a kind of battle axe' in a battle near Pirpaiti.[27] Eventually, the revolt collapsed after half their

private forestry,' Freiburg, Germany, 2–5 September 1991, p. 7.

[24] Dasgupta, 'Adivasi Politics', p. 113.

[25] Ibid., p. 114.

[26] F.B. Bradely-Birt, *Chota Nagpore: A Little-Known Province of the Empire* (London, 1910), p. 4.

[27] K.K. Datta, *The Santal Insurrection of 1855–1857* (Calcutta, 1940), p. 26,

number were reportedly killed. Despite their defeat the *Hul* Rebellion (as it is known among the Santal) 'profoundly influenced the ideological development of many Santal commun ities',[28] and lives on in the songs and oral traditions of the tribal people of the Jungle Mahals.

Toward the end of the nineteenth century many of the estates of smaller landowners were absorbed by large landowners. These included the British-held Midnapur Zamindari Company, the Jhargram Raj, and the Raja of Mayurbhanj. Throughout the later part of the nineteenth and first half of the twentieth century, many forest communities in the Jungle Mahals became increasingly indebted to moneylenders and tax collectors, causing widespread mortgaging and loss of their agricultural lands. McAlpin writing in 1909 observed a 'general transfer of Santhal lands to non-Santhals', noting most sales of Santhal land were due to previous debts and that the land generally was sold for as little as Rs 10 per *bigha*.[29] A report made in 1947, reported that the average agricultural land-holding size of tribals had decreased to 0.5 acre of owned land and 1.2 acres of sharecropped land, noting the precarious nature of such marginal farming operations.[30] The Bengal Tenancy Act and the Zamindari Abolition Act of 1953 which were designed to assist tribal and disadvantaged farmers failed to have the intended effect. In some cases, the acts even facilitated the eviction of sharecroppers. By the early 1970s, many tribals and low-caste people in Midnapore had been reduced to agricultural labourers and sharecroppers.

While the alienation of private lands was an important element in the impoverishment of tribal and low-caste communities, so too was the loss of cash and kind income from forest-based activities as the forests were cleared. Writing in the mid-1850s,

cited in Duyker, *Tribal Guerrillas*, p. 34.

28 Duyker, *Tribal Guerrillas*, p. 35.

29 McAlpin, *Report on the Condition of the Sonthals*, p. 34.

30 K.S. Chattopdhyaya, *Report on the Santals of Bengal* (Calcutta, 1947), p. 35. cited in Dukyer, *Tribal Guerrillas*, p. 44.

Sherwill noted that nearly 20 per cent of the population of Birbhum was involved in tussar silk collection, processing, weaving, or marketing.[31] By the early 1970s, the weaving industry had declined significantly in part due to the need to import cocoons, which had been available in abundance in the area in the past.

Attempts by the government to extract greater revenues and impose increased control over freshwater fisheries throughout the later half of the nineteenth and earlier twentieth century also restricted access of marginal communities over once common property resources.[32] In response to these restrictions Santals in Midnapur and Bankura carried out mass loots on fish-ponds in 1922 and 1923. 'In April 1923, for instance, there was a wave of looting of fish-ponds and violation of forest rights over an area of 200 square miles extending from Jamboni and Gopiballabhpur westward to Ghatsila in Singhbhum district of Bihar and northwards through Silda . . . to Bankura district'. Sarkar quotes an official of the time who noted that the Santal 'will tell you how in his father's time all jungles were free, all *bandhs* (ponds) open to the public, and that this action was simply "carrying on an old tradition" . . . an attempt to bring back the "golden age" '.[33]

## Changes in the Jungle Mahals under the Populist Government

A major shift in the erosion of land control rights of disempowered people in the Jungle Mahals began in 1967 when the United Front Government was elected and announced its intention 'to distribute surplus land among the landless and halt the eviction of

[31] W.S. Sherwill, *Geographical and Statistical Report of the District of Beerbhoom* (Calcutta, 1855), p. 31, cited in Duyker, *Tribal Guerrillas*, p. 146.

[32] See Peter Reeves, 'Inland waters and freshwater fisheries: Issues of control, access and conservation in colonial India', chapter IX, this volume.

[33] Ibid., p. 291, citing Sumit Sarkar, 'The conditions and nature of subaltern militancy: Bengal from Swadeshi to Non-Cooperation, *c.* 1905–22', in Ranajit Guha (ed.), *Subaltern Studies III* (Delhi, 1984), p. 303.

sharecroppers'.[34] Despite a basic agreement on the need for land reform among the fourteen member parties of the United Front Government, the coalition was unable to develop effective implementation programmes for such policies. Policy implementation was also resisted by more conservative party members, and by the need to comply with bureaucratic and judicial procedures. Nonetheless, the announcement of land reform plans stimulated widespread interest in rural areas. Depressed groups began to organize, particularly Santals, who met in groups bringing their traditional weapons with them and often confronting armed police groups. 'Between March and May 1967, nearly one hundred incidents involving *kisans* [peasant farmers and agricultural labourers] armed with bows and arrows, occupying land and symbolically establishing their ownership by ploughing small parcels, were reported to the district police'.[35] The famous uprising at Naxalbari in Darjeeling district took place a few months later, when a local CPI(M) cadre and a tribal leader named Jangal Santhal organized over 600 tribals to attack local government officials and landlords.

The CPI(M), embarrassed by the actions of some of its members, expelled them from the party. Other disillusioned CPI(M) members joined them, ultimately forming a new party, the CPI(ML), generally called the Naxalites. The Naxalites rejected the parliamentary system, and saw no alternative to an armed struggle and a protracted insurgency movement. The Naxalities carried their message of land reform and class struggle to the poorest communities, finding their strongest support among the Santals.

Throughout 1969 and 1970, the violence shifted to Midnapore where Naxalite organizers were encouraging the adoption of Maoist oriented politics, similar to those expressed in Naxalbari. The emerging Naxalite leadership effectively enlisted the support

34 Duyker, *Tribal Guerrillas*, p. 67.

35 'What happened at Naxalbari and why?', *The Hindu*, 12 June 1967, cited in Duyer, *Tribal Guerrillas*, p. 70.

of disenchanted tribal people and landless labourers. The houses of landlords were raided and stockpiled rice redistributed, while killings were also carried out. Some forest communities were also discontented with the Forest Department and its policies of providing elites and contractors with low-cost resource exploitation leases. While forests were logged of timber trees and bamboo, villagers lost the raw materials they required for their subsistence and commercial needs. According to Pritish Dasgupta, a leader of the Midnapore uprising, the Dom tribals in particularly were upset by the high prices contractors charged them for bamboo.[36] The high prices and fuelwood scarcity experienced by potters, blacksmiths, and other caste groups also increased antagonism towards the Forest Department and those who acted as contractors for them.

Many traditional village elites and landowners fled the area and the CPI(ML) began to institute village committees to fill the political vacuum it had created.[37] The extent of broad-based participation was so great that the authorities had difficulty re-establishing control, refraining from directly confronting huge groups of militant labourers, sharecroppers, and small-holders. Gradually, however, Naxalite leaders were rounded up, with over 700 captured by mid-1970. Yet, the resistance and the new political leadership that emerged had a fundamental influence on community attitudes to private and towards public forest land.

## From Conflict to Compromise: Experiences of the West Bengal Forest Department 1972–82

In 1970 the atmosphere in south-east Bengal was tense. Poor tribal people began rapidly cutting the shrinking sal forests as state authority waned in the wake of the Naxalite uprising. While the forest department sought police assistance to protect remaining

[36] Interview with Pritish 'Megnath' Dasgupta, Khargram, 10 November 1979, reported in Duyker, *Tribal Guerrillas*, p. 147.

[37] Ibid., p. 83.

forest lands, they were often met with forcible resistance from community groups. Violent confrontations were resulting in deaths from shooting and injuries on both sides. In Purulia district the situation was particularly explosive. The region had been carved out of southern Bihar in 1956 and was the poorest district in West Bengal. Many tribals from communities in the area were being hired by contractors to cut fuelwood, accelerating deforestation.

In 1970 in another corner of south-west Bengal, A.K. Banerjee, an Indian Forest Service officer, had been appointed chief silviculturist at a small forest research site at Arabari. Experiments were being conducted with sal, teak, eucalyptus and other timber species. The trials were constantly being disrupted by villagers cutting fuelwood and grazing their cattle on the experimental plots. The silviculturist began meeting with members of the eleven villages surrounding Arabari, thirty km to the north of Midnapur. The officer attempted to offer the villagers a comprehensive employment programme, to absorb them in plantation work and inter-cropping in the plantation. In return he asked them to stop grazing and cutting on the field station. Due to limited budget and employment opportunities, he later revised the arrangement, promising them a 25 per cent share of the sal timber and rights to all minor forest products including leaves, medicinals, fibre and fodder grasses, mushrooms, and fruits. This agreement appealed to the communities and local villagers ceased their grazing and cutting, and began protecting the forest from use by outsiders. In 1972 the first Forest Protection Committees (FPC) were born in the villages around the Arabari forests.

While successful examples of joint management agreements were beginning to emerge in Arabari and Purulia during the early 1970s, throughout the decade they remained isolated cases with little effect on routine forest management systems within the state. Nonetheless, these early experiences demonstrated that opening communications with forest communities could effectively reduce conflicts between the Forest Department and forest user groups. Through discussions forest officers were able to identify terms for effective management partnerships. By formulating agreements that responded to the economic needs of forest communities, new incentives were created among villagers which resulted in the emergence of effective controls on forest exploitation. In some communities village men formed volunteer patrols. People who were found cutting green wood or grazing animals were warned by village volunteers. Repeat offenders from the participating villages were fined, and outsiders were turned over to forestry field staff. Most confrontations occurred during the first and second year of protection, after which the restrictions and rights of the protecting communities were generally recognized by outsiders.

Where root stock was still viable, community-based forest protection activities resulted in the rapid regeneration of degraded natural forests. Natural regrowth led to substantial increases in biomass productivity and the enhanced availability of a range of important minor forest products. The capacity of degraded natural forests to rapidly regenerate and produce fodder, fuel, fibres and other valuable materials appears to have been instrumental in sustaining community protection activities.

The effect of these early achievements was, however, limited to small forest tracts. Officers experimenting with joint management were largely working in isolation from one another. As a result the agreements were informal and generally had little validity beyond the term of the individual forest officer, who was usually rotated to a new area every three years. There was little effort to co-ordinate the terms of the agreement in one area with those being offered by forest officers in other territories. Officers exploring new agreements with communities, however, were communicating their experiences to their superior officers and the progress they were achieving, particularly in Arabari, was attracting attention.

In the early 1980s, recognizing the success of Arabari and a few other villagers where management agreements with forest communities were being made, some senior forest officers began to encourage field staff to pursue similar negotiations in wider areas throughout the southwestern part of the state.

In 1986, a District Forest Officer (DFO) who had experimented with joint management groups in Purulia in the early 1970s, was made Conservator of Forests for the south-western forests of West Bengal. His earlier experience in Purulia district and subsequent assignments across the state had further confirmed his opinion that participatory management offered the best prospects for sustainable forestry. He began urging his District Forest Officers to encourage field staff to work with forest communities. To accelerate the formation of local community management groups, the Conservator told range and beat officers that their performance in forming FPCs would be monitored and awards given to those officers who were most successful.

Through informal discussions and small group meetings, the circle Conservator and his DFOs gradually conveyed a message to field foresters that the department was committed to meaningfully involving communities in forest management. Local party and panchayat leaders were also informed of the department's new strategy and began sending this message to communities. The several dozen FPCs existing in 1985 increased to 1611 in July 1990 covering 195,000 hectares of forest land throughout Midnapore, Bankura, and Purulia districts.[38]

The expansion of joint management activities in West Bengal, particularly during the later half of the 1980s, was facilitated by the growth of the department's social forestry programme. These programmes required foresters to negotiate formally with village groups and brought a community extension orientation into these agencies for the first time.

At the same time, small cultivators, landless and tribal families found new authority as the power of landlords and contractors was diminished through political and legislative acts. The growing openness and flexibility of the state Forest Department, and its attempts to minimize corruption, allowed field staff to gain respect in the eyes of the communities. The new joint management initiative promoted by some senior officers urged field staff to

38 Malhotra and Dev, 'History of deforestation'.

stress the environmental problems caused by deforestation and the benefits of sound management, rather than raising expectations with promises of guaranteed forest employment and timber revenues. During this expansion period, senior officers felt the resurrection of 'tree consciousness' among rural communities was among the programme's biggest achievements.[39]

While the officers of the West Bengal Forest Department (WBFD) feel justifiably pleased by community concerns over forest degradation and the willingness of village members to mobilize to protect natural forests, the extraordinary increase in the number of FPCs indicates that a receptive social climate was already present prior to the initiation of programme expansion. Further, many communities in neighbouring Bihar and Orissa are also establishing forest management groups, without similar forest department programmes. While WBFD support certainly supported the expansion and formalization of these organizations, the energy driving this shift in the tenure of public forest lands appears to emanate from the community, the concerns of its members, and their shared history. The historical events outlined earlier in this essay suggest that communities in the area have mobilized repeatedly over the past two hundred years to protect their resource rights from manipulation by outside groups (see Figure 1). To that extent the emergence of community resource management groups in part reflects another attempt by groups with low socio-economic status to reclaim control over their environment. The process of FPC formation and the extent to which it was driven by communities concerned over environmental changes and encouraged by field staff is reflected in the following case studies.

## The Emergence of Forest Protection Committees in Chingra Forest

Ten villages surround the Chingra Mouza forest in Midnapore

[39] Udayan Bannerjee, 'Participatory forest management in West Bengal', in K.C. Malhotra and Mark Poffenberger (eds.), *Forest Regeneration through Community Participation* (West Bengal Forest Department, 1989), p. 4.

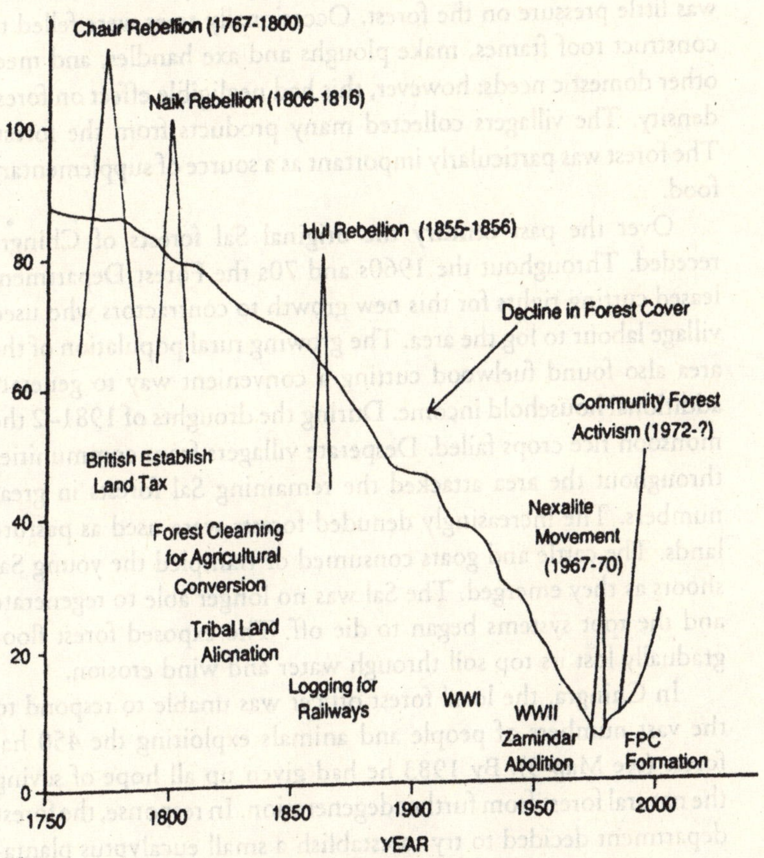


Figure 1. Changes in Forest Cover and Community Activism in Southwest Bengal

district in southwest Bengal, near the borders of Orissa and Bihár. A century ago the Munda tribal community of Chinga was surrounded by dense Sal forest. The trees were of great girth, three to four feet in diameter. The region was sparsely settled and there was little pressure on the forest. Occasionally trees were felled to construct roof frames, make ploughs and axe handles, and meet other domestic needs: however, this had negligible effect on forest density. The villagers collected many products from the forest. The forest was particularly important as a source of supplementary food.

Over the past century the original Sal forests of Chingra receded. Throughout the 1960s and 70s the Forest Department leased cutting rights for this new growth to contractors who used village labour to log the area. The growing rural population of the area also found fuelwood cutting a convenient way to generate additional household income. During the droughts of 1981–2 the monsoon rice crops failed. Desperate villagers from communities throughout the area attacked the remaining Sal forests in great numbers. The increasingly denuded forests were used as pasture lands. The cattle and goats consumed or trampled the young Sal shoots as they emerged. The Sal was no longer able to regenerate and the root systems began to die off. The exposed forest floor gradually lost its top soil through water and wind erosion.

In Chingra, the local forest officer was unable to respond to the vast numbers of people and animals exploiting the 450 ha. forest (see Map 3). By 1983 he had given up all hope of saving the natural forest from further degeneration. In response, the forest department decided to try to establish a small eucalyptus plantation on some of the degraded forest lands near Chingra village. When the healthy saplings reached a few feet in height, however, people from a village near Chingra began cutting them down for fuel. Seeing this, the Chingra villagers thought they should also benefit from the government project and cut down the remaining trees. The local forester was further frustrated by the failure of the plantation project.

Meanwhile, the young men of Chingra were aware of the

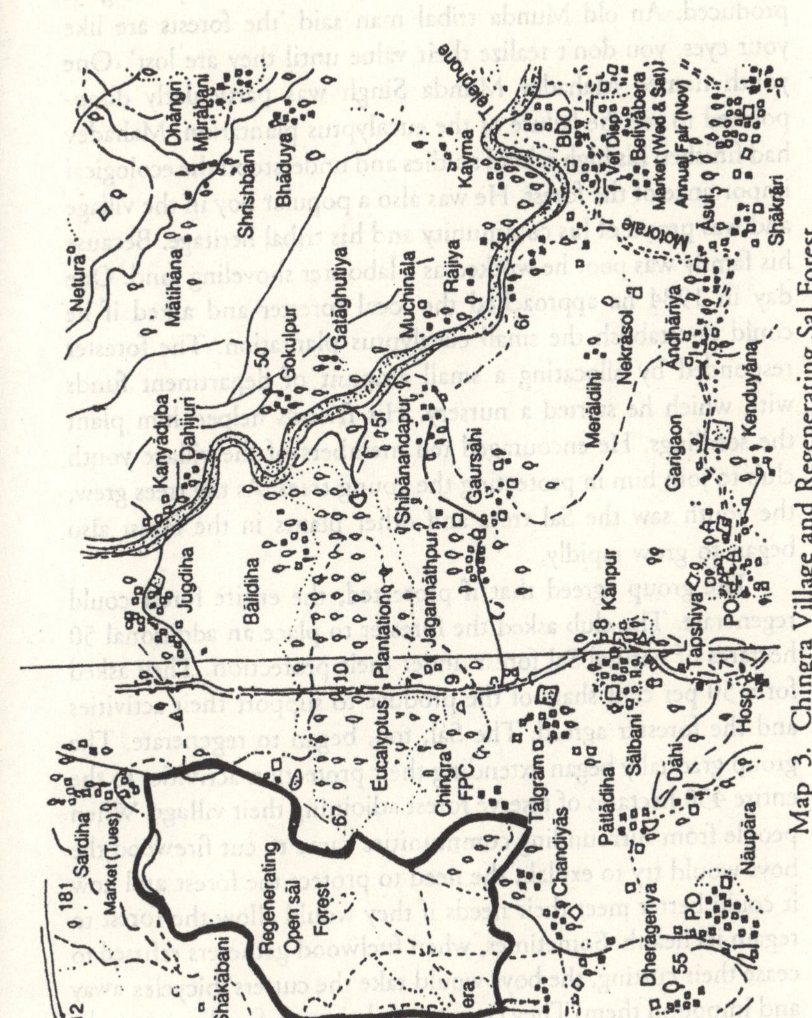


Map 3. Chingra Village and Regenerating Sal Forest.

deteriorating state of their environment. They had often heard the stories from the old people about the beautiful forests that had once surrounded the community and the many things it produced. An old Munda tribal man said 'the forests are like your eyes, you don't realize their value until they are lost'. One youth named Mahadev Munda Singh was particularly disappointed to see the failure of the eucalyptus plantation. Mahadev had finished his high school studies and understood the ecological importance of the forest. He was also a popular boy in the village and was proud of his community and his tribal heritage. Because his family was poor he worked as a labourer shoveling sand. One day in 1984 he approached the local forester and asked if he could re-establish the small eucalyptus plantation. The forester responded by allocating a small amount of department funds with which he started a nursery. His friends helped him plant the seedlings. He encouraged ten members of the village youth club to join him in protecting the young trees. As the trees grew, the youth saw the Sal trees and other plants in the forest also began to grow rapidly.

The group agreed that if protected, the entire forest could regenerate. The club asked the forester to place an additional 50 hectares of natural Sal forest under their protection. They asked for a 50 per cent share of the produce to support their activities and the forester agreed. The Sal, too, began to regenerate. The group gradually began extending their protection activities to the entire 450 hectares of reserve forest adjoining their village. When people from surrounding communities came to cut firewood the boys would try to explain the need to protect the forest and how it could better meet their needs if they would allow the forest to regain its health. Sometimes, when fuelwood gatherers refused to cease their cutting, the boys would take the cutters' bicycles away and impound them. They convinced their own families not to let the cattle graze in the protected forest and chased away cattle from the other villages. After three months the regenerating young Sal shoots had grown to four feet or more in height and were above the reach of the small cattle. Local people began to appreciate the effectiveness of the protection activities being carried out by the club.

People from other villages seeing the success of the Chingra group began thinking of protecting forests near their own communities. Seeing the growth of local interest in forest protection the local forest beat officer began holding meetings with villagers to encourage them. At each meeting he invited Mahadev and his friends to talk about their activities and their hopes for forest regeneration. By 1988, nine of the ten communities surrounding Chingra forests were protecting the forest and the Sal had reached a height of 15 to 20 feet. A dense undergrowth of climbing vines, shrubs, grasses, and small palms emerged.

The rapidly regenerating forest began to attract fuelwood cutters from the neighbouring state of Bihar. One night a band of Bihar villagers came with their axes, bicycles and bullock carts to fell the Chingra forest. The Biharis attempting this 'mass loot' of the forest were soon confronted by Mahadev and his club members, as well as men from many of the neighbouring villages. Mahadev said 'we took our spears, arrows and axes and faced them eye ball to eye ball. We talked and told them the forest was protected now and that the trees were no longer available for commercial cutting'. In the end the Chingra villagers offered to give the Biharis dead twigs and sticks to meet their subsistence fuelwood needs. Later the Biharis organized their own groups to protect forests near their village four kilometres away from Chingra.

Many inter-village meetings have been held over the past three years to work out agreements, settle disputes, repulse outside users, determine territorial protection responsibilities, and establish usufruct rights among participating communities. While eight villages have joined Chingra in protecting the local forests, the community of Talgram has not co-operated. This village is comprised of immigrants from the state of Orissa who were brought into the area by a local landowner as agricultural labourers. On 18 November 1990 a special meeting ('convention') was called by Mahadev and his friends to bring all of the communities together including the Orissa migrants to invite them to join the management group. The panchayat leaders, and range and forest beat officers were also invited. It was hoped this would result in a common understanding regarding management priorities, a clarification of community usufruct rights, and the authorization of the community to use fines and physical force when necessary to protect the forest from outside users.

The Chingra case reflects the decentralized nature of FPC group formation. It also illustrates the way in which village leaders like Mahadev were able to work with field staff and other neighbouring communities to identify forest areas for protection and reach agreements, while turning away outsider users. It appears that the ability of local communities to take the lead in defining management territories was a key to the success of the programme. While field staff helped facilitate this process by encouraging group meetings and authorizing community protection activities, frequently successful FPCs took the initiative in organizing themselves and establishing operational controls over forest access.

### The Emergence of Forest Protection in Chandana

Chandana and Harinakuri villages are located approximately 20 kms. south of Kharagpur, in the state of West Bengal. A 2 km long dirt track off the main road leads to Chandana village after crossing rain-fed rice fields, and passing through regenerating forest lands. Another kilometre down the road bordering the southern extension of the forest is Harinakuri village. The forest lands in the Chandana area total 160 ha., which are surrounded by Chandana and Harinakuri villages on the south, and Nidata and Babunmara villages to the north (see Map 4). The land slopes gradually downward as it drains into the Kele Ghai River to the north of the four villages.

Most of the villages in the area are comprised of low income scheduled castes, tribals, and farming caste families. In Chandana village there are 38 households half of whom are Bhumi tribals, the rest scheduled castes including oil makers. In Harinakuri there

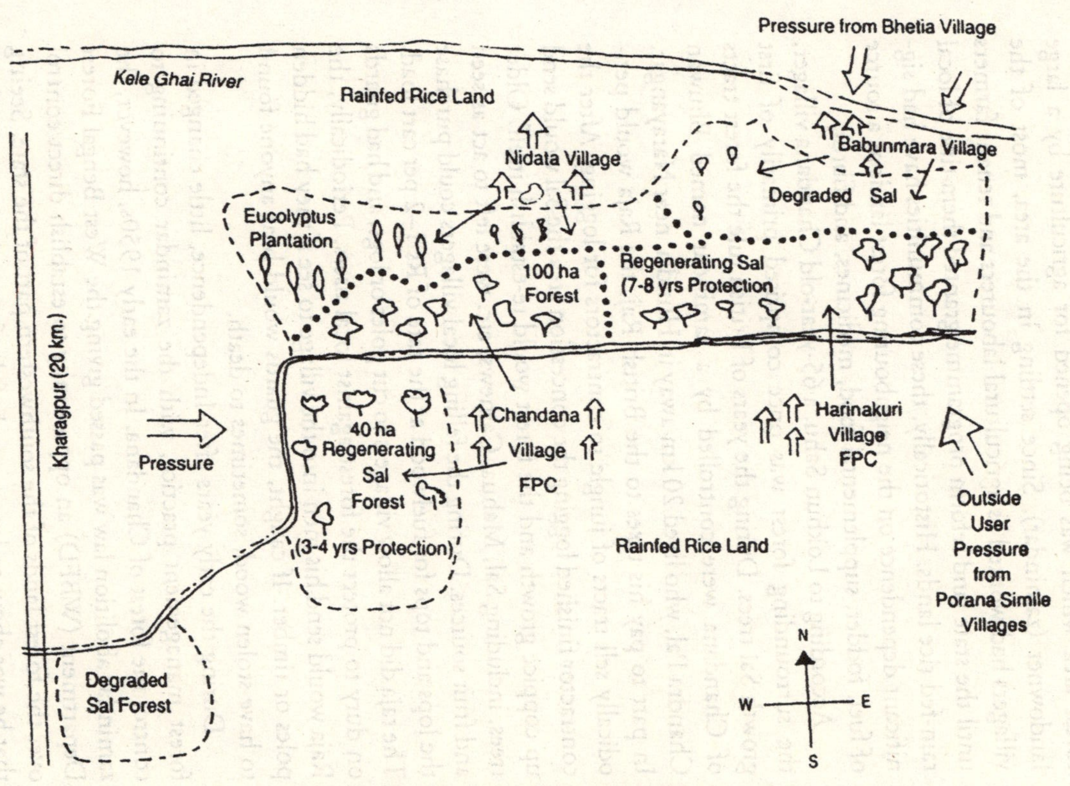


Map 4. Sketch Map of Chandana Forest Beat.

are 31 families, primarily of the Naik scheduled caste. The Naiks claim to have worked as mercenaries for a local raja until approximately one hundred years ago when they moved into this forest area which was being opened for agriculture by a large landowner (zamindar). Since settling in the area, most of the villagers had worked as agricultural labourers and tenant farmers until the state land reform programme granted them title of local rain-fed rice lands. Historically, these communities have had significant dependence on the neighbouring forest lands as a source of fuel, fodder, supplemental food, medicines, and fibres.

According to Lokhun Sahu, a 65-year-old Chandana villager, the surrounding forest was once comprised primarily of first growth Sal trees. During the years of British rule the forest tracts of Chandana were controlled by a zamindar named Bhuwan Chandra Pal, who lived 20 km away in Hundla, near Narayangar. In part to pay his taxes to the British Raj, the Raja would periodically sell tracts of jungle to contractors for logging. After the contractor finished logging the concession area the Sal would send up coppice growth and the forest would re-establish itself. Older trees, including Sal, Mahua, Cashews, etc. were left to act as seed and fruit sources. During the felling local villagers could purchase the lops and tops for fuelwood at the rate of Rs 1–2 per cart load. The raja did not allow villagers to cut poles or logs, and had guards on duty to protect the forest against local users. Periodically, the Raja would send his men into the village to see if they had hidden poles or timber. If caught, the guards would beat anyone found to have stolen wood, sometimes to death.

During the early years after Independence, little changed in forest management practice, with the zamindar continuing to control the forest of Chandana. In the early 1950s, however, the zamindar abolition law was passed giving the West Bengal Forest Department (WBFD) an opportunity to establish direct control over the forest lands of the southwestern part of the state. Seeing that he was about to lose control of the forest, the local zamindar sold off the entire forest tract to contractors who felled the area, leaving only a few fruit trees. For the next six months, communities faced a severe shortage of fuelwood. However, as the coppice growth emerged the forest resource supply also began to recover.

From the mid-1950s through the 1960s the WBFD exerted control over the forests of Chandana. Throughout this period, the WBFD continued the practices of the zamindars by leasing cutting rights to contractors. Consequently, the Sal trees were cut every ten to fifteen years, regenerating through coppice growth. The local field officer complained that the contractors would also often cut the older Sal and fruit trees, a practice that was officially banned, as these trees or standards are important for yielding seeds for natural regeneration. When the forest guard or the villagers attempted to stop the contractors, they were threatened by armed guards. The contractors were also reported to have enjoyed political support, so the field staff and villagers could do little to stop them.

In the early 1970s, Lokhun Sahu, our 65-year-old village informant, said that political organizers began visiting the community. They told the villagers that the forest was community property. In retrospect, Lokhun felt that 'the political leaders misled us to gain our political support'. The villagers began cutting and selling the trees indiscriminately. According to Lokhun, no control system existed and everyone cut where they pleased. The forestry field staff were helpless. They had no support from the community, and contractors often threatened them with physical violence. By the early 1980s, the Sal forests were badly degraded. In some areas, even the root systems had been extracted for fuelwood. Lokhun reported that the temperature seemed to become hotter, while rainfall diminished, and the earth became drier. He felt that the cooling breezes had ceased to blow. The villagers had difficulty finding wood for their spade handles, ploughs, and other agricultural implements. The village ponds and wells dried up faster, making the villagers rely on the water in the river, 2 km away. The forest had been so thoroughly cut, that there were no standing trees outside the village proper and it is said that one could see all the way to the river and beyond.

In 1983 Jyoti Naik, a man from the neighbouring village of

Harinakuri, began visiting Chandana village to discuss forest management problems. Jyoti a 45-year-old, illiterate small farmer, with only two years of formal education, was convinced some action had to be taken to reverse the process of forest destruction. In the beginning, Jyoti visited each house separately in the evening to talk about the problem. He told the villagers of Chandana, that if they didn't begin protecting the forest it would degrade to a point where even fuelwood and leaves would no longer be available. He told them they would be forest people with no forest, nor would their children have forest resources to utilize in their adulthood. Gradually he began organizing village level meetings. By 1984 a sufficient number of Chandana villagers were ready. They called a meeting of the neighbouring four villages to discuss a collaborative management programme. It was decided that each community should take responsibility for the forest area nearest to their village. The subdivision of the 160 ha. forest tract tended to follow footpaths and bullock cart tracts. While the Chandana and Harinakuri villages began actively protecting the forest tracts near their communities, the villages to the north of the forest, Nidata and Babunmara, were less effective in controlling access and commercial fuelwood cutting continued. Jyoti Naik and other village leaders have met with local political representatives from the area and urged them to put pressure on the north side communities to begin protection activities, but Jyoti noted that the politicians are afraid they will lose votes if they do so. At the present time a four village (Chandana, Harinakuri, Nidata, and Bamunmara) FPC co-ordinating board exists. Jyoti Naik currently acts as chairman.

The Chandana Forest Protection Committee has experienced continuing problems in controlling illegal cutting by outsiders. Women from other villages come in groups of five or six every two to three days to cut fuelwood. These women frequently come from Bhetia village across the river to the north, or from Pora and Simildanga villages in the south. When Chandana villagers catch them they ask them to go elsewhere, but when necessary they chase them away with sticks. A more serious threat are the gangs of ten to twelve men who come during the night through the months of August through October and February through May, the slack agricultural season. These groups are interested in cutting Sal poles for commercial sale. When outside cutting groups are active the FPC tends to keep one man patrolling the area on two to three hour shifts. Other villagers are also watchful and notify the community if cutting groups are seen approaching the area. Occasionally, the FPC catches groups in the process of cutting at which time they confiscate their axes and fine them.

Protection experiences in the neighbouring village of Harinakuri are similar. Since the FPC was first formed in 1979, Harinakuri has worked with Chandana and Telebanga village to deter cutting groups from nearby villages in the north and east. According to Jyoti, pressure from outside villages is particularly high because many members of those communities depend on fuelwood headloading as their primary source of cash income. Often tribal and scheduled caste members of these villages are contracted by high-caste families in towns and villages and at the Soluwa Army base to cut fuelwood and timber for them. The cutting groups often band together to overcome local resistance. In response, the Harinakuri FPC had to patrol in a group of eight to ten men armed with bows and arrows and spears, when cutting groups were active. Boys with grazing animals also watch and listen for the sound of the axe upon the tree, so that they can warn the FPC when intruders come. When this occurs the men attempt to encircle the cutting group so that they can catch them. In the cases when this occurred they turned over the offenders to the Forest Department guard. The cutters were later fined by the Forest Department.

Jyoti noted that the decision to protect the degraded forest land had a significant impact on the economy of Harinakuri. Previously, Jyoti and the other villagers had also been engaged in cutting fuelwood for sale. If a number of family members were engaged in cutting, a household might collect two to three 40 to 50 kilogram bundles each day. In 1979 that would generate Rs 35 to 50 per day, while at 1991 prices (Rs 1 per kg) it would yield three times as much. Further, fuelwood cutting and carrying could be done in three or four hours in the morning, leaving time for other work. In contrast to agricultural wage labour, which is only available during certain times of the year, fuelwood cutting would likely generate at least two to three times more wages per unit of time spent. Consequently, it was a considerable sacrifice for the community to discontinue this lucrative economic activity. Based on discussions with villagers in Harinakuri, it appears their decision was partially made on the basis of their concern over the deteriorating environment and also on the recognition that the level of exploitation was not sustainable and that they would have to shift occupations in any case, once the forest resources were exhausted.

The shift away from fuelwood cutting and the lost income it entailed was softened by the land reform programme of the West Bengal Communist Party government, which transferred titles for the rain-fed rice land from the landlords to Jyoti and his neighbours, who had acted as tenant farmers in the past. By not having to share their harvests with the landlord, their incomes rose.

At the same time Jyoti and his neighbours decided to begin producing puffed rice (*chira*) for the local market. This involved buying small stocks of unhusked grain (*dhan*), usually 20 kg at a time, husking and winnowing it, and roasting it under a brushwood and leaf fire. The operation involves three men working from 4 a.m. until 5 p.m. Usually they can process 20 kg of rice grain worth Rs 60, into 10 kg of chira worth Rs 240. This means the hourly income per man from chira-making is approximately Rs 4.60 per hour, or Rs 60 per 13-hour day. This is approximately three times the official minimum daily wage received by agricultural labourers (Rs 24.85 per day). It may also approximate the income generated by fuelwood headloaders if they have sufficient forest resources to exploit. While Jyoti and his neighbours have been successful in finding an alternative, and at least as lucrative a source of income as fuelwood cutting, many neighbours have not been so fortunate and must suffer the lost income or continue to exploit the forest in defiance of their neighbours.

The amount of time Chandana and Harinakuri FPCs spend patrolling the forest and the value of that time in terms of opportunity costs are difficult to calculate. Clearly, much of the time is spent during periods of high threat. These fall after rice transplanting is completed during the months of August through October, and after the rice harvest from February to May, when there is little agricultural work and few paid labour opportunities available. It seemed that no regimented, full-time patrolling system was utilized, rather villagers, especially women and children, engaged in grazing, fuelwood collection, and other forest related activities, acted as an early warning system. When news of illegal activities was given, men would move into the forest for protection activities. While the time involved may not be great, it appeared that many community members were available and alert to possible threats, which they perceived to be significant. The villagers were clearly concerned that as the poles gained value, the threat of a 'mass loot' by a group of outside villagers would grow. They note that the regeneration of the forest has had substantial environmental and economic benefits that will be lost temporarily if the entire area is clear felled. The most important advantages emerging from forest regeneration has been improved ground water infiltration and slowed run-off and the increased availability of such non-timber forest products like tubers, mushrooms, and fibre materials. Finally, the FPC members noted that the re-establishment of standing forest near their village has allowed a large population of birds to nest in the area which are important in controlling insect pests which attack their rice crop. They also felt the forest had a beneficial effect in cleaning the air of disease. They noted that when the forest was degraded the incidence of disease also increased and they associate a healthy environment with a good standing forest.

Despite their success in protecting at least one hundred of the one hundred and sixty hectares of disturbed natural Sal forest adjoining their villages, they continue to be confronted by threats from other villages in the area which depend on fuelwood cutting for a substantial source of their income. The tribal and scheduled caste people who illegally exploit these forests are driven by economic necessity and encouraged by local and urban higher income and caste groups. Until all communities neighbouring the forest can be effectively brought into the joint management programme and their economic needs met, these emerging local management systems will remain threatened and their sustainability in question.

## Conclusion

The case of the Jungle Mahals indicates that the emergence of new community forest management systems in south-west Bengal is grounded historically in tribal and peasant resistance movements. In many parts of rural India, pockets of disempowered people have repeatedly organized to struggle for their survival as their resource base is increasingly captured by local elites, moneylenders, tax collectors, and the state. In the past, each time the movement was crushed or collapsed, after some time it would re-emerge. The people of the Jungle Mahals represent a classic case.

In south-west Bengal, grass roots leadership was effective in mobilizing the communities' commitment to forest protection. The emergence of tribal and schedule caste leaders who could accomplish this under the populist government is a testimony to the broader socio-political changes which have occurred in the state over the past twenty years. Community members clearly are concerned about environmental degradation in their area and are willing and able to take action to respond to the challenge. That they were encouraged by a supportive WBFD programme and helpful field staff definitely facilitated this process.

To the extent that the West Bengal Forest Department has moved more quickly and more successfully than other departments involved with similar efforts, several explanations have been cited. There is little doubt that the socio-political context in the state has encouraged populist programmes and a responsiveness to forest community needs. A new generation of community leaders from small farming, agricultural labour, and tribal backgrounds has emerged. Further, the department's appeal to tribal communities to protect forest resources and its willingness to empower them apparently coincided with a growing desire among these communities to take environmental action. Finally, because the West Bengal programme did not require complex registration and budgetary allocations processes for communities to take action, but rather presented communities with a straightforward opportunity (protect the local forest and enjoy the benefits), it was easier for communities to mobilize. As each community began protection activities it influenced the behaviour of neighbouring villages. Villages were forced to negotiate and discuss management issues and needs with one another, without necessarily waiting for the Forest Department to take action. It is this community based 'chain reaction' or catalytic effect that is apparently a driving force behind the rapid emergence of localized access controls on state forest lands in southwest Bengal. It is likely that similar community concerns over environmental degradation in other parts of India could provide effective support for joint management programmes if initiated by state Forest Departments.

Yet, this most recent insurgency of the disadvantaged, while gaining increasing support from the forest department, remains threatened by both traditional vested interests as well as by neighbouring communities of poor, disempowered peoples. The 'mass loots' experienced by or posing an ongoing threat to West Bengal's forest protection committees is driven by the same poverty and desperation, that led to mass loots and attacks on zamindars and the state in the past. In essence, while a growing political awareness of injustice and the concern over the environment leads some communities to reassert control over forests, the extreme poverty of their neighbours may ultimately undermine and destroy the movement.

# Index